T0365013

THE JOY OF
ENCOUNTERING JESUS

THE JOY OF ENCOUNTERING JESUS:

Living God's Life in a New World

SUNDAY HOMILIES
Years A, B, and C

Hoan Moses Chung

authorHOUSE®

AuthorHouse™
1663 Liberty Drive
Bloomington, IN 47403
www.authorhouse.com
Phone: 1 (800) 839-8640

Published by AuthorHouse 10/28/2017

ISBN: 978-1-4969-7498-3 (sc)
ISBN: 978-1-4969-7497-6 (e)

Print information available on the last page.

NIHIL OBSTAT:
Rev. Msgr. Robert M. Coerver, S.T.L., M.S.
Censor Librorum

IMPRIMATUR:
✝Most Rev. Kevin J. Farrell, D.D.
Bishop of Dallas
February 8, 2015

The nihil obstat and imprimatur are official declarations that a book or pamphlet is free of
doctrinal or moral error. No implication is contained therein that those who have granted the
nihil obstat and imprimatur agree with the contents, opinions or statements expressed.

Unless otherwise specified, all verses from scripture used in this book are taken from
the New American Bible with Revised New Testament and Psalms © Confraternity
of Christian Doctrine, Inc., Washington, D.C. All rights reserved.

CONTENTS

YEAR B

YEAR C

FOREWORD

"Brothers and fathers, listen to me." Such was how Stephen, deacon and martyr, began his first homily in Acts of the Apostles. It was also his last homily. Preachers of the Gospel ought always to keep Stephen and the circumstances of his brief preaching career in mind. Ordained and then quickly arraigned, Stephen bore witness to Christ with not only his words, but with his body too—ready for the sacrifice of martyrdom before he even opened his mouth. "Brothers and fathers, listen to me." These were remarkably brave words, spoken by a man who had already given up his freedom and virtually his life. He preached as a martyr. Preachers ought to remember Stephen. He reminds us what's at stake and of the necessary character of anyone who would dare to preach in the name of Christ.

According to the *General Instruction of the Roman Missal*, after the Scriptures are read at Mass, it's necessary to have a "living commentary on the word" (*GIRM* 29). The homily, in the mind of the Church, belongs to the liturgy itself. Thus, following *Sacrosanctum Concilium*, the homily belongs essentially to the "work of our redemption" (*SC* 2). Preaching, therefore, is obviously important. It's fundamental to the mission Christ gave us to make disciples of all nations, bringing all who are converted by the means of our preaching to the saving waters of baptism and to the kingdom of God itself (Matt. 28:19). "Brothers and fathers, listen to me." It turns out these weren't only brave words; they're words uttered out of evangelical obedience and out of a great love for the salvation of souls.

I bring this up simply to invite you to read the homilies collected here cognizant of the depth of the tradition within which they have been written and spoken. In the Catholic Church the ministry of preaching rightly belongs to deacons as well as to bishops and priests. Deacons bring to this ministry a unique perspective born of the closeness of their mission among the lay faithful. Many deacons labor in the Church and in the world tirelessly and often thanklessly. They offer themselves as did Stephen—in word and in deed. Ordained to serve God, the Church and her bishops, often upon the borderlands of the Church and even in the wilds beyond comforting communities of faith, many of our deacons stand before the world like martyrs—offering their visible fidelity wherever they find themselves—like Stephen, ready to preach even when it's difficult. This is why the preaching of deacons is valuable, and it's why we should hear and hallow their words.

The homilies collected here are the work of Deacon Moses Chung. He has faithfully served out his vocation among the people of Saint Rita Catholic Community for years. Having heard him preach for several years now, I can attest to the quality of his preparation, both intellectual and spiritual. Deacon Moses' homilies are of an uncommon spiritual depth. They reflect a man of prayer, a man open to God and willing to share the grace given him. Deacon Moses is a true preacher, spiritually speaking. Augustine said that whenever someone wanted to preach he should first pray to God that he put just the right words into the preacher's mouth (*De Doctrina Christiana* 4.30.63). This, evidently, is just what Deacon Moses does before he preaches. That's why he's worth hearing. And it's why he's worth reading too.

I'm very pleased to see these homilies in print. I have often gone back to read his homilies with great benefit, and so I am happy that they will be more widely available to our parish family and to others. Good preaching is a blessing from God, and so is this book which is so clearly a work of love and faith.

Fr. Joshua J. Whitfield
Dallas, Texas
February 2015

PREFACE

In the American film classic, *It's a Wonderful Life*, Jimmy Stewart plays George Bailey, a good and honest banker in a small town. At one point in the movie, George becomes the victim of the greedy and vengeful banker, Mr. Potter, and ponders suicide. He thinks he is "worth more dead than alive." At that moment, his guardian angel jumps into the cold river and pretends to be drowning. George, the virtuous man, saves the angel. Then the angel tries to convince George that his life is worth living. George is not convinced and, instead, wishes he had never been born. The angel grants his wish.

From then on, George wanders around the empty world that would have existed if he had not been born. He meets his wife, who is a lonely stranger; his mother, who is a mean old lady; and his close friends, who become wild and wanton without his influence. He also visits his younger brother's grave. His small town has become an amoral and miserable world known as Pottersville. He finally realizes he has a truly wonderful life that touches many people. And he wants to live again. As he returns to his real life, he is happy and joyful.

As I watched George Bailey coming back to life with joy and excitement, I immediately understood he'd experienced a certain resurrection. He'd surely encountered the living God. The resurrection is not a disembodied soul moving on to a blissful life in another world. The resurrection is being grasped by the divine reality. The resurrection means that the Spirit of Jesus Christ continues to live among us. The resurrection of Jesus, therefore, is the source and foundation of a joyful and meaningful life on earth. We can now live God's life in a new world in and through Jesus Christ.

I didn't have an adequate understanding of the resurrection of Jesus until I started to prepare homilies in English about ten years ago. This is not to say that I now fully understand the resurrection. Perhaps we can't have that full realization until we are on the cross. After all, the resurrection is not to understand, but to believe in.

The Word was made flesh for us to live the life of resurrection on earth. And to live the life of resurrection is the goal of life. In this afternoon of my life, I like to live the life of resurrection, too. I hope this book will provide me a foundation for that. This is one reason for preparing this book.

Homilies must be pastoral, not theological. And an important role of deacons is to connect the people to the theology of everyday life. Thus I have included as many stories and poems and prayers as I could. However, because I was born in Korea, and because I was a scientist for a long time, many of homilies may be properly called theological essays or speculative reflections. Now, I would like to present all of them to the Church, hoping they will help spread the Good News of Jesus Christ. This is another reason for preparing this book.

Lastly, some homilies are autobiographical. They reflect who I am. They show consistency in flow and pattern, like a river meandering through mountains, valleys, and meadows under the rising sun. I hope they will remain as a memory of me "on the last day" for those who know me now—my children, grandchildren, relatives, and friends. It is my way to convey the love of God to them and also to let them know their love is sufficient for me. And I will always pray they will be in "touch" with God. Assisting those I love to stay close to God is still another reason for preparing this book.

Having followed Jesus' footsteps from Bethlehem to Nazareth, to Galilee, to Jerusalem, and then back to Galilee, I have concluded that *we* are the holy people of God and that *we* live God's life in a new world. I hope and pray that those who read this book can experience the same inner joy by encountering the risen Jesus. Hence, the title of the book is *The Joy of Encountering Jesus: Living God's Life in a New World*.

Fifty-six homilies cover Advent, Christmas, Lent, Easter, and Ordinary Time, in that order for each liturgical year. In addition, six homilies are grouped in two sets: (1) Christmas Vigil, Christmas Midnight, and Christmas Day, (2) Holy Thursday, Good Friday, and the Easter Vigil. They are included in Year A, B, and C, respectively.

Some homilies have identical or similar theological themes and may be referenced or interchanged. To make cross-referencing easier, the titles of homilies, rather than the names of Sundays, are provided in the Table of

Contents. In addition, other homilies with common or related theological themes are suggested at the end of each homily.

I have often used scriptural passages verbatim. Scriptural quotations that come from Sunday Readings and Responsorial Psalms are directly quoted, whereas other Sunday Readings outside of a particular Sunday are referenced. In addition, Vatican II documents, Encyclical Letters, the *Catechism of the Catholic Church,* and other general articles from *America* are referenced.

To keep the homilies as simple as possible, jargon and/or sentences that interrupt the flow of the prose or that are too theological are kept in parentheses. They are not deleted due to their intrinsic connection to the whole.

For the majority of homilies, I have almost consistently used *Days of the Lord, the Liturgical Year* by Liturgical Press; *Illustrated Sunday Homilies,* Series I and II, (Year A, B, C) by Fr. Mark Link, S.J.; commentaries of Sunday readings by Sr. Dianne Bergant C.S.A. from *America* (2003-2005); and commentaries of Sunday readings by Fr. Daniel Harrington, S.J. from *America* (2006-2008). Fr. Mark Link generously gave me his permission to use a total of ten poems, stories, and prayers from his books, when I visited him at the Columbiere Retreat Center in Clarkston, Michigan in 2012.

I thank the parishioners at St. Rita Catholic Church in Dallas for being patient with me. I also thank Bishop Mark Seitz, El Paso, Texas and Monsignor Robert Coerver, my pastors at St. Rita, for nourishing me. Their guidance and encouragements have been living fountains for my pastoral ministry at St. Rita. I would like to thank Fr. Joshua Whitfield, the Parochial Vicar at St. Rita, for his kind words about this book.

Lastly, I would like to dedicate this book to my wife, Kuenja, who is a writer of spirituality in her own right. For the last forty-five years, she patiently has journeyed with me, while I have brought neither adequate fame nor sufficient fortune. I owe many graces to her.

YEAR A

FIRST SUNDAY OF ADVENT (A)

(Isaiah 2:1-5; Romans 13:11-14; Matthew 24:37-44)

We Are Pilgrims

We are pilgrims. As we begin to celebrate the season of Advent, this revelation that we are pilgrims becomes clear.

During the Advent season, we prepare ourselves for the birth of Jesus Christ and for the second coming of Christ Jesus at the end-time. Liturgically, the Advent journey culminates in the celebration of Christ's ultimate victory at the Feast of Christ the King. And so, today we begin the yearly re-enactment of the drama of salvation; we take our first step of the Advent journey as pilgrims.

Some of us may have made pilgrimages to Jerusalem, to Rome, or to the shrines of Our Lady of Guadalupe, Fatima in Portugal, or Lourdes in France. But all of us are on a pilgrimage—a faith journey—toward salvation from pride and self-centeredness, as well as from insecurity and uncertainty. During the season of Advent, we renew our commitment to this salvation once again as pilgrims.

Today, the Church asks us to reflect upon Christ Jesus, who came once in flesh and who will come again in glory. When Jesus comes, we will "climb the Lord's mountain" and live the life of God together with Jesus. However, Christ Jesus will come suddenly and unexpectedly. He has said, "As for the exact day or hour, no one knows it, neither the angels in heaven nor the Son, but the Father only" (Mt 24:36, Mk 13:32).

So we must wait. We don't know how to wait calmly and patiently, not even knowing how long we wait. It is natural for us to want to know when the Lord will come; such uncertainty can be cause for anxiety. But wait we must.

The Lord's coming is like that of a dear friend who calls us one afternoon and simply tells us he will one day pay us a surprise visit. We will, then, always be ready to receive our friend, knowing that he will not be offended

2

by our performance of daily tasks when he finally arrives. In the same way, it is not a question of being bored with waiting, but of being active. We know each passing day draws us closer to the coming of the Lord.

We also need to be vigilant for the Lord's coming. St. Paul says, "It is the hour now for you to awake from sleep; the night is far gone and the day is near." To those who have already seen the light but still remain caught in the endless battle between light and darkness, he asks that they put on "the armor of light."

In this battle between the spirit and the flesh, we need to hold on tightly to our faith, hope, and love. In faith, we find the light. In hope, we hold the light. In love, we live the light.

Among faith, hope, and love, it is appropriate to reflect upon hope during the Advent season. Students go through difficult courses and exams because they hope for a bright future. A young couple goes to the altar because they hope in a blissful life together. We come to the table of the Lord's Supper because we hope to encounter the risen Lord.

Moreover, hope allows us to move toward the future with joy and confidence. Hope brings the future into the present. Hope is the heart of our lives. To live is to hope. We live as long as we hope; we live as much as we hope.

In this season of Advent, we must also live well today, because how we live today decides tomorrow. We must be prepared today so we will not be surprised by the unexpected coming of the Lord. Let us not sleep in the darkness: "Let us put on the armor of light; let us conduct ourselves properly as in the day." ✝

[2nd Advent (C)]

SECOND SUNDAY OF ADVENT (A)

(Isaiah 11:1-10; Romans 15:4-9; Matthew 3:1-12)

John the Trailblazer

John the Baptist cries out in the desert, "Repent, for the kingdom of heaven is at hand!" John is the trailblazer for Jesus and lays out the vision of the new age.

The new age that Jesus will preach is so different and so shocking that people must turn their value-system around to understand it. The new age Jesus will establish is so strange and so unfamiliar that people must change their heart to understand it. So, John needs to bridge it step by step. He baptizes people with water so that Jesus baptizes them with the Holy Spirit. John, the trailblazer, is "preparing the way of the Lord." John is fulfilling the prophecy of Isaiah.

John the Baptist lived all his life in a desert (Lk 1:80). Like Elijah, he "wore clothing made of camel's hair and ate locusts and wild honey." The Pharisees dared not question John's authority, because people respected him immensely. According to the Gospel of John, John the Baptist introduced two of his own disciples to Jesus. Most likely, Jesus himself was associated with "the school of John the Baptist."

In the Bible, the desert is a special place to purify heart. Moses spent years in the desert before taking up God's command. The Israelites spent forty years in the desert before they reached the Promised Land. John the Baptist stayed in the desert before preparing the way of the Lord. Paul stayed for three years in a desert in Syria before joining the Christian community in Antioch. Jesus was tempted in the desert before he began his public ministry.

The desert is a dry, dusty, and empty place, where distractions and noises are minimal. The desert is simple, silent, and solitude place, where ordinary necessities are stripped down to bare essentials. The desert is a place to form a new consciousness in the deepest part of our mind.

The world we live in has too many problems and too many conflicts. The world is interested only in accumulating wealth, power, and fame. Jesus must come again. The world we live in is filled with too much greed to satisfy and too much delusion to gratify. Never-ending wars and selfish political maneuvers around the globe clearly point at the absence of Christ. Jesus must come again. Therefore, the happiness and authentic wholeness, called salvation, can only be possible by re-discovering and re-inventing spirituality. St. Paul said, we "must not be conformed to this world, but be transformed by the renewing of our minds" (Rom 12:2). Jesus must come again.

In this season of Advent, we like to get rid of our false selves and recover our true selves. In this season of Advent, we like to find God once again in this confused world. In this season of Advent, we like to awaken to the silent voice of God, for the Lord is coming.

When the Lord comes into this world, he will turn it upside down once again and make it anew. In this new world, "the wolf shall be a guest of the lamb, and the leopard shall lie down with the kid; the calf and the young lion shall browse together, with a little child to guide them." In this new world, "the cow and the bear shall be neighbors, together their young shall rest; the lion shall eat hay like the ox."

In this new world, Jesus will once again be at the table with the sick and the poor and the marginalized. Jesus will once again love his enemies. Jesus will once again gather sins and evils of the world and carry them unto the cross. Above all, Jesus will once again ask us to do likewise.

During this season of Advent, we need to prepare ourselves in a desert. Advent is the time for us to attend to the words of John the Baptist: "Repent, for the kingdom of heaven is at hand!" Advent is the time for us to transform our consciousness from self-centeredness to God-centeredness. Advent is the time for us to reflect seriously on what it means for God to take up human flesh. ✝

[2ⁿᵈ Advent (B)]

5

THIRD SUNDAY OF ADVENT (A)

(Isaiah 35:1-6a, 10; James 5:7-10; Matthew 11:2-11)

Rejoice, We Are the Holy People of God

As we wait for the coming of the Lord, we pause briefly today and take a look at the spectacular, panoramic view before us, reminding ourselves that we are the holy people of God.

In the first reading, the beautiful poetry of Isaiah reveals the hope of the Israelites, who would return to Zion. When the prophecy was fulfilled, not only would deserts and arid lands be covered with trees and green grass, but also the blind would see, the deaf would hear, the lame would walk, and the mute would sing. All would meet with joy and gladness in the absence of sorrow and mourning. The prophet Isaiah was concerned with renewing terrestrial forms of life when the Israelites returned from Exile.

In the gospel reading, John the Baptist in prison inquires about Jesus, "Are you the one who is to come?" Jesus sends his answer: "The blind see, the lame walk, lepers are cleansed...." Jesus reminds John he has fulfilled the prophecy of Isaiah, by revealing himself as God's revelation. Jesus is the revealer as well as the revelation.

Jesus' revelation, however, is not restricted to the terrestrial forms of life, as in the first reading from Isaiah. His revelation extends to the celestial and cosmic splendors of God's kingdom. Accordingly, we pause today to catch a glimpse of the spectacular vista of God's kingdom.

We can say that Jesus of Nazareth is one of the most influential persons in history. The celebration of Christmas at every corner on earth is simply astounding. Moreover, Jesus' teachings have greatly enhanced the whole humanity, and, as a result, the history of mankind has been shaped according to Christian principles.

In today's gospel reading, however, Jesus declares that John the Baptist is the greatest man who has ever lived. Jesus says, "Among those born of women there has been none greater than John the Baptist." For this reason, of among the saints and prophets, it is John's birthday we celebrate (June 20), along with those of Jesus, Mary, and Joseph (March 19).

Having declared John the Baptist the greatest man who ever lived, Jesus once again surprises us. He says, "Yet the least in the kingdom of heaven is greater than he." This means that we, who now live in God's kingdom, are greater than John the Baptist. This means the least person in God's kingdom is greater than the greatest man on earth, John the Baptist. Therefore, we are ultimately important in the kingdom of God. We are the holy people of God.

This is surprising and unexpected; however, it is only a glimpse of God's kingdom. Speaking of God's kingdom, Paul said, "What eye has not seen, and ear has not heard, and what has not entered the human heart, what God has prepared for those who love him" (1 Cor 2:9). Paul was talking about the kingdom of God fulfilled, when we will see God face to face.

We are the holy people of God because we are created in the image and likeness of God. We are holy people of God because we are brothers and sisters of Jesus Christ crucified and risen. We are holy people of God because we are beloved sons and daughters of God through our baptism. Indeed, we are the holy people of God, the apple of God's eye (Ps 17:8).

The fact that we are holy people of God means we will hug our sons and daughters tightly and show they, too, are the holy people of God. The fact that we are holy people of God means we will look at our neighbors through God's eyes and show them that Jesus loves them, too. The fact that we are holy people of God means it is time to go to Confession, if it has been too long, and to get to know a new dimension of God's mercy. And we live joyfully and reverently because we are the holy people of God. ✝

[3rd Advent (B)]

FOURTH SUNDAY OF ADVENT (A)

(Isaiah 7:10-14; Romans 1:1-7; Matthew 1:18-24)

Joseph the Wise Fool

The Advent hymn, "O come, O come, Emmanuel," has saturated the air for some time. And still, we are waiting for the birth of the Messiah with hope and longing; only one more week to go.

Perhaps this is an opportune time for us to reflect on Joseph, the dreamer, Mary's betrothed (in those days, the term referred to a marriage, although not necessarily a consummated one), who experienced real hope and longing in the midst of doubt, frustration, and treachery. We can learn from Joseph how to hope and how to long for.

Joseph had just learned that Mary was pregnant. He was full of anxiety. He thought of "putting Mary away quietly." (There were three steps in Jewish marriage custom. The first step was engagement, which was worked out by parents. The second step was the solemn promise for the marriage itself; only an official divorce would terminate the relationship. The third step was the physical union. It is in the second step that Joseph learned Mary was pregnant.)

Joseph was anxious and, most likely, angry. Mary told him what the angel Gabriel had said. Still, it sounded absurd; the whole thing was unheard of. Then, in a dream, the same angel came to Joseph, saying, "Do not be afraid.... She will bear a son and you are to name him Jesus." At hearing this, Joseph, a devout Jew, remembered the old prophecy of Isaiah (to King Ahaz) concerning God's promise of Emmanuel, as in the first reading. And so, Joseph caught a glimpse of hope, hope that all Israelites longed for. Joseph was convinced Jesus was not an ordinary child.

In the Book of Genesis, divine messages are usually associated with dreams. Joseph, the son of Jacob and Rachel, who was sold into slavery in Egypt by his brothers, became that country's highest government official because he interpreted Pharaoh's dream (Gen 42). Joseph, the husband of Mary, escaped from many dangerous situations because of his dreams. It happened four times in the first two chapters of the Gospel of Matthew (Mt 1:20, 2:13, 19, 22). We may ask ourselves: Is Joseph a simple and naïve person who obediently does what he is told in dreams? Is this the reason why Joseph is called a "righteous man"?

We know dreams reflect the unconscious mind. Depth psychology, which interprets dreams, has been around for only 150 years or so. In Biblical times, a dream's message was thought to originate in the deepest core of a person's being and considered divine intervention. Dream provides a deeper and higher form of knowledge beyond senses and intellect.

What the angel told Joseph, therefore, concerns his authenticity and fundamental option. And the contents of Joseph's dream had to be tested and then embraced with hope and longing. This means that Joseph did not simply obey in a passive manner and did what was told. He accepted the divine intervention in silence, and yet, he lived out his dream actively, while entrusting his innermost being to God. This, then, is why Joseph was a "righteous man."

We cannot understand Joseph from our twenty-first-century minds. Mystical stories and symbols, such as Joseph's dreams, are beyond reasoning and logical argument. Therefore, we must ask, "What kind of person was Joseph?" The answer is that Joseph was a holy and wise man, possessing divine wisdom. He was simple, carefree, foolish, and yet, wise. He was a foolishly wise man. He was a wise fool, just as the cross was the folly of God's love.

Whenever we celebrate the Eucharist, there are moments reminiscent of Joseph's dream—cloudy, amorphous, intangible or, often, sleepy moments. Perhaps they are those moments when God approaches us through symbols and gestures, through which we may become fools. "For God's foolishness is wiser than human wisdom" (1 Cor 1: 25).

Let us continue to hope and long for the remaining Advent season. Like Joseph, let us continue to hope and long for from the depths of our beings. ✝

[2nd OT (A), 20th OT (B)]

9

THE NATIVITY OF THE LORD: VIGIL (ABC)

(Isaiah 62:1-5; Acts 13:16-17, 22-25; Matthew 1:1-25)

Jesus Christ Comes to Our World

Jesus of Nazareth, the Messiah, has finally come to our world. God's plan to share His divine life with human beings has been fulfilled in the person of Jesus Christ. God has reclaimed the ownership of the whole world through His Son. As a response to God's call, Jesus Christ has inaugurated the kingdom of God.

In today's gospel account, St. Matthew describes the fulfilling of God's plan of salvation through the genealogy of Jesus, which contains many Jewish names difficult-to-pronounce. (The genealogy of Jesus consists of three sections of fourteen names each, distinguishing three historical periods: from Abraham to David; from David to the Babylonian Exile; and from the Exile to the birth of Jesus.) The genealogy summarizes that Jesus is a true son of Abraham in line with the Davidic Messiah.

In the genealogy of Jesus, we recognize names like Abraham, Isaac, and Jacob. But there are many names we don't know. Upon a closer look, we find non-Jewish and even immoral persons. Tamar manipulated her father-in-law to get her twin sons (Gen 38). Rahab was a Canaanite prostitute (Jos 6:25). Ruth was a Gentile woman (Ru 3). Bathsheba, the wife of Uriah (not mentioned by her name) committed adultery with King David and later gave birth to King Solomon (2 Sm 12). Finally, Mary, the Mother of God, was a simple woman in a backwater town in Galilee.

The righteous as well as the sinful, and the clean as well as the messy, find their places in the genealogy of Jesus. Our families may have problems, but Jesus' family was not free of problems. What St. Matthew emphasizes is the incarnation occurred among ordinary people within the real world.

Through the incarnation, God assumed human flesh (hypostatic union) and lived among us (Jn 1:14). As the early church fathers declared that God became human to make us divine, the incarnation gives us a share

10

in God's own life and makes us children of God. So we are brothers and sisters to Jesus Christ, redeemed by his blood and filled with his Spirit.

The incarnation is not easy to understand, however. What does it mean to say that Jesus is fully divine and, simultaneously, fully human? What does it mean to say that the humanity and the divinity of Jesus Christ are distinct but inseparable? The Church teaches that Jesus Christ is fully divine and fully human, not a mixture of the divinity and the humanity. How then do the divinity and the humanity meet in Jesus Christ? We accept this doctrine in faith; we cannot understand. In reality, however, most of us usually think of Jesus as God. Perhaps we are "closet Docetists." In olden days Jesus' divinity was in doubt. In modern days Jesus' humanity is in doubt.

One way to approach this problem and to improve our relationship with Jesus is to consider Jesus as the perfect fulfillment of humanity and follow his footsteps. Jesus is a human being in the most divine way and, at the same time, God in the most human way. Therefore, if we appeal and hold on to Jesus' humanity, as described in the Gospels, then the Spirit of Christ helps us to assent to his divinity.

In his earthly life, Jesus emptied himself freely and followed the will of God without reminder. Jesus' humanity was in perfect union with God; he embodied the human fulfillment of God's love, revealing God's saving plan. In other words, Jesus demonstrated the paradigm of humanity and, accordingly, showed the human face of God. Therefore, in order to find God, we must turn to Jesus of Nazareth. "Only in the mystery of the incarnate Word does the mystery of man truly become clear" (*Gaudium et Spes*, #22).

The baby Jesus is the most precious gift from God. The incarnation is the highest point in the history of salvation. Our world is now filled with the grandeur of God. Tonight is the most joyful night. Tonight is the most silent night. And tonight is the most holy night. ✝

[4th Advent (C), Baptism (C), Christ King (B)]

HOLY FAMILY OF JESUS, MARY, AND JOSEPH (A)

(Sirach 3:2-6, 12-14; Colossians 3:12-21; Matthew 2:13-15, 19-23)

It Takes the Covenant to Raise a Family

There is a beautiful painting about the Holy Family by Rembrandt, the famous Dutch painter. Mary cradles the baby Jesus, who is at the center of the picture, while Joseph, an old man, looks down upon him. Such a painting, although it is great art, is a far cry from the gospel story of the birth of the Messiah we read today.

The Gospel of Matthew shows that, soon after Jesus was born, Joseph had to take Jesus and Mary to Egypt because Herod the Great was trying to kill any would-be Messiah. After staying in Egypt for a while, Joseph could not return to Bethlehem; he had to settle in Nazareth in Galilee, a despised and despicable land. The Holy Family was a refugee family.

Let us focus on Joseph, the lonely man. How would he take care of Jesus and Mary on their journey to Egypt and then back to Galilee? How could he be responsible for the child Jesus, who was not his own? During the journey, there might have been times when they were hungry, when they shivered in the cold of night, and when they were rejected by townsfolk. While taking care of the infant Jesus and the young mother Mary, Joseph certainly experienced hunger, poverty, and rejection.

We are celebrating the Feast of the Holy Family today. The Holy Family is easy to marvel at, but it is difficult even to think about imitating them. The Holy Family is very different from our families. None of us were born after an angelic announcement. If we were to make imaginative projections as we view the Rembrandt painting, it would seem that Mary and Joseph never argued and that Jesus was always obedient to Joseph. Why, then, do we celebrate the Feast of the Holy Family today?

One reason why we celebrate the Holy Family is that our relationship to God is most intimately expressed by the relationships within our own families. The more intimately we are connected to our family members, the closer we are to

God. For example, the first reading teaches us that if a man honors his father, his children will honor him when he gets old, and God will listen to his prayer.

Another reason is that our Savior came to us not with sounds of trumpet or harpsichord, but amongst cold clouds of animal breath in a manger. Our Savior came to us in the form of a human family. Indeed, the Gospel of Christ begins with a human family. We also learn the Holy Family goes through ordinary struggles and typical worries just as we do. For example, returning home from Jerusalem, Mary and Joseph couldn't find twelve-year-old Jesus. Three days later, they found him in the Temple talking to the scribes. We can relate to this type of problem. The Holy Family is a human family.

Holiness begins with humanity. Holiness is not a heavenly thing "far up there." Holiness begins with human strength and weakness. Holiness entails both human sinfulness and God's grace. To be holy, therefore, we must first deal with our own humanity.

It is not at all surprising that our families are holy because we struggle every day to be holy, despite human weakness and the weight of sin. This is exactly what happened to the Holy Family. Therefore, it takes God's covenant to raise a family. We need to learn this valuable lesson from the Holy Family. Pope John XXIII said of fathers, "It is easier for a father to have children than for children to have a father." In the same way, having children does not make a woman a mother any more than having a piano in the living room makes one a musician.

As we honor the Holy Family today, we are reminded once again that our own families are in a covenantal relationship with God. Just as the Holy Family was not a family on its own, neither are our families. Each of our families is part of the holy, catholic, and apostolic communities of the people of God. We are called to form holy families. ✝

[Holy Family (B, C)]

THE EPIPHANY OF THE LORD (ABC)

(Isaiah 60:1-6; Ephesians 3:2-3, 5-6; Matthew 2:1-12)

The Gift of the Magi

O. Henry wrote his short story, "The Gift of the Magi," in 1906. In today's Gospel, the Magi from the East brought gifts to the baby Jesus. The Magi were the first group of persons to give Christmas presents to the baby Jesus. We wonder why O. Henry gave his story that name.

O. Henry's story is about a newlywed young couple, Jim and Della, in New York City. As Christmas approaches, Della wonders what to give Jim for Christmas. She wants to give him a watch chain for his gold watch inherited from his father and grandfather, but she has only managed to save one dollar and eighty-seven cents. Then Della gets an idea of cutting her long and beautiful hair to sell it.

She sells her hair for twenty dollars and buys a platinum watch chain for twenty-one dollars. On Christmas Eve, she holds a box containing the beautiful watch chain and waits for Jim's return home, wondering if he will be disappointed with her short hair.

When Jim climbs the stairs in the evening and notices the scarf on Della's head, he says nothing. After a few silences, Della insists that her hair will grow back quickly. Then Jim hands a small box to her. When Della opens it, she cannot believe what she sees. There, inside the box, is a set of beautiful combs for her long hair. When Jim opens his gift, he cannot believe what he sees, for inside the box is the beautiful platinum watch chain. Finally, Della realizes that Jim sold his gold watch to buy the combs for her hair.

This story is beautiful not because of gifts, but because of the love behind the gifts. Although Jim and Della are left with gifts that neither of them can use, they realize how far they have gone in showing love for each other. They have given unexpected, self-sacrificing gifts of love. It is giving, not receiving, that makes a gift of love. Perhaps this sheds light on why O. Henry named his story "The Gift of the Magi."

The Magi from the East came to Jerusalem under the divine guidance of the star. They wanted to see the King of the Jews. Surprisingly, the King they found was the baby Jesus in a manger in Bethlehem, not a powerful king in Jerusalem. The baby Jesus was a surprising and unexpected king, just like the gifts Jim and Della exchanged.

The gifts the Magi brought to the baby Jesus show, however, what kind of Messiah Jesus would be. They gave Jesus gold, frankincense, and myrrh. Gold is the ideal gift for Jesus the King. Frankincense is for liturgical worship, as we have experienced this morning; it symbolizes the divinity of Jesus. Myrrh is used to prepare the dead for burial. It is a symbol of the mortality of Jesus. These gifts of the Magi suggest who the baby Jesus was and how he would bring salvation to all people.

Today is the Feast Day of Epiphany, and we celebrate the manifestation of Jesus Christ to Gentiles and to the whole world. The baby Jesus has made the world divine. The baby Jesus has reconciled us to God. The baby Jesus has brought heaven down to earth. As a result, we find God where we are. We find God within each one of us (Jn 14:17).

The baby Jesus is the most unexpected and surprising gift from God for us. Jim and Della's Christmas presents—unexpected and surprising—are also like the baby Jesus.

We are Gentiles, not unlike the Magi. And so we ask ourselves: What kind of gift shall we give the Baby Jesus? The answer is love. As a response to God's love in and through Jesus, we must love God, and we must love each other in self-giving ways, like Jim and Della. We must return love for love. I think this is another reason why O. Henry named his story "The Gift of the Magi." ✝

[Epiphany (C)]

THE BAPTISM OF THE LORD (A)

(Isaiah 42:1-4, 6-7; Acts 10:34-38; Matthew 3:13-17)

Jesus Wants to Be One of Us

𝕿he Son of God humbles himself and wants to be baptized by John the Baptist. But John refuses at first. Jesus persuades John and manages to get baptized. The Son of God identifies himself with sinful humanity.

The humility of Jesus Christ is also expressed in the Christ Hymn from Paul's Letter to the Philippians. Having relinquished his divinity, the Son of God assumes the human nature as his own and humbled himself by dying on the Cross. Accordingly, God highly exalted him, giving him the name Lord—and "at the name of Jesus Christ every knee should bend, in heaven and on earth and under the earth" (Phil 2:10).

The Christ Hymn contains the worldview of the ancient Jews that helps us understand Jesus' baptism in today's Gospel. The three-tiered view of the universe is expressed nicely here: "…in heaven and on earth and under the earth." According to this ancient worldview, the top tier, heaven, is where God lived. The middle tier, the earth, is where human beings lived. The bottom tier, the nether world (Sheol, Hades, Gehenna), is where the dead stays, having no relationship with God.

This three-tiered, cosmic view of ancient Israel can also help us understand the scene of Jesus' baptism. During the baptism, the heavens open and the Spirit of God descends like a dove upon Jesus. Then a voice speaks from the heavens: "This is my beloved Son, with whom I am well pleased." It is the voice of God the Father, revealing the Son of God for the saving work of humanity.

We remember that the people of Israel had a constant longing for the fulfillment of God's promise. The prophet Isaiah prayed to God, "You would tear open the heavens and come down" (Is 64:1). The psalmist prayed, "Bow your heavens, O Lord, and come down" (Ps 144:5). God, for whom Israel waited so long, is now speaking to His Son, breaking down the barrier between the heavens and the earth.

In other words, the Spirit of God descends and hovers over Jesus in the form of a dove during the baptism of Jesus. This scene resembles the awesome moment of creation in the Book of Genesis: "In the beginning when God created the heavens and the earth…the Spirit of God was moving over the water" (Gen 1:1). This means that at Jesus' baptism God has re-created the world.

In addition, a voice from the heavens says, "You are my beloved Son." This suggests that Jesus is the new Adam from the new creation. St. Paul called Jesus the second Adam: "The first man, Adam, became a living being; the second Adam became a life-giving spirit" (1 Cor 15:45).

We belong to this second Adam by virtue of our baptism. As St. Paul instructed, "Just as we have borne the image of the man of dust, the first Adam, we will also bear the image of the man of heaven, the second Adam" (1 Cor 15:49). We have within us a part of both Adams. We experience the flesh of the first Adam and the spirit of the second Adam. In other words, we are "spirits in the world." We are embodied spirits. We live in this world with our mortal bodies, but we possess infinite spirits to know and to love. And God is with us always at the "horizon" of our knowing and loving.

In summary, today's gospel passage highlights two points. First, during Jesus' baptism God consents His creation work to the person of Jesus. Second, by virtue of our baptism, we are called to participate in God's creative work as children of God.

Again, we are second Adams by virtue of our baptisms. And Jesus Christ asks us to be his brothers and sisters by completing God's re-creation. Only if we unite ourselves to Jesus Christ can we call God our Father. And only if God is our Father can we then share his eternal life. ✝

[Baptism (B, C), 26th OT (A)]

FIRST SUNDAY OF LENT (A)

(Genesis 2:7-9, 3:1-7; Romans 5:12-19; Matthew 4:1-11)

New and Clean Hearts

The season of Lent is for us to recognize our trials and sufferings, so that we may renew our hearts and transform these trials and sufferings into God's love for us.

The gospel reading today is called "the Temptation of Jesus." Jesus is led to the desert after his baptism, and there the devil tempts him to avoid the trials and sufferings of life. The devil asks Jesus to convert rock into bread (poverty) and to hold power (chastity) and to worship a false God (obedience). Jesus successfully resists these temptations, which the ancient Israelites fell victim to (Dt 6-8). By demonstrating the fullness of humanity, Jesus proves that he is the Son of God.

We have listened to a somewhat different story in the first reading. God created Adam and Eve, just as the potter forms a piece of pottery, and breathed the breath of life into them. God also provided the earth with beauty and nourishment. Yet Adam and Eve wanted to know "what is good and what is evil." Dissatisfied with being creatures, they desired to be like God. This is called the doctrine of original sin.

This doctrine is about the mystery of being human, because we, too, often commit the sins of Adam and Eve. Theologians say that, because of original sin, we have lost the likeness of God but still maintain the image of God. In other words, before the Fall, we knew and loved from our hearts.

What happened to Adam and Eve may be compared to what is happening to us now. We generally pay attention to only what we see and hear. We always understand according to our pre-conceived notions. We always judge with right or wrong consequences. We always act from our self-interests. In all, we emphasize intellect and will, adoring knowledge and freedom. Furthermore, we live in an intellectual, but sophisticated, world controlled by microchip economics. As a result, we end up with huge heads and small, wooden hearts.

Fortunately, we still maintain the image of God, even though we have lost the likeness of God. We often make decisions from our feelings, gut instincts, and intuition. A woman's intuition can shed light on a dark situation. A man's gut instincts can result in a happy ending.

Moreover, we often meet good people who act justly and with virtue and character, not solely using intelligence and knowledge. And we often encounter holy people who love God and neighbors because of their likeness to God and not because of their degree in theology. We can still know and love with our wooden hearts.

As we begin the season of Lent, we need to heal our hearts and transform them into compassionate and loving hearts. As the psalmist sings, "A clean heart create for me, O God, and a steadfast spirit renew within me" (Ps 51:10).

Heart is the center of our being. It is heart that sees God. It is heart that believes in God (Rom 10:10). It is heart that begets love. Love is the sense of "belonging together" among other attributes.

Love allows us to recognize God within us; love allows us to walk with God among the evening breezes in the Garden of Eden; love creates a new heart in us. Therefore, when we are in love, we cannot separate heart from intellect and will. What we sense, what we understand, what we judge, and what we act—all of these naturally come from our hearts. As a result, God is not understood in terms of ideas or concepts, but in terms of habits of the heart. If and when this happens, we have acquired new and clean hearts.

Jesus' triumph over his temptations in the desert is the paradigm for us to follow. By attaining new and clean hearts, we can stand firm against temptations in our daily lives. Lent is the time to recognize trials and sufferings, so that we can renew our hearts and transform these trials and sufferings into love. ✝

[4th Lent (A), Holy Trinity (C), 8th OT (C)]

SECOND SUNDAY OF LENT (A)

(Genesis 12:1-4; 1 Timothy 1:8-10; Matthew 17:1-9)

We Live between Genesis and Revelation

In our journey of faith, we often experience shining moments. They can be moments of genuine gratitude for joyful events in our lives. They can also be moments of sadness for sorrowful events in our lives.

The apostle Peter had the same kind of experience. Jesus took him, along with James and John, up to Mount Tabor in Galilee. During prayer, Jesus' face dazzled like the sun, and his clothes became radiant with light. Jesus was transfigured. Then, suddenly, Moses and Elijah, who were archetypes of the law and prophets of Israel, appeared and talked to Jesus about his exodus, which would soon occur in Jerusalem. Seeing all these, Peter was excited and wanted the moment to last for a long time. Then a voice from the cloud above identified Jesus as "my beloved Son, with whom I am well pleased." After that, Jesus was left alone, as the embodiment of both the law and prophets. Peter has seen Jesus in glory.

Earlier, Peter confessed that Jesus is "the Messiah, the Son of the living God," but protested against Jesus' prediction of his passion and death (Mt 16:21-28). Peter did not understand the meaning of the Messiah. Accordingly, Jesus rebuked Peter and called him "Satan," just as Jesus rebuked the real Satan during his temptation in the desert. During the Transfiguration, Jesus once again showed a sign of his divine identity, but Peter could not, as usual, comprehend it.

Years later, Peter understood and referred to the event in his letters. He wrote, "With our own eyes we saw his greatness. We were there when he was given the honor and glory by God the Father, when the voice came to him from the Supreme Glory, saying, 'This is my own dear Son, with whom I am pleased!' We ourselves heard this voice coming from heaven, when we were with him on the holy mountain" (2 Pt 1:16-18). Peter was able to comprehend the true nature of Jesus only after he encountered the risen Jesus.

We wonder why Peter made those mistakes, and yet he was characterized as being the gusty and warm-hearted apostle. This is so, not because of Peter's fragile human nature, but because of the goodness of God. God has the primacy over man. Man proposes; God disposes. Paul also confirmed the primacy of God and said that God "saved us and called us to a holy life, not according to our works, but according to his own design," as in the second reading.

Like Peter, we, too, may remember our previous encounters with the Divine much later, although they may not be as glamorous and enchanting as those of Peter's. We often feel truly sorry for others, only some time after we have reflected on what really happened. We often grasp the meaning of true love, only some time after our beloved has departed from us. We often appreciate our parents, only some time after they have passed away from us.

Therefore, the good life we have is not a reward for our righteous living, and the not-so-good life we have is not a penal consequence of our sin. Good or not-so-good, our life is a free gift from God, who always has divine initiatives.

We live, always, between the glorious transfiguration that we have missed and the ultimate resurrection that we hope for. We live between the Book of Genesis and the Book of Revelation. In between, we are like Peter, not really knowing what we should know and not really loving who we should love. In the meantime, the hidden cross is there for us to carry. Indeed, the cross is an absolute necessity in life, as the Transfiguration of Jesus reminds us that the way of the cross leads to the resurrection.

The season of Lent is a time to ask ourselves how well we are doing with our crosses. The season of Lent is a time to ask ourselves how well we let our glorious moments shine before others, so that they may see them and praise our Father in heaven (Mt 5:16). ✝

[2ⁿᵈ Lent (B, C)]

THIRD SUNDAY OF LENT (A)

(Exodus 17:3-7; Romans 5:1-2, 5-8; John 4:5-42)

We Are Made Thirsty

"Everyone who drinks this water will be thirsty again; but whoever drinks the water I shall give will never thirst; the water I shall give will become in him a spring of water welling up to eternal life."

We can go without food for a few days, but when we are thirsty, we need to drink water almost immediately. Our body thirsts for water, and our soul thirsts for the living water, the water that gives life. We are made thirsty.

The gospel story is about the Samaritan woman, who is thirsty for the living water. After a day-long walk, Jesus, who is tired from the journey, asks her for a drink. But in the end, the woman receives the living water from Jesus. In their conversation, the woman misunderstands Jesus repeatedly.

If we consider, however, underlying symbols and different levels of meanings, their dialogue is very much like a harmonious duet in which one instrument plays a key melody and another instrument responds with variations of that melody. Like Beethoven's sonata for cello and piano (#3, op 69), the gospel story begins as a quiet solo and then is followed by a few lively duets. Their duets naturally transform into Jesus' solo performance before the finale of another duet. Jesus and the woman are making musical variations on the theme of the living water.

There is something strange about the woman, however. She comes to the well at noontime to draw water, whereas other women in town do that early in the morning. Considering she had five husbands in her career, she could be despised by her people. And yet, the woman remains attentive to what Jesus says. Jesus, the master teacher, takes their conversation one step at a time, sincerely and seriously. A conversion starts to take place in her heart, as we see her first address Jesus as "Jew," then "prophet" and "the Messiah" and, finally, "Christ." Having attained enlightenment herself, she leaves behind the water jar and runs quickly to share the good news with her people in town. She becomes a missionary for the whole region of Samaria.

In the 1950s western movie "High Noon," Gary Cooper, the marshal of a small town in Kansas, faces off with terrible outlaws at noontime. All the townsfolk, including his newly wedded wife, played by Grace Kelly, desert him. In the end, Grace Kelly returns to help him finish the gunfight. Then, as the townspeople emerge, Gary Cooper throws his marshal's star into the dirt and leaves town with Grace Kelly.

The story of the Samaritan woman is similar to "High Noon." Let us think about why Jesus has chosen this marginalized person. Jesus is tired and thirsty, but he sees a woman who honestly desires and longs for the living water. What kind of emotions and pathos are involved here? Jesus, the sacrificing love, comes face-to-face with the depth of human misery. One may call his reaction pity, empathy, sympathy, mercy, or compassion. Whatever it may be called, all are variations of love. And after all, by saying, "Give me a drink," Jesus meets the woman at the well where Jacob met Rachel (Gen 29:1-14). The love of God never discriminates against people.

It is important to note that today's gospel story also foreshadows another high-noon story. At noontime, Jesus is hanged on the cross (Jn 19:14), and from there he entrusts another woman, his mother, to his beloved disciple (Jn 19:27).

Each one of us has something in common with this Samaritan woman. In our faith journey there have been many wells. Sometimes a stranger waits near one of them and asks for a drink. Maybe this person is sent by God for us to see the face of God, which we might have somehow forgotten. The stranger gives us living water to drink.

"If today you hear his voice, harden not your hearts" (Ps 95:7-8), because "the love of God has been poured out into our hearts through the Holy Spirit who has been given to us" (Rom 5:5). ✝

FOURTH SUNDAY OF LENT (A)

(1 Samuel 16:1, 6-7, 10-13; Ephesians 5:8-14; John 9:1-41)

Can You See with Your Heart?

We have just heard the long narrative about the man born blind. This colorful, poetic story describes how the blind man in his entire life is cured and makes his spiritual journey. It is about us.

The man born blind is a lucky guy. He happens to be in the right place at the right time. When Jesus and his disciples pass by, he becomes an object of discussion. Is he blind because of the sin of his or his parents? There is no mention of anything that the blind beggar might have done to receive Jesus' attention.

It must be around dusk one late afternoon. It is getting dark quickly. This darkness symbolizes the approaching death of Jesus Christ. So Jesus says, "While I am in the world, I am the light of the world." Then Jesus decides to heal the man born blind before the darkness falls in, that is, before his death. "Jesus spat on the ground and made clay with the saliva, and smeared the clay on his eyes."

In the beginning God "formed man from the dust of the ground" (Gen 2:7). Jesus performs a new creation on the man born blind, using his saliva. He can see now, because Jesus is the light of the world. Then Jesus sends him to "the pool of Siloam, which means Sent." In John's Gospel, Jesus is sent from the Father, and the man is sent from Jesus.

With eyes opened, the man born blind slowly begins his spiritual journey. During his journey, he calls Jesus by different names, first calling him "the man called Jesus" and then "prophet." When he is thrown out of the Temple and encounters Jesus for the second time, he calls Jesus "Lord" and accepts him as "the Son of Man." Even when he is summoned to the Pharisees, he proudly suggests them to become Jesus' disciples.

We make a spiritual journey in the same way. When we were first baptized, we opened our eyes and saw things dimly. It takes time to be fully mature and be able to see things hidden in the world. For example, at the beginning of the Gospel of Mark, both John the Baptist and Jesus ask to repent. When I was a child, I understood repenting meant confessing sins. When I was a young man, it meant changing value-systems or world-view. Now at the late stage of life, repenting means to have a pure heart like a child (Mt 5:8).

Heart is the innermost depths of person that can be touched by God. And heart plays a special role (of mind) for perceiving spiritual things in life, such as beauty, love, and wisdom. So, if we have pure hearts, we can know and love things that we cannot see or hear. If we have pure hearts, it does not have to be concrete or tangible for us to grasp its meaning and value. If we have pure hearts, we can know and love things of God.

However, since the Enlightenment of the 18th century, we have been influenced and shaped by intellect and reason. Descartes, the father of modern philosophy, said, "I think, therefore, I am." Since then, we have lived in an age of reasoning for too long. As a result, our heads have overgrown, and our hearts have shrunk: we become smart, sadly not wise.

Fortunately, we are familiar with man's gut reaction and woman's intuition. A stubborn husband is rescued by the wisdom of his wife. A good person knows the right things to do, not because he knows laws or regulations, but because he is virtuous in character and personality. A holy person loves God and fellow human beings, not because of the degree in theology, but because of the disposition to the sacred.

Heart knows and loves intuitively and connaturally. Blaise Paschal put: "Our heart knows reason which reason does not know." Therefore, to repent means to heal our selfish and wooden hearts, and transforms them into compassionate and loving hearts.

Like the man born blind, we like to see, hear, and touch with our hearts. Then we will encounter the Christ, who is always dwelling within us as well as among our brothers and sisters. ✝

[Christmas Day, 1st Lent (A), 15th OT (A)]

FIFTH SUNDAY OF LENT (A)

(Ezekiel 37:12-14; Romans 8:8-11; John 11:1-45)

Jesus Is the Resurrection and the Life

We must experience Jesus of Nazareth as the Christ and the Son of God. Today's gospel reading helps us do that.

The gospel reading today is a well-known story, the raising of Lazarus. It is the final and greatest miracle performed by Jesus in John's Gospel. It also is the direct cause of Jesus' arrest.

The story of the raising of Lazarus consists of many layered, contrasting themes: life versus death, light versus darkness, awake versus asleep, resurrection versus death, the death of Lazarus versus the death of Jesus, Jesus' humanity versus his divinity, Jesus' conversation with Martha versus that with Mary, and so on. All together, the story provides an opportunity for us to personally experience the saving work of Jesus, so that we can call Jesus the Christ, our Lord.

When Jesus first heard about the illness of his beloved friend Lazarus, he stayed for two more days in the Jordan valley (where John the Baptist did his ministry). He knew that he needed to do God's work. Finally, on the way to Bethany, Jesus met Martha, who said, "I know he will rise in the resurrection on the last day." Martha was referring to the typical Jewish understanding of the general resurrection. She did not yet know that Jesus was the Word made flesh. Jesus corrected her, saying, "I am the resurrection and the life; whoever believes in me, even if he dies, will live." (This distinguished Christianity from Judaism.)

Jesus suggests in this declaration that the general resurrection, in which the Israelites have been hoping, has already occurred in him. Thus, the faith in Jesus prevents one from dying and, even if one dies, he will have new life. Martha could not grasp this concept and called Jesus "the Messiah, the Son of God," (a low Christological confession, Jewish general resurrection).

In contrast, when Mary came to Jesus, she "knelt at Jesus' feet" (a high Christological confession of Jesus being the Messiah). This suggests that Mary already had true faith in Jesus. Mary's faith was more mature than Martha's. For this reason, Jesus did not need to teach Mary.

Finally, when Jesus went to the tomb of Lazarus, Martha said to Jesus that her brother had been dead for four days and had begun to decompose. Jesus became "perturbed and deeply troubled." Jesus was sorrowful for the darkness brought by death—Lazarus' death and his own death that was approaching. He wept.

And then, Jesus brought Lazarus back to life (resuscitation). When Lazarus came forth from his tomb, he came with his burial garments, because he would eventually need them. By contrast, when Jesus was raised from the dead (resurrection), he left his garments behind, rolled up in orderly fashion, because he would not need them again (Jn 20:7).

Accordingly, the raising of Lazarus from death is a sign of a deeper awakening to the fullness of life. Jesus said earlier to Martha, "Everyone who lives and believes in me will never die." In other words, Jesus will do for us something even greater than what he did for Lazarus. Jesus will resurrect us. Jesus will give us life that is eternal.

Eternal life is God's life, in which there is no distinction between past, present, and future. Eternal life is the new life of knowing Jesus Christ. Eternal life is Jesus Christ. Eternal life is not a blissful life of soul in heaven, after being separated from body. Pope Benedict supports this view, by saying that eternal life is "not an unending succession of days in calendar" (*Spe Salvi*, #12). Eternal life is the fullness of life in faith, hope, and love. Eternal life is the life with Jesus Christ in the here and now (Jn 14:3). Therefore, those who do not live eternal life today may not enjoy it later on.

Jesus is "the resurrection and the life." So we call Jesus the Christ, our Lord. ✝

[4th Easter (C), 16th OT (C)]

PALM SUNDAY OF THE LORD'S PASSION (A)

(Matthew 21:1-11; Isaiah 50:4-7; Philippians 2:6-11; Matthew 26:14-27:66)

God's Last Word

The cross is the manifestation of God's love and Jesus' response to God's love.

The gospel reading today recounts the passion and death of Jesus and includes elements of betrayal, conspiracy, and murder. In the Gospel of Matthew, Jesus faces his own suffering and death with dignity and as destiny. Even before the passion begins, Jesus announces, "My appointed time draws near." At the Last Supper, Jesus tells his disciples that one of them is going to betray him, and he predicts Peter's denials. In all, Jesus accepts his own death calmly and confidently.

Jesus' death was not an ordinary death, however. He was put to death on the cross. To die on the cross was most painful and humiliating. Jesus' death on the cross was more than physical pain and humiliation, however. Jesus died under the religious curse (Gal 3:13) and outside of the camp (Heb 13:13). It was the shameful and scandalous death of a criminal, because it was executed by irreligious pagans in the absence of God (outside of Jerusalem).

We know very well that Jesus' death changed the history of mankind forever. At the moment when Jesus died, "the curtain of the temple was torn in two, from top to bottom." It means that God became finally available to all people. In addition, "the earth shook, the rocks were split, and the tombs were opened." They were apocalyptic signs of the end-time. Jesus' death marked the end of the present world, where there was no hope and, at the same time, the beginning of a new world, where the Spirit dwells in hope.

Of course, we cannot talk about Jesus' death alone, because his shameful death leads to his glorious resurrection. Theologians, the apostle Paul included, say that Jesus' death and resurrection cannot be isolated from each other; they are one event. To us, it is true that the deeper we pray over Jesus' death, the easier it is to appreciate Jesus' resurrection. The Holy Week is waiting for us to experience that.

In the meantime, let us reflect upon the relationship between Peter and Jesus. It is true, when Jesus was arrested, that Peter was the only courageous one, among the twelve, who followed Jesus into the courtyard, (although Peter was the first apostle who encountered the risen Jesus). What was he doing, however, while Jesus was going through his passion?

Peter denied Jesus by saying, "I don't know him" in the courtyard, not once, but three times (Mt 26:70, 72, 74). Peter denies all the confidence and trust that had been placed in him; he denies his own confession: "You are the Messiah, the Son of living God"; he denies all the leadership that Christ had called him to assume; he denies the intimacy of friendship with Jesus; he denies having ever heard the voice of Father: "This is my beloved Son, listen to him"; he denies all of his history and, ultimately, himself.

On the other hand, the last word of the Gospel does not surround Peter's failure but his reconciliation with Jesus. When the cock crowed, that is, when the light of day defeated the darkness of night, Peter finally remembered what Jesus had said. And he went out and wept bitterly (Mt 26:75).

Furthermore, the promise of reconciliation had already been made at the Last Supper. When Jesus predicted Peter's failure, he promised his companionship with him. Jesus said, "After I am raised, I will go to Galilee ahead of you" (Mt 26:32). Finally, in the lake of Galilee, the risen Jesus appeared to Peter and asked three times, "Do you love me?" (Jn 21:15-19). Jesus forgave Peter three times for his previous three denials. The story of resurrection is the story of reconciliation. The risen Lord takes the initiative to restore the broken bond with Peter and with his people.

God's initiative always comes first with abundant grace. Jesus died in accordance with Scripture, and the cross is consistent with God's plan of salvation. The cross is the manifestation of God's love. ✝

[Good Friday, Palm Sunday (B, C), 13ᵗʰ OT (A)}

Holy Thursday: Mass of the Lord's Supper (ABC)

(Exodus 12:1-8, 11-14; 1 Corinthians 11:23-26; John 13:1-15)

To Serve Is to Love

We are disciples of Jesus and we follow Jesus. To follow Jesus, however, does not mean doing the same things as Jesus did. We cannot imitate Jesus exactly. We cannot do the same exact things Jesus did in this twenty-first century. Ideally, to follow Jesus means to be a human in the way Jesus was a human. To follow Jesus is to be a person very much like Jesus. In order to do this, what is important to Jesus must be equally important to us. To follow Jesus, therefore, we must change ourselves so that we can have the same moral character and disposition as Jesus.

How can we, then, develop moral character and disposition similar to Jesus? We do it by discerning ethical paradigms from stories about Jesus' actions and deeds recorded in the Scriptures. The gospel reading today provides an excellent example for that.

On the night when he is betrayed, Jesus is fully aware of his origin in God and his imminent return to the Father. Loving his own to the end, he gets up from the table, takes off his outer robe, picks up the bowl and towel of a servant, and begins to wash the disciples' feet. This act of hospitality is normally performed by Gentile servants. Jesus turns the Jewish practice upside down.

Obviously, his disciples are astonished and dumbfounded. Peter objects wildly, "Master, you are not going to wash my feet." He thinks that Jesus is not fit to do the servant's work; however, that is precisely why Jesus wants to wash Peter's feet. Jesus insists, "Unless I wash you, you will have no share with me." Faced with the risk of losing the tie with Jesus, Peter yields. When it is all done, Jesus spells out the meaning of his scandalous act: "I have given you a model to follow, that you also should do as I have done to you."

To follow Jesus is, therefore, to perform acts such as the washing of feet, just as Jesus did for his disciples. What drove Jesus to wash his disciples' feet? It is love. Because of his love for humanity, after washing the disciples' feet, Jesus lays out his new commandment: "Just as I have loved you, you also must love one another" (Jn 13:34). To Jesus, to love is to serve, even if it includes washing the feet of the lowly.

Let us ask ourselves, "What is love?" Is love affectionate emotion? Yes, love has something to do with the heart. Is love justice? Yes, there is no justice without love. Is love respect? Yes, love always entails honor and respect. Is love belonging? Yes, the sense of belonging and togetherness is fundamental in love. We can talk a lot about love, but we cannot nail down exactly what love is.

The New Testament does not define what love is, at least not in a few simple words, although Neo-Platonism broadly defines love as the force that moves the world.

The best explanation of love comes from St. Paul, who illustrates more than a dozen virtues to explain love: "Love is patient; love is kind; love is not envious or boastful or arrogant or rude..." (1 Cor 13:4). Paul's explanation of love suggests that love is the foundation of all virtues. All good traits become virtues only through love. Conversely, to love is the most efficient way to acquire other virtues in life.

Jesus himself does not spell out what love is. Rather, he shows what love is by his actions. To Jesus, love is washing his disciples' feet. This is why Jesus says to his disciples, after he washed their feet, "If you know these things, you are blessed if you do them" (Jn 13:17). Love means to do what Jesus has shown us—to serve all, especially the lowly and the marginalized.

On the night when he is betrayed, Jesus washes the disciples' feet. By doing so, Jesus shows us what love is and, consequently, how to follow him. To love is to serve others. To love is to serve others with dignity, self-sacrifice, and mutuality, even if they are the lowly, the marginalized, and the vulnerable. To love is not to lord over others (Mk 10:42-44, Lk 22:25-26, Mt 20:25-27). To be the disciples of Jesus is to follow him and to serve one another, as he has served us. ✝

[3rd OT (B), 9th OT (A)]

EASTER SUNDAY (A)

(Acts 10:34-43; Colossians 3:1-4; John 20:1-9 or Luke 24:13-35)

Easter Affirmations

Easter Sunday is the most important day for Christians. The resurrection of Jesus has changed everything. The singular word "Alleluia" expresses joy and happiness on this Easter Sunday.

The gospel reading today makes three great affirmations. First, the tomb of Jesus was empty. Second, Jesus appeared alive to some of his followers. Third, through faith we share in the new life of the risen Christ. These are our Easter faith.

The first Easter affirmation is the empty tomb. On Good Friday, Jesus died on the cross. The body of Jesus was taken down from the cross and laid in a new tomb. Mary Magdalene and other women saw his body being buried. Three days later, in the early morning of Sunday, which was the first day of the week, Mary Magdalene went to the tomb and found it empty. She suspected that Jesus' body was stolen. Peter saw Jesus' burial clothes neatly folded in the empty tomb, but drew no such conclusion; the beloved disciple "saw and believed."

The second Easter affirmation is the appearance of the risen Christ. Mary Magdalene said repeatedly, weeping three times, "They have taken the Lord from the tomb, and we do not know where they put him" (Jn 20:2, 11, 13, 15). When the risen Jesus appeared to her, she didn't recognize him because, by clinging to her previous perceptions, she did not see the reality and significance of his death (Jn 20:17). Mary's love ultimately did allow her to witness the risen Jesus.

The risen Jesus appeared again to some disciples. Peter's speech, which we heard earlier today in the first reading, is a good example of the early Church's faith. At the center of his speech is the proclamation that God raised Jesus from the dead on the third day and that the risen Jesus appeared to the witnesses chosen by God.

The third Easter affirmation is a new creation with the risen Christ. On the first day of the week, the risen Jesus appeared to Mary Magdalene (Jn 20:1). Mary saw the risen Jesus as the gardener standing outside the tomb (Jn 20:15) in the garden where Jesus was buried (Jn 19:41). The garden represents the Garden of Eden, and the gardener represents the new Adam. On another first day of the week, the risen Jesus appeared to all eleven disciples, including Thomas (Jn 20:26). Just as God created the world on the first day of the week (Gen 1:1); so does the new creative work of God appear through the risen Jesus.

In addition, when the risen Jesus appeared to the disciples, he breathed the Holy Spirit into them, as God did to Adam in the beginning (Gen 2:7). Therefore, the resurrection of Jesus signifies the beginning of the Jewish end-time, that is, the new creation and the new life with God.

The resurrection of Jesus is an eschatological event that happens on the other side of the cross. The resurrection of Jesus is God's affirmation of Jesus' life, passion, and death. The resurrection of Jesus means that the whole person of Jesus—body and soul—has been raised to the final, full, and eternal life of God. It means that God has begun a new creation and that there is a life after death.

Because of the resurrection of Jesus, we are able to see the depth, height, and width of God's love for us. Because of the resurrection of Jesus, we are beloved sons and daughters of God. Because of resurrection of Jesus, we hope that we, too, will be raised on the last day, as Paul said to the Romans, "We will certainly be united with him in a resurrection like his" (Rom 6:5).

Actually, we "have already been raised with Christ," as we have listened to the second reading from the Letter to the Colossians. This realized resurrection contrasts to the future resurrection in the Letter to Romans mentioned earlier. Because we have already been raised with Christ, we must seek what is above, not what is on earth. The resurrection of Jesus is the source and dynamism of our ability to partake in God's life here and now. †

[Easter (B, C), 3ʳᵈ Easter (B), 32ⁿᵈ OT (C)]

SECOND SUNDAY OF EASTER (A): DIVINE MERCY SUNDAY

(Acts 2:42-47; 1 Peter 1:3-9; John 20:19-31)

Faith in Resurrection

At this time of year, we are surrounded with signs of spring everywhere. We see new, green leaves sprouting from barren trees. We hear the songs of many birds in the wake of the gentle breeze from the south. We do not know how these things happen; we may not even notice that spring is here already.

Our inner world, too, is full of wonders and mysteries. We are often enchanted by finding ourselves immersed in something true or something beautiful. We are joyful as we search for something holy and something divine. Above all, we are blessed when we love and are loved. All of these feelings and emotions, which transcend logic and reasoning, are habits of the heart.

From today's gospel reading, I am glad to learn a person like Thomas was a disciple of Jesus. Thomas, who believed only tangible and concrete proof, remained skeptical of Jesus' resurrection when he first heard of it. He was a "doubter," who was unfamiliar with transcendental things in life. When the risen Jesus appeared for the second time, he asked Thomas to poke his side and touch his wounds. Then Thomas cried out, "My Lord and my God!" That is the highest profession of faith in Scripture. Soon after, Jesus said to his disciples, "Blessed are those who have not seen and yet have believed." These words of Jesus are for us to listen to, because we, too, believe in Jesus we never met.

Once again, I am glad to know that Thomas was one of Jesus' disciples, because then I can be a disciple of Jesus, too. You see, I have performed science research for so long that I have become a habitual linear thinker. I like to explain things based upon their causes and effects. I can understand only what can be explained in terms of logics. Therefore, just like Thomas, it is difficult for me to accept transcendental or spiritual events that are beyond human logic and reason, such as the resurrection of Jesus. I am sure that all of us have a Thomas within us. We believe only those things that we can see, hear, touch, and explain. Apostle Thomas opens up the possibility for us to be disciples of Jesus.

On the other hand, if we pause and listen to our hearts carefully, the resurrection of Jesus parallels the signs of spring. We can encounter the risen Jesus. We can encounter the risen Jesus in our hearts like new green leaves shooting from tree branches or songs of birds suddenly present in the wind. In other words, we can be poetic and contemplative, rather than intelligent and speculative.

The resurrection of Jesus is not like a mathematical equation requiring proof. The resurrection of Jesus is the revelation of the divinity of Christ that has been hidden in the humanity of Jesus. The resurrection is the divine manifestation of the living God. The resurrection of Jesus is the proof of God's love, stronger than death. We remember that when the risen Christ appeared to Mary Magdalene and the disciples, they did not ask Jesus, "How did you do that?" Instead, they realized overwhelmingly that something awesome and remarkable had occurred. The evangelist John reported, "The disciples simply rejoiced when they saw the Lord" (Jn 20:20).

The second reading from the First Letter of Peter says that faith and hope in the resurrection of Jesus "guarantees the inheritance kept in heaven and also the salvation that is ready to be revealed on the last day." This exhortation reflects a profound faith and hope of the spiritually mature Peter who, after having failed in the hour of trial, first encountered the risen Jesus.

Thomas didn't believe the risen Jesus at first, and Peter denied the passion of Jesus at first. On the other hand, the first word of the risen Jesus to his disciples was "Peace be with you," not once but twice. And he continued to say, "Receive the Holy Spirit. Whose sins you forgive are forgiven, and whose sins you retain are retained."

As we celebrate the Divine Mercy Sunday, let us remind ourselves that the risen Jesus never brings up our past failures and short-comings; he is always forgiving and merciful. The resurrection of Jesus is like the spring that has already arrived. Christ Jesus already dwells within us, so that we may live the life of God. ✝

[2ⁿᵈ Easter (B)]

35

THIRD SUNDAY OF EASTER (A)

(Acts 2:14, 22-23; 1 Peter 1:17-21; Luke 24:13-35)

On the Road to Emmaus

The gospel story today, the Walk to Emmaus, is a long and beautiful story of the resurrection of Jesus. It makes up almost one half of Luke's resurrection account with mature theological themes.

It was afternoon of the first day of the week. Two disciples of Jesus decided to go home to Emmaus. Their dreams to free Israel and themselves had been badly crushed, because their Messiah had died on the cross. Some women claimed Jesus has been raised, but it had to be silly gossip.

On the road to Emmaus, a stranger suddenly joined and engaged in conversation with the two disciples. They complained to the stranger that they "were hoping that Jesus was the one who was going to redeem Israel." They explained to the stranger why they were so frustrated, for their would-be Messiah was dead. It was a real dead end. To those frustrated disciples, the stranger "interpreted all the scriptures, the things concerning the Messiah, beginning with Moses and all the prophets."

When the two disciples arrived in a small village at dusk, they invited the stranger to stay. The stranger humorously pretend to go on. Then he quietly assumed the role of a host at the table—taking, blessing, and breaking the bread. At that moment, the disciples' eyes were opened and recognized the risen Jesus, who then vanished immediately from their sights.

At that very moment the two disciples were able to make sense out of what Jesus had told them on the road. So they simply recalled, "Did not our hearts burn within us while he talked to us on the road, while he opened to us the Scriptures?" They belatedly realized that their hearts had been moved when they first saw the risen Jesus. They were finally enlightened; they finally found the living God in the depths of their being.

So they decided to return immediately to Jerusalem. The two disciples told other disciples in Jerusalem, "We have met the risen Jesus who has broken bread with us." Other disciples in Jerusalem responded, "The Lord has truly been raised and has appeared to Simon."

Scripture scholars say that the two disciples in the story could be husband and wife (Jn 19:25). If so, the Emmaus story is the reverse of the story of Adam and Eve in the Book of Genesis. After being tempted by the serpent and having eaten the fruit, "their eyes were opened" and they became like God (Gen 3:7). By contrast, on the road to Emmaus, when Jesus broke the bread, "their eyes were opened," but they share in a new life with God.

We, too, are on the journey to Emmaus. The risen Lord always comes into our lives when we are in trouble. He rarely asks us to come to him; instead he comes to us. When he comes, he usually comes as someone we do not recognize. Whenever the risen Lord disguised as a stranger comes to us, he interprets our life stories. Moved by the Holy Spirit, we then find ourselves in a prayer. Being grasped by the grace of God, we receive appropriate consolations.

For example, during the Eucharistic celebration, we are moved by the risen Lord unknowingly. He always takes bread, blesses and breaks it, and gives it to us. And then he disappears. Where does he go? When will he come again? He has disappeared within us, but he will appear again, whenever we give (break) ourselves for others.

Therefore, if we look closely at ourselves, the risen Jesus is within us. When we work for others, together we will see the risen Jesus, alive and personalized, within us. And as Jerusalem was the place where our dreams and hopes were crushed and frustrated, we will start again from there, the lowest point of our lives.

We, too, are on the journey to Emmaus. In the middle of the disappointment and frustration of daily life, we come to this sacred place to listen to the Word of the Lord and to share his body and blood. In doing so, we realize that the risen Jesus has been with us all along, blessing, consoling, and encouraging us. ✝

[3rd Easter (B)]

FOURTH SUNDAY OF EASTER (A): GOOD SHEPHERD SUNDAY

(Acts 2:14, 36-41; 1 Peter 2:20-25; John 10:1-10)

The Good Shepherd

The responsorial psalm, the most famous one, shows that the image of God is a shepherd, who nourishes and protects his flock: "The Lord is my shepherd; I shall not want. He makes me lie down in green pastures; he leads me beside still waters; he restores my soul." What a comfort and security this psalm portrays! God is so gentle and nourishing that we want to "dwell in the house of the Lord for years to come."

In the gospel reading, Jesus, the Good Shepherd, says, "I am the gate." To understand this saying of Jesus, let us describe a sheepfold. To take care of the sheep in the wilderness, they are put at night into a cave or a closed sheepfold. A sheepfold consists of stone walls several feet high, with a narrow entrance. After the sheep were enclosed in the sheepfold, the shepherd would lie down at the narrow opening, so that no sheep could escape the sheepfold and no wild animal could enter it. The narrow spot is the gate. When Jesus says, "I am the gate," he means that he puts his body in that narrow spot and protects his flock from wild animals. Jesus is the Good Shepherd, and we are his flock.

Sometimes, a single sheepfold may contain multiple herds of sheep for the night. In early morning, shepherds call out for their own sheep. When sheep hears the voice of their shepherd, they follow him. Occasionally, a false shepherd imitates the voice of another shepherd. If there happens to be a sheep which follows the false shepherd, sadly it will not return to the sheepfold that night. Being able to recognize the shepherd's voice is a matter of life and death.

We, the sheep, know how to recognize the voice of the Good Shepherd. This is particularly true in this globally pluralistic society we live in; not only many different Christian denominations but also numerous non-Christian religions claim that each of them alone possesses or represents the Good Shepherd.

(To illustrate how to discern the voice of the Good Shepherd, I like to share with you a story. One cool summer night, a Zen master and his student were walking under a full moon. In the middle of their conversation, the master suddenly raised his finger and pointed at the moon. Then, the student's eye immediately turned to the master's finger, instead of looking at the moon. He ought to look at the moon, not the master's finger. The moon, not the finger, is the truth.)

As we celebrate the Good Shepherd Sunday, we know, of course, Jesus being the Good Shepherd. But we must go beyond this traditional cliché. When we say Jesus is the Good Shepherd, it sounds like an introductory catechism, as if we still believe that the sun is circling around the earth. Realizing that the earth is only one of many planets circling around the sun, the image of the Cosmic Christ, "in him all things in heaven and on earth were created" (Col 1:15)," is better suited in our time. It will help us develop global consciousness. And when Paul says, "It is no longer I who lives, but it is Christ who lives in me (Gal 2:20)," this Christ who lives in us is the Cosmic Christ.

To understand the meaning of the Cosmic Christ, let us remind ourselves that the Christian faith claims that all people in the world come from the same origin, God. And the incarnation of the Word shows that Jesus Christ is the center that joins God and humanity.

Finally, the death/resurrection of Jesus brings everything in heaven and earth into one with the Cosmic Christ. The Cosmic Christ is neither objective Christ out there in the cosmos, nor subjective theological assent to the risen Christ. The Cosmic Christ is the living Christ in the cosmos to which all people belongs to. With the Cosmic Christ, man and the cosmos have become one in distinction, but without separation. Therefore, the Cosmic Christ points at the fact that there is an inner similarity and commonality among all people in spite of their differences in races and colors. The Cosmic Christ, the Good Shepherd, is not only for Christians, but also for Buddhists, for Hindus, for Moslems and even for atheists, so that all "might have life and have it more abundantly." ✝

[4ᵗʰ Easter (B, C)]

FIFTH SUNDAY OF EASTER (A)

(Acts 6:1-7; 1 Peter 2:4-9; John 14:1-12)

"I Am the Way and the Truth and the Life"

On the night before he died, Jesus was concerned about how his disciples would remember him. Thus he revealed himself by revealing the Father. To his disciples, Jesus said, "I am the way and the truth and the life. No one comes to the Father except through me."

We are on a journey of faith to the Father in heaven. Our journey to the Father is possible only if we believe that Jesus is the way to the Father, the truth about the Father, and the life of the Father. Jesus is indeed "the way and the truth and the life," and this is the foundation of Christian faith. Let us look closely at these three attributes of Jesus.

First, Jesus is the way to know God as the Father. Jesus says, "No one comes to the Father except through me" (Jn 14:6). The early Christian movement was simply called "the Way" (Acts 9:2, 19:9). Jesus reveals the way to the Father. Accordingly, we follow Jesus, who is the way.

Second, Jesus is the truth that will free us from sins and selfishness. Jesus says, "I am in the Father and the Father is in me" (Jn 14:10). Jesus signifies the truth about the Father. Accordingly, we grow in love with Jesus, who is the truth.

Finally, Jesus is the fountain of Christian life. Jesus says, "Whoever eats my flesh and drinks my blood has eternal life, and I will raise him on the last day" (Jn 6:54). Jesus embodies the life of the Father. Accordingly, we live the life of God through Jesus, with Jesus and in Jesus.

All of us journey to the Father together, not individually. That Jesus chose his disciples and that Jesus founded the Church are credible and convincing tenets when based only on the solidarity of all people of God.

The second reading concerns the common priesthood of the faithful, in contrast to the ordained priesthood (*Lumen Gentium* #10). St. Peter's statement to the newly baptized Gentiles is remarkable: "You, however, are a chosen race, a royal priesthood, a holy nation, a people of God's own." Indeed, by virtue of baptism, we are called to share God's life and participate in the common priesthood of Jesus Christ *in persona Christi*. We are "the priestly people of God."

The common priesthood was exercised for establishing a new order of diaconate in the Church, as we heard in the first reading. When the Church grew large and changed her face, she embraced the Greek-speaking Jews and Gentiles. The Church of Christ changes herself prudently as she reads the signs of the times, while still remaining as the Body of Christ.

The common priesthood was founded by Jesus, whose entire life was a total surrender to the Father's will. And it was upon the cross that Jesus revealed both the boundless gift of God's love for humanity and the perfect human response of self-sacrifice to God. On the cross, Jesus gave himself completely, both to the Father and to all human beings. Therefore, the common priesthood requires a prerequisite of carrying the cross.

The common priesthood manifests itself most perfectly through the Eucharist. At the Eucharist, the priestly nature of the faithful is exhibited most vividly. The second reading exhorts Christians "to offer spiritual sacrifice acceptable to God through Jesus Christ." We bring this spiritual sacrifice to the Eucharistic celebration, presided over by an ordained priest *in persona Christi capitis* (in the person of Christ as Head of his Body, the Church.)

Our journey to the Father always includes the cross (of varying size, weight, and shape), because Christian life is marked by the cross. Our journey to the Father also requires us to share in the priesthood of Jesus Christ, because Jesus is the way and the truth and the life. Jesus is the way that leads to the true life. **✝**

[Corpus Christi (B)]

41

SIXTH SUNDAY OF EASTER (A)

(Acts 8:5-8, 14-17; 1 Peter 3:15-18; John 14:15-21)

How to Keep Jesus' Commandment

Realizing that there was not much time left, Jesus gave the last directive to his disciples: "If you love me, you will keep my commandments.... Whoever has my commandments and observes them is the one who loves me" (Jn 14:15-21).

As the disciples of Jesus, we are ready to account to Jesus by keeping his commandments. To remain faithful to Jesus and to hold Christian values firm require a great deal of courage, however.

Scripture helps us grow in courage and enables us to do what our conscience dictates. Scripture shows stories of God's love for human beings. Scripture shows how Jesus lived God's life and revealed the face of God. Scripture shows how early Christians followed Jesus Christ.

Scripture does not, however, provide adequate answers to all moral and ethical situations such as AIDS, internet theft, weapons of mass destruction, and so forth. An approach based on "do this and don't do that" may not address today's moral issues adequately. Moral theologians say that it is time to emphasize how to do things and why, rather than merely what to do.

To search for this "how to do," we must start with the most precious thing at the depth of the human heart—love. And love is mutual and requires action. This is why Jesus says, "If you love me, you will keep my commandments."

In the same way, Christian discipleship can be viewed differently. To follow Jesus is not just to do what Jesus would or would not do. We cannot do exactly the same things as Jesus did. To follow Jesus is to experience the reality of God manifested in the person of Jesus. To follow Jesus is to take seriously what Jesus took seriously. To follow Jesus is to build the kingdom of God, especially among the people in need of justice and reconciliation.

To take Jesus seriously is to follow him, not because he acts this way or that way, but because it is the way to respond to God's love. To take Jesus seriously is to follow him, not because some authority tells us to do so, but because it is the way to heal wounds. To take Jesus seriously is to follow him, not because we want our souls to go to heaven, but because we wish to build the kingdom of God on earth.

To illustrate how to follow Jesus, I would like to share a story. In the early 1940s, when World War II was at its most intense, the theological ethicist H. Richard Niebuhr put out a serious of articles in the magazine *The Christian Century*. In those articles, he asked questions such as "What is God doing at war?"

Those articles offended many readers of the magazine who thought that America and the Allies were doing God's work by punishing the war's unjust aggressors. Historically, when the Assyrians invaded Israel, the prophet Isaiah regarded it as God's judgment upon the faithless Israel. In a similar way, Niebuhr thought the crisis of the World War could be a means to discover God's healing judgment for both the Allies and their enemies. He called for repentance rather than retributive justice based on self-righteousness. Niebuhr tried to follow Jesus rather than being naïvely patriotic.

(What can we learn from this story at this juncture of the world's history? What is the United States doing now in several war fronts in the world? On this Memorial Day, we must not only honor the souls of departed soldiers but also recognize the dignity of soldiers who are alive.)

We give thanks to God, who is love, for what he has done through His Son, Jesus Christ. We hope and pray that our minds and hearts are filled with God's love, so that we may wisely discern the moral and ethical issues of today. ✝

[3rd OT (B), 6th OT (A)]

SEVENTH SUNDAY OF EASTER (A)

(Acts 1:12-14; 1 Peter 4:13-16; John 17:1-11)

The Law of the Cross

"Father, the hour has come. Give glory to your Son, so that your Son may glorify you."

The "hour" is the hour of the death of Jesus on the cross. Why in his hour of death is Jesus asking the Father to glorify him so that he may glorify the Father? Is the suffering on the cross related to glory? Glory refers to the brilliance and splendor of God. Suffering constitutes unbearable pain in body, mind, and spirit. Why, then, the reference to glory and suffering together? Not just the gospel reading, but all of today's readings refer to the connection between glory and suffering.

The first reading shows how the disciples and Jesus' family gained a new perspective on Jesus' suffering and death when they saw Jesus being taken up to heaven. All the original disciples (with the exception of Judas Iscariot) and some women were present, along with Mary, the mother of Jesus. It is important to note Mary's presence to the end. It makes her the most faithful disciple, even though her soul was pierced with the sword (Lk 2:35).

The second reading shows that early Christians were excluded from Roman society and suffered because of their faith in Jesus Christ. It is understandable why a murderer, a thief, or an evildoer should suffer, but to suffer because of the faith in Jesus Christ is not right. Suffering for Christ glorifies God.

The Gospel reading today is a part of Jesus' priestly prayer. On the night before he was betrayed, Jesus prayed that the offering of his own self would glorify God the Father for the life of the world. Having revealed the name of God to his disciples, Jesus consecrated them to eternal life. They were no longer "of the world," although they were still "in the world." In their journey coming without Jesus, they may face suffering, persecution, and even death. Then, they must glorify God by suffering for Jesus.

44

Glory and suffering appear to be opposite from each other. But they are closely related to the death of Jesus on the cross. On the cross, Jesus gave himself completely both to the Father and to the whole human race. On the cross, Jesus revealed both God's unconditional love for humankind and the perfect human response of self-sacrificing love for God. On the cross, Jesus responded to God's love most perfectly as a human being. On the cross, Jesus revealed the breadth and length and height and depth of God's love, love that allowed His Son to die (Eph 3:18). Therefore, on the cross, the glory of God was manifested most effectively by the death of Jesus.

The death of Jesus on the cross is not just any suffering, however. It is self-sacrificing suffering, rather than self-seeking suffering. It is the suffering through which we are redeemed, giving glory to God. It is suffering for others. It is redemptive suffering.

This redemptive suffering for others is expressed by the Law of the Cross (Bernard Lonergan), which states: Sin leads to death. And death, if accepted out of love, is transformed. This death transformed receives the blessing of a new life, eternal life. Eternal life is to know Jesus and to live as Jesus lived. The Law of the Cross depicts precisely the life, death, and resurrection of Jesus.

The Law of the Cross is applicable exactly to us in our everyday lives. A housewife, who is patient with her husband who is blind to the things of God, will eventually be vindicated by his later conversion. A mother who struggles to rear her children will be rewarded later by their constructive contributions to society.

We are in the world, but we are not of the world. And we share the suffering of Christ in the world by means of the Law of the Cross. Let us remember that Jesus Christ always remains with us in our redemptive sufferings, and so we give glory to God. ✝

[22nd OT (A)]

PENTECOST (A)

(Acts 2:1-11; 1 Corinthians 12:3-7, 12-13; John 20:19-23)

The Gift of the Holy Spirit

Paul said to the Corinthians, "No one can say, 'Jesus is Lord,' except by the Holy Spirit." This means that Jesus, who has shown us the face of God the Father, is the Christ (Messiah) in the power of the Holy Spirit. Those who believe that Jesus is the Christ also believe that the Spirit of God is bestowed in him.

In the Bible, the Holy Spirit appears as the dove at Jesus' baptism (Lk 3:22) and as the tongues of fire at the Pentecost (Acts 2:3). And the concept of the Holy Spirit varies from one person to another. To some, the Holy Spirit is the Spirit of God, a distinctive identity within the Trinity. To others, the Holy Spirit is the Spirit of the risen Jesus. Now, the risen Jesus, the Christ, sits at the right hand of the Father and exists since the beginning of creation. Thus the Holy Spirit is the Spirit of Christ.

Among the three persons of the Trinity, the Holy Spirit is least known. The Holy Spirit does not have face or shape. The Holy Spirit does not use words. St. John Paul II called the Holy Spirit the "hidden God," hidden behind God the Father and Jesus Christ. However, whenever we invoke or pray to Jesus or to the Father, we always pray in the Holy Spirit. Without the Holy Spirit, nothing of the divine can happen at the liturgy, in the Church, or in the world.

Have you ever wondered why Jesus sent the Holy Spirit? After his resurrection, Jesus stayed with his disciples for fifty days. Why, then, did Jesus send the Spirit? Perhaps, if Jesus had remained among the disciples after resurrection in his visible human presence, their faith would never have grown as it needed to. It was necessary for Jesus to withdraw his presence so the disciples could continue to grow in faith. Jesus said to his disciples, "It is better that I go away, for if I don't go away the Spirit will not come to you" (Jn 16:7).

Jesus gave us the Holy Spirit, not once, but three different occasions. First, on the cross he gave the Spirit to his mother and his beloved disciple (Jn 19:30). Second, on the first day of the week he gave the Spirit to his disciples, as we heard in the gospel reading (Jn 20:20). Third, after being with the disciples for fifty days (Acts 4:4), he gave the Spirit to all people in the world, as we heard in the first reading today.

The Holy Spirit is "Lord, the giver of life," as in the Creed. The Holy Spirit is the gift (*charisma*) of God. Jesus said to the Samaritan woman, "If you knew the gift of God and who it is that is saying to you, 'Give me a drink,' you would have asked him, and he would have given you living water" (Jn 4:10). The Holy Spirit is the living water and the gift of life from God, as the down payment (earnest money) for us to fulfill the kingdom of God (Eph 1:14, 2 Cor 5:5).

We cannot see or touch the Holy Spirit. But we are Christians precisely because of the presence of the Holy Spirit within us. The Holy Spirit illuminates our hearts and helps us understand the Scriptures and teachings of the Church. And the Holy Spirit helps the Church read the signs of the times and interpret them in the light of the Gospels. In other words, the Holy Spirit ensures that the Church will be faithful to the original apostles.

The Holy Spirit has no face. Jesus said, "The wind blows where it chooses, and you hear the sound of it, but you do not know where it comes from or where it goes" (Jn 3:8). Just as the wind can only be known by its effect, so goes the Holy Spirit. This is why we pray *in* the Holy Spirit, not *to* the Holy Spirit. We come to know the presence of the Holy Spirit by its fruits: love, joy, peace, patience, kindness, generosity, faithfulness, gentleness, and self-control (Gal 5:22-23).

The disciples of Jesus needed the Holy Spirit to complete the work Jesus initiated. We, too, need the Holy Spirit. We must be guided, refreshed, and strengthened by the Holy Spirit. The power of the Holy Spirit worked wonders in the lives of the first disciples. The power of the Holy Spirit has worked wonders in the lives of many believers throughout the ages. *Veni, Sancte Spiritus!* ✝

[Pentecost (C)]

47

THE MOST HOLY TRINITY SUNDAY (A)

(Exodus 34:4-6, 8-9; 2 Corinthians 13:11-13; John 3:16-18)

God Is for Us

"The grace of the Lord Jesus Christ, and the love of God, and the fellowship of the Holy Spirit be with you all!" This is the best-known blessing from Paul, found at the end of his Second Letter to the Corinthians. It is also the greeting used at the beginning of Mass. It is a brief and concise Trinitarian confession of faith

To explain the doctrine of the Holy Trinity, three different phases of water is often used. As the water exists in gaseous steam, liquid rain, and solid ice, so the Godhead subsists in three distinct persons: the Father, the Son, and the Holy Spirit. St. Ignatius portrayed the doctrine in terms of three musical notes that harmonize together to make a single chord. St. Patrick used three leaves of a clover to convey the idea of the unity of the Father, the Son and the Holy Spirit.

Let us look closely at Paul's blessing. The first point regards the grace of the Lord Jesus Christ. We can know God only from what Jesus Christ has revealed. God's revelation is this: "God so loved the world that he gave his only Son." Therefore, the Son has shown us the face of God through his life, death, and resurrection. Jesus Christ, the Word Incarnate, is the proof of God's love for us.

The second point describes the love of God. Scripture emphasizes that God loved us first and that our love for God is our natural response to God's love. As in today's first reading, God is "merciful and gracious, slow to anger and rich in kindness and fidelity." Every word of this statement stresses that God cares for us and loves us. God is for us. God, the Father of Jesus Christ, however, always keeps His transcendence and remains the Absolute, the Infinite, the Ineffable, the Silence, the Ultimate Concern, and the Holy Mystery. Our understanding of God the Father is based only on His Son, Jesus of Nazareth. Through Jesus of Nazareth, God has entered into the salvation history of mankind.

And the third point regards the fellowship of the Holy Spirit. The Holy Spirit guides, empowers, and teaches in place of Jesus Christ. The Holy Spirit brings us together in faith, hope, and love. And the Holy Spirit shapes and animates the life of the Church, by reminding what Jesus of Nazareth did for us.

The doctrine of the Trinity is about the trinitarian nature about God. The Father, the Son and the Holy Spirit dwell within one another without distinction and separation. There is no Father without the Son and the Spirit; there is no Son without the Father and the Spirit; there is no Spirit without the Father and the Son. The Holy Trinity is relational and interconnected. The Father creates through the Son in inspiration of the Holy Spirit. The Son, sent by the Father, is made flesh by virtue of the life-giving Spirit. The Spirit comes upon us, as being sent by the Father at the request of the Son.

The Holy Trinity is the trinitarian Ultimate Reality. Another trinitarian reality is that of God, man, and the world (cosmotheandric). God cannot be God without man and world; man cannot be man without God and world. World cannot be world without God and man. There are more trinitarian realities: Man is the trinitarian unity of body, mind, and spirit: mind is the trinitarian unity of intellect, affection, and will; theological virtue is the trinitarian unity of faith, hope, and love, the ideal of humanity is the trinitarian unity of truth, beauty, and good. Time is trinitarian unity of past, present, and future. All realities are inseparable trinitarian in nature.

The final point of the doctrine of the Trinity is that the personhood of the Father, the Son, and the Holy Spirit is the perfect personhood, and the communion within the Holy Trinity is the prototype for all human communities. Accordingly, we follow Jesus, because Jesus is the parable of God, and because he has shown us the most perfect paradigm of humanity. Pope Benedict in his Encyclical Letter said, "Jesus Christ has shown us who man truly is and what a man must do to be truly man" (*Spe Salve*, #6).

Let us close with the Sign of the Cross, the Trinitarian sign. ✝

[Holy Trinity (B, C), 8ᵗʰ OT (B)]

THE MOST HOLY BODY AND BLOOD OF CHRIST SUNDAY (A)

(Deuteronomy 8:2-3, 14-16; 1 Corinthians 10:16-17; John 6:51-58)

The Reality of the Eucharist

When the Israelites journeyed the Sinai Desert during the Exodus for forty long years, they were hungry and thirsty, and their bodies began to feed on themselves. They wanted to go back to Egypt, where they had, at least, something to eat. Then God gave them manna, the food from heaven. God also gave them water from the rock (Dt 32:51). God provided food and water to the Israelites when they were hungry and thirsty.

In the same way, we are on our own Exodus journeys. We travel the way of salvation from ego to wholeness, from sin to grace, and from death to life. However, it is very difficult to get rid of resilient egos and self-centeredness. As soon as we have cultivated some virtues, we are trapped by the darkness of vices. As soon as we feel whole and focused, we become prisoners of envy and anxiety. As a result, we are always hungry and thirsty. Our journeys of salvation, therefore, require the tangible form of God's love.

In the gospel reading, Jesus says, "I am the living bread that came down from heaven; whoever eats this bread will live forever." Jesus compares himself to the manna in the desert but, unlike the manna, Jesus himself becomes the bread that satisfies hunger and thirst. And so Jesus instituted the Eucharist at the Last Supper on the night he was betrayed and commanded to do it in memory of him.

We believe that Jesus Christ is present in the consecrated bread and wine. However, the consecrated bread and wine remain the same in appearance. If they don't change in appearances, how is Jesus Christ present? What does "real presence" mean, anyway? Let us reflect upon the reality of the Eucharist.

The presence of the risen Jesus in the consecrated bread and wine is just like the incarnation of God. Through incarnation, the Word was made flesh. In the same way, through the Eucharistic consecration, the bread and wine are transformed into the body and blood of Christ. We remember that when Jesus was on earth, he said, "It is good that I leave (Jn 16:7)." Now, the risen Jesus is in the Eucharist by the power of the Holy Spirit. In fact, whenever we eat the bread and drink the wine, we manifest each other the face of Christ present within us.

We also remember that the presiding priest offers the Eucharistic prayer *in persona Christi*. When he quotes, "This is my body… This is the cup of my blood," he goes back to the Last Supper and reenacts what Jesus asks him to do. The presence of Christ Jesus is the reality of the consecrated bread and wine, as well as the reality of the act of consecration itself.

Reality is not always what we can see. Oftentimes, it is what we cannot see. For example, when we look up stars at night, it seems that we see them in their fixed positions. This is what we see. Actually, the reality is that we see them in their previous positions, depending on how far they are from the earth. Each star gives off light that takes time to reach our eyes; some several hundred years, and others several million years. Therefore, what we see is not the stars' absolute fixed locations, but their relative moving positions.

The consecrated bread and wine are like that. They are what we see, but they are the divine reality of the risen Jesus that we cannot see. In the same way, we can see the priest offering the Eucharist prayer, but we cannot see the risen Jesus who is doing the actual consecration.

As the incarnation is bodily, God's love for us also has to be bodily, because we are embodied spirits. Therefore, if we believe that Jesus Christ is the Word made flesh, then we also believe that the consecrated bread and wine are the body and blood of Jesus Christ.

The Eucharist is not the flesh and blood of Jesus, the young Palestine Jew. The Eucharist is the body and blood of Christ, who is "the image of invisible God." The Eucharist is the fullness of the mystery of Christ. Therefore, by receiving the Eucharist we can embody Christ in ourselves, that is, Christ can become our own life. ✝

[Corpus Christi (B, C), 18ᵗʰ OT (A), 19ᵗʰ and 20ᵗʰ OT (B)]

SECOND SUNDAY IN ORDINARY TIME (A)

(Isaiah 49:3, 5-6; 1 Corinthians 1:1-3; John 1:29-34)

"Where Is the Lamb?"

"Behold, the Lamb of God, who takes away the sin of the world." Calling Jesus "the Lamb of God," John the Baptist testifies the imminent coming of Jesus Christ on the Jordan River.

In order to understand Jesus being the Lamb of God, we need to consider the Jewish custom of animal sacrifice. The Jews offered daily animal sacrifices at the Temple as a way of restoring a right relationship with God. Every morning and every evening, a lamb was sacrificed in the Temple (Ex 29:38-42). This ancient Jewish custom of animal sacrifice may appear to be somewhat cruel and uncivilized. However, before the practice of the animal sacrifice the eldest son of a family was sacrificed in neighboring regions.

Surely, the sacrifice of Isaac in the Bible was intended to teach a lesson against such an ancient practice. Let us take the sacrifice of Isaac as an example. God had promised Abraham that he would have numerous descendents, as many as the stars at night and sands in seashore. So Abraham and Sara, at their very advanced ages, had a son Isaac. Then God, unexpectedly, asked Abraham to sacrifice Isaac (—the very seed for future numerous descendents). Abraham, once again, obeyed God and took Isaac to the mountain where God dwelled. On the mountaintop right before the actual sacrifice, the young Isaac asked Abraham, "Where is the lamb?"

This age-old question, "Where is the lamb?" which summarizes the entire Hebrew Bible, was answered by John the Baptist. John foretold that Jesus was the sacrificial lamb for the salvation of mankind. And Jesus eventually died as the Passover lamb on the "hour" (Jn 19:31).

Returning to the story of the sacrifice of Isaac, it ended with, as we know, God's intervention not to sacrifice him. God, who spared Abraham's only son Isaac, did not rescue His only Son, Jesus. Even as the psalmist pleaded so ardently, "Bow your heavens, O Lord, and come down" (Ps 144:5), God did not come down and rescue His Son. God let Jesus die on the cross. The Son of God was the Lamb of God.

We wonder, if God was almighty and all-powerful, why didn't He rescue His Son on the cross? God was definitely present on the Calvary Hill, but He remained utterly silent. Perhaps, God respected human freedom, not arbitrarily meddling with human affairs. Perhaps, God was weak and vulnerable, not almighty and all-powerful.

Indeed, God has been weak and vulnerable all along. For example, when God created human beings in His image, God took a foolish risk. Consequently, simply because Adam and Eve were created in the image of God, they obviously wanted to be like God. Even now, we, too, try to be like God. Another example of God's vulnerability is that, before the Word was made flesh, God had to seek permission from a young country girl, Mary.

We are familiar with the Greek notion of God, which is opposite to the portrayal of human beings, based on the duality of Greek philosophy. We are weak; so God is omnipotent. We are confined in a place; so God is omnipresent. We are limited in knowledge; so God is omniscient. We suffer changes; so God is immutable. We are bound in time; so God is eternal.

If some of us are still holding on such notion of God, let us remind ourselves that God has taken human flesh and become one of us. This is all about Christmas we celebrated a few weeks ago. Moreover, even now, the incarnation continues; the almighty God descends, takes human flesh and suffers. Therefore, the omnipotent and omniscient God is, paradoxically, weak and vulnerable. The story of Jesus is our story.

We may ask, "How come the utterly transcendent God takes human flesh and suffers with us even now?" This is so, because God is love. Love always seeks others. Love always self-sacrifices. Love always becomes more and more. Naturally, therefore, when we are in love, we suffer, because love makes us weak and vulnerable. Indeed, it is a terrible thing to fall in love with God. The story of Jesus is our own story. ✝

[4th Advent (A), 2nd Lent and 20th OT (B)]

53

THIRD SUNDAY IN ORDINARY TIME (A)

(Isaiah 8:23-9:3; 1 Corinthians 1:10-13, 17; Matthew 4:12-23)

Called Together to Follow Jesus

Jesus enters into the lives of four disciples—Peter, Andrew, James, and John—who are engaged in their ordinary profession by the Sea of Galilee. They are fishermen. When Jesus simply says to them, "Follow me," they drop everything and immediately follow him.

We may consider fishing a low-ranking profession, and the word "fisherman" seems odd and perhaps even dangerous. First of all, fishermen catch fish to feed people, although it is clearly bad news for the fish. And then, there are those words in English linking fishing with uncommon and unsavory human activities. A deal sounds "fishy." A drug dealer tries to "hook" innocent people. A "hooker" "lures" someone.

The image of fishing in today's English is not the same as it was for the first-century Israelites. They used fishing nets to gather fish. Thus the word "fishermen" did not refer to "catching," "hooking," or "luring," but "gathering." In addition, fishing refers to a new level of consciousness, as the fish is moved from under water into an open-air environment. In the Bible, the sea symbolizes a chaotic and disordered situation. Therefore, fishing symbolizes a gathering of the people "who are in the darkness" so they "see a great light," as we heard in the first and gospel readings.

The reason for this discussion on fishing is that, if we regard fishing as a low-ranking profession (*eisegesis*, not *exegesis*), we are likely to be either boastful for being chosen by Jesus or be confident of a future conversion. We may think that if even the fishermen in Galilee were chosen, we would be natural picks for the disciples of Jesus. In short, pride can make us stumble, as in the second reading.

Jesus didn't choose a rabbi or a scribe. But he chose a tax collector (Matthew) and a political radical (Judas). Jesus wasn't partial in his saving work. After all, the four fishermen were average people who already had good character traits—endurance, patience, and courage, suitable virtues for missionary work.

Jesus Christ wants to share his divine light with us and wants us to live God's life—the true life—in him, with him, and through him. Jesus Christ is our light and salvation. Our task, therefore, as disciples of Jesus Christ, is to respond to this call from Jesus.

How can we respond to Jesus' call? To help find an answer to this question, I would like to share a story with you. The chapel at the Central American University in San Salvador is named after Archbishop Oscar Romero. On the outside of the chapel are inscribed his words: "If they kill me, I will rise again in the Salvadoran people." Those words were broadcast days before his assassination.

On the inside walls of the chapel, the traditional fourteen Stations of the Cross appear. Instead of the customary pictures of the passion of Jesus, however, there are fourteen ink drawings of Salvadorian victims of torture—men, women, and children who have been stripped, beaten, and executed. The message is clear and direct. The death and resurrection of Jesus continues today in the passion of the people of El Salvador.

The power of this story comes from the belief that Jesus Christ continues to work in the same way as in the gospel story. The chapel at Central American University is filled with religious symbols that connect the crisis in El Salvador today to the stories of Jesus in the Bible. The people of El Salvador find Jesus Christ in their own situations because they identify with Jesus.

Have we identified ourselves with Jesus in our daily lives? Have we identified ourselves, in even a small way, with our sons and daughters, with our brothers and sisters? We cannot hesitate in answering this question, because we are disciples of Jesus Christ. ✝

[3rd and 30th OT (B)]

55

FOURTH SUNDAY IN ORDINARY TIME (A)

(Zephaniah 2:3, 3:12-13; 1 Corinthians 1:26-31; Matthew 5:1-12)

Ethics in the Kingdom of God

The gospel reading today is about the Beatitudes, the summary of Jesus' Sermon on the Mount. The Beatitudes describe the life of Jesus and point at those attitudes and dispositions necessary for Christian life. The Beatitudes are the ethical paradigm of the kingdom of God.

The Beatitudes describe what kinds of persons are blessed and happy and what they can hope for in two major parts. The first part declares that those who display certain attitudes or values are blessed. They are the poor in spirit, those who mourn, the meek, the hungry and thirsty for righteousness, the merciful, the pure in heart, the peacemakers, and the persecuted because of Jesus. The second part explains that the reward is living God's life in the fullness of God's kingdom.

The Beatitudes are contrary to what is often valued and respected in this world. God does not conform to the standard of this world and turns them upside down. The Beatitudes sketch the way of life that might be deemed foolish by the world, but not by those who truly love God.

Among the eight virtues listed in the Beatitudes, let us consider three examples: the poor in spirit, the merciful, and the pure in heart.

First, the poor in spirit are the people who are humble and have found God in their hearts. Only those who are poor in spirit are strong enough to detach themselves from worldly things and to attach themselves to divine things. The poor in spirit are found among the least as well as the most successful people.

An example of the above is Pope John XXIII. One of Pope John's first visits, after he became Pope, was to a prison in Rome. He told the prison inmates, "You could not come to me, so I came to you." He also told them that the last time he went to a prison was to visit his cousin. The next day, the Vatican newspaper omitted the reference to his cousin; the paper kept silent on the fact that a papal relative was in jail. St. John was one of the world's most successful persons, yet he was a down-to-earth man who was poor in spirit.

Let us consider the merciful. Mercy is the willingness to enter into the chaos of others. It is love in action. We often pray the Jesus Prayer: "Lord, Jesus, have mercy on me." And we ask Jesus to be with us among our flaws and sinfulness. Mercy is a uniquely Catholic virtue, as Pope Francis published a book entitled "The Name of God Is Mercy."

Finally, let us consider the pure in heart. Heart is the innermost core of our being. Thus, the pure in heart simply follow their conscience, because conscience is where we are alone with God. So if our hearts are pure, then our lives are in harmony within ourselves and with others.

Babies have pure hearts. They don't have so many attachments and desires; when hungry, they eat; when tired, they sleep. By contrast, we eat, even if we are not hungry; we cannot go to bed, because we have things to finish. Again, observe the children watching cartoons, where animals talk and laugh and sing songs and dance. By contrast, we, grown-ups are not that pure, that innocent. We spend our energy chasing dreams and, sometimes, fantasies. Day in day out we desire things temporary; we look for things camouflaging the true reality.

Those who are pure in heart, as St. Paul said, can perceive even invisible things in the world (Rom 1:20), that is, they find God in all created things, because they can see God in them. The purity of heart is not a simple moral injunction; it is an existential requirement for Christians. If we maintain the purity of heart, then Christ is born within us. If our hearts are pure, then God dwells within us.

In summary, the Beatitudes are the ethics of the kingdom of God and the confession of our ultimate dependency on God (CCC, #1723). With the Beatitudes, the risen Christ comes into our hearts. Without the Beatitudes, we cannot be called Christians. ✝

[11th OT (B), 17th OT (A)]

FIFTH SUNDAY IN ORDINARY TIME (A)

(Isaiah 58:7-10; 1 Corinthians 2:1-5; Matthew 5:13-16)

Orthopraxis in God's Kingdom

Jesus sacrificed himself against evil forces of the world and showed us the way how we can be authentically human. As disciples of Jesus, we follow him in his sacrificial act of love and attain salvation from God.

In the gospel reading, Jesus tells us that we are the salt of the earth and the light of the world. Salt is the source of sacrifice necessary in the world, so we are to serve others in this world. Light contrasts to darkness, ignorance, and the ungodly, so we are to radiate with our virtuous acts. Therefore, "to be the salt of the earth and the light of the world" is to let "our light shine so brightly before the world that they can see our good works and glorify God the Father."

Jesus, however, does not tell us to *become* the salt and the light. Rather, Jesus tells us that we already *are* the salt of the earth and the light of the world. This teaching of Jesus is about our dignity and responsibility as disciples of Jesus. It is about living out the gospel values under our sociopolitical conditions rather than being doctrinally sound Christians. It is about orthopraxis, not orthodoxy.

Jesus himself demonstrated orthopraxis. On the night before he died, Jesus washed the disciples' feet. As Peter protested, he said, "Unless I wash you, you have no share with me." When it was done, Jesus said to his disciples, "If you know these things, you are blessed if you *do* them" (Jn 13:17).

In the first reading, the prophet Isaiah says, "Share your bread with the hungry. Shelter the homeless. Clothe the naked." This doctrine of the preferential love for the poor is one of the basic tenets of the Scriptures, seen in passages such as the Magnificat, the Beatitudes, Isaiah 61, and the Last Judgment (Mt 25). God has shown a special form of primacy to the lowly and the marginalized. Therefore, as the salt of the earth and the light of the world, we need to care for the poor and the marginalized.

The late Cardinal Stephen Kim in Korea was a man of humility and piety. He said in his book that one thing he missed in his life was actually living together with the poor and the destitute. However, his duty at office didn't allow him to reside in an orphanage or a shelter. As the head of the Korean Catholic Church, he played a very critical role for holding justice, peace, and human rights against military dictatorships in the 1960s and 1970s.

As we come close to God through Christ Jesus, we attain peace of mind, maintain the right way of living, and give thanks to God. These are signs of liberation from evil and of reconciliation with the human existential conditions of finitude and contingency. At this stage, we are more or less concerned with personal and ethical issues of Christianity. As we make progress, although we long for God's kingdom, we become more concerned with issues of justice and peace. And we become more sensitive to issues surrounding social and political aspects of Christianity. In other words, orthopraxis, not orthodoxy, constitutes the ground of God's kingdom.

Cardinal Kim had a deep-seated desire and yearning to be with God. He earnestly wanted to live with the poor and the marginalized. He wanted to live the life of orthopraxis. He was the salt of the earth and the light of the world.

As we have heard in the second reading, St. Paul approached his ministry "in weakness and fear and much trembling." He did so because he knew that it was God's power at work. He practiced orthopraxis. He was the salt of the earth and the light of the world.

We, too, are the salt of the earth and the light of the world. Let us act and live out our lives according to what we are—the children of God. The world will see us as we are. Seeing the good we do, the world will give glory to God the Father. ✝

[9ᵗʰ OT (A), Christ King (A)]

SIXTH SUNDAY IN ORDINARY TIME (A)

(Sirach 15:15-20; 1 Corinthian 2:6-10; Matthew 5:17-37)

Is It Too Difficult to Follow?

According to theologians, the goal of life is to find "authenticity" or the "true self" that God created. If we find our authenticity or true self, then we will be in union with God and in perfect harmony with our fellow human beings.

Jesus of Nazareth, the Wisdom of God, teaches us how to achieve the goal of life without using sophisticated words such as "authenticity" and "true self." To achieve the goal of life, Jesus gives us the Sermon on the Mount—the ethics of the kingdom of God.

Today's gospel passage is a part of the Sermon on the Mount that deals with the ethics of murder, reconciliation, adultery, and oaths. Some say that these are lofty ethical exhortations, difficult to carry out. For example, Jesus says, "If you bring your gift to the altar and there recall that your brother has anything against you, leave your gift at the altar, go first to be reconciled with your brother, and then come and offer your gift." If we stick to the literal meaning of this teaching, most of us gathered here must go back to where we were before and offer reconciliation to our brothers or sisters. Only after that, we come back to this altar.

In a similar way, Jesus says it is wrong to entertain thoughts of adultery, not to mention doing it. Once again, most of us are either adulterers or victims of adulteries. How, then, can we understand these teachings of Jesus? This question brings up a special problem, because we live today in an age where people don't fear God and have weak awareness of sin and guilt. People today do not bother with questions about sin and sinfulness. Then, what is the point of Jesus' teaching, we ask?

In the gospel reading, Jesus says several times, "You have heard...I say to you..." This means that Jesus himself is the new Torah and thus provides new moral and ethical paradigms. Furthermore, the history of salvation shows that God, who offers the divine life to share, has been the innermost center of human existence. Whenever we long for something in self-reflection, God fills that emptiness. Thus, if people can accept the inescapable love of God, then they can grasp what sin and sinfulness mean. The closer we come to God, the clearer we know who we really are. Moreover, we are already redeemed in the person of Jesus Christ. We are called to live God's divine life.

How to live God's divine life? There certainly are multiple answers to these questions. One answer is to convince ourselves that the risen Christ dwells within us and that we try to unite with him in everyday life. Then, we will not wait for God's grace to come down from on-high. In other words, we, as moral agents, try to follow those very examples Jesus has shown us in the Bible.

The Church teaches that we have in our hearts "a law inscribed by God" (*GS* #16). This law is the risen Christ with whom we can be united in our conscience. Hence, we have sacred obligation to maintain our conscience clean, pure, and straight. Otherwise, we end up either blindly following someone else or obediently listening to the authority conditioned by rules and regulations.

So we are called to follow Jesus Christ, by loving God and our neighbors. Loving God and neighbor is to do good and virtuous acts, because what we do transforms us into who we are. By doing good and virtuous acts, we become disciples of Jesus Christ. Therefore, we try to be persons who want to perform good and virtuous acts habitually, instead of being anxious for doing things morally right and not doing things morally wrong.

The Sermon on the Mount is closely related to who we are, as opposed to what we do or don't. Jesus Christ, the absolute and definite bringer of salvation, wants us to be virtuous persons who obey God's law naturally and spontaneously. When we keep the Sacred Heart of Jesus in our hearts all the time, then we have found our "authenticity" and become "true selves." †

[6th Easter (A), 4th OT (A), 16th OT (C), 28th OT (B)]

SEVENTH SUNDAY IN ORDINARY TIME (A)

(Leviticus 19:1-2, 17-18; 1 Corinthians 3:16-23; Matthew 5:38-48)

Jesus and Girard's Theory on Violence

"When a person strikes you on the right cheek, turn and offer him the other." This is, no doubt, an unrealistic saying of Jesus. It is, however, the exact description of the earthly life of Jesus.

Many scriptural passages say "Jesus died for our sins" (Gal 1:7, 2:20, 3:13, 1 Cor 15:3, 2 Cor 5:14, 1 Jn 2:2). These are theological conclusions and do not explain exactly how Jesus' death saves us and why. To early Christians, who were familiar with the Passover and animal sacrifices, Jesus' death on the cross was a sacrificial act to God; besides, Jesus never preached that his death was the remedy for our sins and the cause of our salvation.

Why, then, did Jesus suffer and die for us? How does Jesus' death on the cross save and redeem us? How can we, as his disciples, participate in the saving act of Jesus? Today's gospel passage provides answers to these questions.

The phrase, "eye for eye, tooth for tooth," was a warning against excessive revenge (Lv 24:17-20). For example, during a war, ten enemy hostages were killed for each soldier who died. The whole families of one betrayed politician were killed. Thus, "an eye for an eye" was a proper way of revenging, no more and no less than what was necessary.

On the other hand, Jesus says, "When someone strikes you on your right cheek, turn and offer him the other." He also says, "Love your enemy." Jesus teaches us not to return violence for violence, but to eradicate the very roots of violence in human history.

According to Rene Girard, the origin of violence is rooted in human desire and envy. A professional envies his coworker's promotion. A housewife envies the next door neighbor's new car. A child envies another child's toy. People instinctively desire what others do or have. These imitative or mimetic desires naturally generate conflict and violence. And violence spawns more violence, until a scapegoat is identified and victimized. Then, the system is pacified, but only until another mimetic violence occurs. In this way, human history has been filled with seemingly unstoppable desires, envies, conflicts, and violence.

In the world where Jesus of Nazareth lived, his words and deeds were controversial, provocative, and revolutionary. Some Jewish leaders were worried about whether Jesus was perverting the faith of Israel. Others were afraid of the Romans and nervous about whether Jesus would cause another uprising. Still others were threatened over whether they would lose their own power and status. Naturally, Jesus was identified as an ideal scapegoat by the Jewish religious leaders.

Jesus willingly and conscientiously became the scapegoat, although he was innocent, and sacrificed himself. Jesus freely accepted his own death out of love for *Abba* and his fellow human beings. Jesus chose the cross against the source of violence — the human desire and envy. Therefore, the self-sacrifice of Jesus provided a non-violent way of establishing peace in human history by eliminating imitative desires and mimetic violence.

Jesus demonstrated the authentic way of being human based on non-violence and self-sacrifice. Jesus exemplified the paradigm of self-sacrificing love. By doing so, Jesus showed us how to be truly human. Pope Benedict XVI says, "Jesus tells us who man truly is and what a man must do to be truly man" (*Spe Salvi*, #6).

God vindicated Jesus by transforming his death into a new life of resurrection. And the risen Jesus, the second Adam, brought forth a new age for us. In summary, Jesus responded to God's love and lived human life perfectly and showed us the human face of God. This is why we confess that Jesus died for our sins.

We are called to follow Jesus, the parable of God, who showed us how to be truly human. Let us remember what Jesus says: "Be perfect, like the heavenly Father is perfect." ✝

[5th Lent (C), 10th and 22nd OT (A), 22nd OT (C)]

63

EIGHTH SUNDAY IN ORDINARY TIME (A)

(Isaiah 49:14-15; 1 Corinthians 4:1-5; Matthew 6:24-34)

Money, Money, and Money

Recently, I helped my daughter's family settle in Dallas from Washington, D.C. They bought an old house that was remodeled some years ago, and I hired workers for general repair works. One of the most surprising things we discovered was that there were three unused air-conditioning return ducts underneath the house. One was a ghost duct that was exposed to the open air; the other two were still attached to walls. This meant that during hot summers, the air conditioner pumped the warm air from the crawl space for some years.

Anyone who has remodeled or repaired a house may have had a similar experience. After the work has been completed, no homeowner crawls underneath the house to inspect the quality of the work done. In general, workers are interested in money rather than in doing the work correctly and honestly. To make money, they may cut corners, lie, or cheat.

My experience, perhaps an extreme case, illustrates that money is the most important thing in life nowadays. This is the dark side of the world we live.

By contrast, I like to share with you another story that illustrates something other than money is important in life. It also shows a blissful and peaceful side of the world we live.

Fr. Pedro Arrupe was the Superior General of Jesuits some years ago. He visited a poor slum in Latin America. During his visit, he celebrated Mass for the local people in a small building where cats and dogs wandered in and out during the service. Afterward, Fr. Arrupe was invited to the house of one of the church members. Following, in his words, is the rest of the story.

"When it was over, a big devil whose hang-dog look made me almost afraid said, 'Come to my place. I have something to give you.' I was undecided; I didn't know whether to accept or not, but the priest who was with me said, 'Accept, Father, they are good people.' I went to his place; his house was a hovel nearly on the front of collapsing. He had me sit down on a rickety old chair. From there I could see the sunset. The big man said to me, 'Look, sir, how beautiful it is!' We sat in silence for several minutes. The sun disappeared. The man then said, 'I didn't know how to thank you for all you have done for us. I have nothing to give you, but I thought you would like to see this sunset. You liked it, didn't you? Good evening.' And then he shook my hands."

"As I walked away, I thought, 'I have seldom met such a kindhearted man.' I was strolling along that lane when a poorly dressed woman came up to me; she kissed my hand, looked at me, and with a voice filled with emotion said, 'Father, pray for me and my children. I was at that beautiful Mass you celebrated. I must hurry home. But I have nothing to give my children. Pray to the Lord for me; he is the one who must help us.' And she disappeared running in the direction of her home." (*One Jesuit's Spiritual Journey* by Pedro Arrupe, S.J., p. 35-36).

This is a beautiful story of the poor people who give thanks to God. The poor are close to God, and so God is close to them. In today's Gospel, Jesus says, "No man can serve two masters… You cannot give yourself to God and money." By pointing out birds of the air and the grass in the fields, Jesus says, "I tell you, do not worry about your life." Jesus reminds us that, unlike birds in the air or grass of the fields, we hold the image and likeness of God, the dignity for being human.

Jesus asks us to have confidence in God and his kingdom rather than building a kingdom of money. As long as money is the central focus in life, it is impossible to build God's kingdom. And Jesus says, "Whoever is not with me is against me" (Mt 12:30).

So we sing together with the psalmist, "Only in God is my soul at rest; from him comes my salvation. He only is my rock and my salvation, my stronghold; I shall not be disturbed at all." ✝

[25th OT (C)]

65

NINTH SUNDAY IN ORDINARY TIME (A)

(Deuteronomy 11:18, 26-28, 32; Romans 3:21-25, 28; Matthew 7:21-27)

Putting into Practice

During the ordination of permanent deacons of my class in 1997, Bishop Emeritus Charles Grahmann placed the Book of Gospels in candidates' hands and said, "Receive the Gospel of Christ, whose herald you now are. Believe what you read, teach what you believe, and practice what you teach." That was a clear and concise command: "Believe what you read, teach what you believe, and practice what you teach." Among the three acts—to believe, to teach, and to practice—the most difficult one is to practice. We can read, study, and teach Scripture, but to practice what is in it is extremely difficult and nearly impossible.

In today's gospel reading, Jesus says that putting into practice is the most important. "None of those who cry out, 'Lord, Lord,' will enter the kingdom of God but only the one who does the will of my Father in heaven." Those who pray with lips will not enter God's kingdom, unless they put words into practice. Those who prophesize or perform miracles will also be rejected, unless they perform the will of God. Jesus asks us to put his teachings into practice.

Let us look at some more examples from Scripture. First, according to the Gospel of John, on the night before he was betrayed, Jesus washed his disciples' feet. And then he said to them, "You are blessed, if you do [these things]" (Jn 13:17). Jesus commands his disciples to put into practice what he has just demonstrated, even though it is work normally performed by a servant. On the night before he was arrested, Jesus showed his disciples how to serve his flocks. At the most critical moment of his life, Jesus put the kingdom of God into practice and asked his disciples to do the same.

Second, according to the Gospel of Matthew, the condition of the Last Judgment is whether we feed the hungry, give a drink to the thirsty, welcome the stranger, clothe the naked, or visit the prison (Mt 25). Once again, it is action that counts at the Last Judgment.

Our last example is from the Letter of James: "What good is it, my brothers and sisters, if you say you have faith but do not have works? Can faith save you? If a brother or sister is naked and lacks daily food, and one of you says to them, 'Go in peace; keep warm and eat your fill,' and yet you do not supply their bodily needs, what is the good of that?" (Jas 2:14-16).

Some years ago, a young man wanted to teach religion in a Catholic school. When the principal asked him if he were a practicing Catholic, he replied, "No, I am not; but I know Catholic teachings thoroughly. I went to Catholic schools all my life." The principal explained to the young man that the heart of Catholicism is not knowledge but living the Catholic faith. Even though the head is filled with knowledge, the heart can be devoid of God. Knowledge needs to be translated through heart into action. Theology must be based on the life lived and experienced.

This story demonstrates why it is so difficult to put faith into practice. The good practice (orthopraxis) comes from the sound faith (orthodoxy) that is based on the life stories of Jesus and shaped by the faith tradition. In other words, putting faith into practice is putting the kingdom of God into practice, as Jesus has done.

The kingdom of God is built upon actions and practices, not on ideas and theories. This means that we cannot seek an individual relationship with God apart from our family, friends, and neighbors. To be Christians is to establish relationships with our brothers and sisters. We live with our brothers and sisters and learn each other how to serve, how to love, and how to be loved. Together with our brothers and sisters in the Church are we saved.

Jesus calls us to be his disciples. And Jesus asks us to love one another in action, as he has loved us in action, that is, on the cross. ✝

[Holy Thursday, 5ᵗʰ OT (A)]

Tenth Sunday in Ordinary Time (A)

(Hosea 6:3-6; Romans 4:18-25; Matthew 9:9-13)

God in the Postmodern Age

The closer we come to God, it seems to me, the farther away God is from us. If we come to know something about God, it is no longer about God. God is the Mystery, the Holy Mystery.

If we listen to God's words and try to put them into action, there are always aspects we cannot comprehend. For example, we hear today from the gospel reading that Jesus calls Matthew, a tax collector. Matthew immediately leaves his post and follows Jesus. To most people, this choice of a sinner, without any evidence of conversion, is a source of scandal. What is more, Jesus and his disciples joined the party later at Matthew's house with many more tax collectors and sinners.

Tax collectors worked for Rome. They made a living by ripping off their own people. They were public sinners. In addition, the Jews paid taxes to the Temple only. Paying taxes to the Roman emperor constituted giving what belonged to God. No wonder Jews hated tax collectors. Hence, when Jesus called Matthew, it was truly absurd.

If we look closely at ourselves, however, we have our own built-in mechanisms by which we understand things the way we like. We think that we are righteous on our own merits. We think that we have good health and fortunes on our own lots. We think that the only way for others to enter the heavenly banquet is through the way of "righteousness" like ours. In short, we are fundamentally self-centered. This is so, partly because we have been influenced by the intellectualism and rationalism of modernity for the last several hundred years.

We no longer live in the modern age; we now live in the postmodern age. The modern industrial economy has been replaced by the postmodern, microchip economy. It is hard to define the postmodern age. The postmodern mentality could be defined in terms of oppositions— movements of thoughts opposed to the world as we know it now. In general, postmodernity favors experience over logic, body over spirit, emotion and feeling over intellect and scholarship, spontaneity over deliberation, unconscious over conscious, temporal over eternal, personal choice over objective values, search for pleasure over traditional morality, and so on.

Postmodernity, even with its not-so-good aspects, has some aspects precisely identical to Jesus' teachings. Jesus does not say, "Search for the meaning of life." Jesus does not command, "Build a good human relationship at work." Jesus says, "Love one another, as I have loved you." What is esteemed now, in this postmodern age, is very similar to Jesus' teachings. It is love. And love does not belong to any intellectual category or rationality. We cannot put love into a mathematical equation.

God's love and mercy for people is also found in the Book of Hosea, as we heard from the first reading. God's love is like the dawning light of day, always filled with promises. God's mercy is like the spring rain that waters all living creatures on earth.

God is not happy with superficial religiosity based on rigid doctrines under tightly controlled, institutional supervisions. God expects piety and religiosity grounded in genuine love, not in sacrificial offering (Hos 6:6).

Therefore, to know and to experience God is not the result of speculative knowledge acquired by studying the Bible and theology books. To know and to experience God is to see and hear the goodness of God, and then to try to live the life of God daily. Even though we see the image of God dimly and hear the voice of God faintly, we must live God's life.

The closer we come to God, it seems, the farther away God is. This is so, not because God runs away from us, but because we come to know ourselves better. God is love and draws us in mysteriously. God is the Holy Mystery. ✝

[5th OT (C), 16th OT (B)]

ELEVENTH SUNDAY IN ORDINARY TIME (A)

(Exodus 19:2-6; Romans 5:6-11; Matthew 9:36-10:8)

Do You Trust God?

Do you trust God? Do you trust God in His love and care for you? I don't mean whether you believe in God, or whether you have faith in God. I mean whether you trust God. Do you trust God, even if you may not avoid pain and sufferings in life? Do you trust God, even if you may not attain eternal life or go to heaven?

A man saw an angel walking down the street. The angel was carrying a torch in one hand and a bucket of water in the other. "What are you going to do with that torch and that bucket of water?" the man asked. The angel stopped, looked at the man, and said, "With the torch I am going to burn down the mansions of heaven; and with the bucket of water, I am going to put out the fires of hell. Then we are going to see who really trusts God." The angel's point is that people believe in God out of the fear of punishment in hell and out of the hope of reward in heaven.

Trust is the main theme in today's readings. The first reading concerns the early part of Israel's journey in the Sinai desert after the exodus from Egypt. God would let them go to the Promise Land in a few months. But God wanted to keep them in the desert for a long time and offered them the Ten Commandments. God wanted the Israelites to trust Him.

In the gospel reading, Jesus is moved with pity for his people who become "like sheep without a shepherd." And he says to his disciples, "The harvest is good but laborers are scarce. Beg the harvest master to send out laborers to gather his harvest." Jesus chooses the twelve disciples and empowers them to expel demons and to cure all diseases and infirmities. Jesus trusts his disciples.

In the Letter to Romans, Paul says that the death and resurrection of Jesus Christ reveal God's love and care for His people. They are reconciled to God by the mystery of the cross. They must trust God, who will continue to care for them.

To trust is to accept someone with heart. To trust is to share something spiritual. To trust is to be affectionate and confident beyond belief and faith. To trust is not to be afraid. Mary trusted God when the angel Gabriel said, "Do not be afraid." Mary's trust commenced the Incarnation of God. The same trust in God helped St. John Paul II end the communism.

It was only fifty or so years ago that God was all-powerful and all-knowing and present everywhere; God was a grandfather with a beard, always scooping our sins. We now have different images of God in the Bible. God, the Father Jesus of Nazareth has shown us, is neither a judge nor a grandfather. Like the father of the Prodigal Son, God is forgiving love and mercy. Like the Good Samaritan, God is self-sacrificing love. Jesus washed the disciples' feet, so God is a lowly servant. Jesus died on the cross, so God is weak and vulnerable. God, the Father Jesus has shown us, is love and mercy.

These images and notions of God are very important in this twenty-first century for developing a sound theology as well as spirituality, which is based on Jesus of Nazareth who lived God's life on earth. In addition, the social and communal dimension is an inseparable element of our faith journey. We cannot be wholesome and integrated if we remain solitary individuals. We must trust each other as community. Without trust, we will be a collection of individuals filled with disputing desires, egos, prides, and ambitions.

It is true that morning newspapers and evening television are full of bad news: cheating, burglaries, forgeries, murders, shootings, and the like. Deep in our hearts, however, we know that the world is still full of good news of trust.

God has shown His personal love and mercy to His people continuously and permanently. To respond to this justice of God, we must trust God in return. We must trust God for creating us in His image and likeness. We must trust God for sending His Son. We must trust God, who will raise us on the last day. ✝

[11th and 12th and 18th OT (C)]

71

TWELFTH SUNDAY IN ORDINARY TIME (A)

(Jeremiah 20:10-13; Romans 5:12-15; Matthew 10:26-33)

Love and Self-Image

When I was a little boy, my mother said to me, "You are more important than sparrows flying in the sky." Today's gospel passage reflects what my mother said. While I was preparing this homily, I became absorbed to the memory of my mother. In the old days, only the Gospel of Matthew was read during Mass. She must have heard that gospel passage from a priest's sermon.

My mother was an uneducated farmer born at the end of the nineteenth century. I remember that, when I was a small boy, one cold morning on Christmas Day, she took me to church, holding my tiny hand. My mother, uneducated though she was, taught me Catholicism. And she always gave me everything she had. My mother was very special to me, simply because she was my mother.

Today's gospel reading is about Jesus' instruction on God's care for sparrows and his disciples, as he sends them on their missions. The world will hear the good news of salvation through Jesus Christ, who is the new Adam, the redeemed mankind (Gal 6:15). People can now participate in the new humanity God re-created. But they may still adhere to the old Adam, the fallen mankind.

The Gospel of Jesus Christ always challenges the world. Disciples of Jesus will most likely face confrontation from and persecution by the world. Therefore, Jesus asks his disciples to lead simple lives and to stand firm for gospel values. Jesus also assures them that God, who is attentive even to sparrows, will certainly care for them.

From the first reading, we heard that the prophet Jeremiah demonstrated tremendous courage in prophesying God's words. He criticized rulers and leaders who neglected the poor and relied on foreign powers instead of God. Because of that criticism, they put him into a cistern (Jer 38:1-13).

Even there, he relied upon God and made a confession: "The Lord is with me like a mighty champion." Jeremiah provides a model discipleship.

As the disciples of Jesus, our mission is to spread the Gospel of Christ to the world. The Gospel, unless shared with others, fails to be the revelation from God. For the Gospel to be God's word, it must be accepted and answered. Salvation from God occurs only when the Gospel of Christ meets human hearts. Our task is to spread the Gospel of Christ throughout the world.

We must also remember that the Christian mission begins at home. All of us have mothers and fathers who love us and care for us. In return, we must love our children. What we receive from our beloved ones we pass on to our own loved ones.

Love is a pure and selfless gift to another person. If he or she is not valuable and lovable, we do not give of ourselves. Conversely, if we do not think that we are valuable or lovable, he or she will not accept our love as a gift. Moreover, love is the source of life that moves the world forward. Love is the ground of salvation from God. Accordingly, if we love someone, that person will develop a strong and positive self-image. If someone loves us, we feel worthy and satisfied. In other words, those people who are capable of loving and being loved develop strong and positive self-images of themselves.

Psychology tells us that self-image is an important factor in a person's success. A person with a positive self-image is bound to succeed. A person with a negative self-image is bound to fail. In other words, if we love our children, they will develop strong self-images and most likely succeed in life. Otherwise, they will develop negative self-images and probably fail at what they do.

If God cares for and loves sparrows, how much more God cares for and loves us and our children. God cares and loves us, so we care and love our children. This is the Good News. We must proclaim it to the end of the world. ✝

[6th Easter and 7th Easter (B), 30th OT (A)]

73

THIRTEENTH SUNDAY IN ORDINARY TIME (A)

(2 Kings 4:8-11, 14-16; Romans 6:3-4, 8-11; Matthew 10:37-42)

The Cost of Discipleship

"He who will not take up his cross and come after me is not worthy of me."

This is the heart of Jesus' teachings. It is about the necessity of carrying the cross as a requirement of following Jesus (Mt 10:38, 16:24, Mk 8:34, Lk 9:23, 14:27). In the Gospel of Luke, the words "deny themselves" and "daily" are added. And so it reads, "If any want to become my followers, let them *deny themselves* and take up their cross *daily* and follow me."

We are disciples of Jesus by virtue of baptism. We have died to sin, and risen to a new life with God. For disciples of Jesus, the new life is not simply a happy and joyful life, however. The new life in Christ Jesus is the blessed and virtuous life that comes only with carrying the cross. There is no exception to this imperative.

The cross is the most essential element of Christian life. It was Jesus' cross that saved and redeemed the human race. In the same way, we need to carry the cross for our salvation and redemption. Many people are hungry for the truth. But not many of them obtain the truth, because they are unwilling to carry the cross. Many people search for eternal life. But not many of them attain eternal life, because they are unwilling to carry the cross.

The cross we carry daily is to be grateful for the gifts we have received from God. The cross we carry daily is to strip down our primitive ego and ambitious self-centeredness in the process of fulfilling our true selves. The cross we carry daily is to surrender ourselves to God. The cross we carry daily is to self-transcend ourselves to God. Therefore, the cross is the absolutely necessary prerequisite of following Jesus.

Dietrich Bonhoeffer, the German Lutheran theologian who plotted to overthrow the Hitler regime, wrote the book *The Cost of Discipleship*. In it, he says, "When Jesus calls a man to come, he asks him to come and die." The cost of discipleship is the death on the cross. For Bonhoeffer, the discipleship actually cost him his life. He died just before the Allies liberated him from the prison. His discipleship required the "costly" grace, whereas the vast majority of European Christianity at that time was silent in "cheap" grace. Needless to say, the salvation earned by Jesus for us was the "costly" one.

We are neither Dietrich Bonhoeffer nor other Christian martyrs. We are just common people. Our discipleship of Jesus must cost us the cross, however. In other words, we must die before we are raised. One may ask, "What kind of death is it?" It is the death of the desire to have more money and more material things. It is the death of the desire to have the power to control others. It is the death of the original sin that adheres to "old selves" "covered with "garments of animal skins."

Ultimately, to die is to live for others. We live for others because our faces are made for others. Even though we look at our faces in a mirror, it is only a snapshot. Our face is for others to see. We are made for others. To follow Jesus, therefore, is to live and to sacrifice for others.

Who are the others? They are our children, spouses, parents, and grandparents. They also are the poor, the sick, the lonely, and the marginalized in society.

To follow Jesus is to respond to God's love manifested in the person of Jesus of Nazareth. To follow Jesus is to experience the reality of God in everyday life. To follow Jesus is to experience God's love and mercy among all God's holy people here and now.

Paul wrote at the end of his letter to the Galatians, "I carry the marks of Jesus branded on my body" (Gal 6:17). After all arguments and justifications on the Gospel of Christ and on true discipleship, the last criterion of discipleship is whether one bears the cross of Jesus or not. To follow Jesus is to live for others with the cross. ✝

[Palm Sunday (C), 13th OT (B and C)]

FOURTEENTH SUNDAY IN ORDINARY TIME (A)

(Zechariah 9:9-10; Romans 8:9, 11-13; Matthew 11:25-30)

ABC of Prayer

Today's Gospel begins with Jesus' prayer of thanksgiving to God the Father. Jesus praises God for revealing him to the "little ones" and for keeping him hidden from "the wise and the learned." The "little ones" are his followers—the simple and the uneducated. "The wise and the learned" refer to the scribes and the Pharisees. Jesus, the revelation, reveals and, at the same time, hides himself.

Jesus says, "Come to me, all you who labor and are burdened, and I will give you rest." And he continues, "Learn from me, for I am meek and humble in heart. You will find rest for yourselves." In this beautiful prayer, Jesus teaches us how to encounter him through our own prayers. Today we will consider some aspects of prayer: why we pray, how to pray regularly, and the goal of prayer.

Before we begin, we must remember that God exists within us—in the very depths of our beings. To the Ephesians, Paul says, "May Christ dwell in your hearts through faith" (Eph 3:17). To the Galatians, Paul says, "God has sent the Spirit of his Son into our hearts" (Gal 4:6). To the Romans, Paul also says, as in the second reading, "The Spirit of God dwells in you." Thus the Spirit of Christ, dwelling within us, is the fountain and source of Christian life and allows us to pray (Rom 8:26). Therefore, we must find the hidden God in the depths of our own beings, rather than in someone else's words or in someplace beyond the earth. If we find God within ourselves, we may be able to avoid the separation of the subject and the object in our prayers, in the way which God and we are on the same sphere so that a holistic approach of a union is possible.

The first aspect of prayer to consider is why we pray. Because God is in the depths of our beings, nobody else can penetrate. We alone can do it by praying. Prayer also maintains a relationship with God. Therefore, prayer is not an option but the essence of Christian life. As long as we maintain a relationship with God and as long as we live, we pray.

The second aspect of prayer to consider is how regularly we should pray. In prayer, we typically ask for what we want. In time, we gradually seek a deeper relationship with God and begin to let God decide what we ask for. The Holy Spirit within us teaches us how to pray (Rom 8:26). And then, the prayer changes from head to heart and from self-centered to self-emptying. The prayer, which began as obligation, transforms itself into a habit and becomes a spontaneous and connatural response to God's love.

We need to pray unceasingly because we are tempted and tested always by our egos and selfishness (1 Th 5:16). Adam and Eve have always been a part of us; and so the need to pray constantly.

The third aspect of prayer to consider is the goal of prayer. Prayer is the means of maintaining our relationship with God, who dwells in the depths of our beings. And prayer transforms our minds and hearts in conformity with God. Jesus is the paradigm in this transformation. This is why we pray in Jesus' name (Jn 16:23). We desire to encounter Jesus. We want to be one with Jesus in love and faith. Jesus says, "Learn from me, for I am meek and humble in heart." Through prayers, we learn how to see as Jesus sees, how to hear as Jesus hears, and how to think as Jesus thinks. Ultimately, through prayers, we have "the same mind as Jesus" (Phil 2:5).

In summary, with prayer, we become "the little ones" to whom the revelation is revealed. Without prayer, we become "the wise and learned" to whom the revelation is hidden. With prayer, we find God within us, and life is meaningful and fruitful. Without prayer, we find our ambitious egos within us, and life is void or filled with envy and greed. Let us end with a prayer of Mother Theresa:

> *The fruit of silence is prayer.*
> *The fruit of prayer is faith.*
> *The fruit of faith is love.*
> *The fruit of love is service.*
> *The fruit of service is peace!* †

[17th and 28th and 29th OT (C), Pentecost (C)]

FIFTEENTH SUNDAY IN ORDINARY TIME (A)

(Isaiah 55:10-11; Romans 8:18-23; Matthew 13:1-23)

The Prodigal Sower

Rain and snow help seeds grow into plants. More rain and snow help plants produce fruits. To the ancient people, this simple cycle of farming was the work of nature, not the work of their labor. They also believed that God's words, like rain and snow, brought life to those who heard it.

The prophet Isaiah depicts a beautiful image of God's word, using rain and snow. The psalmist is joyful with the fruits of God's word: "The fields are garmented with flocks and the valleys blanketed with grain. They shout and sing for joy."

Jesus tells a story, in the gospel reading, how God's word produces results similar to those of rain and snow. A farmer spreads seeds to different grounds: a path, rocky ground, a thorny field, and good soil. In this parable the farmer is Jesus, and the seed is God's word. Different grounds receiving the farmer's seeds represent different people who hear God's word. Some people reject it immediately. Others receive it initially but do not cultivate it because of hardship or persecution. Still others receive it but abandon it right away because of worldly ambition. Only those, who receive God's word and treasure in their hearts, produce a hundredfold or sixtyfold or thirtyfold.

The farmers in ancient Palestine first sowed seeds on soils and then plowed (Joachim Jeremias). The farmer sows seeds on all kinds of soils generously. Even though he may lose some seeds in bad soils, he gathers remarkable harvests from good soils. In the same way, the word of God is sown freely to all of us, but not everybody welcomes it. Only those who receive God's word in their hearts will produce abundant harvests. Furthermore, God is contended with each equally bountiful harvest: thirtyfold, sixtyfold, and hundredfold. God doesn't demand that we should always produce hundredfold.

Today's gospel passage is a beautiful story about God as the prodigal Sower. Jesus speaks in parable because he wants to appeal to the heart, not to the head. The heart does not understand intellectual, logical, and speculative languages, as Paschal said: "Heart has reason that reason doesn't understand."

Perhaps how well we receive God's word in our hearts is related to how close we are to nature. Nature provides an excellent opportunity to encounter divine mysteries. To the ancient people, God and nature were intimately connected. The rain and snow helping seeds to grow, the sun rising in the morning, and the sun setting in the afternoon—all belong to God's providence. All things in nature manifest the power of God (Rom 1:20).

On the other hand, we understand what happens in nature precisely in terms of rational and scientific knowledge. We drive cars door-to-door. We hardly look stars at the night. The only time we may move closer to nature is when we buy organic foods at a local grocery store. At best, we go to mountains or beaches for vacation once a year or so. We stay far away from nature. As a result, God's word and nature are disconnected.

In the second reading, Paul talks about the new age where "all creation is groaning in labor pains" by virtue of the resurrection of Jesus. All creatures, not just human beings, have been affected by the resurrection of Jesus. Thus all of creation painfully waits for their resurrections. This means that all creation converge through Christ at the Omega Point, according to Fr. Pierre Chardin. This concept of the cosmic Christ and the Omega Point were developed from a profound understanding of nature; Fr. Chardin was a famous paleontologist.

Today's readings remind us that everything about us is a part of nature, even our understanding of God. As with all creatures on earth, we depend on rain and sunshine. We came forth from nature, and we will return to nature. Perhaps, to be more receptive to God's word, we must be close to nature. ✝

[Christmas Day, 4ᵗʰ Lent (A), 25ᵗʰ OT (A)]

SIXTEENTH SUNDAY IN ORDINARY TIME (A)

(Wisdom 12:13, 16-19; Romans 8:26-27; Matthew 13:24-43)

Weeds, Wheat, and Mustard

The central message of the Gospel of Jesus Christ is that God the Father has at last reclaimed the whole world as his own in and through Jesus Christ. Jesus' response to this call is to initiate the kingdom of heaven. God's kingdom is the main thrust of Jesus' teaching and also the ultimate goal of Christian life.

What is the kingdom of heaven? Is it a place where saints and godly people live? Is it a state in which the good and lovely triumph over the evil and misery? Or, is it a state at which "death will be no more; mourning and crying and pain will be no more" (Rv 21:4)? If the kingdom of God is here in this world, how do we build it? What happened to the kingdom Jesus inaugurated anyway?

The gospel reading today gives us some clues to these questions. Jesus says that the kingdom is like a field where the wheat and weeds can grow side by side. And Jesus commands us not to get rid of the weeds because, if one pulls up the weeds, it hurts the wheat.

The Church is also like a field where both the wheat and weeds grow together. Would it be all right, then, to weed out some people from time to time? Would it be good to shake people up and try to make them more committed? If we build a church exactly the way we want, then we may be building our kingdom, not the kingdom of God.

Besides, who decides to shake up whom? Some who were thought to be righteous are not really righteous, and others who were overlooked before are found righteous later. And as always, there always is a possibility of repentance and conversion.

God alone can judge. (Even the Vicar of Christ in Rome cannot judge. Pope Francis said famously, "Who am I to judge?") God alone can remove weeds. God will, however, remove weeds at the harvest time. Until then, we are the holy people of God, on a journey in God's kingdom.

Hence, we need to get along with people who do not meet our expectations and standards. We need to be content with a church where saints and sinners live side by side. Actually, the Church is made of sinners and repentant sinners, rather than saints and sinners. And so, we need to reconcile with each other and with God again and again. A church that is full of saints might be a nice church, but it is not the Church of Jesus Christ. Jesus says, "The sun rises on the evil and on the good, and it rains on the righteous and on the unrighteous" (Mt 5:45).

Let us also remember that, through the cross of Jesus, the kingdom of God has already come. And Jesus has never considered the possibility that God's kingdom would be fulfilled without the cross. Therefore, we too must carry our cross. The cross strips away disguise and pretension and makes us humble and simple. The cross helps us empty ourselves. The cross is the "subjective condition of possibility" for us to build God's kingdom.

God's kingdom is designed not to take us away from this world but to transform it by our participation in God's creation. God's kingdom is the horizon toward which Christians look and live day by day. Furthermore, God's kingdom is not something we complete. God will complete it in His time. The kingdom of God is here already, but has not yet been completed.

Accordingly, how God's kingdom is realized on earth depends on how we reconcile with each other in peace, justice, and love. Our reconciliation, in turn, depends on whether we carry our cross or not. Jesus has established the kingdom of God on earth. It is now for us to build God's kingdom in a wheat field with many weeds. ✝

[11th OT (B), 17th OT (A)]

SEVENTEENTH SUNDAY IN ORDINARY TIME (A)

(1 Kings 3:5, 7-12, Romans 8:28-30, Matthew 13:44-52)

The Kingdom of God

God the Father has reclaimed the ownership of the whole universe through His Son, Jesus Christ. In response to God's call, Jesus Christ has inaugurated the messianic kingdom of God on earth—"They will be done on earth as it is in heaven.".

In the gospel passage today, Jesus describes what this kingdom of God is like. The first two parables show that the kingdom of God is like a priceless treasure and pearl that must be purchased at any cost.

The third parable is about the dragnet story of fishing, drawing all kinds of fish—large or small, useful or useless. This means that the kingdom of God gathers all kinds of people. It is inclusive. Moreover, in the kingdom of God to judge who is good and who is bad is up to God, not us. The kingdom of God is where God alone claims governance and sovereignty, not we. In the kingdom of God, God reigns.

In addition, the kingdom of God is transcendent, because it belongs to God. The kingdom of God is God's reign. The kingdom of God also is eschatological, because it will be fulfilled at the end of time. The kingdom of God looks to the future. As long as we live in this world, we can only catch a glimpse of it. We will never grasp it fully. The kingdom of God is "already" here but "not yet" fulfilled.

In the kingdom of God, however, "all things work for good for those who love God." For those who love God, all things—even tragedies and calamities—do work toward good. Furthermore, God often transforms crooked lines into straight ones. In the kingdom where God reigns, if we focus only on what is important to God, the rest of our concerns will be solved naturally. In the kingdom of God, all things are intelligible in the light of God.

Today's first reading provides an excellent example. King Solomon asked for an understanding heart to govern his people and to distinguish right from wrong. For a king, it was an unusual request. He could certainly have instead asked for a long life or revenge upon his enemies. At this humble request, God granted Solomon not only the understanding heart he had asked for, but also riches and honor and a long life (1 Kgs 3:13-14), which he did not ask for. King Solomon was at home in the kingdom of God.

The kingdom of God is the existential and ultimate reality for Christians. It is not a special place for some selected people. It is a life of God; it is a life of respect and service to others. The kingdom of God is a place where we love each other in the here and now. Thus the kingdom of God is among and within us (Lk 17:21).

The kingdom of God, which is the most sought-after in life, also has to do more with the quality of interior life and less with the outward advancement of civilization. So we ask, "Has the kingdom of God been improved upon in proportion to the advancement of human civilization?" Obviously, the kingdom of God, along with the well-being of humanity, has not kept up with civilization. Therefore, we need to rethink our Christian vocation for completing the kingdom of God on earth.

God's kingdom is most ideally tasted through the Eucharistic meal. And the Eucharist is the symbol of God's kingdom par excellence. When we break the Lord's bread and share it together with the people of God, we are truly in the kingdom of God. By partaking in the Lord's Supper, we not only encounter the risen Jesus (Latin Church), but we also are deified and sanctified as sons and daughters of God (Eastern Church).

We have seen the kingdom of God in the lives of people who have kept their hearts open to God. Indeed, we have met many people who live in the kingdom of God. We hope and pray the kingdom of God is realized more and more in our lives here and now. It is the grace of God that we live in God's kingdom. ✝

[11th OT (B), 16th OT (A)]

Eighteenth Sunday in Ordinary Time (A)

(Isaiah 55:1-3; Romans 8:35, 37-39; Matthew 14:13-21)

We Are Hungry and Thirsty

Let us imagine the scene described in today's gospel reading. A large crowd of five thousand people, not counting women and children, are gathered on a hillside of Galilee one hot summer afternoon. They have followed Jesus all day long, until the sunset nears. They are hungry and thirsty.

Jesus and his disciples are hungry and thirsty, too. The only food around consists of five loaves of bread and two fish, belonging to a boy. When Jesus learns of this, he calls the boy. The boy trusts Jesus and gives him all that he has. In the end, all five thousand eat fully and heartily, leaving behind twelve baskets of bread.

Scripture scholars say that this miracle story foreshadows Jesus' institution of the Eucharist at the Last Supper. This is a doctrinal view of the Church. However, from the viewpoint of ordinary believers who need to experience God in their daily lives, this story tells us that a great many people have been satisfied from hunger and thirst. Indeed, Jesus has multiplied five loaves of bread and two fish to feed five thousand people who are hungry and thirsty.

Material poverty is only one type of poverty. What about culturally poor people imprisoned in a flat earth without music, literature, or fine art? How about spiritually poor people who simply live day by day without dreams, hope, and imagination? How about emotionally poor people who only want to be accepted and loved? And what about morally poor people unable to break the vicious circle of disgrace and self-contempt?

Now, if we look closely at ourselves, we find that we, too, are poor. We are hungry and thirsty one way or another. Realizing that we are hungry and thirsty is good, because we can hear the voice of Isaiah shouting, "All you who are thirsty, come to the water! You who have no money, come, receive grain and wheat."

Let us share a story about a woman who was really thirsty and then came to the water. For the former hostage Ingrid Betancourt, a normal everyday experience—such as taking a hot shower, something most people take for granted—is a potent symbol of new freedom after seven long years of captivity in the jungles of Colombia. Ingrid remarked, "I had not been in contact with hot water for nearly seven years, so the first shower I had, it was a strange feeling because it hurt." She considered the hot-water shower a "spiritual bath" that "got rid of all bad memories" she wanted to flush away.

I looked at several pictures of Ingrid via Yahoo and noticed several wonderful pictures of her holding the rosary she made during captivity. It was a beautiful rosary. During her captivity, she hit the very bottom of weakness and powerlessness. She had been hungry and thirsty for a long time. For this reason, she was able to encounter the living God.

We do not normally experience such a dramatic event. We are pilgrims. We slowly make our way along the journey of faith. We love, but our love needs to be more mature; it needs to be purified. We trust God, but generally not with such unshakable confidence in God's love. We bear witness to religious virtues we cherish, but we are without prophetic witness. We are pilgrims in faith journeys. We hunger for food and thirst for water. Yes, we too desire to go to the hillside in Galilee, one hot summer afternoon, where Jesus feeds thousands of people. We would simply like to be fed by Jesus.

In this cool Sunday morning, we suddenly realize that Jesus has indeed fed us. We will be fed with the body and blood of Jesus. So we say along with St. Paul, "What will separate us from the love of Christ? For I am certain that neither death nor life, neither angels nor principalities, neither height nor depth, nor any other creature, will be able to separate us from the love of God that comes to us in Christ Jesus, Our Lord." So we pray, "Thank you, Lord, for your generous gifts of your body and blood. You have fed us abundantly." ✝

[17th and 18th OT (B)]

85

NINETEENTH SUNDAY IN ORDINARY TIME (A)

(1 Kings 19:9, 11-13; Romans 9:1-5; Matthew 14:22-33)

"Little Faith!"

All of us encounter God one way or another. It could be through solitude in silence or through a prayer at dark night. It could be through sickness or death within our own families.

Today's gospel reading shows how Peter encountered God in Jesus of Nazareth. Peter and his colleagues struggled all night long in the Sea of Galilee. In the early morning, after a heavy storm, Peter saw Jesus walking on the water. The fishermen first thought he saw a ghost because they had left Jesus earlier on the other side of the lake.

Having seen Jesus walk on the water, Peter got excited and wanted to walk on the water too. So he asked Jesus whether he could. Jesus granted his wish. Peter succeeded momentarily; however, he had to be rescued by Jesus almost immediately from drowning.

In the Bible, a storm on the sea symbolizes a chaotic condition. Walking on the water during a storm means creating order from chaos. Thus, it is natural for Jesus to walk on the water. An interesting point of the story, however, is that Peter wanted to do the same thing as Jesus does. Why did Peter want to walk on the water and why did he then nearly drown before being rescued?

To answer this question, we must return to the first reading. Elijah fled for his life forty days and forty nights, only to arrive at Mount Horeb, where Moses had encountered God (Ex 33:17-23). There was a strong wind, an earthquake, and fire, but God was not in any of them. Soon, "there was a tiny whispering sound." Then Elijah heard God's voice at the entrance of the cave. The "tiny whispering sound" with which God appeared is translated as "the whistling of a gentle wind" or "a sound of sheer silence" in other versions of the Bible. I wonder whether a sound can be tiny, gentle, or silent, but this is a way of trying to say something about the presence of God, using human languages.

Elijah's encounter with God can be summarized with two key words: "cave" and "silence." These two words are important metaphors for Christian spirituality. The cave symbolizes the deep unconscious self inside of the psyche where God resides—the center of being. The silence symbolizes the condition that is necessary for the soul to meet God at that center of being.

To encounter God deep inside of us, therefore, we must maintain interior silence, not only by bringing an order of conscious thoughts, but also by eliminating unconscious noises. Only when we recognize and renounce thoughts and desires in silence (*samadhi*), can we hear the tiny voice of God from the depths of the innermost being (Johnston, *America*, 11/19/2007).

This brings us back to Peter's story. Peter was a gutsy man with a big heart. Only a man like Peter would ask of Jesus such a favor. To walk on water, however, Peter had to journey deep inside of his inner world where God could be found. Alas, he was distracted momentarily. Perhaps he became frightened. Perhaps he was trapped by a noisy ego (Jungian) once again. Therefore, Peter's attempt to walk on water was by the sheer grace of God, even if it lasted only a very short time. Peter was, in fact, privileged to do that.

This story of Peter is also our story. We encounter Jesus, during a prayer, in the depths of our beings. Quite often, however, we are possessed by worldly thoughts. Then we are away from our true selves. Encountering with God is solely by virtue of God's grace.

Jesus called Peter a man of "little faith" after he rescued him. The "little faith" is surely better than no faith. The little faith is a tiny mustard seed that grows into a huge tree with many beautiful bird's nests. If we have the little faith, we will be fully grasped by the incomprehensible Mystery, who takes initiative and establishes a personal relationship with us. Only by grace is God present within us as the living God. ✝

[21st OT (A)]

TWENTIETH SUNDAY IN ORDINARY TIME (A)

(Isaiah 56:1, 6-7; Romans 11:13-15, 29-32; Matthew 15:21-28)

A Dandelion Flower

Today I would like to share a story about myself. I hope this story can help us penetrate deeply into the mind of the Canaanite woman, a Gentile, in today's Gospel reading. The story is about a dandelion flower in the middle of green grass. It is about me, a Korean immigrant.

One early morning not long ago, I noticed a yellow flower at the far corner of my lawn. I approached and found a small dandelion. I tried to pull it out, but it refused to come out. I gazed at it. It was a yellow flower like the rising sun in the morning calm. "Why don't you like me?" I asked. In its smile was a cynical message. The dandelion said, "You don't like me because I represent you." I felt sad and didn't ask any more questions. I stood on the lawn and looked mindlessly at the flower, feeling no spirit. Gradually, I returned to my childhood in Korea.

I was born and educated in Korea, where dandelions bloom in early spring all over the countryside. When other plants begin to produce their flowers in early spring, dandelions have already produced their seeds. The yellow flowers change into white cottons in the midst of warm Texas sunlight. Most of the seeds scatter nearby, but one was driven by a strong wind. Soaring high into the sky, it floated with the clouds, flew over mountains, crossed the Pacific Ocean, and finally arrived in the great country of America.

It was certainly a strange place for the dandelion seed, landing in the middle of the green grass as it did. The seed was afraid to land, but it had no choice. The wind died down, and the dandelion seed could no longer stay in the air. When the seed settled and covered itself with dirt, the grass said, "You are not to settle here. This is only for us." "You are not serious," said the dandelion. "I'll tell you the truth. You belong to the roadside," the grass responded. "But everyone has the right to live wherever he is destined to," the dandelion protested and continued, "It seems that one cannot freely choose where he wants to live. It is only according to the fundamental option." The final warning came from the grass: "Next spring you will know what I mean."

Regardless of what the green grass said, the dandelion seed settled in the yard and covered itself with dirt to prepare for the winter.

The winter came. And the dandelion thought, "Without a flower, it is not worth living." The dandelion decided to sprout again as soon as the spring came. It was a short winter in Texas, and the spring came.

While the grass and trees in the yard still slept, the dandelion worked from early morning until late at night and penetrated its roots deeply into the soil. The dandelion had to prove itself in a new place. By the time other plants and grasses started to come up from the ground, the dandelion had already produced bright yellow flowers. The dandelion was proud of them.

In the mean time, the owner of the house came into the yard to get a fresh air and saw the yellow flower, he did not appreciate it. He said, "I thought I weeded these out last fall." He then tried to pull the flower up. The plant was rooted so deeply that no part of it came out. The grass, seeing what happened to the dandelion, said, "I told you so last fall. You don't belong here. Go away." But the dandelion said nothing. Some of its leaves were already taken away, and the tall and handsome flower-stem was knocked down. The dandelion could go nowhere.

In spite of what happened to it, the dandelion believed that it was called to settle where the wind had carried it. Then the dandelion dreamed. In the dream, the dandelion became the man who was looking at the bright yellow flower in his hand with no spirit. The man was a Korean-American, who lived in Dallas for a long time. ✝

[16th OT (B), 16th OT (C), 26th OT (B)]

TWENTY-FIRST SUNDAY IN ORDINARY TIME (A)

(Isaiah 22:19-23; Romans 11:33-36; Matthew 16:13-20)

Peter the Rock

Simon Peter is a gusty and impulsive man with a big heart. And he is an ordinary man with ordinary shortcomings. But he is the rock on which the Church of Christ is built.

The gospel reading of two weeks ago tells how Peter, after seeing Jesus walking on the water of the Sea of Galilee during the storm, wants to do the same (Mt 14:22-33). Scholars say that walking on the water symbolizes God's creative act that brings order to chaos. We can certainly understand Jesus walking on the water. But it is absurd to imagine Peter walking on the water. Peter is that gusty and impatient man.

The gospel reading today is called Peter's confession at Caesarea Philippi, a Gentile town in northern Palestine. From there, Jesus begins his long journey to Jerusalem. After having avoided the crowd, Jesus devotes himself exclusively to the twelve disciples. He is about to reveal the true nature of the Messiah and the mystery of the passion. So Jesus asks the disciples, "Who do people say that the Son of Man is?" Jesus wants to know who he is as told from others. He wants to confirm his own divine son-ship. Multiple answers float.

Jesus singles out Peter and asks, "Who do you think that I am?" Jesus does not ask, "Who am I?" or "Do you know who I am?" It is an existential question that will provide the ultimate meaning of life to both Jesus and Peter, "You are the Messiah, the Son of the living God," Peter answers. However, he does not yet understand what the Messiah really means.

What is more surprising is that Jesus says next to Peter. Reaching out to Peter, Jesus says compassionately, "Blessed are you, Simon, son of Jonah... You are the Rock, and on this rock I will build my church." Two weeks ago, Jesus called Peter a man of "little faith" when he tried to walk on water. Today, Jesus says that he will build the Church of Christ upon Peter, as fulfillment of the prophecy of Isaiah (Isa 28:16). Obviously, there seems to be inconsistency in Jesus' dealings with Peter, because Jesus is going to build the Church on the man who has "little faith."

Peter is an ordinary man. He is gusty and impulsive, but ordinary. Yet he has a big heart, and his faith will grow. Peter does not understand the true nature of the Messiah, so he will betray Jesus three times during the passion (Mt 26:69-75). It is only after encountering the risen Jesus that Peter understands the true nature of the Messiah and becomes the fearless preacher of the Gospel of Christ. It is only through the death and resurrection of Jesus that Peter becomes the apostle among apostles.

Let us imagine or at least conjecture, if we can, how Jesus takes on the situation in Caesarea Philippi. Jesus must have confidence in Peter, hoping that he will eventually understand and follow him. Jesus knows that he must make a journey to Jerusalem to lays the foundation for God's kingdom. He must build the Church as an extension of his body. So Jesus is not asking, but begging Peter. This is the way how God works for human salvation. We also remember that God asked Mary's consent for the incarnation of His Son.

Fr. Raymond Brown talks about three special occasions that Jesus grants to Peter in the Gospel of Matthew: First, Peter is rescued from drowning during the storm. Second, Peter is designated as the Rock for the Church of Christ. Third, Peter denies Jesus three times during Jesus' passion. These are privileged moments for Peter, because he is able to be intimately associated with Jesus and subsequently raises Jesus' blood pressure. Eventually, we know that Peter became the apostle among apostles. This is the Divine Paradox.

Peter is an ordinary man: he believes in doubt and suspicion; he hopes through failure and frustration; he loves in the midst of hatred and rejection. Peter also knows his own weakness and the redeeming love of God. We are ordinary persons with flaws, faults, and even sinfulness. But we are loved and chosen by God. God always chooses ordinary persons like you and me. ✝

[19th OT (A), 20th OT (B)]

91

TWENTY-SECOND SUNDAY IN ORDINARY TIME (A)

(Jeremiah 20:7-9; Romans 12:1-2; Matthew 16:21-27)

Peter the Stumbling Block

Jesus asks Peter, "Who do you say that I am?" in Caesarea Philippi, a town at the northern tip of Galilee. Peter answers, "You are the Christ, the Son of the living God." Then Jesus says to Peter, "Blessed are you, Simon, son of Jonah….you are Peter, and upon this rock I will build my church…." This is a summary of the Gospel last Sunday.

This Sunday, we have heard the continuation of the same Gospel passage. Right after Peter's confession, Jesus oddly predicts that he must go to Jerusalem to suffer greatly and die. To Peter, it does not make sense at all for the Messiah to die on the cross. How could the Messiah be subjected to terrible suffering and die? Peter says, "God forbid, Lord! No such thing shall ever happen to you."

Peter is disappointed and frustrated with Jesus' prediction of a dark future. Hence, Peter tries to breathe into Jesus his own idea, his own desire, and his own worldly ambition. Jesus understands what Peter is doing and rebukes him, "Get behind me, Satan, you are a stumbling block." The rock, which the Church of Christ will be built on, suddenly becomes a stumbling block. A stumbling block is an obstacle that becomes more attractive whenever one stumbles against it. By interjecting his own idea, Peter sets himself up to be a stumbling block for Jesus. This rivalry—more precisely, a power struggle between Jesus and Peter—has something to do with the origin of violence.

According to Rene Girard, we desire and envy the same things others have. A child desires a toy in the hand of another child. A professional envies his coworker's promotion. A housewife envies her neighbor's new car. These desires and envies yield rivalries and conflicts that, in turn, yield violence. At the peak of violence, an unwitting scapegoat is identified unknowingly and sacrificed as a victim. Peace is then temporarily established until the next contagion of rivalry. This (mimetic) theory of the origin of violence shows the dark side of the humanity; a primordial example is the doctrine of original sin.

What Peter wants is to share with Jesus his own idea of a worldly Messiah. If Jesus were to accept Peter's suggestion, they would compete for leadership of an earthly kingdom. Then, the kingdom of God would be wiped away. But Jesus does the Father's will (Jn 10:30). Jesus knows that his death is the divine consequence of his solidarity with his people and loving service to them. Jesus knows that his death is an essential part of God's saving plan. Therefore, Jesus firmly says, to Peter, "Get behind me, Satan!" Jesus wants Peter to stay out of his way and follow him behind, as a disciple.

Jesus' death on the cross proves that Jesus, by himself becoming a scapegoat, has eliminated the source of violence. Jesus accepts his death as self-sacrificing love and allows it to be the very means to end the cycle of violence in human history. This is a reason why the cross of Jesus has saved us and why Jesus' life is the paradigm for all human beings. (Having formulated this theory, Girard later became a Roman Catholic.)

We need to carry the cross in this world filled with all kinds of desires and envies. If we carry the cross, that is, if we love others and sacrifice for them, then we will be transformed and raised by God. This law of self-sacrificing love is called the Law of the Cross (Fr. Bernard Lonergan). It defines our relationships with loved ones: spouses, children, parents, friends, neighbors. In the Bible, it means: "Whoever wishes to save his life will lose it, but whoever loses his life for my sake will find it."

Jesus shows us how to be a true and authentic person by (1) not desiring the same thing others desire and by (2) carrying the cross for others. The life and death of Jesus "tells us who man truly is and what a man must do to be truly man" (*Spe Salvi*, #6). This is why Jesus is the paradigm for all human beings. This is why we confess that Jesus of Nazareth is the Christ, the Lord, and the Savior. ✝

[5ᵗʰ Lent (C), 7ᵗʰ Easter (A), 7ᵗʰ OT (A)]

TWENTY-THIRD SUNDAY IN ORDINARY TIME (A)

(Ezekiel 33:7-9; Romans 13:8-10; Matthew 18:15-20)

Christian Life

$\mathcal{I}$ndividualism is a dominant characteristic in our culture. We value individual rights and freedom, and we respect a self-made man. We practice capitalism with minimal government control. We support the justice system based on "innocent until proven guilty." These aspects of individualism have, no doubt, created American culture, which honors creativity, independence, and personal achievement.

If we get carried away, however, individualism transforms itself into egotism and narcissism. These forms of self-centeredness require no relationship with God and with neighbors. And the absence of these relationships naturally justifies the absence of ethics and morality. Fr. Albert Nolan, O.P., in his book *Jesus Today* points out that individualism is the most disturbing factor in Christian life.

Christian life is rooted in the collective spiritual growth of a community. Today's readings show how to bring peace, harmony, and reconciliation out of selfishness, dishonesty, and sinfulness in a Christian community.

The first reading describes the role of the prophet in a community to assist a person who is morally sick. Not to do so is to commit a serious sin.

The gospel reading today provides a three-step process for settling a dispute in a community. The first step is to confront an opposing party privately, with love and mercy. The second step is an official intervention, with many witnesses. The third step is to treat the person as a tax-collector or a Gentile, that is, as legitimate God's people, after expulsion from the community. The goal of this procedure is not to condemn, but to restore peace and harmony in the community.

The gospel passage ends with these words of Jesus: "Where two or three are gathered in my name, there I am in the midst of them." The Gospel of Matthew begins with the announcement of the birth of Emmanuel, which means God is with us (Mt 1:23), and ends with the promise of the presence of the risen Lord to the disciples: "Behold, I am with you always, until the end of the age" (Mt 28:20). The Gospel begins and ends with emphasis on the presence of God. Where God is present, all Christians form one body in the Lord.

In the second reading, Paul insists that Christians cannot merely care for themselves only. Everybody is responsible for the spiritual well-being of the entire community. If we truly love our neighbors, then we will not commit adultery, murder, theft, or coveting of another's property. This is why Paul said, "Love is the fulfillment of the Law" (Rom 13:10) and "Christ is the end of the law" (Rom 10:4).

When we pray "Our Father," we do not start with "O, Father, who art in heaven" or "My Father, who art in heaven." We start with "Our Father, who art in heaven." We pray together with our brothers and sisters, even when we recite it alone. No person is an island of selfishness and indifference to others. Everything we do is communal, never individual. When we pray together with our families at home or with our brothers and sisters in this sacred place, we grasp the spirit of our common tradition and history. We pray and worship together; we are redeemed and saved together.

Most of all, we celebrate the Eucharist together. At the table of the Lord's banquet, we forgive and are forgiven and reconciled to each other by exposing any hidden ignorance, contempt, and division. The Eucharist is the most effective liturgy through which our Christian identity is fostered.

We should not be deterred by individualism. Self-accomplishment, self-responsibility, and self-fulfillment are all good and necessary. We must also remember that, as sons and daughters of God, our task is to build a community of forgiveness and reconciliation in God's love and mercy. Let us walk together in the presence of the Lord. ✝

[17th and 26th OT (C)]

Twenty-Fourth Sunday in Ordinary Time (A)

(Sirach 27:30-28:7; Romans 14:7-9; Matthew 18:21-35)

"How Often Must I Forgive?"

It is hard to apologize when we have offended someone. It is even harder to accept an apology when someone has offended us. And yet, we always pray, "Forgive us our trespasses, as we forgive those who trespass against us." To forgive and to be forgiven are mutually related. Today's readings provide more details on this dynamic relationship between forgiving and being forgiven.

In the gospel reading today, Peter thinks that forgiving a brother sinner seven times is more than enough. Surprisingly, Jesus tells him, "I say to you, not seven times but seventy times seven," meaning there is no limit to forgiveness. In other words, it is impossible to forgive within human power; it is possible only with the grace of God.

Jesus continues with the story of the merciless servant. The point of the gospel story is that the servant, who has already been forgiven by the king for his own astronomical amount of debt, turns around and demands justice on a tiny sum of money from his fellow servant. That incident of mercilessness is reported to the king, who then takes the first servant into harsh judgment, saying, "Should you not have had mercy on your fellow servant as I had mercy on you?"

An irony is that both servants use the same words of forgiveness: "Be patient with me, and I will pay you back." This means that both servants have the same magnitude of sincerity for being forgiven. This parable, therefore, illustrates that petitions for forgiveness are granted insomuch as they are directed to God, but not to a human being. We owe God a great deal, yet God always forgives. In contrast, we owe each other very little, but we hardly forgive. God's justice and mercy are incomparable to our justice and mercy.

Finally, the story points out the basic dynamics of forgiveness. In order to forgive others, we need to be with them in their points of view. If we want

96

to forgive and be forgiven, we must be able to understand each other that we are beloved sons and daughters of God.

Forgiveness is a social virtue requiring two parties: one that forgives and the other that asks for forgiveness. The humble person asks for forgiveness, and the generous person offers forgiveness. Forgiveness also is a necessary virtue for repairing and rebuilding mutual relationships in a community.

We live in a culture of individualism that tends to shy away from communal and social obligations. Healthy individualism makes a person independent and self-confident. But unhealthy individualism produces egotism and selfishness, which are not conducive to the spirit of forgiveness.

Erich Fromm, a psychologist who is not a Catholic, says in his book *The Sane Society,* "Protestant countries have a much higher suicide rate than Catholic countries." One explanation for this may be that the Catholic Church provides adequate means, through the Sacrament of Reconciliation, for dealing with a sense of guilt and for experiencing forgiveness.

Forgiveness also draws us closer to God and allows us to remain in the kingdom of God. This is why Jesus always forgives first, before he cures the crippled and heals the sick. Forgiveness is to participate in the ministry of Christ Jesus, who is the Son of God and, at the same time, a human being who walks with us. Ultimately, it is not us, but the Spirit of Christ Jesus who dwells within us, forgives. St. Paul exclaimed this truth as follows: "If we live, we live for the Lord, and if we die, we die for the Lord. Christ is the Lord of both the dead and the living."

As we build God's kingdom on earth, so we must try to forgive and to be forgiven. If we do not, we will remain victims of injustice, with angry and bitter hearts. To forgive and to be forgiven provide the ultimate meaning of human existence before God and the "reason to hope" in everyday life (1 Pt 3:15). ✝

TWENTY-FIFTH SUNDAY IN ORDINARY TIME (A)

(Isaiah 55:6-9; Philippians 1:20-24, 27; Matthew 20:1-16)

Is Our Generous God Fair?

Sometimes the Bible says something unusual or even absurd. We continue, however, to think about it, and suddenly, a new realization of the true meaning hits home. Then, humbled, we bow our heads and revere the Bible as the Word of God.

Today's gospel passage, the parable of the vineyard workers, is an excellent example. In ancient Israel, people harvest grapes during the month of September, just before the rainy season. If torrential rains come before the harvest, the entire crop can be lost. Thus, picking the grapes becomes a race against time. One morning, the owner of the vineyard wakes up and sees a dark sky with stormy clouds. He rushes to the marketplace to hire workers to pick the grapes. He goes out again at nine o'clock in the morning, at noon, and at three o'clock in the afternoon. Surprisingly, he goes to the marketplace again near the end of the day.

After the work is completed, the owner pays the workers who came at the eleventh hour a full day's wages ahead of the early workers. On the contrary, we expect the owner will pay a full day's wages to the early workers first and hourly wages for the late workers. The early workers are bound to complain and get mad.

Obviously, the owner did not act properly. We think that workers should be paid based upon the results produced. We think of justice and fairness in terms of individual autonomy and personal accomplishment. By contrast, in the Bible, justice is to form a right relationship in love.

Let us look closely at the situation during the first century in Palestine. The life of a worker was hard. His family lived a hand-to-mouth existence. If a worker failed to get employment one day, his whole family went hungry the next day. If he found work in the morning, his whole family rejoiced all day. It is against this background that we can see how God's justice plays out in today's gospel story.

The owner of the vineyard is God the Father. The early workers are the Pharisees, who are satisfied with their own views of the world; they are deaf to Jesus' teachings. The late workers are sinners and outcasts; they accept Jesus' teachings and reform their lives.

Today's parable shows the clash between two different moral perceptions— our justice and fairness versus God's grace and generosity. Actually, the owner was fair and just, because he freely gave of his own, and because all workers were paid as initially agreed. Furthermore, the owner is within his right to pay a full day's wages to the late workers; his generosity comes from an abundance of grace. God's grace is a free gift, and the abundant grace of God is not for us to judge. God's grace is not proportional to human efforts. The early workers should not be envious of God's grace (generosity).

In today's parable, Jesus teaches us the relationship with God, who pays the same wage to both the early and the late workers. Those who come to God late will receive the same abundant grace of God as those who come early. This means that all people are equally related to God, and God deals with each person individually. Each person has one soul only. And God takes care of each soul to its fullest potential.

We thought initially that God was not just, because we did not understand God's grace. Now that we have understood God's grace and generosity, we need to wake up from our usual moral perceptions. We need to transform ourselves and change our hearts. This is why Jesus speaks parables and appeals to our dispositions and imaginations. Jesus speaks to our hearts and unconscious minds.

Today's gospel passage proves that the Bible is the Word of God and, furthermore, presents a new paradigm for us to transform our moral perceptions. We need to transform ourselves continuously toward Jesus in accordance to the moral ideals and ethical perspectives of the Gospel. ✝

[15th OT (A)]

Twenty-Sixth Sunday in Ordinary Time (A)

(Ezekiel 18:25-28; Philippians 2:1-11; Matthew 21:28-32)

The Principal Virtue of Christianity

Humility is the most important virtue in Christianity. In humility, God became man. In humility, man can exists in union with God.

Philippi in Macedonia was the first city in Europe that received Christianity from Paul (Acts 16:9-12). The people in Philippi were influenced by die-hard Jewish Christians who demanded the Jewish way of becoming Christians. In his Letter to the Philippians, Paul asked them to know Christ Jesus correctly and, through Christ Jesus, to recognize God's grace and justice. The second reading includes the Christ Hymn, which is a part of that letter.

The Christ Hymn, which was composed only twenty-five years or so after the death of Jesus, provides a remarkable insight into how the earliest Christians understood Jesus. Furthermore, scholars say that Paul did not compose the entirety of it; he edited what was then a popular song among Jesus' followers. It shows that the essence of Christology began very early on and has remained the same for the last twenty centuries. Jesus of Nazareth is the Christ, the Son of God. At the same time, it shows how to be Christians.

The Christ Hymn consists of two modes: one is the descending mode of God's incarnation in Jesus of Nazareth, and the other is the ascending mode of Christ Jesus being glorified in his resurrection. In other words, the Hymn celebrates Jesus Christ as the Son of God who humbled himself by taking the form of a servant, suffered death on the cross, and was exalted in his resurrection. Therefore, Jesus is the Lord.

When the Son of God assumed human nature as his own, he did away with all of his divine privileges. He made himself available to others. He never boasted, and he refused any kind of human entitlement. Instead, he chose to be the servant for all. When he died, he did not demand or claim any human dignity. He died as he lived. He truly emptied himself. God raised him up for that. The divinity of Jesus Christ was revealed through his perfect humanity. As a result, in the person of Jesus, God shares his divine life with us.

In the same way, Christian life consists of two distinctive modes: one is the descending mode of partaking in Jesus' humanity, and the other is the ascending mode of being deified or sanctified (*theosis*) in and through Jesus Christ. If we empty ourselves by getting rid of our egos and selfishness (*kenosis*), we will then be with God and recover our true selves.

In essence, the Christ Hymn summarizes the fundamental principle of Christianity. Like the Philippians, we have pride and self-centeredness deep inside us; we often boast of ourselves in our relationships with our brothers and sisters. The Christ Hymn is for us to reflect seriously, as Christians, how humble we are.

The gospel reading today shows two types of people. The first son was slow at first, but eventually turned his life around in response to Jesus' teachings. He represents tax collectors and prostitutes. The second son appeared to be faithful at first, but actually was not. He listened to Jesus but not acted upon his message. He represents chief priests and elders. Another way to interpret this parable is to ask who is more humble among those inside of the Church and those outside of the Church.

Why did chief priests and elders reject Jesus in the end? What was special about tax collectors and prostitutes who accepted Jesus? The answer is humility. Humility constitutes the basic attitude and disposition of human beings in relation to God. Humility enables us to understand our finitude and contingency as God's creatures, by destroying our egos and selfishness. Humility enables us to empty ourselves, as Christ has done on the cross. Humility allows us to accept Jesus Christ as the Savior of mankind.

We must be humble, and then we will be in communion with God through Jesus Christ. Those who are self-sufficient or self-centered cannot look beyond themselves and search for God who transcends. Humility is the principal virtue of Christianity. ✝

[Christmas Midnight, Baptism (A), Palm Sunday (C), 22ⁿᵈ OT (C)]

TWENTY-SEVENTH SUNDAY IN ORDINARY TIME (A)

(Isaiah 5:1-7; Philippians 4:6-9; Matthew 21:33-43)

God's Vineyard

How is our vineyard coming along? Our vineyard could be ourselves, our family, our work, or our parish. Actually, our vineyard belongs to God, not to us. We don't own it; we are only tenants.

Do you know that our vineyard was carefully prepared by somebody else? God cleared away rough stones and wild bushes, and tilled the soil for tender young vines to spread their soft roots. God did all these things with his own hands, without using any machine. God put a great effort into preparing the soil and planting the vines in our vineyard. God also made the sun rise and sent rain to ensure a rich and abundant harvest. For our part, we simply prune the vines and weed out wild grasses in order to let them produce abundant sweet grapes.

Today's readings are all about our vineyard. The first reading and the responsorial psalm show that the vineyard of the Lord is the house of God's people, Israel. The gospel reading is called the parable of the vineyard, how God's people are cared for.

In the gospel account, the owner was deeply concerned over his tenants' care of his vineyard, especially when the tenants produced wild and sour grapes. The owner sent his servants over and over again, but every one of them was beaten or stoned by the tenants. Finally, the owner sent his son, who was seized and lynched. In ancient Palestine, whoever owned land for some time could eventually gain possession. Obviously, in order to possess the land, the tenants killed the owner's son. At last, the owner came in person and replaced the old wicked tenants with new tenants. The vineyard was safeguarded under new management after all.

Vineyard is an image of Israel as a bride. So this parable depicts the entire history of salvation using symbols and metaphors. The religious leaders of Israel did not take good care of the vineyard of the Lord, so God sent many prophets. The leaders badly treated or killed them, one by one. God was still deeply concerned with His vineyard, so God finally sent His Son. They killed him. God's care for His vineyard was so serious and important that He sacrificed His own Son.

The point of the parable is that God always cares for His vineyard. Starting with the creation, through the incarnation and the death and resurrection of Jesus, and up to the future fulfillment of the eternal kingdom, God maintains a personal relationship with His vineyard. The psalmist expresses God's care during the creation in this way: "What are human beings that you are mindful of them, mortals that you care for them? You have made them a little lower than the angels, and crowned them with glory and honor" (Ps 8:3-5).

The Son of God, Jesus Christ, has shown us the face of God and exemplified how to take care of God's vineyard. In order for us to live the life of God, Paul demonstrated to all Christians that the Spirit of God dwells within us (Eph 3:17, Gal 2:20, Phil 2:13, Rom 8:9, 2 Tm 1:14). In short, the entire history of salvation points out that God is deeply and seriously concerned with His vineyard, which He has entrusted to us.

In the vineyard of the Lord, God wants to show us the early morning sunrise; God wants to walk with us in the evening breeze; God wants us to enjoy the riches of His harvest. What God asks us to do in return is to look after His vineyard faithfully and diligently. We are to produce abundant, choice grapes from His vineyard so that excellent wines are made from them.

God's vineyard is all that we are and all that we do. God's vineyard is our families, for which we love and care. God's vineyard is our works, which we honor and respect. God's vineyard is our parish, which we belong to and serve.

How is our vineyard coming along? I mean, how is God's vineyard coming along? Are we taking care of it diligently and faithfully? ✝

[5ᵗʰ Easter (B)]

103

TWENTY-EIGHTH SUNDAY (A)

(Isaiah 25:6-10; Philippians 4:12-14, 19-20; Matthew 22:1-14)

God's Banquet

Today's readings are filled with languages that symbolize banquets. The first reading is about God's invitation of people to "a feast of rich food and choice wines" on the sacred mountain. The responsorial psalm, the most famous Psalm 23, shows "the (banquet) table" in a green pasture prepared for us by God. The gospel reading is about a king who invites people to his son's royal wedding banquet.

In the Bible, a banquet is a metaphor for the fulfillment of God's kingdom at the end-time. At the end-time when the Messiah comes, God's promises will be fulfilled. At the end-time, the present world order will end, and God will invite people to His banquet.

For our twenty-first-century minds, it is difficult to understand what the end-time is and when it will come. The ancient Israelites had no clear distinction in time and place. The present and the future were combined together, as well as this world and the next. Furthermore, in Hebraic thinking, the concept of time is circular, whereas in Greek thinking it is linear. For example, the resurrection is the fulfillment of the incarnation. Therefore, according to ancient Jewish thoughts, the end-time is when God's promises are fulfilled in the end. So the end-time is the fulfillment of the creation. The end-time is neither the end of the time nor the end of the world, as often claimed by some evangelical circles.

For Christians, God's promises have already been fulfilled in the person of Jesus Christ. This is why the Gospel is the powerful good news of Jesus Christ. According to the Gospel, Jesus ate and drank with sinners, prostitutes, and tax-collectors as a proof of the arrival of God's kingdom. And the Last Supper was Jesus' last banquet on earth right before his own death.

The Gospel continues to say that God has raised Jesus Christ who now sits at the right hand of the Father. This means that God's creative work continues now in the presence of the Holy Spirit, the Spirit of Christ.

Therefore, for Christians, the creation is no longer a past historic event; the creation continues on and on now. When Jesus talks about the birds in the air and lilies in the field, he is not simply praising them aesthetically, he is reminding us the dignity and worth of human beings who can participate in God's creation. We must celebrate for our being humans, because by giving glory to God, man is perfected.

As we participate in God's creative acts, we experience God directly. If we can experience God, then God's own self must dwell within us. During a deep and objectless meditation, we can see ourselves meditating or a particular theme we are meditating. This ability of "I see myself meditating" is caused by the presence of God within us. St. Paul put it in this way: "It is no longer I who live, but Christ who lives within me."

The indwelling God within us is actualized implicitly in our acts of love, faith, and hope. If we love our neighbor, God within us loves the person, and naturally we love God in tandem. Whenever we turn in love to our neighbor, not only God within us loves the person through us, but also the same God within us is the source of our love of neighbor. In other words, the love of our neighbor is the combination of the love of God within us and through us, as the concomitant expression of the two modes of God's love. Therefore, by loving our neighbor, we can really experience and encounter God in our daily lives.

For Christians, the invitation to the banquet is not a future event far away from the present time. God has already invited us to His banquet through His Son and with His Son. And so we live God's life, not our life. We live God's life with the risen Jesus Christ.

In a few minutes, we will celebrate the Lord's banquet, the Eucharist. During the celebration, we are invited to the Lord's banquet to forgive and reconcile one another (CCC, #1846). And we will foretaste the heavenly banquet that will be fulfilled at the end-time (CCC, #1000, 1344). Let us go forth and gather together at the table of the Lord's banquet, and give thanks to the living God. ✝

[32ⁿᵈ OT (A), 33ʳᵈ OT (B), 33ʳᵈ OT (C), Christ King (C)]

Twenty-Ninth Sunday in Ordinary Time (A)

(Isaiah 45:1, 4-6; 1 Thessalonians 1:1-5; Matthew 22:15-21)

Religion and Politics

"Give to Caesar what belongs to Caesar and to God what belongs to God."

This saying of Jesus appears to mean that religion is one thing and politics is another. Thus, if we fulfill our religious duties, we may not be bothered with other political and social issues. If we achieve our political goal, we may not be concerned with its religious implications. Such an interpretation is the consequence of dualistic thinking.

During the first century, the world was not divided into one part for God and the other for Caesar. People knew that human beings were created in the image of God. All creatures were under God's sovereignty, and human beings had a special role in God's ongoing creation.

In the Bible, there is no separation between politics and religion. Jesus himself counseled his disciples to pay attention to the Pharisees and the scribes because "they occupy the chair of Moses" (Mt 23:2). Jesus died as "the king of the Jews" by Roman soldiers, because of his non-violent policy of God's kingdom. St. Paul said, "Jesus is the Lord," which means "Caesar is not the Lord." Therefore, if we remove the politically charged death of Jesus from the Bible, there is no Christianity. If we remove politics from the Bible, there is no Christianity.

When Jesus says, "Give to Caesar what belongs to Caesar and to God what belongs to God," he is not speaking of whether one pays taxes to Caesar or not. He is asking them to pay tax after having recognized the obligation to God. The point Jesus makes is this: If you are so concerned about paying taxes to Caesar, how much more concerned should you be about your service to God as our creator? The duty toward God always binds all and applies everywhere. Only then does the remainder—civil duty—come.

The gospel passage today does not suggest that we do not value our political system. It suggests that fidelity to both religious tradition and political

106

systems is not only possible, but is God's will. Jesus makes it clear that we have a dual citizenship. We are citizens of two mutually inclusive worlds: the kingdom of God and the civil government.

The Archbishop Angelo Roncalli, the papal nuncio to France, was a good politician as well as a religious man. As we know, the Archbishop later became Pope. John XXIII.

I would like to share with you two stories about him. As a bishop, a diplomat, and a politician, his life was full of deep experiences of the love of God. Although he was elected as a "transitional pope," he announced his intention for an ecumenical council only three months after his Installation. He did so against fierce protest from the Curia and other cardinals and bishops. On the night when he announced his plan to convene the Second Vatican Council, Pope John had trouble falling asleep. He later admitted he talked to himself that night: "Giovanni, Giovanni, why can't you sleep? Is it the pope or the Holy Spirit who governs the church? It's the Holy Spirit? Well, then, go to sleep, Giovanni!"

St. John also was a man of humor. One day he visited a hospital in Rome, the Hospital of the Holy Spirit. Shortly after he entered the hospital building, he was introduced to the nun in charge of the hospital. "Holy Father," she said, "I am the superior of the Holy Spirit." St. John responded delightedly, "You're very lucky. I'm only the Vicar of Christ."

God's kingdom has been inaugurated in this world where we live. Accordingly, we have a duty and a responsibility as citizens of both God's kingdom and this world. †

[20th OT (C)]

THIRTIETH SUNDAY IN ORDINARY TIME (A)

(Exodus 22:20-26; 1 Thessalonians 1:5-10; Matthew 22:34-40)

The Greatest Commandment

In the gospel reading today, the Pharisees challenged Jesus and asked, "Which is the most important law?" That was a critical issue, because the people of Israel were confused with a lot of dos and don'ts from the Torah. Jesus wisely chose the love of God (Dt 6:5) and the love of neighbor (Lv 19:18) and said, "The whole law and the prophets depend on these two commandments." In other words, these two commandments provide a key to the understanding of God's will and, more importantly, prove that Jesus is the new Torah.

We often think of the law as a collection of regulations we must obey. For example, we think that we must love our neighbor because it is God's commandment. The best way to avoid such legalism is to understand why we have the law in the first place. Furthermore, some people consider the love of God and the love of neighbor are two different laws. Today, we reflect on why we love God and how the love of God is related to the love of neighbor.

God loved us first (1 Jn 4:19), so we love God. Not because it is a commandment, and not because it is a moral law, but because God loved us first, do we love God. Our love for God is a natural response to God's love for us. The love we might have felt for the "first" time in our youth was, actually, the second love. The first love with God is still hidden in our hearts. God's love is imprinted in our hearts permanently. As a result, we can never grasp the love that lasts forever. In this life on earth, our love reflects only a glimpse of the love of God for us.

Another way to consider the relationship between God's love for us and our love for God is that God exists in the depths of our beings (Gal 2:20, 1 Jn 4:13). Moreover, the love we have is the one poured out into our hearts by the Holy Spirit (Rom 5:5). In other words, we love God with the love of God that was already put into our hearts. It is, in a sense, not we, but God within us who responds to God's love. God's creative love for us and our responsive love for God are two distinctive aspects of one love of God. St. John of the Cross said, "God loves us so that we can love Him by means of His own love" (The Spiritual Canticle, *32*, 6).

God is love (1 Jn 4:8 and 4:16), and God's love is our understanding of God. Therefore, by loving God we become holy. As we become holy, we come to be in union with God. The union with God cannot be fully realized in this life, however. When the kingdom of God is fulfilled, our union with God will be fulfilled. This is why we do not yet fully appreciate God's love on earth. While on earth, we must respond to God's love for us.

To do so, we need to understand the nature of love and the relationship between the love of God and the love of neighbor. Love is the mother of all virtues, and love embraces and generates all other virtues. And love cannot stand by itself. The love within us is always actualized by reaching out to others. Love is mutual.

When we are in love with God, we also are in love with our neighbors, because God's love has already poured into our hearts, as well as theirs, through the Holy Spirit. Moreover, we cannot say that a part of us loves God, while another part of us loves neighbor. If we love our neighbor, we are already in love with God. Conversely, if we are in love with God, we naturally love our neighbor. The love of God is the source of the love of neighbor, and the love of neighbor is an expression of the love of God. Therefore, the love of God and the love of neighbor are two distinct aspects of one love, God's love (*Deus Caritas Est*, #18). We come into union with God, who is love, by becoming one with our neighbor in love.

The greatest commandment, the love of God and the love of neighbor, is our spontaneous responses to God's love for us. God alone creates, redeems, and sanctifies. The success of a union with God depends on the desire to develop this capacity to love to the best of our abilities. This is the reason why Jesus' commandment on love is the summation of the Judaic Law and other human laws. ✝

[6th Easter (B), Pentecost (B), 4th OT (C), 12th OT (A), 31st OT (B)]

THIRTY-FIRST SUNDAY IN ORDINARY TIME (A)

(Malachi 1:14-2:2, 8-10; 1 Thessalonians 2:7-9, 13; Matthew 23:1-12)

Church Leadership

As the liturgical cycle is about to come to an end, so does Jesus' journey to Jerusalem. At this juncture of his ministry, Jesus is very concerned with the church leadership.

In today's gospel passage, Jesus teaches his disciples not to behave like the Pharisees and scribes, although he asks them to recognize the Pharisees and scribes on the chair of Moses. The first reading also shows that, through the prophet Malachi, God warns temple priests not to exhibit partiality in their ministry. Thus the message of today's readings is about how to treat each other with dignity and respect in the Church. It also is a warning against leadership that harms the Church, then and now.

The word "leadership" includes all members of the Church, in a collective sense. All members of the Church, not just bishops and priests, are responsible for the church leadership nowadays. Any church leader has sacred responsibilities to serve the people of God. All of us, as disciples of Jesus Christ, must be accountable for the salvation of the whole community.

People from all walks of life come to the Church, so some sorts of structure and organization are necessary within the Church. Otherwise, the Church would be filled with individual ideas and personal interests. Evil forces of human nature could potentially drive the Church into a chaotic mess. In spite of these human weaknesses, because the Church is the Body of Christ, the abuse of power and authority must not creep into leadership. The Church is always in danger of exercising her authority, rather than serving the flock. The Church is a pilgrim church.

If we look closely at ourselves, it is true we expect church leaders to provide us examples of a life lived in the image of Jesus Christ. And we would like to receive the body of Christ, instead of trying to be the Christ for others. We also recognize the truth too soon and hold on to it too long. We need to be saved and redeemed.

To understand the human side of the Church, I will share with you some observations. One is that we always emphasize a particular virtue at the expense of other contrary virtues. For example, when we talk about loyalty and obedience, we tend to forget equality and justice. If we adhere to the past, we are slow in reading the signs of the times. Another pbeservation is that people who control or oppress others habitually were already controlled or oppressed by someone else in the past.

Jesus repeatedly says to his disciples, that is, church leaders, "Those who try to make their life secure will lose it, but those who lose their life will keep it" (Lk 17:33). In fact, this saying is a short summary of Jesus' life according to the Synoptic Gospels. To put it differently: "If you want to gain power, you will lose it. If you lose power, you will gain it."

Paul is the prime example of leadership. His leadership is that of a "nursing mother who cares for her children." His leadership comes from the strong conviction of "being in Christ" and thus sharing the life in the Spirit among brothers and sisters of Jesus.

"The Church is like a sacrament of communion with God and of unity among all men" (*Lumen Gentium*, #1). This beautiful statement from Vatican II shows Jesus' intention of having founded the Church on earth. It also reminds us that we must build the kingdom of God through the Church, following the footsteps of Jesus Christ.

Let us end by quoting Jesus' instruction to his disciples as he approached Jerusalem during his final days on earth. Actually, Jesus was not *saying* it; Jesus was *begging* it to all his disciples. "You know that the rulers of the Gentiles lord it over them… It will not be so among you; but whoever wishes to be great among you must be your servant, and whoever wishes to be first among you must be your slave" (Mt 20:25-27). ✝

[4th Easter (A), 29th OT (B)]

111

THIRTY-SECOND SUNDAY IN ORDINARY TIME (A)

(Wisdom 6:12-16; 1 Thessalonians 4:13-18; Matthew 25:1-13)

Jesus' Lamp Burns Our Oil

As we come close to the end of the liturgical year, we meditate on the theme of the second coming of Jesus. Jesus will come again, and we must prepare ourselves for his second coming by doing what we must do with courage and in confidence.

The second coming of Jesus, called *parousia*, is fulfillment of the kingdom of God at the end-time (*eschaton*). The end-time is neither the end of time nor the end of the world. The end-time is the time of fulfillment of God's promise (Bergant, *America*, 10/03/2005). At the end-time, God's promises will be fulfilled, the present world order will end, and God will be all in all (1 Cor 15:28).

Jesus himself says that he will come again (Mt 24:27, 37, 39). Hence, many people in history have questioned and even predicted when the end-time will come. Jesus says that he doesn't know exactly when it will come. He says, "About that day and hour no one knows, neither the angels of heaven, nor the Son, but only the Father" (Mt 24:36). If Jesus doesn't know the day and hour, nobody can predict it. Therefore, everybody should be ready, because it will surely come "like a thief in the night" (1 Thes 5:2). We must stay awake and pray (Mt 24:42, 26:41).

Today's gospel reading, the parable of the foolish bridesmaids, shows how to prepare for the second coming of Jesus. During a Jewish wedding, which takes place at the bride's house, the bridegroom sometimes does not show up until midnight. Tired from waiting, some of the bridesmaids may fall asleep only to be awakened by loud voices from the procession nearby. In the parable, soon after being awakened, the bridesmaids light their lamps immediately. Some foolish bridesmaids, who have no oil of their own, ask others to share the oil. They meet with harsh rejection: "No, there will not be enough for us and you."

This parable is about the suddenness of Jesus' second coming and our readiness for it. The bridegroom is Jesus, who will come again at the end-time, whereupon God will provide a wedding banquet. The wise bridesmaids are those who have prepared the oil for the lamps, whereas the foolish bridesmaids are those who want to borrow the oil from others. The oil represents the good deeds performed.

One way for us to reflect upon the end-time is to compare it with our own mortality. We know that we will die someday. When we die, we will join in God's eternity. We will not add or change anything in our life after death. In other words, our true identity is established only after our death. Therefore, death is the completion of life, rather than the end of life. Because death is the completion of life, we must continue to live fruitfully and be good to others until the very last moment.

In the gospel story today, when the bridegroom comes, the foolish bridesmaids want to borrow oil for their lamps from the wise bridesmaids. These foolish ones cannot join the wedding banquet in God's kingdom, whereas the wise ones can.

The questions we need to ask of ourselves, therefore, are: Are we more like the foolish bridesmaids or the wise bridesmaids? In other words, are we going to love and do good deeds for others until the end-time, or are we going to waste our talents and time? The answers to these questions should be obvious. Jesus says, "You are the light of the world.... Let your light shine before others, so that they may see your good works and give glory to your Father in heaven" (Mt 5:14-16).

Jesus also says, "I am the light of the world" (Jn 8:12). If Jesus is the light of the world, have you ever wondered where Jesus gets the oil for his lamp? We are his disciples; we are his oil. "Jesus' light burns with the oil of our lives" (Schillebeeckx, *Christ*, p. 846). ✝

[1ˢᵗ Advent (C), 28ᵗʰ OT (A), 33ʳᵈ OT (C)]

THIRTY-THIRD SUNDAY IN ORDINARY TIME (A)

(Proverbs 31:10-13, 19-20, 30-31; 1 Thessalonians 5:1-6; Matthew 25:14-30)

To Fear the Lord

As Jesus approaches Jerusalem and nears the end of his life, he becomes somber and serious. Jesus is very concerned with how the disciples will follow up his teachings.

In the same way, the Church asks us to reflect seriously on how we have used the talents God has given us, as we approach the end of the liturgical year.

Last week we were advised to wait for the end-time with constant readiness. This week Jesus tells us that, while waiting for the end-time, we cannot simply sit back and wait. Blessed with our God-given talents, we must keep on working while we wait. We must go on doing something positive, something constructive, and something life-affirming. We must be accountable for God's gifts to us.

The gospel reading today is called the parable of the talents. A wealthy man entrusted his servants with his money, giving them no instructions, and he went on a long journey. The first servant received five talents, the second servant two talents, and the third servant one talent. When the wealthy man returned, he required accounting of the entrusted money. The first two servants produced twice the money they had originally received. Sadly, the third servant buried the money in the ground and made no profit.

The wealthy man who went on the journey is Jesus, who will ascend to heaven after the resurrection. He will return again at the end-time. The servants are you and me, all of us. And the money represents our God-given talents.

The word "talent" refers to one's abilities and gifts. It also was a Roman currency of about 6,000 denarii; one denarius was equivalent to a day's wage. So the one talent the third servant received is equivalent to an ordinary retirement income nowadays. All three servants were entrusted huge amounts of money, suggesting that the grace of Gad—that is, our God-given talents, are huge and enormous.

But the third servant did not do anything at all with his talent. He wanted to preserve what was given to him. Therefore, this lazy and non-productive servant was sent to the place where there was "weeping and grinding of teeth," an extremely harsh punishment in the First Gospel (8:12, 13:42, 13:50, 22:13, 24:51, 25:30).

(St. Matthew says elsewhere in his Gospel, "For to those who have, more will be given, and they will have an abundance; but from those who have nothing, even what they have will be taken away" (Mt 13:12).)

We may ask ourselves, "What is it that will lose its value when buried and will gain its value when used?" The answer is love. When we love, love multiplies. When we do not love, love dies. In the gospel story, it is love that could not be multiplied. This is why the owner was mad at the lazy and conservative servant.

The woman in the first reading is quite the opposite of the lazy servant in the gospel story. She is faithful, industrious, and responsible. She is a model of wisdom (*sophia*) who fears the Lord.

The phrase "to fear the Lord" appears frequently in the Old Testament. To fear the Lord is to respond positively to the love of God. "To fear the Lord is the beginning of wisdom" (Sir 1:14). To fear the Lord is an attitude of expressing proper respect to God. To fear the Lord is not to violate God's transcendence. To fear the Lord is to love the Lord.

We fear the Lord, not because we must obey God's rules and regulations, not because there will be judgment, but because we are responsible for our lives. We fear the Lord, and we diligently do our shares in our family, church, and society, not being lazy and depending on others. Being faithful to our gift of life is to fear the Lord. "Happy are those who fear the Lord." ✝

OUR LORD JESUS CHRIST THE KING (A)

(Ezekiel 34:11-12, 15-17; 1 Corinthians 15:20-26, 28; Matthew 25:31-46)

The Last Judgment

Jesus has shown us the face of God and has lived the authentic human life. Jesus is the sacrament of God and the paradigm of humanity. We believe in him and follow his way of life.

We have listened to the gospel account which is Jesus' last testament. Jesus asks us to feed the hungry, to give drink to the thirsty, to welcome the stranger, to clothe the naked, to comfort the sick, and to visit those in prison. These are traditionally called the corporal works of mercy. Those who perform such works will neither receive much publicity nor become rich and famous. These services to others, however, require the grace of God, who will free us from selfishness and individualism.

We ask, "Why do we have to perform such works of love and mercy?" We do so because we desire to live the life of God, by reminding ourselves the following three points. First, we desire communion with God. Second, we wish to love God and our neighbor. Third, we want to be merciful to the poor and the lowly.

First, we desire to be in union with God. God is one nature comprising three persons; we are individual persons sharing one human nature. Therefore, the goal of our Christian life, which is to breathe God's breath and live God's life, already implies that we are communal and social beings. The communion with God we strive is not "me and God," but "God and us" and "God in us."

Second, Jesus sums up all commandments in terms of the love of God and the love of neighbor (Mt 22:37-39). And Jesus gives us the new commandment, which is to love one another as he loves us (Jn 13:34). The love of neighbor is realization of the love of God. Conversely, the love of God is the source of the love of neighbor. Hence, the evangelist John has said, "Those who say, 'I love God,' and hate their brothers and sisters are liars; for those who do not love a brother or sister whom they have seen, cannot love God whom they have not seen" (1 Jn 4:20).

Because God is love, love is the foundation of all virtues, and mercy is realization of love. Mercy includes all forms of justice. Consequently, without mercy, there is no love of God and love of neighbor.

Third, God is merciful to the weak and the poor in contrast to the strong and the rich, as in the first reading. Jesus Christ also has identified himself with the poor, the marginalized, and victims of injustice. The truth of the Gospel is that God consistently reveals preferential love (option) for the poor and the marginalized because the poor, who are neglected by the society, are closer to God. Therefore, "God's heart has a special place for the poor" (*Evangelii Gaudium*, #199).

The poor, however, include not only those lacking economical sustenance; issues surrounding the poor also concern social, cultural, psychological, and spiritual aspects. The poor have many faces.

Today's gospel message shows that the love and mercy we show to the least among us constitutes the condition of our last judgment. With the least of our brothers and sisters, we not only recognize Jesus Christ, but also seek to be in communion with the triune God. Therefore, we will be judged on how well we serve Christ Jesus in the least among us. On the last day, there is only one thing that will be counted—the love and mercy in our hearts.

On this last Sunday of the liturgical year, we celebrate the Feast of Christ the King. Jesus has established the kingdom of God on earth. Jesus also leads his people by love and mercy, inspiring them to join him in completing the kingdom of God.

We are called to complete the kingdom of God. We are called to follow Jesus of Nazareth, who is the King of kings.✝

[26th OT (C), 32nd OT (B)]

YEAR B

FIRST SUNDAY OF ADVENT (B)

(Isaiah 63:16b-17, 19b; 64:2b-7; 1 Corinthians 1:3-9; Mark 13:33-37)

We Are Always Born-Again Christians

A friend of mine, a Protestant fundamentalist, had a strong opinion against the Catholic liturgy. He was so knowledgeable with scriptural passages that he defended his position well. He was, as he called himself, a born-again Christian. I once asked him, since he was a born-again Christian, whether he no longer had selfish and worldly desires. He admitted earnestly that he still had those desires. I told him that he should have been born again and again. What I meant was that union with God is a lifetime task; a born-again status is simply the commencement of a journey of faith.

As we begin the season of Advent, this story lends itself to interesting reflection. Advent is the season we prepare for the first and historical coming of Jesus Christ and also for the second coming of Christ (*parousia*). Two thousand years ago, on Christmas Day, God came to us in the person of Jesus Christ. The second coming is the fulfillment of that first coming.

On the other hand, we wonder why Jesus has to come again. This question relates back to the story of my fundamentalist friend. If the first coming of Christ, the incarnation of God in the person of Jesus, can be compared to being born again, then the second coming of Christ parallels our union with God.

We live in a very troubled world. Not only are there continuous wars and conflicts around the globe but also constant declines in fundamental values of humanity. To name a few, I would like to point out the respect for human life from the moment of conception, the sanctity of marriage according to God's design, the inevitable and providential suffering at the end of life, and the dignity of all persons. In fact, people want to be gods once again and do not understand that "we are the clay and you are the potter," as we heard in the first reading. The world in which we live is indeed confused and in distress. And humanity is in danger.

Jesus needs to come again, even though he once came two thousand years ago. We need another Christmas desperately, and the world we live in must be redeemed once more. If Jesus comes to redeem us once again, then we will learn from Jesus how to find genuine humanity (*humanum*) and how to live fully, glorifying God.

We live in an age of identity crisis, and so we search diligently for our identity instead of identifying ourselves more closely with our brothers and sisters. A born-again Christian represents an effort to find such an identity.

Jesus was not concerned with his identity, however. Jesus' identity was not a problem for him, only for his followers. Jesus identified himself with everyone he met: the Samarian woman, the rich young man, the centurion, the tax collector, the prostitutes, the Pharisees, the scribes, the blind, the crippled, the sinners, and so on. Jesus identified himself with everyone even on the cross. By identifying himself with everyone, Jesus revealed his own identity.

The history of Christianity also reveals, in a striking manner, that those who follow in Jesus' footsteps identify themselves with others, especially with the poor, the outcast, and the rejected. We, too, must learn—once again—from Jesus how to identify ourselves with others.

This brings us back to my fundamentalist friend. His claim of being a born-again Christian is an open admission of conversion. Conversion, however, is not a final, once-and-for-all accomplishment. Conversion is identifying ourselves with the person of Jesus in response to God's love. Conversion is a life-long process of "being born from above" (Jn 3:7) and, ultimately, "having the same mind that was in Christ Jesus" (Phil 2:5).

Let us close with a prayer: "God our Savior, help us to follow the light and live the truth. In you we have been born again as sons and daughters of light: may we be your witness before the world" (Week I, Wednesday morning prayer). ✝

[33rd OT (B)]

121

SECOND SUNDAY OF ADVENT (B)

(Isaiah 40:1-5, 9-11; 2 Peter 3:8-14; Mark 1:1-8)

How Do We Repent?

"The beginning of the Gospel of Jesus Christ, the Son of God." With these words, St. Mark begins the Gospel. The evangelist continues on to pronounce that John the Baptist is the messenger who will pave the way for the Messiah, as Isaiah had prophesized.

The prophet Isaiah says in the first reading, "Every valley shall be filled in, every mountain and hill shall be made low; the rugged land shall be made a plain, the rough country, a broad valley." This beautiful poetry describes how God prepares a straight highway in the desert, between Babylon and Jerusalem, for the Jews returning from Exile. The prophet Isaiah hoped for and dreamed of the coming salvation from God (the Exile from Babylon).

In the same way, St. Mark declares we will be joyful and comforted because John the Baptist prepares the way for the Messiah, as Isaiah's words reverberate with the masterpiece of music--Handel's Messiah.

John the Baptist, a voice from nowhere—never heard before—is the trailblazer for Jesus Christ. John performs the work of repentance by baptizing people with water, and the Messiah will fulfill the actual work of salvation.

To prepare the way for the Lord, John has lived in the desert all his life, "feeding on locusts and honey and clothed in camel's hair." John has completely detached from the world.

We, too, await the Messiah as we celebrate the Advent season. We would like to see light from darkness; we would like to attain joy from sorrow; we would like to be comforted from troubles and worries. And so, we sing with the psalmist, "Lord, let us see your kindness, and grant us your salvation."

As we wait for the Messiah, however, St. Mark's message clearly suggests we find a place where we can detach ourselves from the world. We need to get away from the busyness of daily life and find a still point. We need to, alone with God, think about ourselves and repent.

To repent is to turn away from our way of thinking and value systems to those of God. To repent is to turn from self-centeredness to God-centeredness. To repent is to prepare ourselves to listen to the Good News of Jesus Christ, because it will turn our world upside down. To repent is to renew our hearts.

In doing so, however, we must avoid some extremes. One extreme is that of regretful repentance by putting an emphasis on God's judgment and wrath; perhaps this is a way to dispense of our guilt by chalking up our sinfulness to human weakness. Another extreme might entail appreciation of life's goodness by emphasizing God's love and mercy, but perhaps this only results in a complacent, self-absorbed Christianity.

Actually, to repent is to renew the commitments to our lives in God's kingdom, which has already been inaugurated by Jesus Christ. If we have placed our work ahead of our families, then we must correct the situation. If we have placed success in the world ahead of our personal relationship with God, then we must change that. We can, and must, correct, improve, and straighten ourselves up. We are moral agents.

In addition, we must always remember that John the Baptist points to Jesus Christ. While John looks forward to God's kingdom, he recognizes that the task of inaugurating God's kingdom on earth belongs to Jesus. John is a man of humility.

We, too, must be humble and remain God's creatures, by letting God be God. Like John the Baptist, we must point to Jesus the Messiah, begging God to show us mercy and grant us salvation (Ps 85:/). ✝

[2nd Advent (B)]

123

THIRD SUNDAY OF ADVENT (B)

(Isaiah 61:1-2a, 10-11; 1 Thessalonians 5:16-24; John 1:6-8, 19-28)

Rejoice in the Lord

𝕿oday, we celebrate the third Sunday of Advent, a joyful Sunday. All of today's readings reflect themes of joy. The first reading contains a sentence that proclaims, "I rejoice heartily in the Lord." The responsorial psalm resonates repeatedly, "My soul rejoices in my God." The second reading contains the sentence "Rejoice always." The gospel reading does not contain the word "joy," but John the Baptist rejoices in his role of witnessing. John says that he is neither the Messiah, nor Elijah, nor a prophet; he simply gives joyful testimony to the Messiah who is coming.

Today is indeed a joyful day, because we celebrate three comings of the Lord: (1) two thousand years ago at Bethlehem, when the Son of God was born of the Virgin Mary; (2) today in our world, where he is always present as the Word Incarnate; and (3) tomorrow when he will return in glory.

The joyfulness we celebrate today, however, is not an ordinary joyfulness. It is not a simple happiness charged with emotions. It is the blessedness and satisfactying hearts—the centers of our beings. It is a paradoxical joyfulness, inviting us into a world of reversal. The coming new world beholds captives freed, hungry people filled, and the rich sent away empty. Indeed, our joy is that of a new world where things are turned upside down.

This new world offers God's justice and peace. God's justice is different from our justice. Our justice is, basically, "I keep mine, and you keep yours." God's justice concerns the right relationships in God's eye. For example, John the Baptist refuses to make himself the center of attention. After finishing his task of preparing the way of the Lord, John said, "I am not the Messiah. But I have been sent ahead of him. For this reason my joy has been fulfilled. He must increase, but I must decrease" (Jn 3:28-30). John, a humble man, maintained the right relationship with God.

In order to grow in God's justice and peace, however, we need to first transform ourselves and be converted. This is why John the Baptist calls for repentance—changing of the heart. Make straight the way of the Lord! Remove any obstacle that might deter his arrival. Eliminate greed that takes advantage of others. Get rid of arrogance that tries to set us above others. Abolish power that makes us abusive. Purge selfishness that satisfies our interests alone.

Deep down in our hearts, we need to ask ourselves: Are we willing to step forward, or are we afraid to have our world turned upside down? Are we the brokenhearted who will be healed, or are we the ones who have broken others' hearts? Are we the captives who will be freed, or are we the captors who have restrained? Are we the poor who hear the good news of reversal, or are we the ones responsible for poverty? We need to ask ourselves on which side of these reversals we stand.

Pope John XXIII was a joyful and pious man who trusted God. On the night when he announced his plans to convene the Second Vatican Council, he had trouble falling asleep. He later admitted that he talked to himself on that night: "Giovanni, Giovanni, why don't you sleep? Is it the pope or the Holy Spirit who governs the church? It's the Holy Spirit, no? Well, then go to sleep, Giovanni!" St. John was able to find joy in a dark night with the help of the Holy Spirit.

During Advent, we search our hearts to discover what we need to change and transform ourselves and how. We heal our personal brokenness, our fractured families, our troubled church, and our bleeding world.

During Advent, we are also joyful, because we know the Messiah is coming. If we can open our hearts to his saving power, we can indeed transform ourselves, our families, our churches, and our world. ✝

[3rd Advent (A)]

Fourth Sunday of Advent (B)

(2 Samuel 7:1-5, 8b-12, 14a, 16; Romans 16:25-27; Luke 1:26-38)

God Becomes Man

When man encounters God, God speaks first and ask questions. In the Old Testament, God asks Adam and Eve, "Where are you?" as they hide, after being expelled from the Garden of Eden. In the New Testament, Jesus asks Andrew and another disciple, "What are you looking for?" as they follow Jesus in the Jordan River. God asks questions to establish a proper relationship with man. God is always in search of man.

Jewish theologian Abraham Heschel, in his book *God in Search of Man,* says, "The human history as described in the Bible may be summarized in one phrase: God in search of man." This statement sounds very strange to us, because normally we think we are the ones who are in search of God. We search for joy and happiness in life; we search for love; we search for truth; we search for the meaning of life. Because God is the source of love, joy, life, and truth, we rightfully think that we are in search of God.

Surprisingly, however, we are saying that God is in search of us! If we pause for a while and think about it, God is indeed in search of man. Both the Old and New Testament begin with God's questions in search of man.

God, who is in search of man, has finally assumed the humanity to live among us (Jn 1:14). God has become a simple person to make us one with him.

Today's gospel passage, the Annunciation, describes how God entered our human world. The angel Gabriel appears to a young woman, Mary. The angel announces the birth of her son, who will be named Jesus and inherit the kingdom of David. Mary sees that God's promise to David is going to be fulfilled through her; therefore, she says in fear and doubt, "How can this be, since I am a virgin?" The angel answers, "The power of the Most High will overshadow you." The angel then tells Mary that her cousin, Elizabeth, has conceived a son in her old age. Moved by the power of God already at work in Elizabeth, Mary says, "May it be done to me according to your word." Soon after, Mary travels to the hill country in Judea to attend to Elizabeth. Having been filled with God's grace, she naturally wants to do God's work of charity.

The incarnation of Jesus shows that God's love—infinite, irreversible, and unconditional God's love—has been realized, in an ordinary way, within human history. Now, God is in search of us in the very human way. God is near us as well as far away from us. This means that we can experience God in our ordinary daily life and find who we really are. This also means that we will eventually be in union with God. This, however, does not mean that we will be free from joy and sorrow, sadness and happiness, struggling and suffering in life. These are a part of human adventures of being in love.

Another aspect of God's love is that we will be changed in hearts and be transformed into simple persons who fall in love with God. In this regard, Mary is the archetype of humanity because she was the first person moved by God's grace. Mary's consent to God's quest made the salvation of all human beings possible.

Let us then remind ourselves, once again, why Mary is important in the salvation history of mankind. We have heard that God's power "overshadowed" Mary during the Annunciation. This means that Mary was filled with the active presence of God (*Shekinah*). In the Book of Exodus, the mysterious cloud "overshadowed" or "covered" the tent in which Israel kept the ark of the covenant (Ex 40:34). Accordingly, Mary's body is equivalent to the tent, her womb is equivbalent to the Ark of God, and the baby Jesus in her womb is equivalent to the Ten Commandments. Mary carries the Son of God for a new creation in her womb. Mary is the New Eve.

Let us be joyful and give thanks to God. Let us listen to Christmas songs, while preparing the manger for the baby Jesus in our hearts. Indeed, it is joyful to hear the footsteps of Jesus, coming to us day by day. ✝

[4th Advent (C), 3rd OT (C)]

THE NATIVITY OF THE LORD: MIDNIGHT (ABC)

(Isaiah 9:1-6; Titus 2:11-14; Luke 2:1-14)

Heaven and Earth Are Fused Together

We have listened, today, to the beautiful story—the Infancy Narrative—from the Gospel of Luke. It is a story about how Israel's hope for the Messiah was fulfilled in the person of Jesus. It is a story about how the Word was made flesh and dwelt among us. It is a story about how the heavens and the earth were fused together.

On the surface, this beautiful story sounds charming, and perhaps romantic. Beneath its soothing surface, however, harsh realities may be readily detected.

An imperial decree ordered a census of all the people within the Roman Empire. Joseph and the fully pregnant Mary had to travel from Nazareth in Galilee to Bethlehem in Judea. It took them about ten days in a caravan through tortuous, meandering roads along the Jordan valley. Finally, the baby Jesus was born in a barn in Bethlehem, because Mary and Joseph were too poor to rent a room somewhere else. So they placed the newborn child in a manger. The word "manger" appears not once, but three times, in the gospel narrative. And the first human witnesses to the child were shepherds—a group of social outcasts.

At the same time, Jesus was no ordinary child. Angels surrounded him and identified him as the "Messiah and Lord," announcing Jesus' birth and gave glory to God. When the heavens were glad and the earth rejoiced, the Word was made flesh and dwelt among us. Our Savior, Jesus Christ was born.

On this joyful night, let us reflect on the deeper meaning of God's incarnation. A little while ago, I said, "On this Christmas night, the heavens and the earth are fused together." The incarnation means that the Son of God emptied himself and came to us in the person of Jesus of Nazareth. The fullness of divinity is united with the fullness of humanity in the person of Jesus Christ. In the beginning, God created human beings in his image and likeness. Now, the Son of God assumes the human form as his own.

The incarnation consists of two modes: the descending mode of taking on human flesh from God's side and the ascending mode of being sanctified from man's side. These modes are two distinct—but not separate—aspects of one great mystery. As a result, we partake in the divinity of Jesus Christ, who humbled himself to share in our humanity. God has become one of us, and so we "become participants of the divine nature" (2 Pt 1:4).

Now, we can reach God where we are. Now, we can embrace God when we want. Now, we can live God's life. This is what is meant by "the heavens and the earth being fused together." This is called the holy (marvelous) exchange. By virtue of the incarnation, God is radically open to humanity. Therefore, "only in the mystery of the incarnate Word does the mystery of man truly become clear" (*Gaudium et Spes*, #22). Jesus Christ holds the key to how we can be truly man.

God's word has been spoken once and for all. "The Word became flesh and lived among us" (Jn 1:14). And the history of mankind becomes the history of salvation. Accordingly, when we want to talk *about* God, we do it *with* Jesus Christ. When we want to talk *to* God, we do it *through* Jesus Christ.

In a few minutes, during the Eucharist celebration, the celebrant will pray, "Today in him a new light has dawned upon the world: God has become one with man, and man has become one with God. Your eternal Word has taken upon himself our human weakness, giving our mortal nature immortal value. So marvelous is this oneness between God and man that in Christ man restores to man the gift of everlasting life" (old Christmas Preface III).

Tonight is the most holy and the most joyful night. God has truly become one of us, so that we can partake in the divine life of God. We pray that the grace of the infant Jesus may dwell in the "mangers" of our hearts.✝

[4th Advent (C)]

HOLY FAMILY OF JESUS, MARY, AND JOSEPH (B)

(Sirach 3:2-6, 12-14; Colossians 3:12-21; Luke 2:22-40)

An Ordinary Human Family

The Holy Family consists of Jesus, Mary, and Joseph. They are very different from our families. Jesus is the Son of God. Mary is the Mother of God. Joseph is the husband of Mary. So we may ask, "Why are we celebrating the Feast of the Holy Family?" Today, we are going to reflect on the Holy Family and find out just how ordinary they are.

The gospel reading today tells us that, as any typical Jewish family would do, Mary and Joseph took Jesus to the Temple in Jerusalem (Lk 12:6). They presented "a pair of turtledoves or two young pigeons," the gifts offered by a poor family.

In the Temple, the family encountered two ancient people, representing the aged Israel. Simeon, the old man, took the child Jesus in his arms, blessed him, and offered a prayer. Anna, the old woman, approached the Holy Family and praised God. St. Luke suggests that a new age will begin with the infant Jesus. To Mary and Joseph, however, such encounters were unexpected; they were simply amazed (Lk 2:33).

Let us also remember that, when Jesus was twelve years old and during a later visit to the Temple in Jerusalem, Jesus was lost for three days. When Mary and Joseph finally found him in the Temple, Jesus was with the elders and scribes. Mary chastised him, and Jesus responded: "Did you not know that I must be in my Father's house?" Mary and Joseph "did not understand what he said to them" (Lk 2:50). Perhaps they were not yet firmly convinced that Jesus was the Messiah.

In summary, when Mary and Joseph presented the infant Jesus in the Temple and when, years later, they found the child Jesus in the Temple, they didn't know for sure Jesus was the Christ. We conclude, therefore, the Holy Family was an ordinary family who had doubts and worries just like our families.

If the Holy Family is an ordinary family like ours, we wonder, then, why we celebrate the Feast of the Holy Family. Perhaps the holiness of the Holy Family was not suddenly bestowed upon them by God. Or, perhaps they were not holy from the beginning. Mary, Joseph, and Jesus worked on it. They earned it, so to speak.

For example, Mary, as a mother, was concerned and worried. When the shepherds told Mary what they had heard from the angel, Mary "treasured all these words and pondered them in her heart" (Lk 2:19). When Mary spoke to Jesus after she and Joseph found him in the Temple, she once again "treasured all these things in her heart" (Lk 2:51). On both occasions, was Mary, unlike our own mothers, engaging herself in purely contemplative prayer in simple obedience to God's will, accepting all things occurring? Did Mary never fret or doubt? Most likely, Mary was very worried about Jesus, exactly like our mothers, and tried to figure out what was going on with him.

As for Joseph, he was responsible for rearing Jesus in wisdom and in years (Lk 2:52). During the years of his life as a public figure, Jesus frequently prayed alone. But his prayer habit was not suddenly acquired. It must have been taught by Joseph.

In conclusion, Mary and Joseph struggled with, and worried about, problems typical for a human family. Jesus, Mary, and Joseph comprise an ordinary human family.

Holiness is not a static and passive state of sainthood, but a dynamic and active process of being taken up with things of God. This means that our families have a chance of being like the Holy Family. Yes, our families can grow to be holy. This is the reason why we celebrate the Feast of the Holy Family today. ✝

[Holy Family (C), Baptism (C)]

THE EPIPHANY OF THE LORD (ABC)

(Isaiah 60:1-6; Ephesians 3:2-3, 5-6; Matthew 2:1-12)

The Fourth Wise Man

We know today's gospel story very well. Three Magi from the East traveled through deserts and found the baby Jesus in Bethlehem. After they presented their gifts to the Savior, they returned home. This is the story of the non-Jews who paid homage to the baby Jesus for the first time. This is also the story of our faith journey.

I would like to share with you a story called "The Fourth Wise Man."

There lived in ancient Persia a certain man named Artaban. He was a member of the community of Zoroastrian scholars known as Magi. Zoroastrians were astrologists and believed in the search of goodness and light. Artaban told his friends that he would join three other Magi soon. Together they would search for the newborn King of Israel. Selling his possessions, Artaban bought three jewels—a sapphire, a ruby, and a pearl. He wanted to give them as gifts to the King.

Thus began Artaban's journey. He was supposed to meet his three companions at the Temple of the Seven Spheres. But on the way to the temple, Artaban came upon a dying man lying on the road. Artaban stopped to cure him. Astrologists were also physicians. At last, the man regained his strength, but this delay caused Artaban to miss the caravan and his friends. He was forced to sell his sapphire in order to buy a train of camels and provision for his journey.

When he arrived in Bethlehem, the soldiers of King Herod were killing the baby boys. Artaban found a mother with her child in a house. The woman told him that it was now the third day since the three wise men had appeared in Bethlehem. They had found Joseph, Mary, and the baby Jesus, and had laid their gifts at his feet. Then they had disappeared as mysteriously as they had come. Joseph had secretly gathered up his family that same night, fleeing far away into Egypt.

Suddenly, there was a wild confusion of sounds. The woman said, "The soldiers of Herod are killing the children." Artaban went to the doorway and witnessed soldiers hurrying down the street with dripping swords and bloody hands. The captain approached the door, but Artaban stopped him, giving him the ruby and requesting to leave the mother and baby alive. Then Artaban went to Egypt, searching everywhere for the family that fled before him from Bethlehem.

For thirty-three years Artaban continued looking for the King, all the while helping the poor and the dying. At last he came to Jerusalem. There was a great feast of the Passover in Jerusalem. Suddenly, a slave girl, being dragged by soldiers, broke away from her tormenters and threw herself at Artaban's feet. Taking the last of his treasures, the pearl, he gave it to the girl. He said, "This is the ransom, daughter! It is the last of my treasures that I kept for the King."

While Artaban spoke, a powerful earthquake shook the city and he was struck by a roof tile. Artaban knew he was dying. The slave girl, holding the dying man, heard a sweet voice and then saw Artaban's lips move. Artaban said "Ah, Master. I have long sought for you. Forgive me. Once I had gifts to give to you. Now I have nothing." Then another voice said, "Artaban, you've already given your gifts to me." Artaban replied, "I don't understand."

But the unmistakable voice came again; the slave girl heard it clearly. "When I was hungry, you gave me to eat. When I was thirsty, you gave me drink. When I was a stranger, you welcomed me. When I was naked, you gave me clothing." Artaban said "O no, my Savior, I never saw you hungry, nor thirsty. I never welcomed you home. I never gave you clothing." The voice continued, "Whenever you did it for the least of my brothers, you did it to me." A long breath of relief exhaled from Artaban's lips. His journey just ended. ✝

[Christ King (A)]

133

THE BAPTISM OF THE LORD (B)

(Isaiah 42:1-4, 6-7; Acts 10:34-38; Mark 1:7-11)

We Are Beloved Sons and Daughters of God

Jesus shared our humanity through his baptism so that we might share his divinity through our baptism.

Baptism is the most important sacrament for Christians. Through baptism, we are grafted into Jesus Christ. Through baptism, we become Christ-like persons—that is, Christians. Through baptism, we become members of the mystical Body of Christ, the Church.

Whenever I have a chance to baptize infants, it is a great joy for me to meet those innocent angels; it also is a tremendous honor to witness the sacred moments of christening and rebirthing as part of Christ's mystical body. I always emphasize that, through baptism, children become prophets, priests, and kings. By virtue of baptism, they become sons and daughters of God. By virtue of baptism, they become brothers and sisters of Jesus Christ. By virtue of baptism, they live the life of God as Christians.

Let us take a close look at Jesus' baptism, the supreme model for our baptism. Jesus began his public ministry after his baptism by John the Baptist. He wanted to join in humanity, although he was the Son of God. He wanted to acknowledge that the whole human race, of which he was a part, needed to admit that it had sinned and was in need of conversion.

The baptism of Jesus raises some questions, however. Why did he begin his public ministry at the age of thirty? Why not started at twenty or fifteen? Jesus remained in Nazareth for thirty long years while the whole world cried out for his teachings. Why did Jesus wait so long to begin his ministry? Jesus grew in wisdom and personhood. The long hidden life of Jesus suggests that Jesus had to be a fully grown man before he preached the Gospel. In other words, the Word of God was not like a thunder coming down from heaven; it was born out of a genuine mature humanity.

Historically, the people of Israel did not practice baptism. Only those who came to Judaism from other faiths went through baptism. Jews considered themselves God's chosen people and did not need baptism. Baptism was for sinners only.

Around the time of John the Baptist, however, Jews were cognizant of their own sins and wished to repent. That was the moment for which Jesus was waiting. In other words, Jesus waited until the people were ready to repent. Jesus waited for John the Baptist, who prepared the people for their repentance.

Another important aspect of Jesus' baptism is that the Triune God acted in unison during the baptism. The heavens were torn open, the Spirit descended on Jesus, and God the Father said, "You are my beloved Son. On you my favor rests." At this voice of God, Jesus was able to convince himself that he was the beloved Son of God. That was precisely why, when he was driven into the desert, after the baptism, to be tempted by the devil, he was able to triumphantly reject the devil's temptations. Jesus lived God's life.

There is another place in the Bible where we find the same voice of God to Jesus: when Jesus was transfigured on a high mountain, God said, "This is my beloved Son" (Mk 9:7). Here, God affirmed Jesus' Son-ship once again when Moses and Elijah talked about Jesus' exodus in Jerusalem—his death and resurrection.

Finally, during our baptism, the same Trinitarian God acts in unison. As Jesus of Nazareth has revealed that he is the Son of God, we become beloved sons and daughters of God in and through Jesus Christ.

By virtue of baptism, we are prophets, priests, and kings. By virtue of baptism, we are brothers and sisters of Jesus Christ. By virtue of baptism, we are sons and daughters of God. The success of our spiritual journey as Christians depends on how deeply and seriously we understand who we are by virtue of our baptism. ✝

[Baptism (A, C), 14ᵗʰ OT (B)]

FIRST SUNDAY OF LENT (B)

(Genesis 9:8-15; 1 Peter 3:18-22; Mark 1:12-15)

Somewhere over the Rainbow

Let us imagine that we represent Dorothy in the Wizard of Oz and sing along,

> *Somewhere, over the rainbow, way up high,*
> *there's a land that I heard of once in a lullaby.*
> *Somewhere, over the rainbow, skies are blue.*
> *And the dreams that you dare to dream really do come true.*
>
> *Somewhere, over the rainbow, bluebirds fly.*
> *Birds fly over the rainbow, why then – oh, why can't I?*
> *If happy little bluebirds fly beyond the rainbow,*
> *why, oh, why can't I?*

This is the song of Dorothy, who wants to escape a sticky situation in a Kansas farm. This is also a song for us, because we want to transcend our existential conditions. The rainbow in the sky is a symbol for us—a sign to reach out to God in his divinity.

In today's first reading, after the Flood ceased, God gave Noah the rainbow as a token of God's covenant. According to the Book of Genesis, human sinfulness was so awful that God regretted having created human beings on earth (Gen 6:1-22). God decided to cleanse the earth with a gigantic flood. After the Flood, the rainbow marked a new beginning, connecting heavens and the earth, which had been disconnected before by human sin. By means of the rainbow, humans could once again reach out to heaven.

We often think that the most important story in the Book of Genesis is the creation story of Adam and Eve. Scripture scholars, however, point to Noah's Flood as the most important story. God regretted his creation and decided to start over, suggesting the persistent and unyielding love of God. No matter how sinful man may be, God creates again and again. In addition, the Flood prefigures Christian baptism. During baptism, we die with Jesus by going into the water, and we rise with Christ by coming out of the water.

The story of the Flood is not a story just for children. It provides a new cosmic order, and it highlights the role of human beings within that order. God's promise was made, not with Noah alone, but with Noah's many descendants. God's promise was made, not with humankind alone, but with all living creatures on the earth. God is decisively joined to all creatures, until the end of time.

The situation of the world we live in, however, suggests we may need another Flood. Newtonian physics insists that the world consists of matter and forces, not spirits and souls. This worldview allows exploitation of all natural resources on earth, in whatever manner we deem. As a result, the good earth is threatened by thousands of nuclear weapons and pollutions everywhere, air, land, sea, water, beach, etc. It is no wonder that the New Heaven and New Jerusalem, which are found at the very end of the Bible, symbolize an ecological utopia for Christians.

Other reasons for a new Flood revolve around modernity's intellectualism and rationalism, along with individualism and consumerism. We have heavily relied on intellect and reason for the last several hundred years. As a result, our heads have become very large and our hearts have become very small.

Jesus Christ wants to help us renew our hearts and recover our original innocence. So Jesus asks us to "repent, and believe in the Gospel." To repent means to change our worldview. To repent means to transform our wooden hearts into loving and compassionate hearts, as the psalmist sings, "A clean heart create for me, O God, and a steadfast spirit renew within me" (Ps 51:10).

Lent is a time to put things back into order. Lent is a time for each of us to look at our role in the world as one of God's creatures. Lent is a time to transform our hearts and to recover our dreams and rainbows. Indeed, somewhere over the rainbow, skies are blue. Indeed, somewhere over the rainbow, little bluebirds fly. ✝

[1ˢᵗ Lent (A)

137

SECOND SUNDAY OF LENT (B)

(Genesis 22:1-2, 9, 10-13, 15-18; Romans 8:31-34; Mark 9:2-10)

God's Plan of Salvation

Abraham was a man of faith. God promised Abraham numerous descendants, as many as the sands in a beach and the stars at night. Abraham believed in God's promise, but the promise never materialized.

Abraham still believed in God, however. The fullness of time finally arrived. Abraham knew Sarah, and she bore Isaac, their only fruit, through which all of their generations would be blessed. There was joy in Abraham's household.

And yet, God decided to test Abraham's faith one last time. God asked him to sacrifice Isaac, the only son, through whom the promise would be fulfilled. Abraham obeyed God; he decided to give up his hope for numerous descendants, all the while holding on to the love for his only son, Isaac. Now everything would be lost! Everything in his life was about to be wiped out—the hope, the dreams, even God's promise. But Abraham believed in God and held fast to God's promise.

Some scholars interpret that the whole episode took place in a dream of Abraham. Among many dreamlike features in the story, Sarah, Abraham's wife, was present nowhere, and Moriah was a fictitious mountain. It could have been a dream in which Abraham screamed and shivered, while sweating, one dark night. It could have been a dream like the one Jacob had, in which he wrestled with the angel before he faced his brother Esau (Gen 32:22-32). After that dream, however, although limping from his hip injury, Jacob became a fully mature man and found his "true self."

Abraham, too, was able to prevail over his inner demons, through the dream at Mount Moriah. In other words, his faith grew to the fullest maturity. Perhaps he found his true self, or recovered authenticity, or achieved "individuation" in psychology, or attained "enlightenment" in Buddhism. That was why God no longer tested Abraham since then.

Abraham believed in God and kept God's command, not really understanding how and when God would fulfill his promise. According to St. Paul, God, who ultimately did not want Abraham to sacrifice his only son, "does not withhold his own Son, but gives him up for all of us" (Rom 8:32). Paul used this argument as the proof of God's love for mankind and the mystery of God's plan of salvation for human beings. The death of Jesus did not stop there; it led into the resurrection, through which God created a new humanity.

In the gospel reading, Jesus takes three disciples—Peter, James, and John—to Mount Tabor in Galilee. Suddenly, Moses and Elijah appear, and they talk with Jesus about the Exodus that is going to happen soon in Jerusalem. Peter, having glimpsed the heaven, wants to hold on to that ecstatic moment for a long time. Peter does not comprehend God's plan of salvation in Jesus Christ.

In Mark's Gospel, this account of the Transfiguration occurs on the way to Jerusalem, shortly after Jesus' first passion prediction. Therefore, the story of the Transfiguration is related to the agony in Gethsemane with an anticipation of the cross.

If we apply this gospel story to our situation, the Lenten journey should also point to the cross we must bear in our daily lives. To know God's plan of salvation in Jesus Christ is to take up our cross. We must not abandon or reject our cross. Perhaps Jesus knows the weight of the cross is unbearable, and thus he allows us to get a glimpse of ecstasy in our journey through the Lenten season.

In our Lenten journeys, one way to find the cross is to offer proper sacrifice to God. Lenten sacrifices like fasting and "giving up something" do not revolve around ice cream and French fries, or the lack thereof. The Lenten sacrifices are about paying attention to our inner worlds, so that we can be more spiritually mature, integral, and wholesome. ✝

[2ⁿᵈ Lent (A, C), 2ⁿᵈ OT (A)]

THIRD SUNDAY OF LENT (B)

(Exodus 20:1-17; 1 Corinthians 1:22-25; John 2:13-25)

The Mystery of the Cross

Lent is a time for us to pray over the mystery of the cross of Jesus and our own cross.

Generally speaking, we are morally and ethically "all right." However, if we examine ourselves carefully, we are lost and found many times a day. Sometimes we insist on our own ways because God's way is different from our own. Sometimes, our conscience is weak because things of the world overpower our moral standards. No wonder we need to follow certain rules and regulations!

The Ten Commandments were given to the Israelites by God. The Ten Commandments deal with moral principles, essential for the Israelites. They represent God's Law, which applies to all cultures and civilizations. The significance of the Ten Commandments, therefore, is that the nationhood of Israel was founded on them. In other words, Israel was founded not by the Israelites, but by God.

The Israelites carried the Law too far, unfortunately. They adhered to the Law as fervently as the Greeks revered their philosophy. They forgot the Law was a symbol of their covenantal relationship with God. They emphasized the external observations of the Law, rather than their heartfelt commitments. One example concerns the commercial activities within the Temple proper.

As we heard in the gospel reading, Jesus expels money changers, along with their sheep and oxen, from the Temple. Moreover, he overturns their tables and spills the coins. This violent act of Jesus in the most holy Temple is not meant to renounce the Law, as the temple authority perceives. Instead, Jesus defends the holiness of the Temple. The Temple is where God resides and it represents salvation from God. The Temple ought to reflect the light and glory of God to the Israelites. Thus, Jesus says that those commercial activities will "destroy this temple and in three days I will raise it up" (Pope Benedict, *Jesus*, p.21).

Obviously, the Temple authorities are furious. In the Synoptic Gospels, this episode occurs right after Jesus' entrance into Jerusalem; it becomes the ground for the arrest of Jesus and, ultimately, his death on the cross. In John's Gospel, this episode occurs at the beginning of Jesus' public ministry. It symbolizes that the Temple is replaced by the body of Jesus, Jesus being the new Temple of Israel.

The person of Jesus is the "horizon" of Christian ethics. Christian ethics are grounded on the words and deeds of Jesus. Jesus rises up violently against evil, even when it causes resentment and anger among religious authorities. Filled with the Spirit of God, Jesus shows his never-ending love and mercy to the poor, the sick, and the lowly. Jesus has pity on the repentant tax collector, but not on the proud and law-abiding Pharisees (Lk 18:9-14). On the cross, Jesus suffers for all men and women. Jesus is the manifestation of the universal love of God, in the form of a human person. Jesus is the end of the Law (Rom 10:4) and has truly shown us the face of God.

Christian faith is to believe in the person of Jesus of Nazareth. Christian life is to live as Jesus lived. Simply put, it is a life lived for others, rooted in self-giving love. Inevitably, it means to suffer in solidarity for, and with, others for the sake of God's cause.

The life for others, however, requires the cross. Through the cross, God realizes his salvation and justice. The cross, "a stumbling block to Jews and foolishness to Gentiles," is "the power and the wisdom of God." The cross is the divine logic of the salvation for all peoples.

Lent is a time for us to examine ourselves and reflect on whether we have followed Jesus. Lent is a time for us to examine our consciences and reflect on whether we have carried our own crosses properly in our relationships with God, with ourselves, and with our neighbors. ✝

[5th OT (B), 23rd OT (C), 25th OT (B)]

FOURTH SUNDAY OF LENT (B)

(2 Chronicles 36:14-16, 19-23; Ephesians 2:4-10; John 3:14-21)

God's Merciful Love

"By the streams of Babylon we sat and wept when we remembered Zion. On the aspens of that land we hung up our harps.... How could we sing a song of the Lord in a foreign land? If I forget you, Jerusalem, may my right hand be forgotten."

It is a heartbreaking song, filled with a deep longing for Jerusalem during the Exile in Babylon, which was the most humiliating event for the Israelites. About seventy years later, Cyrus, the Persian king, defeated the Babylonians and allowed the Israelites to return home. Cyrus, an instrument of God, was called a messiah (Is 45:1). God allowed the Israelites to return to Jerusalem and rebuild the Temple. Of course, the Israelites fully realized God's love much later in history.

The same thing happens to Nicodemus in today's gospel reading. Nicodemus, a Pharisee and a high official of the Sanhedrin, wants to see Jesus. He has a deep longing for something right, something holy, something sacred. He is looking for God from his lonely and confused heart. He decides to go and talk to Jesus at night, as he is afraid other people see him.

Jesus says to Nicodemus, "God so loved the world that he gave his only Son, so that everyone who believes in him might not perish but might have eternal life" (Jn 3:16). This verse is the most famous scriptural passage, one that often appears in sport arenas.

Nicodemus, unfortunately, does not understand how God gives his only Son. He is further confused by Jesus' comments on being born again and on saving life by looking at the bronze serpent of Moses. As a devout Jew, Nicodemus cannot accept reincarnation. He cannot accept Jesus yet; he is not ready to commit himself fully to Jesus. His heart has not yet been moved. On the other hand, Jesus neither condemns him nor invites him to follow; Jesus leaves him alone.

142

Thus Nicodemus nearly disappears from the Gospel. Later on, he briefly appears and defends Jesus before his fellow Sanhedrin officials (Jn 7:50). He appears, finally, underneath the cross of Jesus. He helps Joseph of Arimathea to bring down Jesus from the cross and prepares the body of Jesus for burial with a mixture of myrrh and aloe, weighing about one-hundred pounds—sufficient amount for a king's burial (Jn 19:39-40). At last, Nicodemus comes to the light, only after Jesus is lifted up on the cross.

One lesson we are to learn from today's Gospel is that religious conversion takes time. It takes time to transform our ways of life from God of Torah to God of life. It takes time to reorient our ethical paradigm from God of rules and regulations to God of mercy and love. It takes time to cultivate our prayer from individual well-being to loving care for others. It takes time to develop ecological insights from God of human beings to God of all living beings. Then everything we touch is turned into prayer. The white clouds in the sky are our prayer, the unknown songs of birds are our prayer, and the wind in the trees is our prayer, because God is all in all, and because we find God in all things.

If we look hard at ourselves, we can see we are very much like Nicodemus. We don't really know what being born again is, even though we have been baptized a long time ago. We don't really understand what eternal life is, even though we have lived in it for some time. At the same time, however, we hope that we will find what we really long for, and we know that we will see the light someday.

We are very much like Nicodemus. What we long for is the Garden of Eden, where we used to walk with God in the evening breeze. We long for the Garden of Eden, because our hearts are made in God's image. Our longing for the Garden of Eden itself is a gift from God, and we gain access to this gift from God through faith, because, as Paul says in the second reading, "by grace we have been saved through faith." ✝

FIFTH SUNDAY OF LENT (B)

(Jeremiah 31:31-34; Hebrews 5:7-9; John 12:20-33)

The Hour Has Come

At last, Jesus has arrived in Jerusalem to celebrate the Passover. This will be his last Passover celebration. Soon he will become the Passover lamb.

To prepare for his final hour, Jesus goes out to pray in Gethsemane. The evangelist Mark describes Jesus' agony and suffering in this way: "And going a little farther, he fell on the ground and prayed that, if it were possible, the hour might pass from him. And he said, 'Abba Father, all things are possible to you; remove this cup from me; yet not what I will, but what you will'" (Mk 14:35-36).

The Letter to the Hebrews in the second reading also shows Jesus in torment: "He offered prayers and supplications with loud cries and tears."

By contrast, Jesus embraces his death calmly and solemnly in today's reading from the Gospel of John. He does not pray to God the Father to save his life, and he identifies himself with the grain of wheat that dies in order to bear much fruit. He knows that, by dying on the cross, he glorifies God and that God, in turn, will glorify him. The hour of death is the hour of glory; in that hour, Jesus will draw all people to salvation from God. Jesus says, "Once I am lifted up from earth, I will draw everyone to myself." The "lifting up" of Jesus on the cross means the glorification of Jesus and the salvation of all people.

This universal salvation was prophesized a very long time ago. In the sixth century B.C., the prophet Jeremiah warned the Israelites that they would soon be victims of the Babylonian invasion. Jeremiah also announced a more glorious renewal of God's covenant, the "new covenant," by conveying, "I will be their God, and they shall be my people." The new covenant that Jeremiah once hoped for is finally realized in the hour when Jesus is lifted up. Jesus is the new covenant that Jeremiah so fervently hoped for.

A little while ago, we talked about Jesus' agony in Gethsemane as described in the Gospel of Mark. And we compared it to Jesus' glory at Calvary from the Gospel of John. We did that in order to understand our own pain and suffering.

So let us ask ourselves this question: If our pain and suffering are like that found in the Gospel of Mark, can they be purified into glory such as that found in the Gospel of John? Can our pain and suffering in everyday life be transformed into Jesus' own pain and suffering? Can our pain and suffering be redemptive? The answer to these questions is definitely "yes," because the new covenant prophesized by Jeremiah has already been fulfilled, at the hour of Jesus' death.

This is exactly what we do every time we celebrate the Eucharist. All Eucharistic prayers contain the following sentence: "This is the chalice of my blood, the blood of the new and eternal covenant." Whenever we celebrate the Eucharist, we remember Jesus' death and resurrection— the new covenant prophesized by Jeremiah. This new covenant has been written in our hearts, so that it can transform our pain and suffering.

We have almost finished our Lenten journey, and next week we begin Holy Week. Jesus' hour is around the corner. So we sing the responsorial psalm: "Have mercy on me.... Wipe out my offense.... Create a clean heart in me." In today's language, we say: "Help me to accept what I am bothered by in others.... Heal me in my stubbornness, my selfishness, and my pride.... Help me to see the beauty and truth in other persons."

As we are about to finish our Lenten journey, we must ask ourselves whether we are ready for *our* hour. Our hour is coming soon. Our hour is around the corner. ✝

[7ᵗʰ OT (B)]

145

PALM SUNDAY OF THE LORD'S PASSION (B)

(Mark 11:1-10; Isaiah 50:4-7; Philippians 2:6-11; Mark 14:1-15:47)

What Is Holy about It?

We have just heard the passion of Jesus according to the Gospel of Mark. It is not a story about a mystical or fictional character. It is a story about a real, historical person—Jesus of Nazareth.

It is the story about Jesus sold by Judas, denied by Peter, abandoned by his disciples, accused of blasphemy by priests, rejected in favor of a murderer by the crowd, and mocked, spat upon, and struck by the Sanhedrin and Roman soldiers. It is the story about Jesus' death on the cross as "the King of the Jews" one dark afternoon, forsaken by God and watched over by only a handful of women, who had followed him from Galilee. It is a story of betrayal, denial, mockery, and bloodshed on the cross.

Some of us might wonder, then, why we listen to the story of Jesus' suffering and death on this first day of Holy Week. What is holy about it? Surely, it is not just the suffering and death of Jesus that makes this week holy. The love behind the suffering and death makes this week holy. Because of this love, mistaken and misunderstood, we begin Holy Week.

Scripture scholars say that the evangelist Mark placed the way Jesus died, not his resurrection appearances, at the heart of his Gospel. The death of Jesus on the cross was the final act of his selfless love and service totally committed to others. The death of Jesus on the cross was the complete and unconditional surrender of the whole humanity to God's cause. The death of Jesus on the cross is the key for recognizing Jesus of Nazareth as the Son of God. Therefore, the cross is the final and concrete manifestation of God's love and mercy (in Mark's Gospel.)

Soon after Jesus died on the cross, God raised him up from the dead. Without the cross, therefore, we cannot see the face of God in Jesus. Without the cross, we cannot appreciate the kingdom of God on earth. Without the cross, we cannot live eternal life. Without the cross, we cannot be Christians.

The cross is not just a mere symbol of the historical execution of Jesus of Nazareth. The cross also shows us the way in which we may find the meaning of life and hope for the future.

Scripture scholars also say that Mark's Gospel has not yet ended, because the women who visited Jesus' tomb did not tell Jesus' disciples what the young man in white told them to do (Mk 16:8). Therefore, the passion of Jesus continues until the women tell to his disciples about the risen Jesus.

We are Jesus' disciples, waiting to hear from the women. Rather, we are the woman who will deliver the message to the whole world.

In the meantime, the passion of Jesus continues in the suffering of every child of God. The passion of Jesus continues in the suffering of every victim of social injustice and war. The passion of Jesus continues in the suffering of single parents whose love was rejected. The passion of Jesus continues in the suffering of the lonely elderly in nursing homes. The passion of Jesus continues in the suffering of all of us. The passion of Jesus is our story.

The passion of Jesus teaches us how to live with the aging elderly, how to live among the homeless, how to deal with ignorant and selfish young people, how to get along with coworkers, how to love our friends and enemies, and how to hope for the future. The passion of Jesus is our hope of salvation, because only through the trial and suffering on the cross, are we saved and redeemed.

The passion of Jesus is all about how to love and how to be loved yesterday, today, and tomorrow. ✝

[Palm Sunday (A, C)]

GOOD FRIDAY OF THE LORD'S PASSION (ABC)

(Isaiah 52:13-53:12; Hebrews 4:14-16, 5:7-9; John 18:1-19:42)

The Glory of Jesus' Death

Jesus died at the hour of glory. When he died, a soldier pierced his side. Blood and water gushed out, signifying a new life. Through his death, Jesus gives us a new life.

The long story of the passion of Jesus concerns the painful suffering and cruel death by crucifixion in Jerusalem about two millennia ago. It is the story told by the risen Jesus Christ. The passion of Jesus would never have existed as it does today if Jesus had not made it part of his Easter revelation. Jesus himself, raised from the dead, told the story of his passion and death.

Today we celebrate the death of Jesus on the cross. Despite the somber atmosphere, today is not solely a day of sorrow and mourning. As evident in its name, Good Friday is a day of joy and hope. It is a day of thanksgiving for the infinite love that God shows to the world through his Son.

The mysterious "hour" that is alluded to throughout John's Gospel is finally realized today on the cross. For this hour, "the Word became flesh and lived among us" (Jn1:14). So we celebrate the hour of glory; as Jesus says, "When I am lifted up from the earth, I will draw all people to myself" (Jn 12:32). Today is a sorrowful day, but it is also a joyful day.

The Gospel of John, when compared with the Synoptic Gospels, contains no Anointing at Bethany, no account of the Last Supper, and no Agony in Gethsemane. To the evangelist John, Jesus is the Word made flesh and is sent to reveal the love of God for the whole world. And the most compelling expression of God's love is, paradoxically, the death of Jesus.

As we have heard in the passion narrative, Jesus faces his death calmly, freely, and willingly. Through the passion and death, Jesus fulfills his mission, which is the revelation of God's love to the world. Even before the arrest, Jesus announces, "I lay down my life and I take it up again; no one takes it from me" (Jn 10:17-18). During the trial, Jesus uses the divine phrase, "I AM," and Pontius Pilate shuttles between the Jews and Jesus as if he, not Jesus, is the one who is about to be sentenced. Jesus takes up the cross alone. Jesus' kingship is universal witness; "the King of the Jews" written in Hebrew, Latin, and Greek—all languages of the world.

The Beloved Disciple and Mary, the Mother of God, are with Jesus under the cross. Jesus gives them his last instructions. Mary becomes the Mother of the Church. And then the blood and water flow from the body of Jesus, as a soldier pierces his side, symbolizing a new life—the Eucharistic and the baptismal life.

As the Word made flesh completes this mission and returns to the Father, his death on the cross becomes the glorious exaltation. The last words of Jesus on the cross, therefore, are "It is finished." The task to redeem humanity is finished. The task to glorify God the Father is finished.

(Jesus has also finished the prophecy of Isaiah regarding the mysterious "suffering servant," as we heard in the first reading. This, the Servant Song, played an important role for Jesus' disciples in identifying Jesus as the Messiah. Jesus indeed suffered and died on the cross, as Isaiah had prophesized: "…through his suffering, my servant shall justify many and their guilt he shall bear.")

The passion of Jesus is the story of God's salvation for us. The passion of Jesus also is the story that brings us hope. The passion of Jesus tells us how to live, how to love, how to hope, and how to die. The Word made flesh is glorified today. Today is a sorrowful day, but it is also a joyful day.

We will venerate the cross in a few minutes. Let us now cite the prayer together: "We worship you, Lord. We venerate your cross, we praise your resurrection. Through the cross you brought joy to the world." ✝

[Palm Sunday (A, B, C)]

EASTER SUNDAY (B)

(Acts 10:34, 37-43; Colossians 3:1-4; John 20:1-9 or Luke 24:13-35)

Alleluia! The New Life with God

The narratives on the resurrection of Jesus appear at the very end of the Gospels. The resurrection itself, however, including the outpouring of the Holy Spirit, was the event that triggered the writing of the Gospels and the birth of Christianity. After encountering with the risen Jesus, the disciples discovered new meanings for those words and deeds they had shared with Jesus. Convinced of the vision of the kingdom of God, they put Jesus' words and deeds into writing. Without the resurrection of Jesus, there would be neither Gospels nor the Church.

As soon as Jesus was arrested, all of the disciples deserted him and fled (Mk 43:50). When Jesus died on the cross, only a few women looked on from a distance (Mk 15:40). The one expected to be the Messiah was now a dead criminal on a cross. Hope had been utterly dashed. All had been for nothing. The disciples of Jesus were completely done with Jesus, and some of them decided to go back to where they came from before they met Jesus, scattering or hiding. Jesus died in vain.

It was not just disappointment and frustration the disciples had to cope with, however, but also guilty consciences. One of their members had turned Jesus over for execution. Another, the one they had regarded as their leader, had openly sworn three times that he did not even know Jesus. Not one of them stood under the cross of Jesus. Not one of them stepped forward to claim the body of Jesus.

Suddenly, however, the disciples heard that Jesus had appeared to Mary Magdalene on the first day of the week. They tried to brush off the strange and unbelievable rumor. But on the next first day of the week, the risen Jesus once again appeared out of nowhere. Actually, the risen Jesus appeared to the disciples from the presence of the living God. God gave the risen Jesus to the disciples who did not deserve. This gift of the risen Jesus was not only gratuitous but also forgiving and reconciling, as Jesus greeted them with "Peace be with you." The risen Jesus appeared as totally forgiving love.

As the disciples encountered the risen Jesus, they then began to understand his death on the cross. Conversely, only after they understood the death on the cross as the manifestation of God's love, they encountered the risen Jesus. Jesus' death on the cross was inseparable and necessary element for his resurrection. Perhaps this is why St. Paul always talks about Jesus' death and resurrection as one event; it seems that Jesus died into his resurrection.

Jesus gave himself so totally and completely to God the Father that the earthly tomb could not hold his body. Perhaps this is why his tomb was empty.

Accordingly, the resurrection of Jesus is God's recognition of Jesus' sacrificial offering on the cross. The resurrection of Jesus is vindication of the victimized Jesus on the cross. It is not just Jesus' life coming back after death; it is the totality of Jesus' new and whole personhood, which remains forever in a new existence. The resurrection of Jesus is the manifestation of the divinity of Christ Jesus, which has been hidden behind the humanity of Jesus.

The resurrection of Jesus shows us that God's love is stronger than death. The resurrection of Jesus is God's invitation for us to participate in His new life, by carrying our own cross daily. The resurrection of Jesus is God's invitation for us to live God's life by living for others.

The risen Jesus has also brought us the Holy Spirit—the breath of life transforming us into the image and likeness of God. By the power of the Holy Spirit, the risen Jesus Christ allows the love and mercy of God to be present forever in our midst. We are children of God; we participate in God's divine life. The resurrection of Jesus verifies that God is love and mercy. The resurrection of Jesus proves that we are God's children and we live God's life. The resurrection of Jesus convinces that we will be raised on the last day. ✝

[Easter (A, C), 3rd Easter (B), 32nd OT (C)]

SECOND SUNDAY OF EASTER (B): DIVINE MERCY SUNDAY

(Acts 4:32-35; 1 John 5:1-6; John 20:19-31)

Thomas, the Doubter?

Easter Season consists of seven weeks between Easter Sunday and Pentecost. During this long Easter Season, we are called upon to affirm and strengthen our Easter faith. The way the apostle Thomas encounters the risen Jesus will help us do that.

On the evening of the first day of the week, Jesus appeared to his disciples, while Thomas was not there. The disciples told Thomas that they had seen the risen Jesus, but he could not believe it. He wanted to not only see the risen Jesus, but also touch his wounds. One week later, when Thomas was with them, Jesus appeared again. Jesus literally grabbed Thomas's hand and pushed his fingers into the wound, as Thomas did not himself dare to touch Jesus' wound. Thomas cried out, simply, "My Lord and my God!" It was the highest confession of faith in the Scriptures.

Thomas' faith appears to be potentially inferior to that of other disciples, because he needs to see and touch before he believes. For this reason, Thomas has gone down in history as "the doubter." Is Thomas really the doubter? If so, what makes him a doubter?

First of all, the Gospels show us that Thomas is not the only one who doubted. In Luke's Gospel, the women who went to Jesus' empty tomb told disciples what happened, "but they did not believe" (Lk 24:11). Again, two disciples on the road to Emmaus could not recognize the risen Jesus until the bread was broken (Lk 24:31). In Matthew's Gospel, before the commissioning of the disciples in Galilee, "they worshiped him, but some doubted" (Mt 28:17). The resurrection of Jesus can easily be doubted.

Actually, the risen Jesus is not readily recognizable. He appears only to those who have faith in him. He passes through walls and doors. He disappears as soon as being recognized. The risen Jesus is the glorified God.

Let us look at closely what is at stake. Thomas could not accept the risen Jesus until he experienced him personally. If Jesus was raised, as they said, how could it be possible that he suffered death? Could God suffer and rise? Where was God when Jesus died? How was Jesus raised? Thomas was faced with issues of a God who died on the cross. Therefore, he doubted until he changed his concept of God—Jewish monotheism. He doubted until he convinced himself that God's love was manifested on the cross. He doubted until he convinced himself that the risen Jesus was the Crucified One. Thomas was an honest and realistic believer.

As the risen Jesus appeared, along with his exposition of the wounds in his hands and side, Thomas saw God in the face of Jesus. Now, the risen Jesus was the Christ. Now, the death and resurrection of Jesus is one and the same event. Now, Thomas' intellectual honesty helped him experience the divinity of Jesus. Thomas acquired the "costly" faith based on both the divinity and humanity of Jesus.

We often consider faith and reason separately. Some people insist that faith alone is the key to Christianity. Because Thomas could not believe right away and doubted, his faith appeared to be inferior to that of the other disciples. On the other hand, isn't it true that "cheap" faith exists, faith that is based on emotion alone? Isn't it true that "blind" faith exists, faith that dances along with the crowd? Strong faith needs strong intellectual foundations.

The resurrection of Jesus is the gift of God, requiring both faith and reason—heart and head. We doubt intellectually in order to strengthen our faith. Perhaps this is exactly what Thomas did.

Today is the Divine Mercy Sunday. Mercy, a uniquely Catholic virtue, means to involve with or engage in the chaos and disorder of others. God is merciful for sending his Son and for raising him from the dead. Jesus, the Divine Mercy, calls us to be his disciples. Let us pray that we continue to strengthen our faith in the resurrection and be merciful to our brothers and sisters. ✝

[2nd Easter (A, C)]

THIRD SUNDAY OF EASTER (B)

(Acts 3:13-15, 17-19; 1 John 2:1-5; Luke 24:35-48)

"Have You Anything Here to Eat?"

Peter's profession of faith, as we listen to the first reading, is somewhat crude and primitive. By contrast, the Profession of Faith we recite at Mass is theologically profound and well organized. Both professions of faith, however, point out that the Crucified One is the Lord and the Son of God. The death/resurrection of Jesus is the summit of God's revelation and the fulfillment of God's promises.

Today's gospel reading describes the appearance of the risen Jesus in Jerusalem. It is the continuing story of Emmaus (Lk 24:13-34). As we recall, two disciples of Jesus were frustrated, because their would-be Messiah had died on the cross in vain. Some women went to the tomb early in the morning and found it empty. That stirred up some rumors. With all these confusions and frustrations, they simply wanted to go home in Emmaus, forgetting the whole thing.

On the way to Emmaus, the risen Jesus appeared to them and explained that the Messiah had to die. At sunset, they arrived in a village and, somehow, kindly invited Jesus in. There, as soon as Jesus broke bread, they recognized him as the risen Jesus, who then disappeared instantly. The two disciples immediately returned to Jerusalem and informed the other disciples what had happened.

The risen Jesus in Jerusalem even asked for food to eat. After the meal, Jesus explained once again that he had to die and be raised according to Scripture. On the road to Emmaus, Jesus first explains Scripture to the two disciples and then breaks the bread. In both stories, reading Scripture and breaking bread are two major tasks the risen Jesus performs. It is natural that Mass consists of the Liturgy of the Word and the Liturgy of the Eucharist.

When Jesus appeared again to all disciples, the risen Jesus showed his wounds and convinced them he was the same Jesus on the cross. The disciples opened their eyes right away and recognized that God's love was manifested in the sacrificial death of Jesus on the cross. In other words, when they accepted the death of Jesus on the cross as the glory of God, they could encounter the risen Jesus. So they became one with the risen Jesus and began to live the life of resurrection.

The resurrection of Jesus means that the Spirit of the risen Jesus continues to live among us. The resurrection of Jesus means that God, the author of life and death, gives a new life. The resurrection of Jesus means that God will do to us what He has done to Jesus Christ.

In the mean time, let us remember what Jesus said: "Unless a grain of wheat falls into the earth and dies, it remains just a single grain; but if it dies, it bears much fruit" (Jn 12:24). This means that only those who die on the cross are raised. Only those who sacrifice for others, while alive, can experience the resurrection. Just as the kingdom of God is already with us, the resurrection of Jesus is the Good News for those who want to live life fully here and now. The resurrection of Jesus allows us to share in God's divine life (2 Pt 1:4). The resurrection is for the living, not for the dead.

Indeed, we live now a new life of resurrection. Having passed from death to life at baptism, and by dying to sin daily, we live a new life of resurrection and wait for its fulfillment (Co 2:12, 3:1). This is our hope, and this is our driving force for transforming the world. Paul says, "If God is for us, who can be against us?" (Rom 8:31). What God has done with Jesus, God will do again for us. This is our resurrection faith.

Let us close with a prayer, reminding ourselves that we, too, sometimes want to go back to Emmaus (Tuesday evening prayer Week IV).

> *Stay with us, Lord Jesus, for evening draws near, and be our companion on our way to set our hearts on fire with new hope. Help us to recognize your presence among us in the Scriptures we read, and in the breaking of bread. Amen.* ✝

[Easter (A), 3ʳᵈ Easter (A)]

FOURTH SUNDAY OF EASTER (B): GOOD SHEPHERD SUNDAY

(Acts 4:8-12; 1 John 3:1-2; John 10:11-18)

Following the Good Shepherd

It happened some years ago when I was a chaplain at St. Paul Hospital. I was about to conclude a visit to a Christian lady of middle age. I said to her, "Jesus is always with us, and I hope that you will get well soon." Then she responded, "Yes, Chaplain, I believe in Jesus and he will do everything for me."

As I came out of the room, I was very much impressed by her remarkably strong faith in Jesus. At the same time, I felt ashamed of myself for my own lacking of faith in Jesus.

A short while later, however, I began to wonder whether the woman lacked her own will and desire to cope with illness and suffering in life. Perhaps she had a strong faith in God but a weak faith in herself. Perhaps she did not want to take up her own cross and instead wanted Jesus to do it for her. Perhaps she didn't have a sufficiently healthy and constructive understanding of Jesus Christ being the Good Shepherd.

As we celebrate the Good Shepherd Sunday today, this story reminds us what kind image or perception we have about Jesus Christ being the Good Shepherd. Why do we call Jesus the Good Shepherd?

In the gospel reading today, Jesus says, "I am the good shepherd." And then, Jesus explains why he is the Good Shepherd. He says, "This is why the Father loves me, because I lay down my life in order to take it up again." In other words, Jesus loves his sheep and lays down his life for them. Because of this sacrificial act, God loves him and raises him up from the dead. In today's gospel reading, Jesus utters the phrase, "lay down my life" not once, but five times. Therefore, the cross is an inseparable element of being the Good Shepherd.

For the lady I met at the hospital, the Good Shepherd was the one who takes her to the green pasture and fresh waters and protects her from wild

156

animals at night. For her, the Good Shepherd always brings good things only. Apparently she was not informed that the cross is an inseparable element for being the Good Shepherd.

Jesus Christ is the Good Shepherd, because he has perfected the love of God for us. Jesus Christ is the Good Shepherd, because he has demonstrated us how to be genuinely human. Jesus Christ is the Good Shepherd, because he has shown us the human face of God in his death and resurrection. Therefore, we need to once again remind ourselves what it really means by the death and resurrection of Jesus.

The resurrection of Jesus is an eschatological event that happens on the other side of the death on the cross. The resurrection of Jesus is God's affirmation of Jesus' passion and death. The resurrection of Jesus means that the whole person of Jesus—body and soul—has been raised to the final, full, and eternal life of God. The resurrection of Jesus means that God has begun a new creation and that we now can live the divine life of God.

Therefore, the death and resurrection of Jesus are intimately connected each other in our daily life. The death of Jesus reminds us that we are constantly tempted by the apparent good, rather than the proven evil, in this world. In contrast, the resurrection of Jesus, on the other hand, reveals that we can transcend our human weakness and temptations. The death of Jesus reminds us that our sinfulness is an inevitable aspect of life in this world. In contrast, the resurrection of Jesus reveals that we are created for an ultimate end that exceeds our human nature.

Most importantly, the death and resurrection of Jesus allow us to live life as early Christians did. We are the people who are newly created in Christ as members of God's kingdom, expecting the ultimate coming of Christ. We are the people who live a new life in God's Spirit, perfecting our freedom as God's gifts. We are the holy people of God, announcing the Good news of Jesus Christ, the Good Shepherd. ✝

[4th Easter (A, C), 6th Easter (B)]

FIFTH SUNDAY OF EASTER (B)

(Acts 9:26-31; 1 John 3:18-24; John 15:1-8)

"I Am the Vine, You Are the Branches"

The goal of Christian life is to have an intimate relationship with God through Jesus Christ. The gospel reading today shows how to achieve this goal.

Jesus says, "I am the vine, you are the branches." Jesus is the vine, who provides energy for the whole plant to grow. We are the branches, who draw water and nutrients from the vine to bear fruits. God the Father is the vine grower, who tends the vineyard at all stages of its existence.

The intimacy between the vine and branches suggests that Christian identity is credible only through an organic relationship with Jesus Christ. Moreover, because branches are born out of the vine, Jesus and we share common physiological features. We, the branches, are children, of God through Christ Jesus (1 Jn 3:1-2, not adopted children as in Pauline theology). St. Augustine also says, "The vine and the branches do in fact constitute the same nature" (*Tractatus*, 80).

Jesus also says, "Remain in me, as I remain in you." Because the vine and branches are organically related, we, disciples of Jesus, must abide and remain in Jesus in order to bear fruits. The vine bears fruit through its branches. However, the vine alone cannot bear fruit without branches. And the branches bear the fruit of the vine, not the fruit of the branches. Perhaps Jesus wants to remain with us so ardently that God has raised him up.

The parable of the vine and branches is also an excellent allegory for an ideal Christian community. In our journey of faith within the Christian community, we may have experienced "pruning," or rejection. Such "pruning" was probably necessary because we looked like "dead wood" or withered branches. However, it is important to know that God the Father, not Jesus, did the pruning. The purpose of pruning is to allow the vine to bear abundant fruits. Jesus says, "Every branch that does not bear fruit God prunes, so that it bears more fruits."

In the first reading, we heard that St. Paul, too, was "pruned" and rejected in Jerusalem. And yet, St. Paul was Christ's branch, who spread the words of God and brightened the light of Christ all over the Roman Empire. Can we imagine Christianity without Paul?

Today's parable from the Gospel teaches that the heart of Christian life is centered on Jesus Christ. Jesus is the vine, we are branches. And each one of us is related to Jesus in a way organic and life-giving. If we separate ourselves from the vine, we wither. If we remain ourselves attached to the vine, we will produce sweet grapes abundantly.

When we remain in Jesus Christ, we let him dwell actively in our inmost beings. In other words, to remain in Jesus Christ is to let "God dwell(s) in us through the Spirit who he has given to us" (Gal 4:6, Rom 5:5). Moreover, this mutual in-dwelling is possible only through love: Christ's love for us and our responding love for Christ. Ultimately, the good we do comes from this mutual love. The Spirit of Christ dwells in us, so we abide in God through Jesus Christ.

Through God's grace, we are branches of the vine, Jesus Christ. To bear fruit for the vine is an extraordinary privilege. In a few minutes, we will eat the body of Christ and drink the cup of wine from God's vineyard. All of us together build up one body in God's vineyard. Let us close with a prayer.

> *Lord, the one true Vine,*
> *in you we are Christians.*
> *We are your branches.*
>
> *We bear the fruits of the Vine,*
> *though weak and fragile.*
> *Please ask our Father to prune us gently,*
> *So we can bear your fruits more abundantly.* †

[Baptism (C), 16th OT (A)]

SIXTH SUNDAY OF EASTER (B)

(Acts 10:25-26, 34-35, 44-48; 1 John 4:7-10; John 15:9-17)

"God Is Love"

Today's readings contain three important scriptural passages for Christian life: (1) "God is love." (2) "Love one another as I love you." (3) "I no longer call you servants....I have called you friends." We must thoroughly understand these passages and savor them.

In addition, all three scripture passages are about love. As we celebrate Mothers Day today, we cannot talk about mothers without love. Mothers are the source and fountain of love. And in terms of the hierarchy of love, mothers' love comes the second, only after God's.

So, let us first talk about God's love. The starting point for God's love is stated eloquently in the second reading: "...not that we have loved God, but that he has loved us and sent his Son as expiation for our sins." God loves us by creating us and redeeming us. God loves us and sends his Son, who shows us how to live and how to die.

There is an article in *America* magazine, which says: *"Señor, me has mirado a los ojos; sonriendo, has dicho mi nombre"* (Lord, you have looked into my eyes; smiling, you have called my name). This is the refrain of one of the best-known Latin American hymns, poignantly expressing the belief that God loves us first. The author continues to say that every other theological statement is little more than a footnote to this central belief. Our entire life is a response to the love of God, who has created us, named us, and compelled our response.

St. John of the Cross also wrote in one of his poems: "When you look at me, your eyes imprint in me your grace: for this you love me again, and thereby my eyes are made worthy of adoring you." When we truly realize that God loves us, we cannot but love ourselves in a way that frees us and, at the same time, we cannot but love our neighbors in a life-giving way.

Next, we talk about the love of Jesus for us and our love for one another. Jesus loves all people—those who already accept him and those who do

160

not yet. Jesus' entire life reveals God's unselfish, boundless, and universal love. In love, Jesus empties himself to the Father on the cross, and in love, he gives himself to mankind. Jesus' love proves to us what the love of God is like. Jesus' love for us also sheds light on the kind of love that is expected from us. Therefore, the love of Jesus allows us to remain in God's love.

When the evangelist John wrote his Gospel, scholars say that he knew some of other Gospels. To St. John, the life, death, and resurrection of Jesus revealed God, who is love. St. John simply stated, "God is love." As Christians, we respond to God's love through Jesus Christ. And our discipleship of following Jesus is grounded in God's love. God's love frees us from ourselves. God's love allows us to self-transcend. God's love allows us to attain eternal life. This is why Jesus asks us to "love one another, as I have loved you." Love, indeed, is the existential foundation and principle of life in the universe. This is what St. John meant when he said, "God is love."

Finally, Jesus calls his disciples friends. In addition, Jesus calls God the Father *Abba*, suggesting his own unique relationship with God. And he teaches his disciples "Our Father," suggesting that all of us have the same relationship with God. Therefore, God is our *Abba* Father, and we are brothers and sisters of Jesus. This is why the love of God and the love of neighbors are one and the same love. This unity of love is the foundation of our discipleship of following Jesus.

Our relationship with God is very much like that of the one with our parents, because Jesus is our friend. When we were children, we respected our parents and followed obediently their teachings and instructions. Now that we are grown-ups, we no longer blindly follow them. We are adult friends of our parents in God's household. St. Paul said, "When I was a child, I spoke like a child, I thought like a child, I reasoned like a child; when I became an adult, I put an end to childish ways" (1 Cor 13:11).

God, who is love, has become one of us. God's love has been poured into our hearts. And we are friends of Jesus. We are happy and joyful Christians. Thus, let us love one another, as Jesus loves us. ✝

[7th Easter (B), 4th OT (C), 12th and 30th OT (A)]

SEVENTH SUNDAY OF EASTER (B)

(Acts 1:15-17, 20-26; 1 John 4:11-16; John 17:11-19)

"Deus Caritas Est"

"God is love, and whoever remains in love remains in God, and God in him" (1 Jn 4:16). With these words, Pope Benedict XVI begins his first encyclical letter, *Deus Caritas Est,* or *God Is Love.* This is also the last sentence from today's second reading. Let us reflect on one aspect—the reality of love—from the encyclical letter.

Let us first ask ourselves, "What is love?" In English there is only one word for love, but in Greek there are at least three words: *agape, eros*, and *philia*. *Agape* is God's love, *philia* is the love among friends, and *eros* is the love between man and woman.

These different languages of love generate some confusion. For example, *eros* has a much broader meaning than we think. It entails the desire and passion necessary for expressing beauty and searching for truth. The encyclical letter suggests some important points. First, God's desire to glorify mankind is so intense and passionate that God's incarnation is the manifestation of God's *eros*. Second, God's love to follow his Son even into his death is so intense and sublime that the cross is the climax of God's *agape*.

Contrary to my own understanding, the Pope, a distinguished theologian, says that *agape* and *eros* are not separate from, but inclusive of, each other. It is surprising to learn that God's love, which is generally considered *agape*, can be *eros*, and that man's love, which is generally considered *eros*, can be *agape*. There is no dualistic separation between *eros* and *agape*. On the contrary, both make up the one reality of love.

Another aspect of the encyclical letter concerns the nature of man. God first created Adam from dust and Eve from the rib of Adam. This means that man and woman have the same origin, as well as equal dignity. Therefore, man and woman long for "the other half." This *eros*, which is somehow planted in man's heart, is a possessive and self-seeking love. Therefore, *eros* can and must be purified and transformed into *agape*.

We ask ourselves then, "How to purify and transform *eros* into *agape*?" This question is important, because we know very well that *eros* alone often violates human dignity and degrades it. Accordingly, we long for self-giving and gratuitous love, rather than self-seeking and possessive love.

Pope Benedict answers this question by saying, "Jesus Christ is the source of the unity of *eros* and *agape*." This means that in Jesus Christ and through Jesus Christ we can purify *eros* and transform it into *agape*. In other words, in the redemptive work of Jesus Christ, *eros* finds its own fulfillment in *agape*.

This new understanding of love can free us from our love-phobia. More importantly, it also solves the mystery of love in life. The human heart longs for love that is always satisfying and forever lasting. But we are constantly frustrated, because we cannot find a perfect love in this world. This is so because God loved us first. We can taste a glimpse of God's love. But we can never grasp it. Definitely, the unity of love holds the key to our human struggle.

Jesus has shown us the face of God, who is love. Jesus is the source and the fountain of the unity of *eros* and *agape*. Jesus has created the new meaning of love for all human beings. Therefore, when we love one another, we abide in Jesus Christ. When we abide in Jesus Christ, we abide in God. When we abide in God, we live the life of God. This is why Jesus says that his disciples "do not belong to this world." Disciples of Jesus Christ, although they are in the world, do not belong to the world, where love is often distorted and rejected.

I once asked a priest what Jesus meant to him. He replied that Jesus was everything to him and that he could not live one day without Jesus. As a celibate priest, he practiced the reality of love, all the while following footsteps of Jesus. His *eros* has been purified and transformed into *agape* all along. ✝

[6ᵗʰ Easter (B), 4ᵗʰ OT (C), 12ᵗʰ and 30ᵗʰ OT (A)]

PENTECOST SUNDAY (B)

(Acts 2:1-11; 1 Corinthians 12:3-7, 12-13; John 20:19-23)

The Holy Spirit Dwells within Us

During a retreat based upon the Spiritual Exercises of St. Ignatius Loyola, the retreat master tells us, "Ask God what you want or desire." The words "what you want" are critical because, if we are in union with God, what we want can be the will of God. In other words, what we want during a genuine prayer reflects God's will, because God is found from within, not from without.

The Holy Spirit is the least known and the most mysterious among the three persons of the Holy Trinity. It does not have a face or shape. It does not use any words or gestures. Just like a blowing wind (Jn 3:8), the Holy Spirit is known by its gifts (Isa 11:2-3) or fruits (Gal 5:22-23). However, without the Holy Spirit, nothing holy or divine can happen at the liturgy and anything we do.

In general, we receive God's grace as if it comes from outside us. Because we have dualistic mentality that separates the object from the subject, we, the subject, respond to the object that is outside us. This is why we like to *receive* the Communion during Mass, rather than *be* the body of Christ for others. In the same way, we mistakenly think that the Holy Spirit comes to us from somewhere up on high.

On the other hand, Scripture says that the Holy Spirit dwells within us. Paul said to the Galatians, "God has sent the Spirit of his Son into our hearts" (Gal 4:6). He said to the Romans, "The Spirit of God dwells in you" (Rom 8:9). He also said to the Colossians, "It is Christ in you" (Col 1:27). The evangelist John said, "The Spirit within us enables us to abide in God and also God in us" (1 Jn 4:13). Thus, the Holy Spirit dwells in the depths of our beings. It is the Holy Spirit within us that desires for something holy and something sacred. No wonder it is hard to describe what the Holy Spirit is and does.

In the same way, St. Augustine found God inside himself. After his conversion, he wrote, "Late have I loved you, O Beauty ever ancient, ever new, late have I loved you! You were within me, but I was outside, and it was there that I searched for you…. You were with me, but I was not with you" (*Confession*, Book 10, #38). Augustine searched for God somewhere out there, while loving the lovely things God created in the absence of God. But he found God in the most unexpected place—inside himself. God had been inside him all along, but Augustine had not been inside his own self. And the God he finds is the unchangeable light inside him, as he says: "I enter into the innermost part of myself. …and I saw with my soul's eye an unchangeable light shining above this eye of my soul and above my mind" (*Confession*, Book 7, #10).

According to Thomas Merton, the Holy Spirit dwelling within us is "not of the ontological or inseparable character. It is an accidental character, yet it is more than just a moral union" (*New Seeds of Contemplation*, p. 159). This means that, if we fully self-transcend and completely empty ourselves, then the Holy Spirit manifests or rises up from the depths of our own beings. It is the Holy Spirit within us that our hearts desire something holy, something sacred, something divine.

If we think about it, God has been with us from the beginning. The Father creates us in his image and likeness, the Son comes to us as a person, and the Spirit dwells within us. In other words, God the Father looks like us, the Son is a person like us, and the Spirit exists within us. This means that the Triune God is always with us. We are the very image of God. We are everything, and all things, with whom God is concerned.

If we truly attain to the Holy Spirit dwelling within us, the Holy Spirit actualizes God's love within us and enables us to live God's life (Rom 5:5). We can be mystics in our own unique ways. *Veni, Sante Christus!* ✝

[3ʳᵈ OT (C), 13ᵗʰ OT (B), 30ᵗʰ OT (A)]

THE MOST HOLY TRINITY SUNDAY (B)

(Deuteronomy 4:32-34, 39-40; Romans 8:14-17; Matthew 28:16-20)

God Is for Us

We always make the Sign of the Cross before and after prayers, meals, and all types of liturgies. We do everything in the name of the Father, the Son, and the Holy Spirit.

The doctrine of the Holy Trinity says there are three divine persons—the Father, the Son, and the Holy Spirit. These three divine persons are in communion with each other in such a way that they form one God. The doctrine of the Holy Trinity concerns this Holy Mystery.

Notice that we use the word "person" in describing the Holy Trinity, suggesting that a person is mystery. The word "mystery" does not mean that we don't or can't understand it at all. It means that we know and understand *something*, but never fully. For example, we understand our spouses through the eyes of heart but cannot fully grasp their inexhaustible mystery. The more intimately we know about a person, the more we are drawn to that person's unique mystery. A person is mystery.

If a human person is of mystery, then God in three persons is more of mystery. And among the three persons of the Trinity, the Holy Spirit is the least known. The Holy Spirit has neither a face nor words. The Holy Spirit comes and goes like the wind. The Holy Spirit acts in secret from the depths of the human heart. Without the Holy Spirit, however, nothing divine can happen at the liturgy, in the Church, or in the world.

The word "the Holy Trinity" is not in the Bible. And the doctrine of the Holy Trinity was shaped by the Cappadocian Fathers much later. However, Jesus himself taught the Holy Trinity to his disciples. When Jesus' disciples were on the verge of having their world collapse around them, Jesus spent a serious, quiet time with them in the Upper Room and spoke to them about the Holy Trinity (Jn 16 and 17). Jesus taught them that he and the Father is the same (Jn 10:38) and that he will send the Holy Spirit (Jn 16:7). The Holy Trinity must be an important doctrine in Christianity

166

and, accordingly, must have some practical implications for Christian life. In fact, the Holy Trinity marks the break-away point from the Jewish monotheism.

We have heard the Trinitarian command in Matthew's Gospel today. The risen Jesus goes back to Galilee and commissions his disciples, "Go, then, to all people everywhere and make them my disciples: baptize them in the name of the Father, the Son, and the Holy Spirit." This baptismal formula suggests that, by the time the Gospel of Matthew was edited (around the third or fourth century), the Church firmly practiced the Trinitarian doctrine.

We are familiar with the distinct role of each person of the Godhead; the Father creates the world, the Son died on the cross for our sin, and the Holy Spirit guides us. Actually, the Holy Trinity is a triadic symphony. The Father creates through the Son in the inspiration of the Holy Spirit. The Son, sent by the Father, becomes flesh by virtue of the life-giving Spirit. The Spirit is sent by the Father at the request of the Son. In short, the doctrine of the Holy Trinity says that God the Father creates and redeems the universe in the power of the Holy Spirit through the eternal Word, Jesus Christ.

Even though I have tried to explain the doctrine of the Holy Trinity, we know very well it cannot be ultimately accessed through reason. Reason doesn't reveal the mystery of God. The mystery of God reveals itself to us. Moreover, the mystery of the Holy Trinity is not something we discover. It comes to us as the grace of God. "The Holy Trinity is the mystery from which we come, by which we live, and toward which we strive (Terrance Klein)."

We, too, can live the life of the Holy Trinity. God's creation is not the one-time event that happened in the past. God's creation continues on even now. Whenever we celebrate the Eucharist, Christ Jesus comes to us, so that we may participate in the creative work of the Father in the Holy Spirit. In other words, every time we receive the Eucharist, Jesus Christ is incarnated within us, so that we may partake in the divine creative work of the Holy Trinity. ✝

[Holy Trinity (A, C)]

The Most Holy Body and Blood of Christ Sunday (B)

(Exodus 24:3-8; Hebrews 9:11-15; Mark 14:12-16, 22-26)

"Do This in Memory of Me"

We will begin next week the ordinary liturgical cycle. We are about to take a journey of prayers on Jesus' public life until the Advent season in the late fall. In order for us to prepare the spiritual food necessary for this long journey, we celebrate today the Feast of the Body and the Blood of Jesus Christ.

The gospel reading today is called the Last Supper—the eternal and heavenly banquet that Jesus prepared for us. On the night before he died, Jesus revealed the whole scheme of his perfect sacrifice on the cross. At the Last Supper, Jesus identified himself as the Passover lamb whose blood would be poured out in sacrifice. He took the Passover meal and gave it new meaning, transforming the bread and wine into his body and blood. The Last Supper was the new Passover meal of Jesus Christ himself. Moreover, the institution of the Eucharist was Jesus' last testament in action, the summary act of his whole life, surrendering everything to God.

The institution of the Eucharist at the Last Supper is recorded in all Synoptic Gospels and in the First Letter of Paul to the Corinthians (Mt 26:26-29, Mk 14:22-25, Lk 22:15-20, 1 Cor 11:23-25). In the Gospel of John, the lofty discourse of the Bread of Life appears at great length. Through all these instances, we see that the Eucharist was celebrated in early Christian communities.

When we celebrate the Eucharist, we renew (and make present) the sacrificial death of Jesus sacramentally. At the central point of the Eucharistic prayer, the priest, representing Christ, quotes the same prayer Jesus offered to the Father during the Last Supper, consisting of four verbs: *take, bless, break,* and *give.* And these words appear precisely in all Synoptic Gospels and Paul's Letter.

Therefore, the Eucharistic celebration is neither a passion play ritualized nor a memorial service of Jesus' death and resurrection. During the Eucharistic celebration, we continue the paschal mystery of Jesus, in the power of the Holy Spirit, through the mediation of the Last Supper.

At the Last Supper, however, Jesus did not simply transform the bread and wine into his body and blood. Just as the bread was the product of the wheat dead in the ground and the wine was the result of the grapes crushed, Jesus broke his own body and passed it around to be eaten, and he handed the cup of his own blood to be drunk. The Eucharist is the sacrificial Passover meal of Jesus himself—already broken and crushed.

Now, Jesus Christ asks us to do the same—to take ourselves, bless them, break them, and give to others—that is, to be the life-giving bread and wine for others. Jesus asks us to become his Eucharistic body and blood, broken and shed for others. It is precisely in "the body broken" and "the blood poured out" that we are in communion with the risen Christ and become the Body of Christ (1 Cor 10:16-17). The Eucharist is the sacrificial Passover meal.

Furthermore, the Eucharist is for us to be transformed into his body. The Mass is not meant to transform elements, but to transform people. When he said, "Behold I am with you always, until the end of the world," Jesus was not referring to his real presence in the Eucharist; he was referring to his real presence in his people, the member of his body. (Gerald Martin, *America* March 4, 2000, p. 22)

We encounter the risen Jesus whenever we celebrate the Eucharist—the sacrament of Jesus Christ. Therefore, as the life of Jesus takes hold of us through the consecrated bread and wine, we begin to live the divine life, God's life (2 Pt 1:4). The Eucharist is the sacramental reality in which Christ comes to us in the Holy Spirit. The Eucharist is for us to live the life of God. The Eucharist is for us to build the kingdom of God and the Body of Christ, the Church.

It is important that we show great reverence to Christ in the sacrament of the Eucharist. It is more important that we celebrate the Eucharist so that Christ's sacrificial death may be real in our lives. ✝

[5ᵗʰ Easter (A), Corpus Christi (A. C), 17ᵗʰ OT (B)]

SECOND SUNDAY IN ORDINARY TIME (B)

(1 Samuel 3:3-10, 19; 1 Corinthians 6:13-15, 17-20; John 1:35-42)

"What Are You Looking for?"

Having left those Christmas excitements behind us, we are celebrating today the second Sunday in Ordinary Time. We begin to reflect on how we encounter the new born Messiah in our daily lives.

God is love, so God cannot stay alone all by Himself. God wants to enter into our lives, and so He calls us. And we respond to God's call. This dynamic mutual encounter—God's call and our response—are illustrated nicely in today's readings. In the first reading, God calls Samuel, and in the gospel reading, Jesus calls Andrew and another disciple and Simon Peter.

Let us look at God's call of Samuel. God called Samuel in the Temple, at night. The Temple is God's dwelling place, and the silence at night represents complete detachment from worldly noises. We remember that the prophet Elijah was able to hear the voice of God through sheer silence in the cave at Mt. Horeb (1 Kgs 19:1-21). In the same way, Samuel responded to God's call in silence; however, when God called the young Samuel, he could not immediately discern God's call. Samuel "was not familiar with the Lord." He had to learn from Eli—his spiritual director, symbols, metaphors, and imaginative languages, necessary to listen to God's call.

In the Bible, God usually calls undeserving persons. Samuel was a child when God called him. Moses was slow in speech and tongue (Ex 4:10). David was the youngest and an unexpected child (1 Sm 16:6-13). Jeremiah was a child who did not yet know how to speak (Jer 1:6). Isaiah was a man of unclean lips (Is 6:5). Amos was a shepherd (Am 7:14). God calls undeserving persons like you and me.

In the gospel reading today, Jesus called Andrew and another disciple. As they followed Jesus on the banks of the Jordan River, Jesus turned around and asked them, "What are you looking for?" The two disciples were searching for their master, and so they asked Jesus, "Where do you live?"

wondering what kind of tradition or school Jesus followed. Jesus answered, "Come, and you will see." It was an invitation and a promise.

The two disciples went to Jesus' house. On that night, they let Jesus entered into their lives. We know what happened to them after that. There were times when they were happy and joyful; they had, indeed, met their long-awaited Messiah. There were also times when they were sad and frustrated; they felt their master betrayed them. By following Jesus, they did not acquire authority, power, or principality of the world, but they tasted the kingdom of God. As God entered into their lives, they began to live God's life.

The disciples of Jesus were ordinary people like us. And Jesus' question is also directed to us. Jesus asks us: What is meaning of our life? How can we be worthy and respectful among the people? How can we maintain the peace of world? We are looking for, as disciples of Jesus, a righteous way of living in the world, a community where we want to love and be loved, and a personal and grace-filled relationship with God.

We are God's children. We love God because God first loves us. We seek God because God first seeks us. And so we encounter God in our daily lives. We do not always look beneath the surface and, often, we overlook God's call. Accordingly, we need to prepare ourselves so that we can discern God's call. We must not be too calculating or speculative. We must listen to our friends. We must learn imaginative and figurative languages, such as music and poetry. We must watch the sunrise and sunset over mountains and valleys.

Soon, we will hear God calling us to great things, such as sacrificing ourselves for our children, being patient with our spouses, and providing care for our aging parents. We will also recognize God in other people: the thoughtful people whom we work with, the honest people whom we do business with, and the ordinary people who help us in simple ways. "What are you looking for?" Jesus asks each one of us today. Let us respond to God's call in faith, hope, and love. ✝

[2nd and 19th OT (A)]

THIRD SUNDAY IN ORDINARY TIME (B)

(Jonah 3:1-5, 10; 1 Corinthians 7:29-31; Mark 1:14-20)

Scripture and Discipleship

Jesus has taught us to love God and our neighbor. And he has demonstrated for us how to do it.

It is not easy, however, to put Jesus' teachings into practice. We live in a world where money measures almost everything. Making money is no longer the means of life; it is the goal of life. People are measured by what they eat, what they drive, and where they live. They lose health to make money, and lose money to restore health.

On the other hand, we work hard to see our children grow up morally sound and spiritually upright. When we do a favor for our neighbors, we feel good. When we visit the sick in the hospital, we feel honored and worthy. Above all, we want to love and be loved. In short, our hearts tell us there are such things as eternal life which we long for and the kingdom of God which we search for. This "holy longing" has certainly taken us into a different dimension of life.

The gospel reading today tells us that Jesus enters the lives of four fisherman and simply says, "Come after me, and I will make you fishers of men." Jesus asks his disciples to stay with him and build a life together. Jesus does not teach them the meaning of Israel's faith or principles of Jewish philosophy. In response to his call, the disciples drop everything and immediately follow Jesus.

We, too, are called by Jesus. We are disciples of Jesus. By following Jesus, we commit ourselves to the person of Jesus—his values, his thoughts, and his way of life. Discipleship is to imitate the life of Jesus and to experience how God loves us in and through Jesus Christ. Discipleship is to be human beings in the way in which Jesus of Nazareth was a human being (analogical imagination). As disciples, therefore, the way we live must conform to the life of Jesus recorded in Scripture.

Scripture shows how Jesus lived and what he taught. Scripture, however, does not provide details of moral or ethical norms and guidelines. For example, Jesus asked the rich young man to sell all of his possessions before following him. But he did not make the same demand of Mary, Martha, and Lazarus, who apparently belonged to a rich household near Jerusalem. In fact, nowhere in Scripture do we find that wealth is bad; it becomes an obstacle to our union with God, if held too tightly. "We do not detach ourselves from things (of the world) in order to attach ourselves to God. But rather we become detached *from ourselves* in order to see and use all things in and for God" (Merton, *New Seed of Contemplation*, p. 20).

Jesus commands us "to love one another, as he loves us" (Jn 13:34). The best way to follow Jesus, therefore, is to love. Indeed, the only way to follow Jesus is to love. And Scripture is the manual on how to love. Unfortunately, Scripture does not define what love is in a few words and sentences. Only the apostle Paul describes what love is in terms of more than twelve virtues in life (1 Cor 13), suggesting that love is the mother virtue of all virtues. To find out what love is, the story of Jesus' whole life—from his birth to his death and resurrection—is required.

Fortunately, we learn what love is from Jesus' words and deeds, such as the Washing of Feet (Jn 13:1-20), the Good Samaritan (Lk 9:25-37), and the Prodigal Son (Lk 15:11-32). These stories are summaries of Jesus' life and show us what love is and how to love others as Jesus loves us.

Scripture shows the love of God in action and the life of God lived by Jesus. In order to be disciples of Jesus in our time, therefore, we must internalize gospel perspectives and ideals in our hearts, so that we can respond to God's love spontaneously. Once we form the habit of hearts based on Scripture, we will develop Christian moral characters naturally. We may know how to live without Scripture. But we cannot be disciples of Jesus without Scripture. ✝

[Holy Thursday, 6th Easter (A)]

FOURTH SUNDAY IN ORDINARY TIME (B)

(Deuteronomy 18:15-20; 1 Corinthians 7:32-35; Mark 1:21-28)

The Eschatological Prophet

Jesus of Nazareth is the eschatological prophet. In the Gospel of John, Jesus identifies himself as a prophet like Moses (Jn 5:46), quoting the words from Moses that we heard in the first reading: "God will raise up for you a prophet like me from among your own kin" (Dt 18:15).

Jesus begins his public ministry in the synagogue of Capernaum. There, he encounters a man possessed with an evil spirit. The devil recognizes Jesus as "the Holy One of God" and wants to be left alone. Jesus heals the man from the demonic possession on the Sabbath day.

Jesus always does something forbidden on the Sabbath—such as healing the sick or plucking grains—so what Jesus does in today's Gospel is not surprising. There is, however, a sign of something scary and frightening. As soon as Jesus begins his public ministry, he enters straight into the world of demons and collides with Satan, who recognizes his divine nature. Jesus is portrayed as strong against demons and unclean spirits (Mk 3:27).

Two thousand years ago in Palestine, darkness, despair, evil, and suffering were so severe that something definitely needed to be done. So God sent Jesus into this world as the prophet of the end-time, the eschatological prophet. Jesus was the final word of God and the last prophet sent by God for the salvation of mankind. This means that the message from Jesus is valid at any time, because it will be fulfilled at the end-time.

Jesus was not a priest, nor a scribe, nor a rabbi, but a carpenter's son. Jesus did not preach any special ethics or morality. He left no written document. He preached the kingdom of God for a year or so in northern Galilee, a fleeting point of light in the history of mankind. He called for a new life in light of the imminent coming of God's kingdom. He was convinced that he would be vindicated in the end.

The stories Jesus told about God's kingdom are well known: the wolf and the lamb graze side by side; the lowly are exalted and the rich are sent away; whoever wishes to be first must be a slave for all; the workers who come at the last hour get paid just as much as those who toil all day long. These stories are full of paradoxes and contradictions. Yet, they describe the life of Jesus.

Eventually, Jesus died on the cross outside of the city, and his death was the most scandalous contradiction of all. His followers descended to the hells of their consciences, beating their breasts and pounding their heads. Three days after his death, they encountered the risen Jesus. Only then did they find out that the stories Jesus told were not about another world, but about the new possibility of this world. They experienced the definitive love and mercy of God. They truly understood that Jesus revealed the human face of God and demonstrated the paradigm of humanity in the most divine way.

The story of Jesus is the story of God. In Jesus, God discloses a new world, where we can experience the reality of God. "In Christ and through Christ, God has revealed himself fully to mankind...and in Christ and through Christ man has acquired full awareness of his dignity" (*Redemptor Hominis*, #11).

As we begin to reflect upon the Gospel of Mark this year, we should think seriously, therefore, about what we must do with Jesus in our lives. We must answer for ourselves the very question that Jesus asks Peter: "Who do you say that I am?" We must answer this question, because otherwise it remains in the air until we decide either for or against the possibility of the new life Jesus points at.

Let us also remind ourselves that we are prophets already chosen by virtue of our baptisms. Therefore, Jesus wants us to be familiar with the reversal of values, the hidden paradoxes, and the contradictions in life. Jesus wants us to rebuke the absurdity and emptiness of demonic forces—the sources of evil and suffering in this world. The kingdom of God proclaimed by Jesus is already here, but not yet completed. We are to complete it. ✝

[Baptism (C), 3rd OT (C)]

FIFTH SUNDAY IN ORDINARY TIME (B)

(Job 7:1-4, 6-7; 1 Corinthians 9:16-19, 22-23; Mark 1:29-39)

To Follow Jesus Is to Live for Others

We believe in Jesus Christ and follow him. To believe in Jesus is easy. Even non-Christians can do it. But to follow him is not easy, because it requires living the life for others.

The gospel reading today reveals the busy itinerary of Jesus' Galilean ministry. He heals Peter's mother-in-law, then attends to the sick and those possessed by demons. Early next morning, Jesus goes off to pray alone and renew his intimacy with his Father. Finally, when told by his disciples that everyone is looking for him, he resumes his ministry of proclaiming the kingdom of God.

Jesus spends about three years in public life, according to John's Gospel. In comparison, his ministry lasts only a year or so in the Synoptic Gospels. During this short time, Jesus moves swiftly and hurries everything for others. Jesus is always on the go; he invites his disciples to follow him hastily and urgently. In his journey to Jerusalem, Jesus usually does not explain why he does. He just does. And Jesus always goes ahead of his disciples in a hurry.

Just as Jesus hurried and rushed to Jerusalem, so did Paul. Paul always mentioned the death and resurrection of Jesus, but ignored what Jesus said or did. It is like telling our friends the wonderful news right away, but always the conclusion first. Paul has provided an excellent example about how to follow Jesus, as seen in today's second reading. Paul felt obligated to proclaim the Gospel of Christ under divine compulsion. He was determined to share his experience with as many people as possible.

At the same time, Paul was not concerned with his own comfort and security. He earned his living as a leather worker and tentmaker, not relying on the communities he established. Finally, he met people on their own grounds. He became a servant for all: men and women, slaves and free persons, Jews and Gentiles.

To Paul, the paschal mystery of Jesus is the greatest turning point in salvation's history and the basis of hope for the fullness of God's kingdom. And the good news of God's kingdom liberates everyone from the power of sin and guilt, thus allowing the just and right relationship with God.

Following the example of Jesus, Paul lived his life for others. Why did Jesus and Paul live for others? The answer is love. They lived for others because love compelled them to do so.

We are disciples of Jesus. We know that love is the fundamental virtue of Christian life. We also know that, as love is matured in our hearts, it increasingly shifts attention away from our own needs and accomplishments. Love is self-sacrificing and self-transcending. Love liberates us from individual possessions and accomplishments. Love transforms us to live of others.

We live for others because the love of God allows us to participate in justice and mercy toward others. We live for others because our salvation comes naturally from working for others. We live for others because we encounter God in the life for others.

Who are these others? They are, indeed, the poor, the marginalized, and the vulnerable. But they also are our spouses, our sons and daughters, our brothers and sisters, our parents, our grandparents, and our neighbors. We live for others, being happy and blessed along with all of God's creatures. We live for others, attaining interior poverty and freedom. Jesus teaches us in the Sermon on the Mount, "Blessed are the poor in spirit, for theirs is the kingdom of God" (Mt 5:3). This passage from Matthew's Gospel is an abstract of the entire Sermon on the Mount.

To live for others, in freedom and in spiritual poverty, is to live in God's kingdom. To live for others is to follow Jesus. To live for others is to have the same mind that is in Christ Jesus (Phil 2:5). ✝

[3rd Lent (B), 25th OT (B)]

SIXTH SUNDAY IN ORDINARY TIME (B)

(Leviticus 13:1-2, 44-46; 1 Corinthian 10:31-11:1; Mark 1:40-45)

Compassionate Jesus

𝕵esus Christ is the Lord. We would like to know him more clearly, love him more dearly, and follow him more nearly. One way to do this is to understand Jesus' compassion as a human being. Today, we will reflect on Jesus' compassion so that we, too, may show compassion to our brothers and sisters.

Today's gospel passage tells the story of the leper. When a leper came to Jesus and begged to be cleaned, Jesus, moved with compassion, stretched out his hands and touched him. The leper was cleansed instantly.

In ancient society, leprosy was considered dangerous and highly contagious. Lepers made their shelters outside the city limits for the safety and well-being of the entire community. The filthy leper who came to Jesus violated the law and should have cried out, "Unclean, unclean!"

Having healed the leper, Jesus told him not to tell anyone and to present his clean body to the priest so he could once again join his community. But the leper was so happy that he went out to tell the whole town what Jesus had done for him. An important point of this healing miracle is that Jesus was moved with compassion before he cured the leper.

Let us consider what the word "compassion" means and try to imagine Jesus, as he shows compassion to the leper. The word "compassion" in the Bible means movements of the spirit from one's belly, the bedrock of human emotions and energies, as in "Out of the believer's belly shall flow rivers of living water" (Jn 7:38). In contrast, in this twenty-first century, we value cool judgments mostly from heads and some, if any, loving affections from hearts. To the first-century Jews, belly or stomach was the center of being and more meaningful than minds and hearts.

Compassion is the virtue of suffering with others in faith. Compassion means taking on the pain and suffering of others in love and hope.

Compassion is the deepest emotion of the soul. Therefore, "to be moved with compassion" is to love and care for others from the deepest core of being.

Whenever Jesus cures the sick, he does not just magically perform the task of healing. Before he cures a sick person, he always "has pity on" the person or "is moved with compassion." He always identifies himself with the sick in a compassionate manner.

In addition to Jesus' episodes of healing, we find many examples of compassion in the Gospels. Jesus has compassion for the widow at Nain (Lk 7:13). Jesus has compassion for the hungry crowds before he multiplies the bread for five thousand people (Mk 6:34 and Mt 14:14) and for four thousand people (Mk 8:2 and Mt 15:32). Jesus has compassion for the crowds, like sheep without a shepherd (Mt 9:36). Finally, stories like that of the Good Samaritan (Lk 10:33) and the Prodigal Son (Lk 15:20) have central compassionate characters.

Returning back to today's gospel story, when Jesus is moved with compassion, we can imagine that his eyes sparkle with tears, his face is full of pity, and his heart is ready to take on the leper's pain and suffering. Jesus reveals the caring and loving heart from his deepest inner being. Jesus is compassionate.

Jesus does not simply and magically abolish or eliminate evils and sufferings. Instead, Jesus enters into our innermost beings and helps us to confront those evils and sufferings by encouraging us to find our true selves. Jesus shows that God is not so much a rescuing God, but the redeeming God, the helping God.

Jesus challenges us to be compassionate with others, particularly those in despair and marginal and suffering. To be compassionate is the way to know, to love, and to follow Jesus. ✝

[13ᵗʰ OT (B)]

SEVENTH SUNDAY IN ORDINARY TIME (B)

(Isaiah 43:18-19, 21-22, 24-25; 2 Corinthians 1:18-22; Mark 2:1-12)

Jesus Forgives Our Existential Anxieties

Thomas Merton once said, "Man is not at peace with his fellow men because he is not at peace with himself. He is not at peace with himself, because he is not at peace with God."

In today's gospel reading, a great crowd is gathered around Jesus in a house of Capernaum. Four friends carrying a paralytic man find no easy way to bring him to Jesus. They go up to the roof of the house, open a portion of it, and lower him down to Jesus' feet. Witnessing the faith of these courageous young men, Jesus says tenderly to the paralytic, "Child, your sins are forgiven." Then Jesus heals him.

The paralytic in the story represents a typical human condition that can only be liberated by God. This gospel story illustrates the desperate nature of man's sinful existence and, by contrast, God's unwarranted forgiveness.

In the Gospel of Mark, the compassionate Jesus desires to liberate the whole of humanity from anxiety and despair. Jesus begins his public ministry by healing the man with an unclean spirit (Mk 1:21-28) and is often angry at the sickness, but never at the sick person (Mk 1:41, and 3:5). Jesus has performed many (37, according to the Gospels) healings and miracles. Jesus wants to liberate people from the kingdom of Satan, where terrible bondage and suffering prevails. Jesus has announced the kingdom of God.

We are thrown into this world toward death (Heidegger's *Dasein*). We are finite and temporal and, thus, we long for the infinite and eternal. We are anxious, and we despair. We are not at home. Consequently, we are alienated and estranged from ourselves, from our friends and from our world.

According to Paul Tillich, our finitude and contingency are the sources of our anxieties and despair. We feel empty and meaningless spiritually. We feel guilt and shame morally. And we are bound to face death eventually. These different types of anxieties—spiritual, moral, and ontological—are interwoven together and comprise the existential nature of human beings. Under these existential conditions, like the paralytic man in today's Gospel, not only do we become anxious but we are reduced into mere things; we have lost the sense of transcendence; we don't consider our lives as gifts from God, sacred and entrusted to us.

We wonder, then, "Where is our home and how can we become whole and saved? Can we find eternal life and salvation from things of the world?" We can find eternal life only in God, and we can be saved only by God. St. John Paul II summed up, "When the sense of God is lost, the sense of man is also threatened and poisoned" (*Evangelium Vitae*, #21).

St. Augustine, in his *Confession*, nicely summarized the existential condition of human beings, along with its solution: "God, you have made us for yourself; (therefore) our hearts are restless until they rest in you." This saying has also been the central theme of Christian theology for the last fifteen hundred years. In the midst of life's anxieties and despairs, the restless heart can find home only in God in and through Jesus Christ.

"Jesus Christ is not 'yes' and 'no' but 'yes,'" Paul says in the second reading. Jesus says, "My peace I give to you. I do not give to you as the world gives" (Jn 14:27). The peace Jesus gives is not from this world; it is the free gift from God. Therefore, we can find a true home in Jesus Christ. Indeed, the only way to rescue ourselves from existential anxieties and find our true home is to accept Jesus as the Lord with courage and in confidence.

We are made for God. Without God, our lives are void and filled with envies and desires. If man is not at peace with God, then he is not at peace with himself nor is he with his fellow men. ✝

EIGHTH SUNDAY IN ORDINARY TIME (B)

(Hosea 2:16, 17, 21-22; 2 Corinthians 3:1-6; Mark 2:18-22)

Intellect, Will, and Heart

Jesus of Nazareth often compares himself with a bridegroom as in today's gospel reading. Jesus is happy and joyful, as he exchanges his heartfelt words with his disciples about a bridegroom and his wedding guests. We also find the word "heart" many times in the first and second readings. Let us reflect on the meaning of heart and how important it is in Christian life.

The word "heart" frequently appears in the Bible, although we usually associate it with feeling and affection. This is so because we live in the age of reasoning. We gather as many facts as possible—intellectual and reasonable—and evaluate them before we make a decision. We seldom make a decision moved by heart. We do so because both intellect and will have dominated operation of our minds since the Enlightenment in the eighteenth century. As a result, our rational minds are satisfied only with exact numbers and reasonable logics. It has to be truth only when all speculative reasons tightly fit together. At the same time, we are not easily convinced by things non-logical and non-reasonable. As a result, we have lost the innocence and spontaneity of our hearts. In short, we have huge heads and small hearts, perhaps wooden hearts.

Too much emphasis on intellect and will in the avoidance of heart has developed tensions in our consciousness. Sometimes, we find ourselves in situations where head tells one thing and heart another. This happens when intellect and will are disordered as they are separated from heart. Other times, we cannot express what we have in our minds using mere words and letters. Then poetry, music, story, or metaphor lifts us to a different dimension, where heart is called in to coordinate with intellect and will.

To achieve a harmonized and integrated operation of human mind or consciousness (intentionality), Dr. Andrew Tallon at Marquette University has proposed a model of triune consciousness. According to his model, which is based on the work of St. Augustine, (who understood the inner life of the Holy Trinity in terms of psychological elements: memory, intellect, and will), human consciousness functions as a simultaneous operation of three distinct, not separate, faculties of intellect, heart, and will. Intellect is the basis for thinking, cognition, and reason. Heart is the basis for feeling, affectivity, and imagination, and thus is responsible for innocent, spontaneous, and uncalculating consciousness. Will is the basis for freedom, choice, and volition.

Heart plays the most important role in Christian life. We "believe [in God] with heart" (Rom 10:10). Love and wisdom, which cannot be contained in clear thoughts, are transmitted from heart to heart. Moreover, we know with heads, as well as with hearts. Feelings, guts, hunches, and intuitions still play critical roles in our lives. For example, woman's intuition can still surprise man, and man's gut feeling can often bring woman's smile.

We find the word "heart" in Scripture frequently. The psalmist asks, "God, create a pure heart for me; give me a new and steadfast spirit" (Ps 51:10). The prophet Ezekiel says, "A new heart I will give you, and a new spirit I will put within you" (Ez 36:26). John the Baptist calls for repentance, which is to change heart, so that the Good News of Jesus Christ can be accepted. Heart is the most secret core of being where we encounter God alone (*Gaudium et Spes*, #16).

The goal of the spiritual life is to be good and holy persons with fully functioning hearts. Good persons perform morally good acts because they respond from their whole being, not as the result of academic degrees. Holy persons love God and fellow human beings because they are attuned to divine and sacred things. Obviously, they exhibit holy and virtuous connaturality from their hearts.

God is the Triune God; the Father, the Son, and the Holy Spirit are inseparable in economics of the Trinity. In the same way, the human consciousness entails the collective and synchronized operation of intellect, will, and heart. We need to attain pure and clean hearts, the sources of wisdom and love. Jesus always talks to our hearts, not to our heads or our minds. ✝

[1st Lent (A), Holy Trinity (A), 8th OT (C)]

NINTH SUNDAY IN ORDINARY TIME (B)

(Deuteronomy 5:12-15; 2 Corinthians 4:6-11; Mark 2:23-28)

Sunday and the Sabbath

Jeff Hart from Denver was drilling water wells for the United States Army in Afghanistan. On August 25, 2010, he was called to a gold-copper mine in Chile, where thirty-three miners had been trapped for almost twenty days, the longest on record. Only half a century ago, trapped miners were considered lost causes. A cave-in at the mine would simply be sealed off and crosses hammered into the ground.

Jeff Hart was the best in the world at drilling large holes. He spent the next several weeks on his feet drilling a hole, which was 28 inches in diameter and 662 meters deep, through granite rocks. Hart said, "You have to feel through your feet what the drill is doing; it is a vibration you get so that you know what's happening." He also joked that he thought it was his heart stopping when he felt an unexplained "pop" just before the drill broke through into a chamber far underground.

On October 9, 2010, the drill finally penetrated through the ceiling of the corner where the miners were trapped. On October 13, all thirty-three miners were lifted up, one by one, from the depths of the earth. They had been in darkness for seventy-one days.

Around that same time, the Nobel Committee in Stockholm, Norway, announced its Nobel laureates for 2010. Those distinguished scholars certainly contributed to the advancement of humanity. However, I could not help but think that Mr. Hart, the roughneck driller from Denver, did as well.

The reason why I bring up Mr. Hart from Denver is to wonder out loud whether he stopped working on Sundays. Oh yes, he stopped working for a few days because his drill bit encountered unmapped iron bar. That was also a moment when his heart stopped briefly. A strong magnet was ordered and metal pieces were removed through the hole before the rescue operation was able to resume.

For Jews, it was very important to keep the Sabbath. The Sabbath was a holy day of sacred rest in God's honor. However, Jewish leaders put so much emphasis on observing all 613 laws from the Torah that they forgot the real purpose of resting on the Sabbath. During the time of Jesus, Jews were so sensitive to keeping the laws that plucking a few heads of grain while crossing a wheat field was forbidden. It was considered work. Jesus, however, strongly rejected such regulations. The Sabbath was intended for people to serve God, not the other way around. By enforcing the letter of the law too strictly, Jews lost the spirit of the Sabbath.

On another Sabbath day, according to today's gospel reading, Jesus violated Jewish law again by healing a man with a withered hand. To Jesus, it was proper and natural to heal the man no matter what day it was. Jesus did what God would do. Thus Jesus lamented, "The Sabbath was made for man and not man for the Sabbath." That was also why "the Pharisees went outside immediately and began to plot with the Herodians on how they might destroy him."

The origin of the Sabbath goes back to the creation story in the Book of Genesis. Having completed all creative works in six days, God rested on the seventh day (Gen 2:2). This means that God continues His resting now, not creating another universe. The Sabbath was a day to acknowledge God's lordship over creation.

For Christians, Sunday is the Sabbath. On Sunday, the first day of the week, Jesus was raised from death and appeared to disciples (Mt 28:1, Jn 20:1 and 19). Because the resurrection of Jesus is a new creation, and because Jesus Christ is the Lord, Sunday is the Lord's Day, which is "holy and set apart for the praise of God" (CCC, #2171). On Sunday, we enter into God's rest (Heb 4:10). To enter into God's rest does not really mean to stop working and do nothing. We ought to participate in God's on-going creation.

The real Sabbath does not necessarily come once a week. It can come many times a day, and many days a week. ✝

TENTH SUNDAY IN ORDINARY TIME (B)

(Genesis 3:9-15; 2 Corinthians 4:13-5:1; Mark 3:20-35)

Love Distinguishes Good and Evil

God expelled Adam and Eve from the Garden of Eden because they took the forbidden fruit from the tree of the knowledge of good and evil. Some say that human history would have been different, if Adam had not blamed Eve, and if Eve had not blamed the serpent. Had Adam and Eve stood up and taken responsibility, things would be different today, they say.

Adam and Eve wanted to be like God. They envied God, the owner of good and evil. Theirs is a story of human desire, envy, and covetousness. It is a story about the inherent human condition that turns us away from God. It is a story about the mystery of human nature, which does not let God be God. This story of the disobedience to God's command is called the doctrine of original sin.

The word "sin" does not appear in the story, however. The word "sin" first appears in the story of Abel and Cain (Gen 4:7). We know that the story of Adam and Eve ends with God cursing only the serpent (Gen 3:14). Instead of cursing Adam and Eve, God made garments for them and clothed them before expelling from the Garden (Gen 3:21). We ought to be grateful to God for that.

Actually, there is another story on the origin of sin that appears much later in the Book of Genesis. It tells of the marriage of the sons of God with the daughters of humans (Gen 6:4). This story also suggests that sin is a mystery.

The story of original sin is our story. We participate in sin with Adam and Eve. Sin is ubiquitous in human history. Sin is about our envy and desire, which often awake in the darkness of night. It is about our envy and desire to be like God. It is about our envy and desire not to respect God's transcendence, not letting God be God. As Paul lamented, it is about our inability to do what is right, even when we want to do it (Rom 7:15).

The Gospel of Mark, as we have listened to today's Gospel, vividly shows this dark side of human nature. When we read the Gospel, we feel frightened, like coyotes howling in a graveyard at night (Mk 5). It sends a chill into our spines. Clearly, the world is covered with a darkness of unbelief and a despair of envy. Jesus must, therefore, be the stronger one (Mk 3:27) who confronts the darkness of human nature.

Evil is corrupted and deformed good. And evil is always intimately connected with good. It is difficult to separate the evil from the good. On the other hand, our discriminating and dualistic mind always desires the good and rejects the bad. Consequently, we often admire the Angel of Darkness, because it looks so much like the Angel of Light. Perhaps the inability to separate the good from the evil, because of our selfish envy and desire, is the original sin.

Moreover, we pride ourselves on our judgment upon the evil in the world, while we tend to overlook the evil within our own selves. We must, however, first pay attention to the darkness within us, instead of trying to shine light into the world's darkness.

Jesus Christ heals the sick and expels demons. In today's gospel reading, however, Jesus himself is charged as being possessed by the devil and being an agent of Satan. Even his own family rejects him for being "out of mind." Jesus' heart is broken by this terrible rejection from his own folks and laments, "How can Satan cast out Satan?" Satan is very resilient.

In other words, the evil is always intimately connected with the good. We must not exercise the autonomy in sorting out evil from good; our religious ancestors tried and failed. Only love can separate the evil that is entangled with the good.

God is love. Jesus Christ has shown us that God is love. Only Jesus Christ can distinguish and sort out the good and the evil and thus unravel original sin. ✝

[7th OT (A), 11th OT (C), 22nd OT (A),]

187

ELEVENTH SUNDAY IN ORDINARY TIME (B)

(Ezekiel 17:22-24; 2 Corinthians 5:6-10; Mark 4:26-34)

The Kingdom of God

"The time is fulfilled, and the kingdom of God is at hand," says Jesus at the very beginning of his public ministry (Mk 1:15). The messianic kingdom of God and its absolute nearness are at the heart of Jesus' teachings.

In the fourth chapter of Mark's Gospel, we find three parables about the kingdom of God. Each parable shows a different aspect of God's kingdom. Combined together, we can get an excellent picture on the kingdom of God.

The first parable concerns a farmer who spreads seeds. Some seeds fall on a road, others on rocky soil, some on a thorny field, and still others on good soil. Only those falling on good soil bear abundant fruit. The second parable is the one to which we have just listened. It is about seeds growing beneath soils without the farmer's knowledge. The third parable is also one to which we have listened. It is about a tiny seed that grows into a huge beautiful tree so that birds can safely build their nests in it. All parables are about seeds, symbolizing God's words on which we live on earth.

The first parable shows that the kingdom grows only on good soil. Some years ago, I wondered why these farmers spread seeds everywhere, including useless dry roads, rocky soil, and thorny fields. I thought they were wasting the seeds. Scripture scholars (Joachim Jeremias) say that ancient Palestinian farmers spread seeds first and tilled the soil later. Even though some seed was wasted, the farmer gathered abundant fruit from the good soil. (I interpret the Bible based on my intellect, not on wisdom.)

The second parable suggests that God's kingdom grows in a mysterious manner. We don't know how it grows. Ancient farmers simply accepted plant growth as a mystery, the work of God. They also considered the sunrise and sunset as mysteries of nature. Now we know all about plant science and cosmology. Yet we hardly look at the night stars. This illustrates our need for a new vision and a new heart in order to appreciate God's kingdom.

The third parable reveals that a tiny and insignificant seed of the kingdom eventually grows into a huge and beautiful tree. This poetic expression surrounding the huge tree with its many bird's nests was an attempt to say something holy and beautiful in human words. It also shows hope for the future. When the kingdom of God is fulfilled, it will bring such huge benefits to all.

The kingdom of God is God's, not ours. In God's kingdom, God's mercy, love, and hope prevail—not our own ideas, desires, and dreams. In God's kingdom, God reigns, not we. God's kingdom is also eschatological. This means that God will complete His kingdom in His way, not in our way. The kingdom of God is already here with us, but it has not yet been completed. God's kingdom constantly calls us beyond where we are now and invites us to grow and transcend ourselves. And so, we must "walk by faith sight."

God's kingdom is the "horizon" from which the inner knowledge of God manifests. Jesus identified himself with the kingdom of God. Jesus *is* the kingdom of God. Because the risen Jesus dwells within us as the source and fountain of life, the kingdom of God is also within us (Lk 17:21).

We live between the Book of Genesis and the Book of Revelation. And the Book of Revelation ends with "Come, Lord Jesus!" We are always on a journey of faith in God's kingdom. We cannot possess the things of God firmly and definitely. Our faith has not matured yet. We must trust God and His kingdom, where Jesus has already planted tiny seeds. They will grow into huge trees where birds of the sky will build their beautiful nests.

It is by the grace of God that we gather here in this sacred place, celebrating and worshipping God and hoping for the fulfillment of God's kingdom. With the psalmist, we sing, "It is good to give thanks to the Lord." †

[16th and 17th OT (A)]

TWELFTH SUNDAY IN ORDINARY TIME (B)

(Job 38:1, 8-11; 2 Corinthians 5:14-17; Mark 4:35-41)

Amazing Grace

The sea is dangerous and scary. Sometimes it roars with the colossal amount of water, engulfing even a large ship. What is more, all kinds of beasts and monsters live in the sea. In the Bible, only God calms a storm and rules the sea.

The gospel reading today shows Jesus and his disciples traveling by boat from the western shore (the Jewish territory) to the eastern shore (the Gentile territory) of the Sea of Galilee. When a storm blows up suddenly in the middle of the sea, they are in danger of drowning. Strangely enough, Jesus is sleeping in the stern during the dangerous storm. Finally, they wake Jesus up, and then he rebukes the wind and calms the storm.

John Newton was the son of an English captain. When John was ten, his mother died. He went to sea with his father and learned everything about the sea. Eventually, John became a slave trader.

One night a violent storm blew up at sea. The waves grew to the size of a mountain and tossed around Newton's ship like a toy. Then Newton did something he had not done before. He prayed: "God, if you will only save my ship, I promise to be your slave." It was on that night he sensed there was a God who could answer his prayer.

When Newton reached land, he kept his promise and quit the slave trade. He taught himself Latin, Greek, and Hebrew and became a priest of the Church of England. That was what his mother, who had now passed away many years previous, had wanted him to be.

Among the many hymns he composed, the most famous is "Amazing Grace." This simple and beautiful hymn has the power to inspire and encourage everybody from kings and presidents to the sick and the broken and the misfortunate. The origin of this melody might have been a slave song. John Newton, the self-proclaimed wretch, was saved by amazing grace during a violent storm in the sea. He was once lost, but now he was found.

(We remember another lost-and-found man in the Bible, the prodigal son. He asked his share of inheritance in advance and wasted it away in a distant country. He, too, was at the very bottom of life, feeding himself with pigs' food. There, he felt God's amazing grace.)

We, too, often encounter storms in the middle of life's journey, but these can be occasions that draw us closer to God. This is so because the storm shakes up the basis and foundation upon which our false and camouflaged selves have been built. Our self-centered, ungodly foundations need to be busted open before the grace of God can penetrate. Besides, because genuine faith comes from the depths of our beings where God resides, we cannot know and love God without going into these innermost depths of our being.

The first reading is about the story of Job, who did not lose faith in God even when experiencing terrible agony and misery in life. He was a blameless and upright man who feared the Lord. Unfortunately, he became the subject of uncongenial discussion between God and Satan. He lost everything: all of his family and all of his fortune. In spite of everything lost, he said, "Naked I came from my mother's womb, and naked shall I return there; the Lord gave, and the Lord has taken away; blessed be the name of the Lord" (Job 1:21).

What Job said certainly reveals he was a free, detached, and indifferent person in spite of the misery he faced with. Although he did not understand why he had become so miserable, he persisted in talking to God. The story of Job is not about misery and suffering, but about faith.

Today's gospel reading reminds us that we, the Church, are on a journey in the sea. Our journeys often face violent storms. But Jesus Christ is with us on board and will awake to calm the tempest. ✝

THIRTEENTH SUNDAY IN ORDINARY TIME (B)

(Wisdom 1:13-15, 2:23-24; 2 Corinthians 8:7, 9, 13-15; Mark 5:21-43)

Jesus Grants What We Truly Desire

It happened some years ago when I was a chaplain at St. Paul Hospital. I was about to finish up a visit to a Christian lady of middle age. I said to her, "Jesus is always with us, and I hope that you will get well soon." Then she responded, "Yes, Chaplain, I believe in Jesus and he will do everything for me."

As I came out of the room, I was very much impressed by her remarkably strong faith and confidence in Jesus. At the same time, I felt ashamed of myself for my own lack of faith in Jesus.

A short while later, however, I began to wonder whether the woman lacked her own will and desire for coping with her illness and suffering. Perhaps she had a strong faith in God but a weak faith in herself. Perhaps she did not want to take up her own cross but, instead, wished Jesus to do it for her. After all, there is an old saying that says, "God helps those who help themselves."

Jesus has healed many sick people and even raised the dead. In most cases, however, the desire of the person—the honest and sincere desire—is the most important factor in healings. The desire to be healed is illustrated by two examples from the gospel reading today: one the resuscitation of Jairus' daughter of twelve years old, and the other the healing of the woman suffering hemorrhages for twelve years.

Jairus, a high synagogue official, comes to Jesus, falls at his feet, and pleads for the cure of his daughter. Because his daughter is too sick to come, he asks Jesus to come to his house.

At that same moment, a woman with internal bleeding appears on the scene. Because there is a large crowd, she simply wants to touch Jesus' cloak, hoping it will cure her illness. Jesus, being at once aware that power has been drawn from him, turns around and asks, "Who touched my clothes?" The woman falls down before Jesus in fear and trembling. Then Jesus simply says to her, "Daughter, your faith has saved you."

In the meantime, it is discovered that Jairus' daughter has already died. Now it is too late for Jesus to do anything, and so they ridiculed him. But Jesus goes on to the child's room and resuscitates her by saying, "Little girl, I say to you, arise!"

Both Jairus and the woman are sincere in what they want. Therefore, they are healed and can participate in God's creative act by bearing children. Because they possess an honest desire for life, Jesus cures them and brings salvation to them as well. Jesus has shown merciful acts of God because of their strong desire and faith in him. Jesus grants what they truly desire.

The Word was made flesh and dwells among us (Jn 1:14). St. Paul says, "It is Christ who lives in me" (Gal 2:20). St. John says, "God is in us" (1 Jn 4:13). Therefore, God exists in our innermost beings. If we believe this, we ought to encounter God inside of us, rather than passively waiting for God's healing power from outside. Then God will listen to what we honestly desire in faith. For our part, we ought to prepare ourselves worthy of God's love and mercy.

One way to prepare ourselves is to understand the theology of the cross correctly. Jesus has conquered human suffering and death by the cross. Therefore, only when our suffering is viewed from the mystery of the cross, it has redemptive and salvific power. Through the mystery of the cross, we encounter Jesus in our suffering.

Life is full of suffering. Some of us gathered here have problems to handle, burdens to bear, and worries to confront. To all of us, Jesus says, "Do not be afraid; just have faith." No matter how tough life is, our merciful God will protect us from suffering. We are also confident that God will provide us enough courage and strength to bear with suffering itself. †

[13th OT (A), Pentecost (B), 6th and 22nd and 24th OT (B)]

Fourteenth Sunday in Ordinary Time (B)

(Ezekiel 2:2-5; 2 Corinthians 12:7-10; Mark 6:1-6)

We Are Prophets

One of privileges of being a deacon is baptizing infants. It is a tremendous joy for me to be an instrument for transforming infant babies into prophets, priests, and kings or queens, by the power of the Holy Spirit.

We are already prophets by virtue of our baptisms. In the Bible, prophets do not merely predict the future. Prophets tell people how to live today according to the will of God. Prophets are those who are true and honest in front of God. As prophets, therefore, our lives can be demanding and disappointing, rather than comforting and consoling.

In the first reading, we heard how God called Ezekiel and sent him to the Israelites, who were "rebellious people." They didn't listen to Ezekiel; but God wanted to make sure that the Israelites had a prophet among them. The role of a prophet is simply to prophesize, not to gather the fruits of the prophecy. God will gather the fruit.

As a prophet to the Gentiles, Paul didn't have a comfortable life. He preached the law-free Gospel of Christ, which was rejected by some of his fellow Christians. Throughout his lonely mission, Paul suffered from a "thorn in the flesh," a mysterious physical illness. Whenever he prayed to get rid of it, God said to Paul, "My grace is sufficient for you, for power is made perfect in weakness." Then Paul responded in prayer, "I am content with weakness, for when I am weak then I am strong."

What does it mean to say, "When I am weak, then I am strong"? It means when we are weak, we turn to God. It means when we are weak, we open ourselves to God, who strengthens us. It means when we are weak, we become strong in the power of God.

Ezekiel and Paul were not the only prophets who were rejected. Jesus of Nazareth, the eschatological prophet, also was rejected. The Gospel reading today shows that, when Jesus returned to his hometown with his disciples, his people rejected him. Jesus experienced bitter insult and shame in his own hometown, and it happened at the peak of his Galilean ministry.

As we reflect upon the lives of Ezekiel the prophet, Paul the apostle, and Jesus the Son of God, we may wonder why Christian values are not necessarily compatible to the world. This is so because Christians hold fast to the truth, to the good, and to the beauty. As Christians, we do not compromise with the world, because we have found God, who is the source of the truth, the good, and the beauty. We also have hope in God, who promises, "You will have pain, but your pain will turn into joy" (Jn 16:20).

We are already prophets of God. And we have prophetic missions, which may require serious commitment and undeserving sacrifice. It could be telling people what the recent Pope's Encyclical Letter really means. It could be making a right choice from a lonely conscience. It could be accepting an inevitable death at an old age. Whatever we do as prophets, our goal is "not to be successful, but to be faithful," as Mother Teresa once said. Like Ezekiel, we only prophesize; God decides how and when our prophecy will bear fruit.

As prophets, however, we have to rely on the grace of God, who dwells within us. Grace is an energy which tends to keep us close to God by transforming us. Grace strengthens our conscience and manifests itself in our true selves. Therefore, it is important for us to learn how to release the energy of grace within ourselves.

The world admires the powerful, the rich, and the famous. But we are free from power, money, and fame. What we long for and what we search for are different from what the world offers. As prophets of God, we live a creative life in our mission. We are in the world, but we are not of the world. We are prophets of Jesus Christ. ✝

[Baptism (B), 9ᵗʰ OT (C)]

FIFTEENTH SUNDAY IN ORDINARY TIME (B)

(Amos 7:12-15; Ephesians 1:3-14; Mark 6:7-13)

To Follow Jesus

We are disciples of Jesus Christ and sent for the mission of the Church. God chooses ordinary people like you and me to perform extraordinary tasks.

Amos was a simple shepherd and a dresser of sycamore trees. In our day, he would be classified along the lines of a migrant worker. Yet God chose him as a prophet, and Amos claimed that his vocation came directly from God. The gospel reading today shows the twelve disciples as they are sent to heal the sick and proclaim the Good News of God's kingdom.

God has chosen us, just like the twelve disciples, to follow after Jesus Christ. Our task is to show the world that God is love and, at the same time, to be instruments for the communion of all people with God and with each other. Jesus has shown us how to do all these in the Gospels.

Two thousand years ago, Jesus, a Palestinian Jew, called God *Abba* Father and proclaimed the universal reign of God to the whole world. Jews of the first century wouldn't dare call God *Abba* (Joachim Jeremias). Jesus must have witnessed God's own inner life, and so he lived the life of God. Jesus demonstrated the ethical paradigm of human existence and revealed the human face of God. In other words, Jesus Christ is God in the most human way, and also man in the most divine way.

By following Jesus, his disciples in the first century—as well as countless Christians throughout the history of mankind—have been able to attain freedom from sin and overcome the power of death. Now it is we who must be redeemed by following Jesus.

To follow Jesus means to participate in God's salvation and man's redemption manifested and exemplified in the person of Jesus. To follow Jesus also is to abide the ethical paradigm recorded in the Gospels. For example, at the end of the parable of the Good Samaritan, Jesus said to the lawyer, "Go and do likewise" (Lk 10: 37). We cannot do the exact same thing as the Good Samaritan did in this twenty-first century. But we can do things likewise. We need to experience here and now something similar to what the original disciples experienced two thousand years ago.

By following Jesus, we enter into a radical openness to the will of God and we participate in God's plan of salvation. By following Jesus, we come to know who we are. By following Jesus, we experience salvation from God in Jesus Christ.

While following Jesus, however, we must remember that the person of Jesus is an unattainable goal; he is the Son of God. When Moses begged God to show him His glory, God told Moses that he could only see the back of God, only after God passed (Ex 33:17-23). This means God is always ahead of us. And our very ability to follow Jesus is made possible by Christ Jesus, who is always ahead of us.

To follow Jesus, we don't need to go to a school to learn how to be his disciples. We need not acquire mastery in theology. In fact, if we look carefully at today's gospel reading, Jesus sends out his disciples at a relatively early stage of his ministry. The disciples have stayed with Jesus for only a short while. They have probably learned the Sermon on the Mount and the Lord's Prayer. But they surely do not have any understanding of the death and resurrection of Jesus. Yet Jesus sends them to drive out demons and to heal the sick. (Perhaps we, in this twenty-first century, know more about Jesus than did the original disciples of Jesus.)

In the same way, we are called to follow Jesus, regardless of who we are and what we do. We follow Jesus in order to share his personal relationship with God. We follow Jesus even though it is a task that takes a lifetime. We follow Jesus knowing that our Lord will always be ahead of us and lead us to the bosom of God. Jesus Christ is the way, the truth, and the life (Jn 14:6). ✝

[12th OT (C), 13th OT (A), 13th and 15th OT (C)]

SIXTEENTH SUNDAY IN ORDINARY TIME (B)

(Jeremiah 23:1-6; Ephesians 2:13-18; Mark 6:30-34)

Christianity in the Postmodern Era

Christian mission means to bring a sense of holiness into the world. To do this, we need to know what the world looks like in the first place. A famous person once described the world as follows: "Ours is a time of religious decay; the permanent vitality of religion has been lost, the people have become either superstitious or indifferent to religion; the elite of society are agnostic and skeptical; the political leaders are hypocrites; the youth are in open conflict with the establishment; they are experimenting with eastern religions and techniques of meditation."

What I have just quoted describes the confusion and discontent of the twenty-first century and it appears to be written by a contemporary thinker. Surprisingly, however, it was written two thousand years ago by Tacitus (*Annals*, VI, 7), the Roman historian who wrote the history of Roman emperors including Tiberius and Nero. He also described the execution of Jesus by Pontius Pilate.

I have quoted this because our social and religious condition in this twenty-first century is not too much different from that in the first century. The young generation are restless and rebellious in any generation, and the old-age are stubborn and out-of-touch in any age. Therefore, we have a lot of missionary work to do.

In the gospel reading today, Jesus greeted his disciples back from their mission and asked them to rest. That happy moment did not last long. As Jesus and his disciples tried to find a quiet place, a huge crowd gathered. Jesus' "heart was moved with pity for them, for they were like sheep without a shepherd."

Why was Jesus' heart moved with pity? If Jesus were here with us in this twenty-first century, would his heart not also be moved with pity? Let us look closely at our current situation. Whether we realize it or not, we are swept by the cultural wind of postmodernism, which is protest or revolt against modernity. Modernity promised limitless progress based on human reason and technology. Human reason, however, could not explain the violence and cruelty of two World Wars and the monster that was Communism. Modernity died along with Auschwitz and Hiroshima, and postmodernity came about with the collapse of the Berlin Wall. As a result, we are slowly moving away from intellectual modernity and into foggy postmodernity.

(Postmodernity, in general, is comfortable with relative truth and subjective knowledge, rather than absolute truth and objective knowledge.)

In addition to postmodernity, we wake up every morning with what is called "globalization," which carries with it multi-cultural and multi-racial issues. As a result, some people believe God is dead and that religion has been the "opiate of the masses." Moreover, the rich and powerful are self-sufficient and don't need God. As a result, Christianity is confined to a small group of people. Catholic ethics is ridiculed as a minority opinion. Seeing these chaotic situations, if he were here with us, Jesus' heart would be moved with pity.

As Jesus' heart is moved with pity, our hearts also are moved with pity. So we ask ourselves, "What must we do? What must we do to help make Christianity credible once again?" Christianity holds on to God's love manifested in the person of Jesus; Christianity also maintains hope for the future under the Holy Spirit. As Christians, therefore, we are joyful and blessed in the presence of the living God and would like to see others be joyful and blessed also.

This means we must share with all the people in the world the Gospel of Jesus Christ, who is the sacrament of God and the paradigm of humanity. This means we must also share with them "the joy and hope and the grief and anguish" (*Gaudium et Spes*, #1), as we follow Jesus. Our task in the twenty-first century is not to save souls of pagans and infidels, but to share God's kingdom and eternal life with all peoples in the world. What Jesus asks us to do is to be open to God's love and mercy, and to follow him. ✝

[5ᵗʰ OT (C), 10ᵗʰ and 13ᵗʰ OT (A)]

SEVENTEENTH SUNDAY IN ORDINARY TIME (B)

(2 Kings 4:42-44; Ephesians 4:1-6; John 6:1-15)

"Give Us This Day Our Daily Bread"

It was a long, hot summer day—near dusk. The crowd followed Jesus all day long. They were hungry and thirsty. Jesus took pity on them. There was a boy nearby who carried five loaves of bread and two fish. Jesus multiplied those bread, and the disciples distributed them so that everyone received plenty. When all finished eating, the remaining bread filled twelve baskets, symbolizing the twelve tribes of the Israelites. This story, the Feeding of the Five Thousand, is recorded in all four Gospels, indicating that this miracle of Jesus is an undisputed historic fact.

The multiplication of the bread is interpreted in many ways. Of course, Jesus multiplied the bread in order to show that he was empowered by God the Father to announce the kingdom of God. Of course, it signifies the climax of Jesus' public ministry, because, having been fed abundantly, the crowd expected Jesus to be their king. Of course, it leads into the institution of the Eucharist at the Last Supper. Utilizing all these interpretations, the multiplication of bread provides clues as to how Jesus was concerned with our daily bread.

Let us take a close look at a deeper meaning of this miracle. We need bread and fish to sustain our bodies. We also have other desires to be satisfied, such as art, music, love, fame, friendship, knowledge, and scholarship. These are innate and natural desires that can be satisfied. For example, if we are hungry, we eat. If we are thirsty, we drink. If we hunger for music, we listen to Beethoven, Mozart, or Tchaikovsky.

However, we have a special desire for something divine, something beautiful, something everlasting, something true, and something sacred. We cannot precisely describe what it is, but deep down in our hearts, we desire something better, something different, and something more than before. This desire is "the holy longing," which God planted in our hearts. Until this desire is satisfied, we are left restless and anxious.

According to C. S. Lewis, such holy longing provides a proof for the existence of God. All our natural desires are related to specific objects that can be satisfied. Hunger is satisfied by eating food; thirst is satisfied by drinking water. In the same way, the holy longing is satisfied by God. Therefore, God exists.

In other words, our holy longing cannot be satisfied by any human means. This is why Jesus instituted the Eucharist on the night before he died. Let me explain, using the prayer Jesus taught us.

The Lord's Prayer shows us how our holy longing can be satisfied. As we know, the Lord's Prayer consists of three petitions about God, followed by four petitions about us, which begin with "Give us this day our daily bread." In this particular petition, however, we have an unusual use of similar words twice: "this day" and "daily."

According to scriptural scholars (Brant Pitre), the Greek word that is equivalent to "daily bread" was first used in the New Testament, and it means "super-substantial" (CCC #2837). The New Testament writers wanted to emphasize that the Eucharist is a supernatural food, like the manna from heaven (Ex 16:4), and that the Eucharist satisfies our holy longing. However, in my opinion, the "daily bread" means what it says, because there are too many people in hunger.

The miracle of the Feeding of the Five Thousand has many characteristics, in word and style, similar to those of the institution of the Last Supper. Both are about the supernatural food from God that satisfies our holy longing.

Jesus is truly concerned with what we desire. And so Jesus instituted the Eucharist to satisfy our holy longing. Thus we eat the bread of life and drink the cup of truth to participate in the divine life of God in the most intimate way. We share in Christ's salvation work by eating his flesh and drinking his blood. We encounter the risen Jesus through the Eucharist, which is the sacrament of Christ, our Lord.✝

[17th OT (C), 18th OT (A)]

Eighteenth Sunday in Ordinary Time (B)

(Exodus 16:2-4, 12-15; Ephesians 4:17, 20-24; John 6:24-25)

"I Am the Bread of Life"

We work hard to achieve a certain level of safety and security in life and to maintain social status and recognition. At the same time, we want to love our neighbors as Jesus loves us. However, it is not always easy to do both. It is fair to say that we live a dual life: one is the secular life, and the other the religious life.

For example, we attend Sunday Mass regularly, but our moral dispositions and ethical perceptions can remain more or less the same. Attending a Sunday Mass is like listening to a symphony at the Meyerson Center; high emotion dissipates rather quickly soon after Mass is over. And the love of neighbor is keeping the neighbor at a distance, if possible. When a gray situation develops, we do not want to be uncomfortable with our conscience.

Another example is the recent decline of the popularity of Pope Francis in US. This is most likely because of his Encyclical on climate change and his outspoken critique on the "the idolatry of money." It is indeed difficult to agree to what he says, while maintaining a typical American life-style.

So we ask ourselves: Why is it that our secular life is different from the religious life? How can we put into action what we pray? How can we live God's love, the love we feel during prayers? Today's gospel account provides answers to these questions.

Let us look closely at who we really are. We often hunger for something good deep inside of us; we do not know exactly what. We often long for something holy deep inside of us; we do not know exactly what. This is because, even though we are firmly grounded in this world, we want to transcend ourselves and move toward the unknown divine reality.

In other words, we have a natural desire and longing for God. We have holy longing within us. We are made for eternity. St. Augustine says, "God, you have made us for yourself." Thus only God can provide relief for the deep-down hunger and thirst within us; only God can satisfy that holy longing within us.

In today's gospel reading Jesus says, "I am the bread of life; whoever comes to me will never hunger, and whoever believes in me will never thirst." Jesus wants to satisfy our hunger and thirst; Jesus wants to satisfy our holy longing. So Jesus comes to us in the form of consecrated bread and wine.

The bread of life that Jesus offers is a free gift, however. It depends on neither our own merits nor our own accomplishments, but on God's goodness and gratuitousness. Therefore, the bread of life is always subjected to our own free will, which is often tempted by the world. This is why we remain in tension between God's kingdom and the secular world.

Actually, we live God's life in His kingdom. We may be rich and famous but still feel incredible hunger inside us. Fame and fortune do not satisfy our hearts. Nothing on earth but God can satisfy our hearts. St. Augustine continues to say, "Our hearts are restless until they rest in you."

This is why Christ Jesus continues to come to us in his body and blood. Jesus Christ continues to remind us of his death and resurrection, so that we may be sorrowful together with Christ in our own death, and we may be joyful together with Christ in our own resurrection. Slowly, we are transformed into new and clean hearts, and the spirits within us are renewed. We will be in union with God; we will be transformed into Christ. We will no longer be our "old selves"; we will be our "new selves."

Let us pray for God's grace, and that we will never forget the great truth that our hearts are made for God and will not rest until they rest in God. To forget this truth is to lose sight of one of the most important truths Jesus ever taught, "I am the bread of life." ✝

[19th and 20th OT (B)]

NINETEENTH SUNDAY IN ORDINARY TIME (B)

(1 Kings 19:4-8; Ephesians 4:30-5:2; John 6:41-51)

The Sacrament of Jesus Christ

We thirst for truth; we hunger for eternal life. Christ Jesus is the bread of life that satisfies our hunger and thirst.

In the Gospel passage, when Jesus says, "I am the bread of life," the Jews murmur. They murmur as their ancestors did in the Sinai desert (Ex 15:24 and 16:2). They want more of the same sweet and transitory bread, as their ancestors did. However, what Jesus offers them is the life-giving bread. And Jesus promises that whoever eats his life-giving bread will have eternal life.

The life-giving bread Jesus offers to us is the Eucharist. The Eucharist is the sacrificial meal of communion with God, because it is the action of Christ himself, as well as the action of the Church. And the communion with God in this world of fear, greed, and hatred is possible only with the gratuitous, spiritual food from Christ. Therefore, during the Eucharistic celebration, we continue Jesus' sacrificial suffering on the cross.

Some people may wonder, "Why does Jesus Christ come in the form of bread?" Our response would be, "Why not?" The fact that God is easily available in the form of bread and wine suggests God's complete freedom and, at the same time, His vulnerability. Both God's freedom and vulnerability are attributes of the unfathomable love of God.

For those who consider the Eucharist a mere symbol, and for those who have difficulty accepting that the Eucharistic meal is the real body and blood of Christ, I suggest the following. All Christians believe that Jesus Christ is the Word made flesh. If God has chosen human flesh to bear His Son, why is it not possible for God to let Jesus Christ remain in the Eucharist? If the incarnation is the manifestation of God in the flesh, then the Eucharist is the manifestation of Christ in the bread and wine. As we encounter God in the person of Jesus, so we "taste and see" Christ in the consecrated bread and wine. In other words, because we are bodily creatures, God has come to us in the body of Jesus of Nazareth, and Christ continues to come to us in the bodily form of bread and wine.

As Christ Jesus is the embodiment of God in the form of humanity, so the Eucharist is the embodiment of Christ Jesus in the form of the bread and wine. Christ Jesus is the sacrament of God, and the Eucharist is the sacrament of Christ. During the Eucharistic celebration, we renew the central action that God performs in the world—that is, the death and resurrection of Jesus, so that the Christ is continually present among us.

During the Eucharistic celebration, therefore, we are to participate actively in the paschal mystery of Jesus. Typically, however, we prefer to receive the Eucharist because we are creatures whose instinct is to be on the receiving end. Ideally, we receive the Eucharist in order to become another Eucharist for others. Having received the body of Christ, we fill the world with the glory of God and build the Body of Christ, the Church. In the Eucharistic celebration, the Church accomplishes what she was founded for; we enter into Christ's offering himself to God, and we make Christ present to the world. In this way, the Church draws her life from the Eucharist (*Ecclesia Eucharistica*, #1).

We come to this sacred altar when we are in joy, or fear, or sadness, or sorrow, or loneliness, or boredom, or relief, or hope. And we will surely encounter Jesus, who says, "Do this in remembrance of me" (1 Cor 11:24). So we do what Jesus tells us to do, trusting that God is good and faithful. By doing so together as a community, we transform ourselves into the Body of Christ.

Let us close with a prayer:

> *Thank you God for sending your Son Jesus,*
> *and thank you Jesus for staying*
> *always with us in the Eucharist.* ✝

[Corpus Christi (A, B, C)]

TWENTIETH SUNDAY IN ORDINARY TIME (B)

(Proverbs 9:1-6; Ephesians 5:15-20; John 6:51-58)

Foolish Wisdom

Jesus says, "I am the living bread that came down from heaven; whoever eats this bread will live forever; and the bread that I will give is my flesh for the life of the world."

To Jews, this saying of Jesus was very strange and absurd. It was only one day after that five thousand of them were well fed. Rather than providing them more food, Jesus said he is the bread from heaven (Ex 16). This means in order to attain eternal life, one must eat Jesus' flesh. But the Law was strictly against eating live animals or drinking their blood (Dt 13:23, Acts 15:29). The Jews were obviously confused and even insulted.

In the Bible, Jesus was at times described as possessing "foolish wisdom." He was accused of being insane by his family and being possessed with Satan by his opponents (Mk 3:21-22). So Jesus thanked God for hiding wisdom from the wise and the learned but revealing it to foolish children (Mt 11:25). Jesus of Nazareth reveals and at the same time hides God the Father.

Perhaps we are not comfortable with the idea of Jesus being a fool. We are familiar with the idea of God being almighty, all-powerful, ineffable, incomprehensible, and so on. On the other hand, isn't it true that God took a risk, a foolish risk, by creating human beings in his image and likeness? That is why we, like Adam and Eve, often try to be like God. Another example of God's foolishness is the cross of Jesus. When Jesus suffered on the cross, God would not rescue his only Son but did suffer with him. God had to let His Son die.

Actually, God is not almighty and all powerful all the time. Sometimes, God comes down into our daily life and share our joy and sorrow. God can be a fool. Indeed, God is a fool. God is a fool because God is love. Isn't love the most foolish and, paradoxically, the most powerful force in heavens and the earth?

Now that we accept that God possesses "foolish wisdom," let us look closely at the reality of the Eucharist in comparison with incarnation. All Christians believe that God was made flesh in the person of Jesus. Therefore, as the incarnation is self-emptying of God (Ph 2:5-11), so the Eucharist is self-emptying of Christ. As the love of God is manifested in the flesh, so the love of Christ is manifested in the bread and wine. In other words, the incarnation is the revelation of God in the flesh, and the Eucharist is the revelation of Christ in the bread and wine. God foolishly became man in Jesus, and God foolishly becomes Christ in the Eucharist. Therefore, the Eucharist is God's "foolish wisdom."

In the gospel reading today, Jesus says, "Unless you eat the flesh of the Son of Man and drink his blood, you do not have life within you." This means that the risen Jesus is present sacramentally in the consecrated bread and wine. (To those who must see before they believe, they remain just bread and wine. But to those who believe without seeing, they are the body and blood of the risen Jesus.) The Eucharist is the sacrament of the Christ.

Christ comes to us in the consecrated bread and wine, because he wants to become our flesh and blood. Christ comes to us in the consecrated bread and wine, because he wants us to be transformed into Christ. Indeed, the Eucharist is the simple and straightforward way for us to be transformed into Christ. (Incidentally, there is a classic called *Imitation of Christ*, but we are not called simply to copy or repeat the words and actions of Jesus. We are called to be transformed into Christ and put on the mind of Jesus.)

In a few minutes, we will meet at the Lord's Table and, filled with God's love, we will enter into his "foolish wisdom." At the same time, we are privileged to enter into our own "foolish wisdom," so that we will be liberated from our own egos and selfishness. To lose our selves foolishly in God is to find our true selves. Let us enter into the "foolishness" of Jesus and eat the body of Christ and drink his blood. **✝**

[4th Advent (A), Corpus Christi (B), 18th and 19th OT (B)]

TWENTY-FIRST SUNDAY IN ORDINARY TIME (B)

(Joshua 24:1-2, 15-17, 18; Ephesians 5:21-32; John 6:60-69)

"To Whom Shall We Go?"

The canoe race was added to the Olympic Games in Paris for the first time in 1924. A young man named Bill Havens was a member of the U.S. team. As the Olympics approached, it became clear that Bill's wife would give birth to their first child about the time Bill went to Paris. This presented Bill with a hard dilemma. If he went to Paris, he could not be at his wife's side when their first child was born.

Bill's wife suggested he should go to Paris. He had worked hard all these years, and being in the Olympic Games was his lifelong dream. But for Bill, the decision was made no easier by his wife's suggestion. Finally, Bill decided to withdraw from the team and stay with his wife so that he could be with her when their first child arrived.

To make the story more interesting, the U.S. canoe team won a gold medal. And Bill's wife was late in giving birth to the child. She was so late that Bill could have competed in the Olympic Games and still come home in plenty of time. Of course, some people said, "What a shame!" But Bill had no regrets.

The story of Bill Havens is a story of how one can pay a high price to fulfill his commitments to someone he loves. This story of commitment has a lot to do with today's scripture readings. The first reading deals with the fidelity and commitment of the Israelites to God's covenant before they occupied the Promised Land. The second reading deals with the fidelity and commitment of married couples to their wedding vows.

Finally, the Gospel is about the Eucharist, which is a covenant (Passover) meal that calls for a commitment of faith. After the long discourse of the Bread of Life, many disciples murmured to themselves, including those five thousand who were well fed. Eating the body of Jesus was simply too hard to swallow. They said, "This is a hard saying; who can listen to it?" And then, they decided not to listen to Jesus anymore, and they deserted him. Surprisingly, Jesus let them go, knowing that only faith accepts the Eucharist. This is the only occasion in the four Gospels where Jesus was deserted by his disciples (Brant Pitre, *Jesus and the Jewish Roots of the Eucharist*, p. 107). In other words, Jesus firmly insisted that he is the bread of life, which is convincing only in the commitment of faith.

Jesus told Peter, who represented the twelve, that he, too, could go. Peter answered, "To whom shall we go? You have the words of eternal life." As usual, Peter didn't fully understand Jesus' sayings, but he remained committed to Jesus.

Let us continue with the second half of Bill Havens' story. The child eventually born to Bill and his wife was a boy, who was named Frank. Twenty-eight years later, in 1952, Bill received a telegram from Frank sent from Helsinki, Finland, where the 1952 Olympic Games were being held. The telegram read, "Dad, I won. I'm bringing home the gold medal you lost while waiting for me to be born." Frank had just won a gold medal in canoe racing, the same medal his father had dreamed of winning.

This is a beautiful conclusion to a beautiful story. Bill Havens' commitment twenty-eight years ago became the inspiration for his son Frank who, in turn, made a commitment of his own to show his deep appreciation to his dad. And that is important to remember. The courage and hope with which parents live out their commitments to one another are carefully observed by their children. And children often use these traits for their own commitments.

The Church has been faithful in her commitment to the Eucharist for two thousand years. We, too, are faithful to our commitments in life—at home, work, and church, not because we have certainty regarding the future outcome, but because we have faith in Jesus Christ. "To whom shall we go? You have the words of eternal life." There is salvation in no one else but Jesus Christ. ✝

Twenty-Second Sunday in Ordinary Time (B)

(Deuteronomy 4:1-2, 6-8; James 1:17-18, 21-22, 27; Mark 7:1-8, 14-15, 21-23)

The True Religion

We often do not appreciate the air we breathe and the water we drink. In a similar way, we often do not appreciate that we are Catholics.

There are many different religions in the world. Some of them commit atrocities, even crimes, which cannot be erased from the history of mankind. For example, on November 18, 1978, 910 members of the Peoples Temple (Jim Jones) died from drinking grape juice poisoned with cyanide in Jonestown, Guyana. On April 19, 1993, David Koresh, the head of the Branch Davidians, along with 54 adults and 28 children, died in a fire on the cult's ranch near Waco, Texas.

Today's readings show some biblical characteristics of true religion. Before I point out those characteristics, let us first examine images of God in true and genuine religion in comparison to false and illusive religion. False religion says, "Fear not and trust in God. He will see that none of the things you fear will happen to you." In false religion, God solves problems in life. God is a "fixer." In contrast, true religion says, "Fear not and trust in God. The things that you are afraid of may actually happen to you, but they are nothing to be afraid of." In true religion, God does not solve all the problems in life. God is the "revealer" and "redeemer" and "helper."

Let us now look closely at some characteristics of true religion in today's readings. The first reading reveals one characteristic of true religion. God always takes initiative when communicating with the Israelites. God has primacy over His people. God has the last word in human history.

Another characteristic of true religion is seen in the responsorial psalm, which says, "He who does justice will live in the presence of the Lord." A person of justice lives blamelessly, doing no harm but instead bringing the good to others, and honoring those who fear the Lord. Justice is the virtue that makes love perfect. Love embraces justice and becomes genuine love.

Yet another characteristic of true religion is observed in the second reading. James insists that we should be "doers of the word and not hearers only." The truth of God is not to be admired or contemplated; it is to be acted upon. James also emphasizes the preferential love for the poor, orphans, and widows.

Still another characteristic of true religion is from the gospel reading. Against the Pharisees and scribes sent from Jerusalem, Jesus fiercely criticizes their legalistic attitude for paying only lip service to God, asking them to seek a new relationship with God from their hearts. Jesus insists that the law is not a binding shackle and that it shouldn't be observed rigidly. Jesus has demonstrated that he is the embodiment of God's kingdom and the end of the law (Rom 10:4).

Last, we see one more characteristic of true religion in today's Gospel. Jesus insists that what really defiles a person or not is not what goes into the mouth, but what comes out of the heart. For example, going to church, saying prayers, reading the Bible, and giving alms to the poor do not, by themselves, guarantee holiness. Purity of heart makes a person holy. Without purity of heart, life is illusive and deceptive. The closer one comes to God, the purer a heart one has. The goal of Christian life is, therefore, to attain this purity of heart, which is another name for salvation and redemption from God.

God has spoken to us through his Son, Jesus Christ, who has shown us that "God's love has been poured into our hearts" (Rom 5:5). God is not completely unknown. God is known in and through Jesus Christ.

In summary, true religion allows the living God to act; false religion allows man to act in the name of God. In addition, what counts most in religion is love from the heart. ✝

[6th Easter (B), 13th and 24th OT (B)]

211

TWENTY-THIRD SUNDAY IN ORDINARY TIME (B)

(Isaiah 35:4-7; James 2:1-5; Mark 7:31-37)

We Are Wounded Healers

Jesus Christ heals our wounds so that we can heal the wounds of our brothers and sisters. We are wounded healers. (Fr. Henri Nouwen coined these words in his book *Wounded Healers*.)

The gospel reading today shows Jesus, in a pagan territory, heals the man who is deaf and mute. We do not know his name or where he lives. What's more, the words spoken by him or by the people who brought him are not recorded in the Gospel. It is clear that St. Mark wants us to focus our attention on what Jesus says and does.

Jesus takes the deaf and blind man away from the crowd, and puts his fingers in the man's ears and touches the man's tongue with saliva. And then Jesus looks up to heaven and prays, "Ephphatha!" Jesus takes the man to a quiet and prayerful setting and allows the grace of God to break in by touching him personally.

The Gospel of Mark is unique among the Synoptic Gospels. There are no Beatitudes, no Lord's Prayer, and no parable of the Good Samaritan. Early in the Gospel, we witness Jesus' struggles with demonic forces in a scary and alarming way. Jesus confronts human darkness and misery and acts as an exorcist in the Gospel of Mark more than in any of the other Gospels.

A good example is the one of the Gerasene Demoniac in Chapter 5. The story is about a man possessed by an unclean spirit that calls itself "Legion, for we are many" (Mk 5:9), and he lives in a graveyard with his hands and legs chained, howling like a coyote at night. When we read this particular passage, we may find ourselves that we have dark and untreated emotions (*id* and *libido*) hidden deep in our unconscious psyche. These demonic forces are transpersonal forces that rob our freedom and trap our souls deep in a dark cave. Occasionally, we are imprisoned by such demonic forces. This is the reason why we need to be healed and saved by Jesus Christ.

Healing does not simply mean just getting well physically. Healing is to attain meaning and value in life, no matter what stage of life and condition we are in. Healing is to discover ways in which we can stand against the insecurity of the times. Healing is to find the source of strength to be whole and authentic persons.

Ultimately, healing is measured according to whether we are in communion with Jesus Christ. The ultimate healing must come from faith in the Spirit of Christ who dwells deep in our hearts. This means we are not merely objects of Jesus' healing. We are active moral agents in our existence on earth and can heal others in the Spirit of Jesus Christ. This is why Jesus usually says in his healings, "Your faith has healed you."

Faith in Jesus Christ guarantees not only the love of God in earthly life but also the hope for eternal life. So when we are sick or in trouble, we say, "Come, Lord Jesus."

The prophet Isaiah encouraged the Israelites not to lose hope because the Messiah would come. Isaiah also described the signs that would take place: "The ears of the deaf will be cleared... and the tongue of the mute will sing." As in today's Gospel, Jesus has already fulfilled the prophecy of Isaiah by healing the deaf and mute man.

This story of the deaf and mute man is our story. We are deaf and mute, if not physically, but emotionally, psychologically, or spiritually. Jesus opens our ears. Jesus loosens our tongues. The only difference is in the way Jesus performs miracles. He does not do them through his own hands and words. Rather, he does them through our deeds and our words.

We heal others and, at the same time, need to be healed. We say together, "Praise the Lord, my soul," because the healing ministry of Jesus is still going on today. Jesus heals us, encourages us, and strengthens us through good people just like you and me. We are wounded healers. †

TWENTY-FOURTH SUNDAY IN ORDINARY TIME (B)

(Isaiah 50:4-9; James 2:14-18; Mark 8:27-35)

Ubiquitous Suffering

We are not happy and joyful all the time. Sometimes we have pain and suffering. And we would like to stay away from it, if possible. Peter is no exception. In the gospel reading, Peter correctly identifies Jesus as the Messiah, but doesn't understand why the Messiah has to suffer and die. Jesus himself knows his suffering is inevitable and embraces it. Jesus asks his disciples to do the same, saying, "Whoever would save his life will lose it, but whoever loses his life for my sake and the gospels will save it." This scripture passage appears in all Synoptic Gospels (Mt 10:39, 16:25, Mk 8:35, Lk 9:24, 17:33). Jesus invites his followers to participate in his suffering. In return, he promises that they will be at the kingdom of God.

We see a prototype of Jesus' suffering from the first reading. The mysterious suffering servant, even if his back was scourged, his beard pulled out, and his face spat upon, remained faithful to God and maintained his human dignity. Biblical scholars do not know who this suffering servant was. We do know, however, that this scripture passage helped the disciples to recognize Jesus on the cross as Christ.

Suffering, all different kinds and shapes, is always with us, as a part of life. No one can acquire a virtue without understanding the lack of it. No one can be courageous without confronting fear. No one can be powerful without admitting weakness. No one can love without being hated. No one can possess chastity without suffering inordinate sexuality. Suffering is a natural consequence of being human.

About the constant presence of suffering, Pope Benedict says in his encyclical letter: "Suffering is a part of our human existence. Suffering stems partly from our finitude, and partly from the mass of sin which has accumulated over the course of history.... We must do all we can to overcome suffering, but to banish it from the world altogether is not our own power" (*Spe Salvi*, #36). We cannot avoid suffering, because suffering cannot be separated from joy in life. Suffering and joy are one, not two. They are both sides of one coin.

Accordingly, instead of trying to avoid or get rid of suffering, we ought to accept and embrace it. Pope Benedict continues to say, "It is not by sidestepping or fleeing from suffering that we are healed, but rather by our capacity for accepting it, maturing through it and finding meaning through union with Christ" (*Spe Salvi*, #37). Therefore, we are to learn how to transform our suffering into joy. The Son of Man came not get rid of our suffering, but to redeem it.

Thus the cross of Jesus has definitive redemptive values for us. The cross reminds us that we must die with Christ. Dying with Christ is the fundamental option of discipleship. So we die with Christ when we are faithful to the depths of our conscience, even if the world does not accept us. We die with Christ when we truly love someone who rejects us. We die with Christ when we accept incurable illness at an old age in sheer loneliness.

In the second reading, the apostle James shows how to accept and embrace suffering—by participating in the suffering of our neighbors. This is the mystery of suffering. This is what the cross of Jesus teaches us. This is what it means to die with Jesus Christ.

We are to share with our brothers and sisters their suffering. Otherwise, our faith in Jesus Christ is far from mature, and we will hang on to our own painful, excruciating, and self-centered suffering all the time. "Unless the grain of wheat falls into the ground and dies, it remains alone," says Jesus (Jn 12:24). Let us end with a poem, "Along the Road," from Fr. Link's homily book.

> *I walked a mile with Pleasure;*
> *She chattered all the way,*
> *But left me none the wiser*
> *For all she had to say.*

> *I walked a mile with Suffering*
> *And ne'er a word said she;*
> *But oh, the things I learned from her*
> *When Suffering walked with me.* ✝

[12th OT (C), 13th and 22nd OT (B)]

TWENTY-FIFTH SUNDAY IN ORDINARY TIME (B)

(Wisdom 2:12, 17-20; James 3:16-4:3; Mark 9:30-37)

Will We Recognize Jesus?

"God so loved the world that he gave his only Son" (Jn 3:16). When the Son of God actually came into the world, however, the world could not receive him. The condition of the world was such that it had to oppose and reject him.

What if the Son of God comes again? Will we recognize him and receive him? After all, we made a mistake once before. If we are to be honest with ourselves, many of us may not recognize Jesus even if he comes again. Why not? Why can we not recognize Jesus? We have such a longing for something holy deep in our hearts.

In the Gospel of Mark, Jesus predicts his own passion and death three times on the way to Jerusalem. After each prediction, he gives instructions on how to follow him (Mk 8:27-35, 9:30-37, and 10:32-34). The disciples misunderstand him every time and have wrong ideas about what it really means to be the disciples.

Today's gospel passage is about the second prediction of Jesus' passion. The disciples, as usual, are more concerned with their positions in an anticipated earthly kingdom. Jesus patiently waits for a quiet time until they are "inside the house" in Capernaum, and asks them what they were arguing about on the way. Jesus reminds his disciples that service to others in humility is most important in God's kingdom, and he puts his arms around a child to make his point. Children are pure in heart and solely depend on their parents.

This gospel account raises a few questions. How do we translate and incorporate Jesus' teachings into our own lives? How can we recognize Jesus if he comes again? What must we do to recognize him when he comes?

If we look carefully at ourselves, we see that we struggle between our efforts to secure safety and security in the world on one hand, and God's gift and grace on the other. We also struggle between individualism and selfishness on one hand, and God's love and mercy on the other. Slowly, we begin to listen to the voice of God deep inside us and to encounter the living God. Then conversion starts to take place, and the life of God takes hold of us. We are transformed from self-protection and self-cultivation into self-emptying and self-sacrifice for others. The ultimate end of conversion is to live for others, as Jesus did.

Why live for others? We live for others, because we attain inner freedom from our inherent tendency of narcissistic self-centeredness. We live for others, because we find our true selves by living for others. We live for others, because God is present with others, too. We live for others, because the love of God leads us to participate in His generosity and justice.

If we live for others, then we possess all things in Christ and are happy with all of God's creatures. If we live for others, then we see Jesus in them and walk with them. If we live for others, then we attain inner freedom and the spiritual poverty of what Jesus taught: "Blessed are the poor in spirit, for theirs is the kingdom of God" (Mt 5:3).

The life for others means simply to serve others in everyday life. For most of us, the life for others means that we live for our children, our spouses, our parents, and our neighbors. It means to come to this sacred place often to celebrate the Eucharist.

When we begin to live for others in this way, we begin to become like the Jesus in Scripture. Discipleship is not to follow Jesus by keeping rules and regulations. Discipleship is to change our values and dispositions so that we have the same attitude and character as Jesus. Discipleship is to have the same mind as Jesus (Phil 2:5).

Only when we have the same mind as Jesus, then—and only then—can we recognize Jesus who has been with us all along. ✝

[3rd Lent (B), 5th and 29th OT (B)]

TWENTY-SIXTH SUNDAY IN ORDINARY TIME (B)

(Numbers 11:25-29; James 5:1-6; Mark 9:38-43, 45, 47-48)

Insiders and Outsiders

God created all human beings "in the image and likeness of God" (Gen 1:26). This scripture passage from the Bible is one of the most frequently quoted. It also provides the foundation for social justice issues, as we have heard in the Letter of James for several weeks.

In the gospel reading today, a man is performing a good work. John, a disciple of Jesus, tries to stop him because the man is not one of them. Jesus, in a surprise move, asks his disciple to welcome the man, even though he is outside the inner circle of disciples. Jesus says, "Whoever is not against us is for us." And Jesus firmly lays out stringent instructions not to harm the outsider under any circumstances.

Today's first reading portrays a similar incident. When Joshua complains that two of Moses' assistants are prophesying outside of the "meeting tent," Moses does not agree with Joshua.

Both readings deal with insider-and-outsider tension, that is, the "us against them" attitude, which happens everywhere and in all walks of life. Knowingly and unknowingly, if someone is not one of us, we tend to look down and criticize what he or she does.

We live in a multi-cultural and multi-religious world. Christians and non-Christians of varying traditions mingle together in every corner of the globe. We are proud of being Catholics, but we are not isolationists or exclusivists. We are willing to learn God's goodness from other religions. Non-Christian religions may also provide different aspects of God's grace. No one religion alone can monopolize God, who "desires everyone to be saved" (1 Tm 2:4). "Mother Teresa never tried to convert a Muslim or a Hindu to Catholicism. She told her sisters that their job was not to talk about Jesus or even promote Jesus, but to be Jesus!" (Rohr, *The Naked Now*, p. 100) Nowadays, to be religious is to be interreligious.

According to Arnold Toynbee, a noted English historian, when the historian of a thousand years from now comes to write the history of our time, he will be preoccupied with what happened when Christianity and Buddhism began to penetrate one another deeply, not with the Vietnam War, not with the struggle between capitalism and communism, and not with racial conflicsts (Johnston, *Christian Zen*, p. 1). For example, Christian eschatology can learn from the non-dualistic thinking of life-and-death from Buddhism.

The Church recognizes "anonymous Christians," those who have no knowledge of God's salvation through Jesus Christ but live in a state of God's grace in faith, hope, and love. This pastoral doctrine is based on two principles. Jesus Christ is the only means of salvation from God, and God desires to save all, including atheists and non-Christians. And this doctrine requires a profound understanding of God's love for all and recognition that other human beings are entitled to the same love of God. Vatican II supports this doctrine (*Lumen Gentium*, #16).

In today's gospel account, we heard Jesus' saying, "If your hand causes you to sin, cut it off.... If your foot causes you to sin, cut it off.... If your eye causes you to sin, pluck it out." This firm teaching of Jesus illustrates the urgency of returning to moral and spiritual purity. If our hands hold on to the wrong idea of racial prejudice, if our feet stand on unhealthy religious exclucivism, and if our eyes only look with unfair ecclesial arrogance, Jesus asks us to correct them. It is not coincidental that these firm moral exhortations of Jesus appear immediately after his teaching on the insider-and-outsider..

We treat others as we want to be treated because they, too, are created in the image and likeness of God. We feed the hungry, clothe the naked, and visit the sick, because they, too, are the brothers and sisters of our Lord, Jesus Christ. ✝

[20th OT (B), 21st OT (C)]

TWENTY-SEVENTH SUNDAY IN ORDINARY TIME (B)

(Genesis 2:18-24; Hebrews 2:9-11; Mark 10:2-16)

The Sacrament of Marriage

Those who truly love know what love is. Those who know what love is also understand that God is love.

On the way to Jerusalem, the Pharisees asked Jesus the question of whether a husband could divorce his wife. At that time, John the Baptist was in prison for having criticized King Herod, who was living with his brother's wife. If Jesus answered "No," then he would make Herod angry. If he answered "Yes," he would disagree with John the Baptist, whom the people highly respected. It was a tricky question to trap Jesus.

In answering that tricky question, Jesus did not sink to the level of the Pharisees. Instead, Jesus revealed to them the will of God. Jesus said that people did divorce because of the hardness of their hearts. With the coming of the messianic age, he said, people should listen to God's intention and recover the original purity of marriage in order to find their "true selves."

This gospel passage brings us back to the story in the Book of Genesis. God, who created the heavens and the earth, allowed man to name all living beings by name. Then God realized it was not good for man to be alone. None of the living creatures were suitable as man's partner. So God created Eve from Adam's bone (rib). Adam joyfully welcomed her as his partner of equal dignity.

The story of Adam and Eve is about the mystery of man and woman and the deep-seated attraction between them. This attractive force between man and woman is so powerful that they leave their own mothers and fathers to cling to each other. Where does this powerful force come from? According to the Book of the Genesis, this force comes from God. The Book of Genesis also tells the remarkable story of the origin of human beings, with its lofty vision surrounding the union of man and woman.

The union of man and woman concerns the search for the other half of a person's own being rather than blind, impulsive, and uncontrollable instincts. In reality, however, marital love is often so discreet and confused that its original intention gets lost in the depths of anger, disagreement, frustration, and unfaithfulness.

Marriage is a sacrament. It is a union of two persons who are mysteries. Even though we know and love each other, we can always find something new with our spouses through God's eyes.

Marriage is a sacrament. It joins two persons so that both of them can participate in God's life. Marriage is the communion of love between two persons, as well as with God. In marriage, husband and wife are so fully sanctified and divinized that they are in union with God. Therefore, marriage belongs to the mystery of God.

Marriage is a sacrament. It consists of self-sacrificing, rather than self-seeking, love. Marriage is a sacred means to be in union with God, who is love. Love never completes by itself; love overflows into others; love is mutual and requires action. Love gives itself and hides its pain and suffering. Love is faithful until death and survives beyond death. Love bears all things, believes all things, hopes all things, and endures all things (1 Cor 13:7). Most of all, without love, everything is nothing.

The full meaning of love, however, cannot be understood in this life on earth; we can only foretaste it. As long as we are on earth, our human love is in the process of fulfillment. When God's kingdom is completed, our love will also be fulfilled and satisfied.

The sacrament of marriage means to share God's own life by loving each other. This is the message of Jesus' teaching. We must abide this intention of God and be happy and joyful as sons and daughters of God. We live together in God's kingdom, which can be fulfilled by our mutual love. †

[30ᵗʰ OT (A)]

TWENTY-EIGHTH SUNDAY IN ORDINARY TIME (B)

(Wisdom 7:7-11; Hebrews 4:12-13; Mark 10:17-30)

The Rich Young Man

When we do a favor to our neighbor, we feel good. When we visit the sick in a hospital, we feel honored. And we know there are such things as eternal life and the kingdom of God. We search for something good, and we long for something holy, because we have hunger for God deep inside us.

The rich young man in today's Gospel also has hunger for God. He asks Jesus, "What must I do to inherit eternal life?" The young man asks how to cultivate his hunger for God so that he can be with God. Apparently, he possesses a large tract of land, along with many animals and servants. He keeps God's commandments faithfully, but still thinks he lacks something. He wants something deeper and more fulfilling in his life. He thinks Jesus can provide that.

Having heard from this rich young man, Jesus is happy. Surprisingly, however, Jesus tells him that keeping the commandments is not enough. Jesus asks him to sell what he has and give it to the poor, and then follow him. It is precisely when he is truly empty himself, then he can be infused with God's grace to help the poor. What Jesus wants is his radical commitment for self-emptying so that his heart is filled God's love and wisdom. Therefore, the young man has a choice either to stay on his farm or to follow Jesus on the road.

The rich young man needs to be on the road when Jesus cures the crippled and heals the sick. He needs to be on the road when Jesus is accused by the Pharisees and scribes. He needs to be on the road when Jesus is rejected by his own people. He needs to live his life together with Jesus in order to make what is important to Jesus his own. To know and love Jesus, he needs to follow Jesus on the road (Acts 9:2, 19:9, 19:23, 22:4). Unfortunately, "he went away sad, for he had many possessions."

Like the rich young man, we have hunger for God. We search for our true selves. We want to be authentically human by transcending ourselves. And we want to cultivate our divine nature to be with God. So we must encounter the sacred humanity of Jesus, the Word Incarnate. Jesus is both the fulfillment of God's promise and the perfect paradigm of humanity. Jesus Christ is man in the most divine way and also God in the most human way. Jesus Christ is the human way of being God and the divine way of being human.

St. John Paul II wrote in his encyclical, which begins with the story of the rich young man, states "Christian life (morality) consists, in the simplicity of the Gospel, in following Jesus Christ, in emptying (abandoning) ourselves to him, in letting us be transformed by his grace and renewed by his mercy... in the living communion of his Church" (*Veritas Splendor*, #119).

Therefore, to be able to laugh when Jesus laughs, we need to be on the road with Jesus. To be able to cry when Jesus cries, we need to be on the road with Jesus. To be able to experience how God loves us, we need to be on the road with Jesus.

Ultimately, to be on the road with Jesus, we must first empty ourselves; we must lose everything and have nothing (*todo y nada*); that is, we must prepare ourselves to die many deaths. We must die to ourselves so as to live with God, because only by dying we come to a life. This is what it means by the death and resurrection of Jesus—the unchangeable paradigm of the human face of God.

The German theologian Dietrich Bonhoeffer wrote in *The Cost of Discipleship*, "When Jesus calls a man to come, he asks him to come and die." "What kind of death is it?" we wonder. It is the death of our desire to have more money and higher honor. It is the death of our pride to control and manipulate others. It is the death of our selfishness that wants to adhere to our "old selves" (Rom 6:5) covered with "garments of animal skins" (Gen 3:21).

We have hunger for God. When God's grace breaks into our lives, it demands our responses in the form of discipleship. Therefore, to experience the reality of God in Jesus, we must empty ourselves and then follow him on the road. ✝

[6ᵗʰ OT (A), 8ᵗʰ OT (C)]

Twenty-Ninth Sunday in Ordinary Time (B)

(Isaiah 53:10-11; Hebrews 4:14-16; Mark 10:35-45)

Servant Leadership

"For the Son of Man did not come to be served, but to serve, and to give his life as a ransom for many." This final sentence of today's gospel passage is one of the most paradoxical sentences in Scripture, and yet it succinctly sums up the life of Jesus and the ground of our salvation from God.

Jesus was convinced that he was the embodiment of God and destined to go to Jerusalem. Jesus had to fulfill God's promises to His people. For the disciples, it was unthinkable that their Messiah would suffer and die. They could not understand why Jesus predicted his suffering and death—not once, but three times.

God's plan of salvation was different, however. Jesus had to become the object of human sinfulness and atrocities. Therefore, Jesus' passion and death on the cross was the atoning sacrifice for human sin, as we heard in the second reading.

God raised Jesus on the third day. The resurrection of Jesus defeated sin and death for all mankind, bringing in a new age. The resurrection of Jesus once again joined the heavens and the earth. The resurrection of Jesus allowed disciples to come to the new understanding that Jesus was the Messiah, who indeed did suffer. And the mysterious suffering servant, as the psalmist first predicted, played a critical role in understanding the Messiah who suffered, as we heard in the first reading.

In today's gospel reading, when James and John ask for high positions in an earthly kingdom, Jesus tells them that suffering is inevitable and necessary. In the Gospel of Matthew, it is their mother who asks a special favor of letting her two sons, James and John, to sit next to Jesus, one each on his right and left (Mt 20:20). To their surprise, Jesus offers them a share in his cup of suffering.

In God's eyes, to serve is to suffer. Suffering and service are the same in Christian discipleship. The resurrection of Jesus is a victory over death, but it does not mean that we will not die. In the same way, the passion of Jesus has redeemed human suffering, but it does not mean that we will not suffer.

Accordingly, Christian discipleship is for the service of others. And Christian leaders, who are responsible for Christian communities, must understand and exercise their authority and responsibility not from power, but from servitude. This is called servant leadership, which begins with the conviction that one wants to serve. Then conscious choice brings one, or a few, naturally to lead others.

By contrast, too often in our world, leadership means exercising power over the powerless. Jesus must have known this, because, in Scripture, aphorisms such as "the last will be the first" (Mk 9:35, 10:31) and "do not lord it over" (1 Pt 5:3, Mk 10:42-44, Mt 20:25-27, Lk 22:25-26) appear repeatedly.

There was a boy who came home late from school every day. His father sat him down one evening and told him, "The next time you come home late, you will have bread and water only. Nothing else, understand?" A few days later, the boy came home late as usual. That night when they sat together at the dinner table, the father's and mother's plates were filled with foods of usual kinds, and his sister's plate also. But the boy's plate contained a few slices of bread with a glass of water next to it. With a hungry and twisted stomach, the boy's heart immediately froze, and his eyes opened wide. The father waited for the full impact to sink in. Suddenly, he reached out, took the boy's plate, and replaced it with his own plate. Then they offered the prayer before the meal.

Years later, the boy recalled the incident and said, "What my father did on that night taught me who God is. And I have known God as love and mercy all my life long." This is a love story, because love entails service, and service entails self-sacrifice for others. ✝

[12th OT (C), 25th OT (B), 31st OT (A)]

THIRTIETH SUNDAY IN ORDINARY TIME (B)

(Jeremiah 31:7-9; Hebrews 5:1-6; Mark 10:46-52)

Following Jesus on the Way

We have been on a journey with Jesus for the last six months. This journey, which started from Caesarea Philippi in northern Galilee, will soon end in Jerusalem. In the course of our journey, we witnessed Jesus healing a blind man in Bethsaida, on the eastern shore of the Sea of Galilee. After being healed slowly, the blind man wanted to follow Jesus, but Jesus sent him home.

In today's gospel reading, Jesus heals another blind man in Jericho, the city on a foothill between the Jordan River and Jerusalem, seventeen miles from Jerusalem. Jesus and his disciples were about to depart to Jerusalem, when suddenly, Bartimaeus demanded to see Jesus. The disciples were annoyed by his shouting and yelling, so they told him, "Shut up!" But Bartimaeus did not shut up.

Finally, Jesus called him over and asked, "What do you want me to do for you?" Throwing off his old clothes, Bartimaeus ran to Jesus, saying, "I want to see." Moved by his faith, Jesus opened his eyes. Bartimaeus was able to see instantly who Jesus was and then followed Jesus on the way to Jerusalem. This healing of a blind beggar in Jericho was Jesus' last miracle before his death in Jerusalem.

Between these two healing episodes, Jesus predicted his passion and death three times according to the Gospel of Mark. After each prediction, Jesus taught his disciples how to follow him. Jesus' teachings on the discipleship include topics such as the suffering Messiah, greatness in the community, tolerance toward outsiders of good will, fidelity in marriage, accepting the kingdom of God as a gift, wealth as a potential obstacle for salvation, servant leadership, and so on. The disciples did not comprehend any of Jesus' teachings. Instead, they wished aloud for prestigious positions in an earthly kingdom. On the way to Jerusalem, Jesus revealed God the Father to his disciples by revealing himself. But the disciples did not understand Jesus; they were blind.

Disciples' constant ignorance of Jesus' teachings needs to be considered against the healing episodes of two blind men: one Gentile in Bethsaida, one Jew in Jericho. Particularly, Bartimaeus in Jericho understood who Jesus was, because even before he met Jesus face to face, he called Jesus "the son of David." And after gaining his sight, he followed Jesus all the way to Jerusalem.

We know that the disciples of Jesus also followed him to Jerusalem, but they scattered as soon as he was arrested. Only Peter followed Jesus, denying him three times. On the contrary, Bartimaeus followed Jesus, and perhaps, remained under the cross of Jesus along with John and Mary. So far, we have talked about healing episodes of two blind men against disciples' ignorance of Jesus teachings, as if we are in a Bible study group. What does all these means?

"Opening the eyes of the blind man" is a metaphor for transforming his consciousness from ignorance to accepting Jesus as the Messiah. Of course, "the healing the blind man" is the work of God's grace. And, as Jesus said to Bartimaeus, "Your faith has saved you," it requires human will to manifest and fulfill God's grace. In addition, Jesus uses the word "see" quite frequently in the Bible to invoke his transformative power. In the Gospel of John, Jesus asks Andrew and another disciple, "Come and see." Jesus tells them later, "You will see greater things than these."

The reason why Jesus opened the eyes of Bartimaeus is that Jesus wants him to wake up from his inherent ignorance and see the light of Christ. In the same way, Jesus wants his disciples to wake up from the fouled-up Torah consciousness and see the kingdom of God. Finally, Jesus wants all of us to wake up and live the interior life centered on Christ consciousness, as children of God.

Bartimaeus was able to attain Christ consciousness and lived the life exemplified by Jesus of Nazareth. Strange enough, however, he was given neither a formal title nor an official duty by the Church. I like Bartimaeus, because he was able to see God in the person of Jesus. And I like to be Bartimaeus, because he was courageous enough to follow Jesus all the way to Jerusalem. ✝

[3rd OT (A)]

Thirty-First Sunday in Ordinary Time (B)

(Deuteronomy 6:2-6; Hebrews 7:23-28; Mark 12:28-34)

How Can We Be Good Christians?

We often ask ourselves, "How can we be good Christians?" A variety of answers are possible: go to Mass every Sunday, follow the teachings of the Church, be concerned about justice and peace in the world, experience the gifts of the Spirit, and the like.

Jesus' adversaries confront him with similar questions as he makes his solemn entry into Jerusalem. Pharisees and Herodians ask a question about paying taxes. Some Sadducees demand an answer to a question about seven brothers who shared one wife. In today's Gospel, one of the scribes asks Jesus a question, "Which is the first of all the commandments?"

Jesus' answer to the question is the well-known prayer among the Jews—the *Shema Israel.* "Hear, O Israel! The Lord our God is Lord alone. You shall love the Lord your God with all your heart, with all your soul, with all your mind, and with all your strength."

I would like to share with you the story of Viktor Frankl, the Swiss-born, Jewish neurologist and psychologist who founded logotherapy. The story takes place during Frankl's imprisonment in a German concentration camp during World War II.

As is the usual practice in concentration camps, everything was stripped from him—all his clothes and even the hairs from his body. He was desperate to hide the summary notes that would later become the foundation of logotherapy. But they were eventually confiscated by the Germans. At that moment, Frankl felt that he had lost everything he had accomplished. He felt his whole life had been wasted.

Later on, when he picked up a jacket left by another prisoner, he found a small piece of paper in the pocket. In it, there was a note that said, "You shall love your God with all your heart, all your mind, and all your strength." He immediately realized that his life was worth living, even under the brutal and inhumane conditions of the concentration camp. The presence of the living God brought him a new life.

St. Irenaeus of Lyon said, "The glory of God is the human being fully alive." Therefore, for us to be fully alive, we must love God with all our heart, with all our soul, with all our mind, and with all our strength. In other words, if we realize that God, who is love, is the real and genuine foundation of our being, then we will be fully alive and God will be glorified. Pope Benedict says, "Man needs God, otherwise he remains without hope" (*Spe Salvi*, #23).

Returning to Jesus' answer to the scribe's question, Jesus furthermore gave this second commandment to the scribes: "You shall love your neighbor as yourself." This commandment means that we love our neighbors naturally and spontaneously, as if they are ourselves, because "God makes his sun rise on the evil and the good, and sends rain on the righteous and the unrighteous" (Mt 5:45).

The evangelist John says, "Those who do not love a brother or a sister, whom they have seen, cannot love God, whom they have not seen" (1 Jn 4: 20). The love of God is the foundation of our being, whereas the love of our neighbors is the realization of the love of God. The love of God and the love of neighbors are inseparable and are two sides of the same coin. By becoming one with our neighbors in love, we also become one with God, who is love.

Finally, we are ready to answer the question raised earlier: "How can we be good Christians?" The answer is to love God and to love our neighbors. This Christian love, however, does not concern our desire or conviction to love, but instead concerns the faith that we are loved by God in spite of our unworthiness and sinfulness. It is the love that comes from God, because "God first loved us" (1 Jn 4:19).

Love is the prime gift of God for us to be fully alive. Whatever else is freely given to us becomes a gift only through love. **✝**

[2nd Advent (C), 30th OT (A)]

THIRTY-SECOND SUNDAY IN ORDINARY TIME (B)

(1 Kings 17:10-16; Hebrews 9:24-28; Mark 12:38-44)

The Preferential Option for the Poor

Jesus of Nazareth has finally entered Jerusalem. The long journey, which started from Caesarea Philippi in northern Galilee, has come to an end. To the surprise of his disciples, Jesus cleans the temple as soon as he enters Jerusalem. This angry act is like as if the guest we invited into our house turns the coffee table upside down and throwing away cups and napkins in our living room. In addition to such an angry and provocative act, Jesus confronts Sanhedrin members (Mk 11:28), the Pharisees and Herodians (Mk 12:13), the Sadducees (Mk 12:18), and the scribes (Mk 12:38), upsetting them all. Jesus is a fearless champion of God's cause against the powerful religious leaders.

The gospel reading today concerns what happens the following day. Jesus goes to the Temple and observes two different types of people. One is rich people who give only a small portion out of abundance. The other is a widow who gives all she has—a few coins. The rich people, who have dedicated only a portion of their possessions, will continue to live well with their remaining surplus. But the poor widow has given to God everything she has. Now she has nothing left. She has emptied herself completely. Looking at her, Jesus identifies himself with her, anticipating his own self-emptying on the cross.

We heard the story of another widow in the first reading. Although she had only a handful of flour and a little oil in the midst of a severe drought, the prophet Elijah asked her to make a cake for him. She gave him her last meal. Because of that generosity, God blessed her with abundant flour and oil for the rest of her life.

In an ancient society, a widow was the most vulnerable person. Having no means to support herself, she was shut out of society without hope for the future. She had to rely on God. Accordingly, the widow in the Gospel gave all she had to God. She transcended herself, by emptying her ego and selfishness. She went through a process of losing herself in order to find herself anew (Mk 8:35, Mt 10:39, Lk 17:33, Jn 12:25). On the other hand, the rich people, having all convenient things in life, didn't depend on God. They were proud of what they had, boasting their self-sufficiency and self-absorption.

In order to harmonize the rich and the poor, the Church teaches "the preferential option for the poor." The doctrine is a special form of God's primacy for exercising charity. It says that "God's heart has a special place for the poor." (*Evangelii Gaudium*, #199), and thus the poor are closer to God than the rich. However, this doctrine does not mean that God loves the poor more than the rich, because God is the unconditional love. It is true that the socio-economic system in a society is often tailored by the rich at the expanse of the poor (the critical theory). It is also true that the poor shouldn't sit around quietly, waiting for the free hand-outs from the rich.

Actually, the preferential option for the poor provides an excellent paradigm for Christian charity. We know that Jesus identified himself completely with the whole human race and emptied himself on the cross. In the same way, Christian charity, such as helping the poor, comes from self-emptying, which in turn naturally comes from identifying oneself with the poor. In other words, unless we let go our own selfish ego, we cannot help the poor. Mother Theresa, for example, only after having emptied herself, and then helped the poor, because she encountered the risen Jesus in them. The doctrine of the preferential option for the poor provides a warning against ever-present greed and delusion for both the poor and the rich. God challenges the rich as well as the poor for building the kingdom of God on earth.

Before he faces his own death, Jesus empties himself and indentifies with the poor. The preferential option for the poor summaries this simple act of Jesus in Jerusalem. This doctrine not only confirms the fundamental unity of the love of God and the love of neighbors, but also provides reasons to hope, which is the basis of Christian charity. Accordingly, this doctrine is the way through which we can be union with God here and now on earth. **✝**

[26th OT (C), Christ King (A)]

THIRTY-THIRD SUNDAY IN ORDINARY TIME (B)

(Daniel 12:1-3; Hebrews 10:11-14, 18; Mark 13:24-32)

Apocalypse and Messianic Expectation

Those at the end of a rope or who have experienced extreme hardships in life often achieve remarkable things in later years. In this regard, Helen Keller was an American heroine. She became deaf and blind when she was only nineteen months old. But she became the first deaf-blind person to earn a Bachelor of Arts degree (from Radcliffe College, the Harvard University), and she had a long and productive life as an author and lecturer.

The people of Israel experienced numerous invasions by foreign powers. During the three centuries before and then after the time of Jesus, Assyrians, Babylonians, Egyptians, Greeks, and Romans successively invaded Israel. These times did not span just ten or twenty years, but five to six hundred years. Israel was at the bottom of history's pot. The Jews needed to find a means to endure their sufferings and tribulations. As a result, their dreams and hopes for the future were delegated to the archangel Michael, who waged a war in heaven against Israel's enemies on earth. Of course, the angel Michael won the war; subsequently, only those "found written in the book of life" will be resurrected, as we heard in the first reading.

This literature genre is called apocalypse, and its purpose is to provide reason to hope during extremely troubled times (the apocalyptic imagination). Here, the Jews hope that the present world, with its sufferings and troubles, will end soon. Their hope for a future Exodus also includes the coming of the Messiah (the messianic expectation), who will bring judgment on enemies right before cosmic catastrophes.

Jesus of Nazareth, a first-century Jew, was naturally familiar with the Jewish apocalyptic literature and anticipated the end-time to come. In today's gospel reading, Jesus says that, after the tribulations, there will be cosmic catastrophes such as "the sun will be darkened, and the moon will not give its light, and the stars will be falling from the sky." And then the Son of Man will come "with great power and glory."

Here, Jesus refers to his own death and resurrection. He imagines that the pain and suffering are very much like cosmic catastrophes. He also hopes that God will raise him up on the last day. In the meantime, Jesus asks his disciples to be attentive and persevere, using the "fig tree" analogy.

The apocalyptic imagination and messianic expectation are not just for the ancient Israelites. We, too, cannot escape pain and suffering in life. And we always hope for a better future. We suffer and inevitably persevere, which is the Jewish apocalypse. And we dream and hope, which is the Jewish messianic expectation.

Liturgically, we are about to begin a new year and prepare ourselves for the coming of the Messiah. Therefore, the Church wants us to reflect on our present condition and, at the same time, hope for the future when God's promise will be fulfilled. The Church wants us to sort out our present situations in order to focus on God's future.

The focus on the future is not withdrawal from the world in anticipation of a better future. Rather, it calls for active participation in the present world in order to speed up the coming of the new world.

We hope that God's kingdom will be fulfilled when Jesus Christ comes again. And we look forward to the end-time when Christ will make all things new. Our hope for the future is the key to our present existence. As a result, the present is connected to the future, and the future has a transformative power over the present. For Christians, hope and faith cannot be separated.

St. Peter said, "Always be ready to make a defense to anyone who asks for the reason for the hope that is in you" (1 Pt 3:15). Where there is life, there is hope. To live is to hope. We live as long as we hope. We live as much as we hope. ✝

[1ˢᵗ Advent (C), 28ᵗʰ OT (A), 33ʳᵈ OT (C)]

OUR LORD JESUS CHRIST THE KING (B)

(Daniel 7:13-14; Revelation 1:5-8; John 18:33-37)

The King of Kings

Among the many titles Jesus has garnered—such as Good Shepherd, Messiah, Priest, Prophet, Teacher, the Son of Man, and the Son of God—the title "King" would be least fitting for Jesus in this twenty-first century.

Pontius Pilate, too, was afraid of Jesus being King, and asked, "Are you the king of the Jews?" Jesus accepted Pilate's insight and answered, "My kingdom does not belong to this world." Jesus, however, assured Pilate that his kingdom would stand strong, saying, "For this I was born and for this I came into the world."

On this, the last Sunday of the liturgical year, we remind ourselves that Jesus Christ is the King in whom we have eternal life. Only through Jesus Christ will God save us and help us to find the meaning of life. Let us first review how the disciples of Jesus accepted him as their King.

From our first reading in the Book of Daniel, we heard that the Son of Man, the mysterious heavenly being, comes on the clouds of heaven and is glorified by the Ancient One. This particular scriptural passage was important for the disciples of Jesus to recognize Jesus as the Son of God. The Ancient One was equivalent to God in the Canaanite mythology, and Jesus called himself the Son of Man. Therefore, after Jesus was raised from the dead, the disciples of Jesus were able to recognize Jesus as the Messiah who received "dominion, glory, and kingship" from God the Father.

In addition, some Christians who anticipated the return of the risen Christ composed the Book of Revelation. They identified the risen Jesus as "the Alpha and the Omega and the one who is and who was and who is to come." They also claimed that the risen Jesus made them priests in a kingdom, as we heard from the second reading.

So we wonder what makes Jesus Christ the King in this twenty-first century. Let us first consider what we are, how we are structured, and who we are, and then consider why Jesus is the King.

If we think about ourselves, we constantly search for the meaning of life, and we long for eternal life. Oftentimes we are confused with things of this world. But we make progress slowly and steadily toward salvation in the midst of dark existential anxieties and sinfulness. Salvation here is not some reward for the virtuous life we lived after death. Salvation means to make ourselves whole and authentic in the presence of God. Salvation means to share in God's life (2 Pt 1:4). Deep in our hearts, then we know that our salvation cannot come from things of this world. Only from God comes our ultimate salvation.

Jesus Christ is the Word Incarnate. Jesus Christ is the sacrament of God. Jesus is the mediator between God and man. This means that God's self-giving love in the person of Jesus has become a condition that is necessary for us to be whole and authentic—that is, to be redeemed and be saved. Pope Benedict says in his encyclical, "(Christ) tells us who man truly is and what a man must do to be truly man" (*Spe Salvi*, #6). Therefore, we can be in union with God by transcending ourselves and thus participating in God's plan of salvation in and through Jesus Christ.

Moreover, Jesus Christ has brought us the eschatological hope for the future. This means that the present is always oriented to the future and that the future is always projected from the present. Therefore, we can now live the divine life of God and find the true meaning of life.

Jesus Christ is the source of life. Jesus Christ is what we are looking for and what we are searching for. We can find the meaning of life and be saved only through the person of Jesus Christ. Jesus Christ is the King. He has shown us the face of God, and he has lived the authentic human life. He has made us sons and daughters of God and opened the door of salvation for all. Jesus Christ is the King yesterday, today, and tomorrow (Heb 13:8). †

[1st Advent (C), Nativity Vigil]

YEAR C

First Sunday of Advent (C)

(Jeremiah 33:14-16; 1 Thessalonians 3:12-4:2; Luke 21:25-28, 34-36)

The Son of Man Who Comes in a Cloud

When the disciples of Jesus found out that Jesus was the Messiah, how did they feel? As we begin a new liturgical year and celebrate the first Sunday of Advent, we want to capture the same emotion and conviction as the disciples of Jesus had when they convinced themselves that Jesus was the Messiah.

Advent is the season to prepare for the first coming of Jesus in flesh, as well as for his final coming in glory. Surprisingly, however, in today's readings we do not find any word about "the coming of Jesus," whether it be the first coming or the second. Instead, we hear in the Gospel of cosmic catastrophes—the sun darkens, the moon fades away, the earth trembles, and the roaring sea engulfs the land. We know how terrible these cosmic catastrophes can be as we remember the horrific tsunami damage of Indonesia and Japan in past years.

Those cosmic catastrophes and natural disasters are, no doubt, metaphors for our present confused and destructive situations; they symbolize the end of the world. We wonder, then, why the Church wants us to reflect upon these terrible things. We would rather reflect upon the beautiful Infancy Narratives or the passionate Good Samaritan while we wait for the coming of the Messiah.

The literature genre of today's gospel reading is called "Jewish apocalypse." Apocalyptic literature was popular several hundred years before and after the time of Jesus. Ancient Jews, having been oppressed by brutal foreign powers so long, endured their present miseries by hoping for a bright future (apocalyptic imagination) and anticipating the Messiah, who would free them (messianic expectation). And cosmic catastrophes, which occur immediately prior to the coming of the Messiah, are indicative of imminent judgments upon the enemy.

238

In the Synoptic Gospels, apocalyptic passages appear before Jesus' passion and death. This means the coming event of Jesus' passion and death is equivalent to a cosmic catastrophy, which is followed by a new world order brought in by Jesus' resurrection.

In today's gospel reading, Jesus says, "They will see the Son of Man coming in a cloud with power and great glory." This gospel passage from the Book of Daniel was the key for Jesus' disciples to identify the crucified and risen Jesus. They remembered another passage from the same Book: "To him was given dominion and glory and kingship, which all peoples, nations, and languages should serve him" (Dn 7:14). Because Jesus called himself the Son of Man, who is "the heavenly being" in Jewish apocalyptic literature, the disciples were able to discover that the crucified and risen Jesus was indeed the Messiah, who inherited the dominion and glory and kingship from God the Father.

Hoping for a bright future and waiting for the Messiah are not just for the first-century Jews; we do the same in our daily lives. We have difficulties and problems, and so we hope that things will turn out all right tomorrow. We are confident that we will soon abide God's will, and so we wait for the coming of Jesus Christ.

Accordingly, the Church wants us to look closely at our present situations and aspire to the same conviction as the disciples of Jesus when they recognized the crucified Jesus as the Messiah. In other words, the Church wants us to understand that nothing in this world lasts forever and that the Messiah, Jesus of Nazareth, will bring the ultimate meaning of life. This is why we reflect upon the apocalyptic passages this first Sunday of Advent.

As we begin the season of Advent, we need to reaffirm our discipleship and renew our commitment to Jesus Christ, who has shown us the human face of God. Just as the early Christians realized that Jesus was the Messiah, who brought in a new world, the Church encourages us to embrace the same emotion and conviction, by receiving Jesus as the Christ in our hearts. **✝**

[28ᵗʰ OT (A), 33ʳᵈ OT (B), 33ʳᵈ OT (C)]

SECOND SUNDAY OF ADVENT (C)

(Baruch 5:1-9; Philippians 1:4-6, 8-11; Luke 3:1-6)

Dr. Viktor Frankl

Advent is the season of hope. We hope the Messiah will come into our hearts.

Hope is the main theme in today's readings. In the first reading, the prophet Baruch hoped for the return of the Israelites from Babylon to Jerusalem. To help them come home, God would build a highway by leveling mountains and filling valleys. Joy would spring from misery and sadness. The people of Jerusalem, standing at the highest point of the city, would hail the returning exiles and rejoice at their homecoming.

In the gospel reading, John the Baptist announces the coming of the Messiah, using the same metaphors as in the first reading. Rather than the captivity in Babylon, however, he speaks of the captivity in the old Jerusalem, which has been ruthlessly occupied by the Roman Empire and terribly mismanaged by the temple authorities. Now that the Messiah is coming, John calls for an exodus from the old Jerusalem—a liberation from sin and death. John asks for repentance, *metanoia.*

To hope is not just to expect a bright future by escaping present miseries. To hope is to look for redemption from God, in faith and love. To hope is to accept God's invitation to live eternal life, combining the present and the future together.

To illustrate how to hope in a miserable situation, I will share with you the story of Dr. Viktor Frankl, the founder of logotherapy, an existential psychoanalysis. In his book *Man's Search for Meaning*, Dr. Frankl describes his survival of German concentration camps during World War II. As a result, existential psychotherapy, particularly the meaning of suffering, was tested and shaped. Even under inhumane conditions, Frankl maintained his inner strength and exercised the freedom to choose his own destiny.

According to Dr. Frankl, most prisoners in concentration camps believed that the life's real opportunities ended sadly. Those prisoners, who comforted themselves momentarily by smoking cigarettes, had already lost their hold on life. Because they had lost faith in the future, they were doomed. On the other hand, those prisoners, who searched for the meaning of life, continued to live. They knew that important tasks awaited them.

According to Dr. Frankl, to live is to suffer. Suffering is unavoidable. If there is meaning in life at all, it must come from suffering; without suffering, life cannot be fulfilled. Therefore, to live well is to find meaning from suffering, even in concentration camps.

We can only live the present meaningfully by looking to the future. Dr. Frankl accomplished extraordinary acts that allowed him to transcend his present miseries. For example, knowing that his heart could stop during a cold winter's night, he stayed awake by sheer willpower. He imagined himself giving lectures to college students. He scribbled the outline of future books on scraps of paper. Through imagining his wife, he discovered that love is the only way to grasp another person's innermost core.

Through suffering, we realize how much real joy we have here and now. Furthermore, life's fulfillment is through sharing love with others, discovering tasks that need to be done, and searching for life's meaning— all these can lift us up from the (existential vacuum caused by) unavoidable and inevitable sufferings and anxieties in life. Dr. Frankl endured horrible conditions and survived life-threatening situations with faith and hope for the future. He lived eternal life. No wonder he was greeted warmly by Pope Paul VI.

This Advent season, let us turn from boredom with daily routines, from impatience with progress, and from doubt of the meaning of life. Let us be alert and wait patiently for the coming of Jesus Christ. ✝

[24ᵗʰ and 31ˢᵗ OT (B)]

THIRD SUNDAY OF ADVENT (C)

(Zephaniah 3:14-18a; Philippians 4:4-7; Luke 3:10-18)

Fr. Walter Ciszek

Advent is a joyful season. This Sunday's readings are full of words like "joy" and "rejoice."

In the first reading, the prophet Zephaniah assures the Israelites that they can move forward joyfully into a new age with God. In the second reading, Paul asks the Philippians to rejoice always in the Lord, because Christ has already come. Paul also encourages them to look forward with joy to the second coming of Christ, because the Lord is near.

In the gospel reading, John the Baptist points to Jesus, who will bring the people to the baptism of the Holy Spirit. The people have asked John, "What shall we do?" We might expect John to make radical demands: leave everything and join him in the desert, or perhaps adopt a life of fasting and penance. On the contrary, John does not tell people to do something unreasonable or extraordinary. Instead, he calls upon people to be trustworthy: to those who have plenty, share with those who have less; to tax collectors, be honest; to soldiers, do not take advantage of the vulnerable.

Christian life is a life of joy and gratitude. Joy is serenity of heart and peace of the soul. Joy and salvation are synonymous. God's love and mercy, which are revealed in the life of Jesus, invite us to participate in His divine life as His sons and daughters. We are joyful and thankful, and we look forward to the day when we will see God face to face, knowing that we will be like Him (1 Jn 3:2).

To illustrate what Christian joy really means, I would like to share the story of Fr. Walter Ciszek, S.J., from Shenandoah, Pennsylvania. Soon after his ordination in Rome, Fr. Ciszek entered Russia in 1940 under an assumed name to minister to workers in the Urals. He was caught and accused of being a "Vatican spy," interrogated in Moscow, and sentenced to fifteen years of hard labor in Siberia. He worked in coal mines and factories, performed various construction jobs, and built a city on the tundra in Siberia. Even after he had finished his sentence, the KGB continued to keep him for several more years. Through it all, he never lost his faith in God and his trust in the Lord. Eventually, after nearly eight years of negotiation, he was freed in October 1963.

Fr. Ciszek's book *He Leadeth Me* contains many remarkable stories. In the midst of cold and hunger—even near starvation—and with daily hard labor of twelve to fourteen hours, he did each job as best he could. He worked to the limit of his strength each day and did as much as his health and endurance under the circumstances made possible. We may wonder why? He answered. "Because I saw this work as the will of God for me, I did it. I built a new city in Siberia, not because Joseph Stalin and Nikita Khrushchev wanted it, but because God wanted it." The labor he did was not punishment, but a way of working out his salvation in fear and trembling. Some may say that he didn't have to work so hard; after all, his sentence was unjust. Others may say that he helped the Communist regime. But to Fr. Ciszek, the hard labor in prison camps in Siberia was his vocation, and he was faithful to it. He was a priest of inner joy.

Fr. Ciszek writes that before he was sent to Siberia, he learned how to "empty" himself during his four-year solitary confinement in the famous Moscow prison, Lubyanka. It was there that he learned how to empty himself to the grace of God and how to purify his soul (Levko, *America*, 1/7/2013). In Siberia, he continued to practice his self-emptying in the midst of hunger and starvation among other prisoners, most of whom possessed little other than animal-like instincts. In spite of all this suffering, his life was full of inner joy, peace, and gratitude. No wonder that the Vatican declared the validity of investigation for the sainthood of Fr. Ciszek in March 2012.

We are not prisoners in cold Siberia; we are free persons in warm Texas. And yet we, too, can find the reason for and the source of joy by conforming to God's will in our lives and by breaking away from the status quo of this world. ✝

[3rd Advent (A, B)]

FOURTH SUNDAY OF ADVENT (C)

(Micah 5:1-4a; Hebrews 10:5-10; Luke 1:39-45)

Mary Is the True Ark of God

Christians boldly claim that the Son of God came in the flesh to be the Savior of mankind. Moreover, this claim of incarnation is the fruit of God's long search for man in history. Jewish theologian Abraham Heschel, in his book *God in Search of Man*, says, "All of human history as described in the Bible may be summarized in one phrase: God in search of man."

God, who searched for man throughout the entire history of mankind, finally decided to send His Son in the flesh. In doing so, Mary played a critical role. Had Mary not said, "Let it be done to me as you say," God's search for man would have been in vain. It took Mary's consent for the Son of God to take on human flesh. Therefore, let us reflect upon Mary's role in the history of salvation.

From the first reading today, we have learned that the prophet Micah clearly announced that the Messiah would be born in Bethlehem, the city of David. King Herod, knowing this prophecy, tried to trick the Magi from the East and later "ordered the massacre of all boys two years old and under in Bethlehem" (Mt 2:16).

The gospel passage today concerns the Visitation, which is well known to us. After giving her consent to the angel Gabriel, Mary departs in haste to the Judean country to visit Elizabeth. To get to Judea from Galilee, one has to use roads along the Jordan valley; this takes about ten days on foot with a caravan. But the evangelist Luke is not interested in how Mary traveled the long and tortuous journey from Galilee to Judea. Instead, he immediately describes the encounter of Mary and Elizabeth.

To Evangelist Luke, this is no mere meet-up of two pregnant women, who have a lot to say and a lot to share and a lot to laugh about. It also is the first meeting of Jesus and John the Baptist in the wombs of two women. As soon as Mary utters her greeting, the baby in Elizabeth's womb stirs. The baby, John the Baptist, senses Jesus' presence in Mary's womb and "leaps

244

for joy." Accordingly, Elizabeth says, "Blessed are you among women and blessed is the fruit of your womb. But who am I that the mother of my Lord should come to me?"

One wonders why the baby John in his mother's womb "leaps for joy." The answer to this question comes from the Old Testament. Having established Jerusalem as the capital, and having brought the Ark of God to Jerusalem, King David danced ("leaped for joy") before the Lord (2 Sm 6:14). In the same way, the evangelist Luke wishes to convey that, because Jesus is God's covenant, and because Mary is the Ark of God, John the Baptist, representing David, danced in front of Mary.

Indeed, Mary is the true Ark of God. She carries Jesus, the Son of God, in her womb. We, too, would like to dance in front of her, just as David and John the Baptist did.

Furthermore, the incarnation is a wonderful (marvelous) exchange. Through Mary, God takes on humanity so that we can share in God's divinity. By virtue of the incarnation, Jesus carries the blessings and burdens of our flesh and bone. In exchange, we can partake in God's life by eating the body of Jesus and drinking his blood.

In summary, the earth has become the sacred ground because of Mary's "yes." What we have seen and touched on the face of the earth is no longer belong to us; they are divine and belong to God. As long as this universe breathes, Jesus is permanently present among us.

Let us close with the prayer that combines the initial greeting of the angel Gabriel during the Annunciation and Elizabeth's greeting during the Visitation: "Hail, Mary, full of grace, the Lord is with thee. Blessed are you among women and blessed is the fruit of your womb, Jesus. Holy Mary, Mother of God, pray for us sinners now and at the time of our death. Amen." ✝

[4th Advent (B), Christmas Midnight, 26th OT (A)]

THE NATIVITY OF THE LORD: DAY (ABC)

(Isaiah 52:7-10; Hebrews 1:1-6; John 1:1-18)

Our Savior, Jesus Christ the Lord

"The Word became flesh and made his dwelling among us."

The incarnation is the richest but the most paradoxical event in Christianity. It means the Son of God became flesh. It means the supernatural God is fused with the natural humanity. It means the Word of God is made flesh in the person of Jesus Christ. The incarnation is so strange and paradoxical that the modern world finds it difficult to accept.

The incarnation is not the only paradox in Christianity, however. The Annunciation proclaims the virgin a mother. The Nativity decrees the infant in the manger is a king. The resurrection means there is life in death. The last becomes the first. The lowly are exalted. Christianity is full of many paradoxes. Therefore, we must be familiar with the fact that life's basic truths are grasped as paradoxes.

We are familiar with the bimodal worldview (dualism) with its two distinct divisions or separations, such as soul versus body, spirit versus matter, heaven versus earth, God versus man, nature versus grace, reason versus faith, politics versus religion, and so on. These separating and distinguishing thought patterns, derived from Greek philosophy, were intensified by the heavy emphasis of human intellect and reason since the eighteenth-century Enlightenment. René Descartes, the father of modern philosophy, divided the world into mind/soul (*res cognitans*) and corporeal/substance (*res extensa*), turning man into a "thinking machine."

As a result, we live in a world profoundly divided, oddly separated, and severely dislocated, one that cries out for wholeness, salvation, and redemption. One way to overcome such dividedness and disintegration is to accept the incarnation as an existential ground and a historical reality upon which our human life can be transformed into God's divine life in hope and confidence.

246

The central mystery of the incarnation is that the Word takes on human flesh and becomes identifiable as a mortal man. The incarnation, therefore, is living proof that the apparently incompatible qualities of eternal and temporal, divine and human, and spiritual and corporal can be united in a single reality. The incarnation is the fundamental Christian event that unifies such bimodal and dualistic dividedness and separations.

In Christ Jesus, the Word is made flesh, and so there is no gap between Jesus' life and his teachings. The meaning of the Word comes from the life of Jesus Christ. Not a trace of conflict or difference exists between the Word and the life of Jesus Christ. In the person of Jesus Christ, God and man become one.

The incarnation of God in the person of Jesus of Nazareth is a perfect manifestation of God's love and graciousness. Graciousness is the willingness to form a unity in love with those who are perceived to be inferior. Through the incarnation, God lowers himself and takes on humanity, so that God dwells among his people. Simultaneously, the incarnation offers hope and confidence, so that man can rise and be one with God. That is, Christ Jesus is the condition of possibility for man's humanity and divinity can be combined into one reality.

The incarnation also reveals the humility of God, which, in turn, calls for the humility of man. Humility is the central virtue in Christianity. As Mary sings, "The lowly are lifted up, the hungry are filled with good things, and the rich are sent away empty" (Lk 1:52-53). Christianity invites us to be humble ourselves, so that we can lift up others. (It is not too difficult to understand why ambitious and self-sufficient persons often are not religious. People who are not able to lower themselves or be open to those deemed "inferior" are reluctant to accept Jesus Christ as the Lord.)

The incarnation is the manifestation of God's love, graciousness, and humility for us. The Word is made flesh, so that we can live in union with God in Christ Jesus. Therefore, we are called to let God's love be incarnated in our lives. **✝**

[14ᵗʰ OT (C), 15ᵗʰ and 26ᵗʰ OT (A)]

HOLY FAMILY OF JESUS, MARY, AND JOSEPH (C)

(Sirach 3:2-6, 12-14; Colossians 3:12-21; Luke 2:41-52)

The Teenager Jesus

There are many spiritual tasks we must perform in life—how to be born, how to grow up, what schools to attend, whom to marry, how to grow old, and how to die. Today, we learn that Jesus of Nazareth went through the same spiritual tasks as we do.

The gospel reading today is the third and last Infant Narrative from Luke's Gospel. At the first glance, the story of the Holy Family during their visit to Jerusalem appears to be ordinary.

To go to Jerusalem from Galilee in those days, the Holy Family had to follow meandering roads along the Jordan River, passing Jericho, which was halfway to the Judea hill country. The high, rough mountains between Galilee and Judea could not have lent themselves to an easy path. What's more, because of possible outlaws on the road, they had to travel in caravans with others—several dozens or hundreds.

On the eve of their return to Nazareth from Jerusalem, Mary and Joseph couldn't find the young Jesus, who was twelve years old. Mary and Joseph had to retrace back their steps to look for him. They finally found him in the Temple. He was learning from, not teaching, the scholars there. In their relief, Mary and Joseph could not refrain from reproaching Jesus for his conduct. He had been the cause of such anxiety and worries for three long days! Jesus' answer to his parents was a bit rebellious. The whole story sounds like a typical family episode dealing with a pre-teen.

On a deeper level, this story about Jesus reveals the identity and personhood of Jesus. It is particularly interesting to note that Mary and Joseph did not understand Jesus, when he said, "I must be in my Father's house." In the same way, at the end of the Galilean ministry when Jesus said to his disciples that he must go to Jerusalem, they did not understand him.

This gospel account reveals the mystery of Jesus' personhood in his obedience to the will of God. That Jesus is found in the Temple after three days anticipates the resurrection of Jesus after three days of death. That Mary and Joseph are puzzled anticipates the running away of Jesus' disciples from the cross. However, Jesus' personhood will not be completely revealed until Easter, which is already on the horizon.

Finally, it is at the Temple where the twelve-year-old Jesus manifests his wisdom; it is the same Temple where he will end his ministry. Now, the legal scholars are amazed at Jesus' intelligence and wisdom. Later, they will oppose him and put him on the cross.

On a practical level, however, today's gospel reading is about Jesus growing up to an adult. All of us were teenagers some years ago, and some of us have teenage children now. Certainly, we know that growing out of childhood, the process of forming an independent consciousness apart from parents, is not easy.

Therefore, it is good for us to learn that even Jesus has to grow up by giving a hard time (so to speak) to his parents, not only because it is beneficial for us to see Jesus' undisguised humanity, but also because we can understand that his transition from childhood to adulthood was not unlike ours and our children's.

Concerning the faith in our own families, we always need to grow in faith. The evangelist John, in the second reading, says, "We are God's children now." We must also wait for the second coming of the Son of God, when all will become clear. In the meantime, we must be faithful to our own vocations as members of our own holy families. ✝

[Holy Family (B)]

THE EPIPHANY OF THE LORD (ABC)

(Isaiah 60:1-6; Ephesians 3:2-3, 5-6; Matthew 2:1-12)

We Are the Magi!

We believe in God the Father, who is the Creator of heaven and earth. We believe in Jesus Christ, who is the Son of God. We believe in the Holy Spirit, who proceeds from the Father and the Son. And lastly, we believe (in) one, holy, catholic, and apostolic Church. In other words, while acknowledging our roots in the Hebrew tradition, we believe in Jesus Christ, our Savior. We are Catholics.

All of today's readings concern with the meaning of the word "catholic," which means "universal, all, worldwide." I am proud of being a member of the Catholic Church, because of her doctrinal consistency and historical perseverance, as well as her social justice stance.

In the first reading, the prophet Isaiah foretold that, several hundred years before Jesus, a divine light from Jerusalem would shine upon the whole world and that all the nations would enjoy the light and walk in it. Some would also bring precious gifts of gold and frankincense.

The responsorial psalm repeats, "Lord, every nation on earth will adore you." This means that one day all nations, following the footsteps of the Magi, will pay homage to the baby Jesus, the Messiah.

The second reading shows we are "co-heirs, members of the same body and co-partners in the promise in Christ Jesus through the gospel." St. Paul encouraged all people on earth to be Catholics.

In today's gospel reading, the Magi came to Jerusalem in search of the King of the Jews, the Messiah. The Magi were educated non-Jews, either Persian priests or Babylonian astronomers, who paid homage to the infant Jesus for the first time. They were the first group of Catholics who encountered Jesus the Savior.

For the Magi, the search for the King of Jews was not easy, even though they were under the divine guidance of the star. They had to endure a long journey from a faraway land and be tested by King Herod's cruel political jealousy. Once arrived in Jerusalem, the Magi learned that the King of the Jews was to be born in Bethlehem, and so they went there. However, the Messiah they found in Bethlehem was not the Messiah they had expected. The Messiah was not a powerful king, but a powerless infant in a manger. Borrowing the words of Pope Francis, "the Messiah was a homeless." More surprisingly, the Messiah was the target of a plot between Herod and Israel's religious leaders. The baby Jesus, from the start of his life on earth, had to experience danger and suffering. From the moment of birth, Jesus was a suffering Messiah.

The first group of Catholics who knew of the existence of the Messiah was the Magi, who journeyed difficult and distant roads and, finally, found the homeless baby Jesus in an unexpected and surprising place—in a manger.

The Magi also were those who gave the first Christmas presents to the baby Jesus. Their gifts to the baby Jesus were wise and precious—gold, frankincense, and myrrh. Myrrh was used to prepare the dead for burial; the gift of myrrh was a symbol for the mortality of Jesus. Frankincense was used in liturgical worship. Gold was the gift for a king. These three gifts reveal the real identity of the baby Jesus and how he would bring salvation to all people. The baby Jesus came not only for Israel, but for all the nations of the world.

The Magi were the first group of Catholics who gave Christmas presents to the baby Jesus. We, too, are Catholics like the Magi! So we ask ourselves: What kind of gifts did we give to the baby Jesus on Christmas Day a week ago? What are our roles in welcoming the Messiah into this world? And how do we spread the Gospel of Christ? As the baby Jesus is manifested to the whole world as the Messiah on this Epiphany Sunday, we need to mindful of our dignity as well as responsibility for being Catholics. ✝

[Epiphany (A)]

THE BAPTISM OF THE LORD (C)

(Isaiah 40:1-5, 9-11; Acts 10:34-38; Luke 3:15-16, 21-22)

Jesus was an Ordinary Person

Jesus Christ was baptized, like an ordinary person, by John the Baptist on the banks of the Jordan River. When we think about Jesus' baptism, it is simply amazing and beyond our understanding. The Son of God humbled himself and acted as an ordinary person!

Today, we would like to reflect upon the humanity of Jesus, based on the Infancy Narratives from the Gospel of Luke. Our goal is to find out how the evangelist Luke describes Jesus as an ordinary person and, by contrast, John the Baptist as an extraordinary person.

Our first scene concerns the Annunciation. Near the altar of a temple in Judea, the angel Gabriel appeared to Zechariah the priest and announced the conception of John (Lk 1:5-25). By contrast, in a small cottage in Galilee, the same angel appeared to Mary, announcing the conception of Jesus (Lk 1:26-28).

The second scene is that of the Nativity. When John was born, neighbors and relatives rejoiced with Elizabeth, most likely at her home (Lk 1:58). By contrast, Joseph and the fully pregnant Mary had to travel a long journey from Galilee to Judea, and there Jesus was born in a stable and laid in a manger (Lk 2:1-20). The evangelist Luke emphasized that Jesus was born in a manger by repeating the word "manger" three times (Lk 2:7, 12, and 16).

The third scene is that of the Hidden Life. John went off to live in a desert, away from his family (Lk 1:80). In the desert, John purifies himself in the presence of God. By contrast, Jesus grew up with his family in Nazareth and most likely learned the family trade, the carpentry (Lk 2:41).

The fourth scene concerns public appearance. John appeared in public as an ascetic, like Elijah (Lk 3:7-14). By contrast, Jesus appeared among sinners and penitents (Lk 3:21).

Based on these comparisons, we conclude that John was born and grew up as an extraordinary person, whereas Jesus of Nazareth was born and grew up as an ordinary person. The evangelist Luke wanted to emphasize that Jesus of Nazareth was an ordinary person, like you and me.

St. Luke wrote down his conviction and understanding in his Gospel after he had prayed and reflected on the stories told about those people who had been associated with Jesus. Whenever we read the Gospel, we reverse that process. We first read the life stories of Jesus and reflect upon them prayerfully, and then catch the same conviction and understanding as the evangelist Luke first did.

Whenever we read the Gospel of Christ Jesus, we encounter the human person of Jesus of Nazareth, who is limited and tempted, wants to learn and grow, has likes and dislikes, overcomes hunger and thirst, and has experienced love, joy, fear, and betrayal. Jesus "worked with human hands, thought with a human mind, acted with a human will, and loved with a human heart" (*Gaudium et Spes*, #22).

Jesus is a real person. Jesus is also the norm and paradigm for all human beings. At the same time, Jesus is the visible sign of God and the Word of God spoken for the last time. Thus Pope Benedict writes, "Jesus tells us who man truly is and what a man must do to be truly man" (*Spe Salvi*, #6). Therefore, it is only through the humanity of Jesus that we can experience the reality of God. We often encounter God by entering imaginatively and faithfully into the historic record of Jesus in the Gospels (Ignatian imaginative contemplation). The Word was made flesh in the person of Jesus. Accordingly, we cannot gain access to the Word apart from the flesh of Jesus—the Eucharist.

Jesus identifies himself with the whole of humanity through his baptism. By virtue of the same baptism, we are divinized as sons and daughters of God. Baptism, upon which all other sacraments are rooted, is a tangible expression of God's love for us. ✝

[Christmas Vigil, Baptism (A, B)]

FIRST SUNDAY OF LENT (C)

(Deuteronomy 26:4-10; Romans 10:8-13; Luke 4:1-13)

The Temptation

During our faith journey, we need to rest once in a while. Perhaps we need to drive out into the countryside and look at stars at night. They are much larger, much brighter, and much closer to us than we realize. Perhaps we need to look at green buds on the tree branches in the early morning. They will teach us the mystery of life. Perhaps we need to gaze upon sunsets at day's end. They will whisper to us how to be gracious and humble as we grow old. Perhaps we need to sit still in sheer silence in the living room. We may listen to God's voice there.

The season of Lent is for all of these to happen. It provides us an opportunity to step out of life's routines and be attentive to the voices coming from our hearts. It also provides us opportunities to open our minds and hearts, so that we leave old ways behind by undertaking new journeys. It is a time to recognize that we are hungry and thirsty.

Jesus, also, was hungry and thirsty throughout his forty days and forty nights in the desert. At the end of his fast, the devil tempted him. At first, the devil asked Jesus to convert rock into bread so that he could have food at any time. Then the devil asked Jesus to worship him so that Jesus could possess all the kingdoms of the world. Finally, the devil challenged Jesus to throw himself off the top of the Temple to see if God would rescue him.

To those challenges from the devil, Jesus responded with the same advices and consolations that God had given to the Israelites thirteen hundred years before, when they wandered in the Sinai desert for forty years. As for converting rock into food, Jesus said, "One does not live by bread alone" (Dt 8:3). As for having power and glory, Jesus said, "You shall worship the Lord" (Dt 6:13). As for being the master of his soul, Jesus said, "You shall not put the Lord your God to the test" (Dt 6:16). It is interesting to note that all of Jesus' responses came from Deuteronomy, the new version of Exodus, which was inspired by a new beginning after the Babylonian

Exile. It was thus that Jesus initiated the messianic age, by rejecting the past failures of Jews.

We also remember that the Israelites rebelled against God in the desert three times. First, the Israelites worshiped the golden calf while Moses went up the mountain to meet God (Ex 32:1-8). Second, after the Israelites had eaten manna for some time, they demanded meat. God was angry, but provided quail to them (Nm 11:4-34). Lastly, when the Israelites demanded water at Massah and Meribah, Moses struck the rock twice. God forbade Moses to enter the Promised Land, as punishment for the Israelites' lack of trust (Nm 20:1-13). During the temptation in the desert, Jesus was put to the temptation by the devil, just like the ancient Israelites were. But Jesus got it right this time; he was with God.

We, too, have temptations similar to what Jesus experienced in the desert. We are tempted not to live with Godly things, but with bread alone; we are tempted not to worship and serve God; we are tempted not to discern and accept God's will. At a deeper level, we believe that the embodiment of God's love for us is Jesus on the cross. On the cross Jesus was thirsty, so that we could drink. On the cross Jesus was hungry, so that we could have life in him.

Most of us go about our lives feeling pretty sure that we are not desperate sinners. We do not murder, embezzle, or kidnap children. And yet, occasionally, perhaps after one or two sleepless night, we begin to suspect something is not quite right, and we should have done it differently. If we feel that we lack some spiritual devotions in this way, it is good, because it is a sign for us to advance one step closer to God.

During the season of Lent, let us be alone in stillness, not because we are sinners, but because we hear God's gentle and soft voice. The season of Lent is to get away from the daily routine and be reflective in a quiet place. The season of Lent is to be seriously aware of the living God, who is near us. ✝

[Holy Trinity (C)]

SECOND SUNDAY OF LENT (C)

(Genesis 15:5-12, 17-18; Philippians 3:17–4:1; Luke 9:28-36)

The Transfiguration of Jesus

In the Bible, God dwells on the mountain. Moses encountered God in the burning bush at Mount Sinai (Ex 3:1), and Elijah encountered God in "the sound of sheer silence" at Mount Horeb (Mount Sinai; 1 Kgs 19:8). For the Israelites, Moses represented the Law, and Elijah represented all the prophets.

Jesus takes three disciples, Peter, James, and John, up to Mount Tabor in Galilee in today's gospel reading. During prayer, Jesus' face shines brightly and his clothes become dazzling white. And then, Moses and Elijah appear and talk about Jesus' exodus—the death and resurrection in Jerusalem. Suddenly, God the Father appears in a cloud and says, "This is my Son." (The same words were uttered by God during Jesus' baptism.) After the voice spoke, Jesus is left alone, as personification of both the Law and prophets of Israel.

The season of Lent is supposed to be somber and penitential. Why, then, do we listen to the glorious transfiguration of Jesus today? The answer to this question comes from the context in which we find the transfiguration in the Gospel. The transfiguration of Jesus comes after Peter's confession in Caesarea Philippi and follows several major themes: the first prediction of the passion, the condition of discipleship, and the announcement of the Lord's return.

The transfiguration provides a glimpse into the identity of Jesus, who realized his destiny of the suffering and death that will lead to the glory of resurrection. It is the glorious aspect of Jesus' suffering and death that prefigures the joy of Easter. The transfiguration encompasses both the themes of Good Friday and Easter Sunday.

Joy, glory, and eternal life mean almost the same thing. And joy and suffering are intertwined. Jesus' death and resurrection are often described together as joy (Jn 14:28, 15:11, 16:24, and 17:13, 1 Jn 1:4, 2 Jn 12,

Mt 13:20 and 25:21). Paul writes the words "joy" and "consolation" to fellow Christians who are suffering (2 Cor 2:2 and 7:4). By means of the sorrowful death of Jesus on the cross, the joy of salvation overflows. To Christians, the cross represents a joyful event. We cannot appreciate joy without suffering in life. Indeed, we reflect upon the joy of the cross this second Sunday of Lent.

There is another reason we listened to the story of the transfiguration. This Christ-event is the culmination of all of God's covenants in the Old Testament. The first reading shows that God alone passed like "a smoking brazier and a flaming torch" between animals that were split into two. The one who would betray the covenant would be like the animal split into two. Because God walked alone, God committed himself to the covenant. The death and resurrection of Jesus that Moses and Elijah talked about, therefore, is God's covenant that cannot be broken.

The transfiguration of Jesus prefigures the panoramic view of Jesus' death and resurrection as God's promise, the promise given since the creation of the world. The transfiguration of Jesus, therefore, calls for our readiness to respond to God's plan of salvation.

In the second reading, Paul says to the Philippians, "Observe those who thus conduct themselves according to the model you have in us." In other words, God is revealed to us through the good deeds of others. This certainly is our experience. We all know people who are extraordinary examples of unquestionable integrity and unselfish service to others. Strange enough, these good people do not usually recognize the joy and glory that shines forth from them. They gently insist that they are just ordinary people.

During this season of Lent, we ought to recognize those selfless and joyful people in our lives and be ready to transform ourselves. ✝

[2ⁿᵈ Lent (A, B)]

257

THIRD SUNDAY OF LENT (C)

(Exodus 3:1-8, 13-15; 1 Corinthians 10:1-6, 10-12; Luke 13:1-9)

God Is Our "Abba" Father

The Burning Bush we have just listened to from the first reading is one of the most famous passages in the Hebrew Bible. It is a beautiful and imaginative story which laid a foundation for Jewish mysticism.

Moses, a lonely fugitive, was tending the flock of his father-in-law. When he came to Mount Horeb, he saw a bush on fire, yet not consuming. It defied the laws of nature. As Moses looked closely at the bush, God told him to remove his sandals on a holy ground. Then God revealed himself as the God of Abraham, Isaac, and Jacob, reminding God's covenant to his forefathers. Moses was excited; his heart was pounding. And then God asked Moses to liberate His people from bondage, revealing His name: "I am who am."

This story of the Burning Bush is about Moses' experience of God. To describe the mystical presence of God, Israelites used paradoxical metaphors, such as the burning bush, which shows God's intimate closeness and, at the same time, infinite remoteness.

The significance of this story is that God of Israel, who was hidden in the cloud far away, revealed Himself to Moses for the first time. Since then, throughout the forty-year long journey in the Sinai desert, Moses wanted to see God face-to-face. But God showed him only His back (Ex 33:23), because anyone who saw God's face would die. When Moses appeared to Israelites with the Ten Commandments, his face shone brightly—a sign of having encountered God (Ex 34:29-35). Since then, Israelites always longed for God's face shining upon them (Ps 67 and 80).

This mysterious God of the Burning Bush become known to us through love, which is manifested by the death and resurrection of Jesus of Nazareth. Jesus has shown us the face of God, the compassionate *Abba* Father, (as exemplified by the Parable of the Prodigal Son.) This notion of God's intimate closeness was extremely shocking for the Jews. For that,

Jesus paid the price. Jesus also prays frequently that he will be in us, and we in him. Therefore, whenever we experience the presence of the risen Jesus within us, we have encountered God.

So far we have reviewed a short history of God. We did this in order to reflect on what kind of concepts or images of God we have, because our view on God always shapes up our deepest concerns in life and it can heal the wounds of the world. For example, when we sing "God Bless America," we ought to understand that God blesses even our enemies. Mistakenly, however, we often put more emphasis on the immanent (phenomenal) aspect of God over the transcendental aspect of God, or vice versa, and then we cannot grasp the reality the word God points at.

We need to know about ourselves in search of God. And we need to go beyond ourselves to be in union with God. Most importantly, God is for us. Therefore, we must see, hear, taste, or feel the presence of God in our daily lives. And we must not sacrifice the sense of holiness and sanctity over rules and regulations in our liturgies. Our ideas of God must be compatible with our experiences of God.

The experience of God must be intimately close to us, although God remains totally beyond us. St. Augustine said, "God is closer to us than we are to ourselves" (*Confession*, III, 6, 11). In other words, God should be directly available for us as a divine reality, although God infinitely transcends us. For this reason, God is Trinitarian God: The Father is infinitely beyond us; Christ is personally dwelling within us, (as St. Paul said, "It is no longer I who live, but it is Christ who lives in me (Gal 2:20)); and the Holy Spirit unites all of us as one in love and also with God. We pray to the Father through Christ in the Holy Spirit.

Jesus has shown us that God is our compassionate *Abba* Father, by demonstrating how to live, how to suffer, and how to die. The season of Lent is to remind ourselves once again the life, passion, and death of Jesus, so that we may be joyful and grateful, because with Jesus we can be in union with God who infinitely transcends us. ✝

[17th and 24th OT (C)]

Fourth Sunday of Lent (C)

(Joshua 5:9, 10-12; 2 Corinthians 5:17-21; Luke 15:1-3, 11-32)

Repentance and Forgiveness

Fr. Henri Nouwen, who died suddenly in 1996, was a famous contemporary spiritual writer. He wrote more than forty books, which have been translated into more than twenty languages. Using plain English eloquently, Nouwen wrote so honestly that all readers are spontaneously drawn into his spiritual world.

Why is Henri Nouwen so popular? Of course, he wrote with grace and style. Of course, he taught at Harvard and Yale. Of course, he was a spiritual master. But the real reason why he is still so popular is not because he was a spiritual master and taught at Yale and Harvard. It is because he showed his own weakness and vulnerability and, at the same time, the courage and strength to overcome those weaknesses and vulnerabilities.

In discovering his true self before God, Nouwen does not hesitate to disclose his own flaws and weakness; in other words, by divulging his own personal struggles, he reveals his own intimate and painful inner life. For example, at the peak of his fame, he yearned for the freedom to be himself, away from people's expectations. No sooner than he found himself alone, he started to complain for not receiving letters from his friends. Through personal strength, however, he allowed readers to see his weakness and vulnerability. He was able to place his own struggles in the center of readers' hearts.

Among other writings, Henri Nouwen wrote *The Return of the Prodigal Son*. This book is a personal, spiritual reflection generated as he sat in front of the original Rembrandt painting of the same name for days at the Hermitage Museum in St. Petersburg, Russia. As the painting was one of Rembrandt's final paintings, so the book was one of Nouwen's final books. In this book, Henri Nouwen summarized his own mature spirituality as he stepped into the painting and transformed himself into the prodigal son, the older son, and their father, respectively.

The story of the Prodigal Son is well known. The younger son, the prodigal son, asked his father his share of inheritance in advance, a disgraceful request for a son. And he wasted it away with drink and women in a foreign country. In the end, he worked on a pig farm—disgraceful job for a Jew. He was truly lost, and it was this complete groundlessness that finally brought him to his senses.

When Henri Nouwen identified himself as the prodigal son, he imagined himself being tightly embraced by the Father. He desired to be like the prodigal son so that he could find eternal peace in the Father's bosom. What Nouwen emphasized, therefore, is the ability to say, "I am sorry," the ability to repent, and the ability to empty oneself. By doing so, he must have realized that he truly was a beloved son of God.

Continuing the gospel story, when the prodigal son came home, the father elevated the lost son into a position much higher than before. To this unfair reception of his brother, the older son, responded with such envy that he did not address his parent as "father," calling his brother "this son of yours." Actually, the parable of the Prodigal Son describes the prodigality of the father's love. The father showers his love to both unworthy sons. In Rembrandt's painting, the father is blind; he sees with his heart, not with his eyes. The father's forgiveness is prodigal, too. Therefore, this gospel story shows us the boundless and irreversible love of God: Jesus shows us a new image of God, who is love.

As we approach the end of the Lenten season, we reflect upon our sins and God's forgiveness, which are mutually related. It seems, however, that we do not repent in order to be forgiven by God. Our repentance is not the condition for God's forgiveness. God always, and already, forgives us. We repent in order to find our true selves before God and along with our brothers and sisters. Our sinfulness reflects God's merciful love. And by repenting, we come to know that we are beloved sons and daughters of God. ✝

[24th OT (C)]

FIFTH SUNDAY OF LENT (C)

(Isaiah 43:16-21; Philippians 3:8-14; John 8:1-11)

Stunning the Stoners

𝔉or the last several weeks, we have prepared ourselves for the paschal mystery of Jesus, reflecting upon the goodness of God in our lives. Now we must move forward, knowing that we are in God's hands, not because we have not done enough, but because we have greater things ahead of us. Today's readings reveal God's overwhelming love and mercy, as we come close to Holy Week.

In the gospel reading today, the Pharisees and scribes brought to Jesus a woman who was caught in adultery, and they asked him whether they should stone her according to the Law. If Jesus had said "no," it would be against the Jewish Law. If Jesus had said "yes," it would be against the Roman law and his own teachings of God's love and mercy. It was a no-win situation. Rather than upholding the Law, the Jewish religious leaders "did that to test Jesus" and trap him.

Jesus said to them, "Let the one among you who is without sin be the first to throw a stone at her." This is a remarkably wise and prudent statement, and so we exclaim, "What a response!" Soon after, one by one and beginning with the oldest, the Pharisees and scribes left (apparently the older one gets, the more sinful one is!). Finally, alone with the woman, Jesus showed her the respect she deserved and forgave her sin without denying the sin itself.

This gospel story is about God's mercy, but it raises several questions. What happened to the man in adultery? Why did they let him go? Why did Jesus bend down and straighten up twice? What did he write on the ground?

In the story, Jesus asked the Jewish leaders to throw "the first stone," which is the most difficult stone to throw. Group psychology tells us that, if the first stone is thrown, many more stones will immediately follow and then unstoppable violence explodes. What Jesus said and acted, therefore, prevented a potential violence from igniting. For the same reason, Jesus

262

bent down and wrote something on the ground; he was avoiding the angry and resentful eyes of the Jewish leaders. Jesus knew how to handle explosive situations and thus wisely prevented bloodshed.

However, we know Jesus himself became the victim of violence. Jesus became the scapegoat of the imitative violence orchestrated by the Jewish leaders (Rene Girard) and did freely take up the cross. In other words, Jesus' death on the cross, apart from its excruciating pain and suffering, was the self-sacrificing and non-violent way of resolving the non-stopping imitative rivalry and violence in human history. Jesus was the example par excellence of nonviolence. Jesus was the most perfect human being. This is one of many reasons why God raised him up, and we call him the Son of God.

Jesus showed God's mercy to the woman. So let us reflect on God's mercy briefly in this Jubilee Year of Mercy. We have known all along that God is love. And Pope Francis has recently published a book entitled *The Name of God Is Mercy*. So, "how love and mercy are related?" we wonder. The virtue of love is heavily influenced by Greek philosophy, which is the backbone of the Western culture, whereas the virtue of mercy is more practical, perhaps more Eastern. More importantly, love without mercy would be a brief romance, and mercy without love would be a pure sentiment. (Furthermore, because we ought to love our neighbors, God is love. And because we ought to be merciful one another, the name of God is mercy.)

In this final week of Lent, let us remind ourselves that sin is a failure to love, rather than breaking the law or regulations. Because sin is failure to love, when we are moved by God's love, then we become more sensitive to our sins. And the more sensitive we are to our sins, the more clearly we see God. This is why, by repenting sins, we come to know new dimension of the living God, who is love and mercy.

We prepare ourselves for the Sacrament of Reconciliation, not necessarily because we are sinners, but because we wish to see new dimension of God. Let us prepare ourselves for greater things during the coming Holy Week, by forming good conscience through God's love and mercy. ✝

[7th and 22nd OT (A), 22nd OT (C)]

PALM SUNDAY OF THE LORD'S PASSION (C)

(Luke 19:28-40; Isaiah 50:4-7; Philippians 2:6-11; Luke 22:14–23:56)

Jesus Died As He Lived

For almost two thousand years at this time, Christians have gathered to tell the story of Jesus' passion. This story is about Jesus of Nazareth, who was arrested, tortured, and executed in Jerusalem by Pontius Pilate, the Roman procurator.

The Gospel of Luke portrays Jesus' death as the culmination of his mission, the final act of his selfless love and sacrifice that sealed his life's complete commitment to others. Jesus, in his death, shows eternal trust in God's mercy and love. Jesus, in his death, remains faithful to his own teachings. Jesus, in his death, prays, "Father, forgive them; they know not what they do." Jesus died as he lived.

On the cross, Jesus also shows his trust in God's compassion: "Father, into your hands I commend my spirit." This prayer comes from Psalm 31, which is mostly filled with lamentations on evil and suffering, yet it ends with words of trust and thanksgiving to God. The responsorial psalm today, "My God, my God, why have you forsaken me?" reflects one of Jesus' seven last words on the cross. This lamentation from Psalm 22 is also a hymn of confidence in God, even in the midst of pain and suffering. Jesus' death on the cross reflects the peaceful and providential love of God, rather than excruciating pain and lamentation.

In the Gospel of Luke, we see a compassionate and heartwarming Jesus who exhibits special concerns for women and non-Jews. Following the way of the cross, then, women who have come from Galilee (Mk 15:41 and Lk 23:49) beat their breasts while standing at a distance. Later, they visit the tomb of Jesus, bringing spices and perfumed oil on the first day of the week immediately following the Sabbath (Mk 16:1 and Lk 24:1). Soon after that, the risen Jesus first appears to them.

Jesus dies on the cross with two criminals, and the good thief says, "Jesus, remember me when you come to your kingdom." Jesus responds, "Today, you will be with me in paradise." At the moment of Jesus' death, the sun is eclipsed and darkness spreads throughout the land, and the Temple veil is torn in two. God finds a new home among all people on earth. A new age has dawned.

Today's second reading from Paul's letter to the Philippians is called the Christ Hymn. It first describes incarnation and suffering as the self-emptying (*kenosis*) of Jesus' divinity. Next, it describes the resurrection of Jesus to the point that all creatures worship the risen Jesus as the Lord. This hymn displays the essence of Christianity. As God descends to assume humanity in the person of Jesus of Nazareth, so man can ascend to be in union with God (*theosis*). In other words, "though Jesus was rich, yet for our sakes he became poor, so that by his poverty we might become rich" (2 Cor 8:9).

We can be disciples only through the cross, which symbolizes the trials and sufferings of our lives. The cross strips away our pretenses and disguises and compels us to be self-emptying (self-transcending), thus allowing us to be in union with God.

The cross helps us find our authenticity, or true self. If we discover who we really are, no matter how our hardships and sufferings rally against us, we will be confident of our future resurrection. This principle is termed the Law of Christ (Fr. Bernard Lonergan) and is valid for disciples of Jesus in various situations of everyday life. St. Monica's prayer for her son, St. Augustine, is an excellent example. Another example comes from our parents, who endure hardships and troubles in rearing us.

Life is a sea of suffering, suffering that comes in all different shapes and sizes. The Law of Christ teaches us how to deal with the pain and suffering of life. This is the reason why we listen to the passion story of Jesus. This also is the reason why we follow Jesus of Nazareth. ✝

[Palm Sunday (A, B), 13th and 22nd and 26th OT (A)]

265

EASTER VIGIL (ABC)

(Genesis 1:1-2:2; Genesis 22:1-18; Exodus 14:15-15:1; Isaiah 54:5-14; Isaiah 55:1-11; Baruch 3:9-15, 32-4:4; Ezekiel 36:16-17, 18-28; Romans 6:3-11; Matthew 28:1-10 or Mark 16:1-8 or Luke 24:1-12))

Theodrama and a Symphony of Love

Jesus Christ is risen. Hallelujah, hallelujah!

Hans von Balthasar, a prominent Catholic theologian (1905–1988), wrote a book called *Theodrama.* Perhaps God's work of salvation cannot be adequately expressed by means of human languages, and only a drama can do! For the same reason, Fr. Chris Steck at Georgetown University calls the salvation history "A Symphony of Love" (*America,* 8/1/2005). On this most holy night, we are gathered in this sacred place to play out the divine drama and to listen to the symphony of love.

What happens tonight encompasses everything on earth and beyond; all things of the past, present, and future merge together. What happens tonight includes the Creation, Exodus, Exile, prophets, kings, the birth of Jesus of Nazareth, his earthly life, the kingdom of God, the passion and death and resurrection of Jesus, the fulfillment of God's kingdom, our forthcoming resurrection, and much more.

In actualizing all of these, we use water, fire, bells, candles, incense, white vestments, scripture readings, stories, drama, music, and silence. All together, we, the people of God, participate in the divine drama and perform the symphony of love.

The Easter Vigil is the great liturgical feast, and we enact our collective memory of Jesus Christ and partake in his resurrection. And then, all of a sudden, we encounter the risen Christ during the celebration.

The Easter Vigil also is the feast of love. We sing, "Where true love and charity are found, God is there. *Ubi caritas et amor, Deus ibi est.*" We do not sing this love song unless we have experienced God's love and our love each other.

We also remember that we cannot talk about God's love apart from the resurrection of Jesus. And we cannot talk about the resurrection of Jesus apart from his passion and death on the cross. The risen Jesus did not appear to his disciples and say, "Let bygones be bygones." The risen Jesus appeared with wounds inflicted upon his body. The resurrection of Jesus was bodily, just as the death of Jesus was bodily.

Furthermore, even after the resurrection, Jesus did not forget Galilee. The angel said, "He [the risen Lord] is going before you to Galilee" (Mk 16:7, Mt 28:7). Galilee is a lowly and despised place (1 Cor 1:28) from which no prophet is to rise (Jn 7:52). It is precisely in that poor, lowly, and despised land that we encounter the risen Christ.

Accordingly, whenever we are faced with darkness and anxieties in life, we will encounter the risen Christ. Conversely, if we want to recognize the crucified and risen Lord, we must face the darkness and suffering, even death, in our lives.

Actually, our celebration of the resurrection cannot be confined to one night, no matter how long tonight is going to be. And let us remember that we live between the Book of Genesis and the Book of Revelation. Among the long list of readings tonight, there were none from the Book of Revelation. We will live out the Book of Revelation in the coming fifty days during which we celebrate the Easter Season.

Let us continue the enactment of life on this most holy night. Be absorbed into the feast of God's mercy and love, then ponder and return to life again. ✝

[Easter (A, B, C)]

EASTER SUNDAY (C)

(Acts 10:34, 37-43; Colossians 3:1-4; John 20:1-9)

What Happened?

God has finally raised His Son from the dead, conquering death. The resurrection of Jesus has changed everything. The special word "Alleluia" expresses the joy and happiness of this Easter Sunday.

Three days ago, on Friday, Jesus died on the cross. His body was taken down from the cross and was buried in a new tomb in the garden. Mary Magdalene and the other women who followed Jesus all the way from Galilee witnessed all that.

Three days later, after the Passover rest, on this first day of the week, Mary Magdalene went to the tomb early in the morning and found it empty. She suspected that Jesus' body had been stolen. She informed Jesus' disciples, who ran into the tomb. Peter saw Jesus' burial clothes neatly folded in the empty tomb, and the beloved disciple "saw and believed."

After leaving the tomb, Mary Magdalene, weeping three times (Jn 20:11, 13, and 15), said, "They have taken the Lord from the tomb, and we do not know where they put him" (Jn 20:2, 20:13, and 20:15). She really wanted to say a proper goodbye to Jesus. When Jesus finally appeared to her in the garden and told her not to cling to his old state (Jn 20:17), she recognized him. Mary's love allowed her to see the risen Jesus.

One week later and, once again, on the first day of the week, Jesus appeared to his disciples, including Thomas (Jn 20:26). In the beginning, God created heavens and the earth on the first day of the week (Gen 1:1). Both the creation and the resurrection happened the same "first day of the week." Thus the resurrection of Jesus is another creation, new creation.

Moreover, Mary Magdalene understood the risen Jesus as the gardener who stood outside the tomb (Jn 20:15) in the garden where Jesus had been buried (Jn 19:41). The garden is the Garden of Eden (Gen 3:1), and the gardener is the new Adam—the risen Jesus. Therefore, when the risen Jesus appears to his disciples, he breathes the Holy Spirit into them and recreate them, as God breathed life into Adam's nose (Gen 2:7). The resurrection of Jesus is a new creation.

The resurrection should be interpreted in the light of first-century Jewish thought. At the time of Jesus, Jews believed that the resurrection of the dead was reserved for the day when the kingdom of God was definitely established—in other words, at the end-time. To Christians Jews, the resurrection of Jesus means God's promises are fulfilled and the end-time has arrived in the person of Jesus Christ. It means Jesus is the Christ. It means God's new creation has begun. It means God's new creation begins, as the Christ breathes on disciples and sends the Holy Spirit (Jn 20:22).

The resurrection of Jesus means the whole person of Jesus—body and soul—is raised to full and eternal life. It is not resuscitation similar to the case of Lazarus. When Jesus resuscitated Lazarus, he came out from his tomb wearing burial clothes. When Jesus was raised, his clothes were wrapped nicely inside of the tomb. The risen Jesus no longer needed human clothes.

The resurrection of Jesus is not Jesus' disembodied soul going to heaven (the immortality of soul). The resurrection of Jesus means that the Spirit of Jesus Christ continues to live on with us in this world. The resurrection of Jesus is the work of the living God and must entail meanings and implications here and now, not there and then. Therefore, the resurrection of Jesus means that we have work to do. After a lengthy exhortation to the Corinthians in the earliest account of Jesus' resurrection, Paul simply concludes, "Keep on working at the Lord's work always, knowing that, in the Lord, you cannot be laboring in vain" (1 Cor 15:58). So we should keep on working.

Perhaps we will never understand the resurrection of Jesus until we truly carry the cross. The cross requires love—self-sacrificing love. Indeed, love is the deepest knowledge necessary to understand the resurrection and to celebrate a new life. ✝

[Easter (A, B), 3rd Easter (B), 32nd OT (C)]

SECOND SUNDAY OF EASTER (C), DIVINE MERCY SUNDAY

(Acts 5:12-16; Revelation 1:9-11, 12-13, 17-19; John 20:19-31)

The Resurrection of Jesus

The resurrection of Jesus, the most important event in Christianity, is intimately tied to the death of Jesus. St. Paul always preached the "crucified and risen Christ." The death and resurrection of Jesus are one and the same event of God's revelation. We also call Jesus the Lord because the risen Jesus is the same as the one crucified. The glory of the resurrection of Jesus has reconciled the scandal of the death on the cross.

When the risen Christ appears to his disciples for the second time, Thomas asks Jesus to show him his wounds. Jesus does not say, "Forgive and forget." or "Let's start a new beginning." Instead, feeling pain and grief, Jesus demands his disciples to look at his wounds and even urges Thomas to put his hand in his side. Indeed, Jesus forces the disciples to confront the painful consequence of their betrayal and rejection. Far from implying that the past injury and suffering are healed, Jesus' resurrection actually means that the past injury and suffering are never erased. The wounds remain forever inscribed on the body of Jesus, so that his innocent suffering remains forever a part of the resurrection.

Another incredible aspect of Jesus' resurrection is that the risen Jesus appears to his disciples with open arms and invites them to reconcile. Jesus greets the disciples repeatedly, saying, "Peace be with you." The peace Jesus gives to the disciples is not worldly peace, as in the absence of war. It is the inner joy of living God's life, with God's unconditional and irreversible love. It is *shalom*.

With the peace of God, the risen Jesus welcomes all and commissions all, saying, "Receive the Holy Spirit." This remarkable event happens on the first day of the week, signifying a new creation filled with the Holy Spirit. But what does it mean to be "filled with the Holy Spirit?" It means to acknowledge allegiance by saying, "Jesus is Lord!" This is a religious and political statement. It means, "I choose Jesus, not the Emperor of Rome." It means, "Jesus, not Caesar, is the Lord."

It also means to live good and virtuous lives. The Spirit helps us turn away from vice and walk with virtue. The Spirit helps us participate in Jesus' resurrection and defeat death (1 Cor 15:26).

Finally, Jesus breathes his Spirit into the disciples, founding the Church. This means that an individual is not a recipient of the Holy Spirit. For example, when Thomas left the circle of disciples, he could not recognize the risen Jesus. Only after he returned to the circle of disciples, did he recognize the risen Jesus.

The resurrection of Jesus is the revelation of God's love for Jesus' sacrificial suffering on the cross. The resurrection of Jesus is the source and dynamism of faith in the living God. The resurrection of Jesus is the assurance of hope for our resurrection.

Surely, our future resurrection requires taking up our own cross. This is the lesson we must learn from Jesus' resurrection, which was God's vindication for the sacrificing death on the cross. In his letter to Galatians, Paul also wrote, "I want to…share…his suffering in his death, if somehow I may attain the resurrection from the dead" (Gal 3:10). Therefore, the resurrection of Jesus teaches us how to die while alive, instead of how to live forever after death. The resurrection of Jesus teaches us how to die to our false selves, and how to recover our true selves, and how to live for others.

As we begin the Season of Easter, we see the whole world with a new sense of reality. Easter season is about passing from captivity to freedom and from illusion to what matters most. Eater Season is to realize God's love and mercy for all that we are, so that we can grow in faith, hope, and love.

Today is Divine Mercy Sunday. Mercy is the fundamental nature of God and is the realization of God's love in deeds and words. God is merciful in raising Jesus for us. And Jesus Christ is Divine Mercy, whose Spirit leads us to live God's life. Let us pray that we continue to live the life of the resurrection in and through Christ Jesus and be merciful to our neighbors. ✝

[2nd Easter (B)]

THIRD SUNDAY OF EASTER (C)

(Acts 5:27-32, 40-41; Revelation 5:11-14; John 21:1-19)

Is He Alive within Us?

The gospel narrative today is filled with images and metaphors, indicating God, the Creator, will draw everything back to Him through the resurrection of Jesus. At the same time, it calls for our response of following the footsteps of Peter, the Apostle.

After Jesus died on the cross, his disciples returned to their old profession of fishing on the Sea of Tiberias (Galilee, Gannesareth). But they caught no fish all night long. Early in the morning when the risen Jesus suddenly appeared and instructed them where to throw the net, then they caught abundant fish. Jesus even prepared breakfast with fish for them. Then Jesus asked Peter whether he loved him, not once, but three times.

We may wonder why the risen Jesus lingers on earth. Why not return to God and leave Peter and the other fishermen to resume their old way of living? The risen Lord must have something else in mind.

In the Gospel of John there are two charcoal fires. The first charcoal fire is in the high priests' courtyard, where Peter denies Jesus three times. This charcoal fire is transformed into the second charcoal fire by the Sea of Tiberias. Now, Jesus invites Peter to turn from his previous denials by means of confessing love three times. The risen Lord forgives Peter's weakness and empowers him to be the shepherd, who will nourish and defend his sheep from wolves and thieves and seek the lost ones (Jn 10:1-18).

Jesus certainly does not intend to open a wound in Peter. Jesus is not concerned with whether Peter likes the breakfast or whether Peter wants to be a fisherman again. Jesus is concerned with whether Peter has a warm and compassionate heart, which is otherwise known as love. This love is what the risen Lord looks for from Peter. Jesus is concerned with whether Peter loves him.

Earlier, during their public ministry together, Jesus said, "I do not call you servants any longer, but I have called you friends" (Jn 15:15). Now, on the shore of the Sea of Tiberias, Jesus wants Peter to grow in love as friends.

Earlier on the eve of the passion, Jesus told Peter, "You cannot follow me now, but you will follow me later" (Jn 13:36). Now, on the shore of the Sea of Tiberias, the risen Lord asks Peter to follow him.

Earlier, in the narrative of the vine and the branch, Jesus said, "No one has greater love than this, to lay down one's life for one's friends" (Jn 15:13). Now, on the shore of the Sea of Tiberias, Jesus asks Peter to lay down his life for his friends.

Jesus had to first lay down his life for his friends, so that his disciples could follow him. Now, Peter must begin to prepare for his own "hour," not really knowing, as usual, what that means. Eventually, Peter followed him. Legend says that Peter died near Rome, imitating Jesus, on a cross turned upside down (A.D. 64).

I said earlier that God, the Creator, will draw everything back to Him through the resurrection of Jesus. This is what resurrection means. We often think of resurrection in terms of dualistic notion, as if soul goes to heaven after body is left behind on earth. Of course, our souls will survive death. But the real faith in resurrection is more than the simple survival of soul. The faith in resurrection is that "every creature in heaven and on earth and under the earth and in the sea, everything in the universe" will be raised by God, as in the second reading. In other words, the resurrection of Jesus is God's promise for our future glory of the resurrection of body, the whole person. God creates all things and God will raise up all things.

We are called to follow Jesus. And we know that, in the course of following Jesus, we cannot avoid suffering and death. This is so because death and resurrection together constitute one reality. And one must die first before being raised up. Indeed, to be Christians "is a fearful thing to fall into the hands of the living God" (Heb 10:31). †

FOURTH SUNDAY OF EASTER (C), GOOD SHEPHERD SUNDAY

(Acts 13:14, 43-52; Revelation 7:9, 14-17; John 10:27-30)

Eternal Life

Jesus is the Good Shepherd through whom we attain eternal life. Today's readings are filled with the words "eternal life." In the Gospel, Jesus says, "My sheep hear my voice; I know them, and they follow me. I give them eternal life." In the first reading, "all who were destined for eternal life believed in" what Paul and Barnabas preached. In the second reading, John sees the lamb leading white-robed martyrs to "springs of life-giving water."

To understand that Jesus is the Good Shepherd who brings eternal life, let us describe a sheepfold in ancient Palestine. At night, shepherds put their sheep into a cave or sheepfold to protect them from wild animals. A sheepfold consisted of stone walls several feet high, with a narrow entrance. When Jesus says, "I am the gate," it means that Jesus puts his body in that narrow entrance, enclosing the sheep for the night.

Jesus says, "I know my sheep." This saying of Jesus may be illustrated by a story of motherhood. Several friends gather and exchange cheerful conversations while a baby sleeps in a separate room. Even amidst the depth of conversations, somewhat noisy, only the baby's mother can hear the baby's cry when she wakes up. Like the mother who hears her baby, Jesus hears the voice of his sheep.

Jesus says, "My sheep hear my voice." How sheep hear Jesus may be illustrated by comparing with a mother with a babysitter. No matter how tenderly and diligently a babysitter takes care of a baby, there is a time when the baby wants only her mother and cries until she comes. Like the baby who knows her mother, Jesus' sheep can hear the voice of the Good Shepherd.

We must learn, like a baby, how to listen to the Good Shepherd. The world we live in is full of many voices from false shepherds: It is okay to make money by cutting a corner. Just have fun and laugh it out. Don't be serious about life. Just keep quiet. Treat them as enemies if they have different opinions, and so on. All these noises from our secular and pluralistic world claim to rival eternal life, but they are not the voice of the Good Shepherd.

Jesus also says, "The Father and I are one." This unity between the Father and Jesus is our faith in Jesus Christ. It means the Father and the Son are one and, only through the Son, can we attain eternal life.

Eternal life is God's life. In God's life, the past, the present, and the future are combined and indistinguishable. Eternal life is not an unending life of a soul after being separated from a mortal body. Eternal life is the fullness of life of knowing Jesus Christ. Eternal life is not a future life only, but a present reality with God here and now. Eternal life has already begun. Therefore, those who don't live eternal life now may not enjoy it later on, when it is finally fulfilled.

Eternal life, (the kingdom of God in the Synoptics) is neither apprehensive grasping nor comprehension nor vision. It is hunger and hope, surrender and search, as we slip back and forth from light to darkness. Eternal life is to be grasped with faith, hope, and love. We can only live it in and through Jesus Christ.

Jesus is the eternal life and the Good Shepherd. When we are thirsty, he takes us to fresh waters. When we are hungry, he takes us to green pastures. On the way to green pastures and fresh waters, however, we are not going to be happy and joyful all the time. Sometimes there is cold rain with no cave to shelter. Sometimes there is famine, with no green grass to eat and no fresh water to drink. The Good Shepherd does not guarantee only good things in life. Failure, rejection, setback, poverty, sickness, and even death await us.

On the other hand, with the Good Shepherd hand in hand, we will watch gorgeous sunrises and glorious sunsets and millions of brilliant stars at night. The Good Shepherd redeems our toils and hard works, and he teaches us how to live a blessed, eternal life. ✝

[5th Lent (A), 4th Easter (A, B)]

FIFTH SUNDAY OF EASTER (C)

(Acts 14:21-27; Revelation 21:1-5; John 13:31-33, 34-35)

Love and Mercy Are the Answer

"I give you a new commandment: love one another. As I have loved you, so you also should love one another" (Jn 13:34).

This is the commandment Jesus gave to his disciples after he washed their feet on the night he was betrayed. Jesus concluded his prayer to the Father with these words: "I made your name known to them, and I will make it known, so that the love with which you have loved me may be in them, and I in them" (Jn 17:26). Jesus' love for us is rooted in his love for the Father and reveals the Father's love for us. It is truly remarkable that, simply because we love Jesus, we can be one with the Father.

This love of Jesus for his disciples, in the Gospel of John, is different from the love of neighbor in the Synoptic Gospels (Lk 19:18, Mt 22:37-39). In fact, the love of neighbor is not unique only to Christianity. Other great religions also regard it as a fundamental virtue. The distinctive love in John's Gospel is to love one another, in the same way as Jesus loves us. Jesus Christ is the condition of possibility (prerequisite) of the love of God. Therefore, as Jesus loves us, we ought to love ourselves and our brothers and sisters.

Early Christians believed that the resurrection of Jesus was the foundation of the world to come, which the Book of Revelation calls the "New Heaven and New Earth," where there will be "no more death or mourning, wailing or pain." Furthermore, Christians put this vision into practice. They shared their goods and possessions, and distributed them to all (Acts 2:44). No one claimed a private ownership, but everything they owned was held in common (Acts 4:32). This Christian doctrine on God's love and mercy was the driving force for the spread of Christianity throughout the Roman Empire, like an unquenchable fire. Only a handful Christians early thirties were numbered about 8,000 by the end of the first century.

The first reading describes a brief summary of missionary journey of Apostles. They organized local churches in major cities along Roman roads. In small cities where there was no synagogue, they built house-churches. And then, they appointed "elders," who had persevered in their faith. It was a sort of institution or ordination. And those Christian communities were bound together not only by common rites, but also by common ways of life. This superb spiritual unity and cohesiveness was the second reason for the rapid spread of Early Christianity.

The third reason why early Christianity spread so quickly was their attitude toward human dignity. Christians respected and cared for each other as sons and daughters of God. And so, for Diaspora Jews and Gentiles, Christian doctrines were a liberating force from their old moral and social bondages. Sociologists further suggest that the credible and ordered Christianity was well received by Roman society, because there were too many cults, too many mystery religions, and too many philosophies.

These three features of the Early Church can teach us valuable lessons today, because we have a similar situation in this twenty-first century. Not only numerous Christian denominations but also other non-Christian religions flourish all over the world under the banner of religious freedom. All these religions lift up slogans of love, mercy, justice, peace, and the like. Meanwhile, the world remains in a mess. There will not be peace and justice in the world without peace and justice among religions. Therefore, we must think about what Catholicism can do for the advancement of humanity, by enhancing peace and justice in the world.

One remarkable thing is that, even after the Church made an alliance with Roman Empire and took on hierarchical and institutional shape, these features remain more or less the same throughout the history of the Church. So, we are bound up with the Church, the visible sign of God's grace. Let us keep the light of Christ burning brightly with oils of our lives. ✝

[16ᵗʰ OT (B)]

SIXTH-SUNDAY OF EASTER (C)

(Acts 15:1-2, 22-29; Revelation 21:10-14, 22-23; John 14:23-29)

The Presence of the Holy Spirit

In his farewell discourse, Jesus asks his disciples to love one another as he loves them. Jesus is concerned about how his disciples will continue the Father's work he initiated and how they will maintain the Church he founded. Jesus also promises to send the Holy Spirit to them. The Holy Spirit will inspire and teach them everything they need to know by reminding them of the words and deeds of Jesus.

The Holy Spirit Jesus promised has come when Jesus' side is pierced after his death on the cross (Jn 19:34). The Holy Spirit has also come when the risen Jesus breathes on the disciples (Jn 20:22). This means that the Holy Spirit is the Spirit of the glorified Jesus, who has attained salvation for all human beings.

Another feature of the Holy Spirit is that the Holy Spirit always comes to the Christian community as a whole. The Holy Spirit helps the Church do the saving work of Jesus Christ. St. Irenaeus said, "Where the church is, there is the Spirit of God; and where there is the Spirit of God, there is the church and every grace."

Today's first reading provides an example of how the Holy Spirit works. As we know, Christianity began as a small sect within Judaism. As the Church grew out of Palestine, the question was, "Do the Gentiles need to become Jews in order to be Christians?" In our days, this question seems very strange. But it was a serious issue then. Those who had a deep and heartfelt attachment to Jewish Law strongly insisted that Christians imitate them—in other words, by becoming Jews, and first by circumcision. Thus the Christian community in Antioch, Syria sent Paul and Barnabas to Jerusalem for consultation with James and Peter. That was the so-called Council of Jerusalem, the first ecumenical council.

The Council declared that non–Jews were to follow some aspects of Jewish Law, such as eating, instead of actually becoming Jews. This decision regarding universal salvation for all Jews and Gentiles allowed Christianity to become a major world religion. It was the work of the Holy Spirit.

Today's second reading describes how John the Seer visualizes the New Jerusalem, the redeemed community of God's people. By the time the Book of Revelation was written, Jerusalem had already been destroyed by the Romans. Therefore, the visionary John saw the New Jerusalem in faith. The New Jerusalem needs no Temple, because the Holy Spirit is not confined to one place. The New Jerusalem needs no light, because the glory of God shines through the Lamb, the Son of God.

If we think about the world in which we live, it is true that it is filled with unceasing conflicts, troubles, and wars. Nevertheless, if we look at the world carefully through the eye of God, the world is also filled with a thousand lights of different kinds. We are surrounded by many humble people who devote their lives to others. The Holy Spirit helps us to learn from them. We live between the Book of Genesis and the Book of Revelation, subjecting ourselves to the rule of the Holy Spirit.

Finally, the Gospels are not something to look at, but to look through. The Gospels, like lenses, provide varying intelligible patterns in history. We can, therefore, receive the teachings of Jesus today, in our own unique history, similar to the manner in which they were received by the first disciples. Accordingly, we should be able to write the Gospel of Jesus Christ in our own situations just as John, Luke, Mark, and Matthew did. The Holy Spirit will help us do that.

The Holy Spirit provides us an opportunity to partake of the eternal life of the risen Jesus. Just as Jesus was raised from the dead and sits at the right hand of the heavenly Father, the Holy Spirit inspires us to follow Jesus' footsteps. This is the gift of the Holy Spirit, and we gain access to it through faith. ✝

[Pentecost (A)]

SEVENTH SUNDAY OF EASTER (C)

(Acts 7:55-60; Revelation 22:12-14, 16-17, 20; John 17:20-26)

The First Martyr of the Church

"Father...I made known to them your name...that the love with which you loved me may be in them and I in them" (Jn 17:26). This is the high priestly prayer Jesus offered for his disciples on the night when he was betrayed.

As the hour of his death approached, Jesus shared with his disciples the deepest meaning of his life and laid out his last testament to them. Moreover, Jesus prayed that his disciples would be in union with the Father through him, so that all would be one with Him.

Many of Jesus' disciples indeed followed in their Master's footsteps, even unto death. Martyrdom was very common in the Church's early history and was named "the seed of Christianity" by Tertullian and was considered "the baptism of blood" by Origen.

In today's first reading, we heard about Stephen's martyrdom. The death of the first martyr was extremely important for the early Church; it was described in detail and at length. Stephen died in a way similar to Jesus. As Jesus was crucified at Golgotha, outside of Jerusalem, so Stephen was stoned outside of Jerusalem. As Jesus prayed to the Father, "Father into your hands I commend my spirit," so Stephen prayed to the risen Lord, "Lord Jesus, receive my spirit." Finally, just as Jesus said, "Father, forgive them, for they do not know what they are doing," so Stephen cried out, "Lord, do not hold this sin against them."

At the end of his prayer, "Stephen, filled with the Holy Spirit, looked up intently to heaven and saw the glory of God and Jesus standing at the right hand of God." The fact that Jesus "stands" at God's right hand means that Jesus was with Stephen as Advocate before the judge, God the Father.

God works in mysterious ways. Paul, who once harshly persecuted Christians, watched Stephen dying. For Paul, the seed of faith was already planted then, and soon he became an apostle for the Gentiles.

Our faith has been handed down to us from our ancestors, like Paul and Stephen, who in turn received their faith from the risen Lord. In addition, our faith has been strengthened through the words and examples of others—our families, friends, and acquaintances. Even people we do not know have inspired us, and their commitments to Christian principles have affected us. Our faith is strengthened in the community so that, through all of us, the glory of Jesus Christ is revealed to the world. We may not always reflect upon this, but God works in a mysterious way.

Jesus' prayer near the hour of his death is sublime. Knowing that we are no longer of the world, even though we still are in the world, Jesus prays that we may be in union with the Father through him. Jesus, a poet, prays to the Father for us: "that the love with which you loved me may be in them and I in them." Jesus of Nazareth in the Gospel of John is the risen Jesus.

We encounter the risen Jesus during the celebration of the Eucharist, which will begin in a few minutes. If we believe the Son of God came to us in the flesh, and if we believe that Jesus' death and resurrection occurred in the flesh, it is only through the flesh of the risen Jesus we are healed and saved. The Eucharist is the risen Jesus who comes to us in the flesh. It is only through the flesh and blood of the risen Jesus we can find our true selves.

The risen Jesus comes to us so that we show to the whole world who we are and what we do. We are sons and daughters of God the Father, and brothers and sisters of Jesus Christ. We build the kingdom of God on earth according to the Gospel of Jesus Christ.

Let us enter into God's time in silence and prepare ourselves for the celebration of the Eucharist. ✝

PENTECOST SUNDAY (C)

(Acts 2:1-11; 1 Corinthians 12:3-7, 12-13; John 20:19-23)

The Role of the Holy Spirit

The Easter Season has ended, and we are about to begin a long journey of ordinary Sundays. To prepare ourselves for this journey, the Holy Spirit comes to our aid on this Pentecost Sunday.

(In Judaism, Pentecost, the Feast of Weeks, is the birthday of the nation of Israel, celebrating the reception of the Law of Moses on Mount Sinai fifty days after the Passover. In Christianity, Pentecost is the birthday of the Church, signifying the empowerment of the Holy Spirit after fifty days of Easter.)

In today's gospel reading, the disciples of Jesus received the Holy Spirit as they were commissioned on the evening of the first Easter Sunday. The risen Jesus empowered his disciples to build the kingdom of God and breathed upon them, saying, "Receive the Holy Spirit. As the Father has sent me, so I send you." And "they were all filled with the Holy Spirit."

What does it mean to be "filled with the Holy Spirit?" It means to acknowledge our solidarity with Jesus by proclaiming, "Jesus is Lord!" It means that I choose Jesus, not worldly fame and honor. It means that Jesus is the ethical and moral paradigm. This conviction, however, is a serious challenge for us in this world where comfort and security are valued, money and power are worshiped.

God the Father is the Creator. The Son reveals the Father. The Holy Spirit is the love for both uniting and distinguishing the Father and the Son. The Father never ceases to create, and the Son never ceases to reveal the Father. The Holy Spirit is the permanent expression of this dynamism of continuous creation and revelation.

The Holy Spirit is the Spirit of Christ who dwells in our hearts (Gal 2:20 and 4:6, Rom 5:5 and 8:11, 1 Cor 3:16 and 6:19, Eph 3:16, Col 1:27, 2 Tm 1:14). The Holy Spirit within us enables us to abide in God (Jn 14:17, 1 Jn 4:4, 1 Jn

4:13). The Holy Spirit within us enables us to experience God, just as Jesus experienced the radical union with God (Jn 10:30). The Holy Spirit within us says, "It is no longer I who live, but Christ who lives in me" (Gal 2:20).

The Holy Spirit is God's breath of life and gives life to all things (2 Cor 3:6). The Holy Spirit enables us to participate in God's life. The Holy Spirit ensures the Church to continue the saving work of Jesus Christ. The Holy Spirit is manifested in all sacramental realities of the Church—the Temple of the Holy Spirit.

For example, the Holy Spirit enables us to encounter Christ during the Eucharistic celebration. The Eucharist is the sacramental reality in which Christ appears to us by the power of the Holy Spirit. This is why Jesus said, "It is better for you that I go away, because if I do not go away, the Spirit will not come" (Jn 16:7).

The Holy Spirit is like the wind, which is not to be seen. John writes: "The Spirit (wind) blows where it chooses, and you hear the sound of it, but you do not know where it comes from or where it goes" (Jn 3:8). As it happened on the road to Emmaus, the Spirit of Christ appears and disappears. Thus we pray *in* the Spirit, not *to* the Spirit. And the Holy Spirit can only be known by Her effects.

Finally, it says that in the Second Letter to Corinthians "where the Spirit of the Lord is, there is freedom" (3:17). Conversely, where there is fear, there is no Spirit. And what is free cannot be manufactured arbitrarily. This is why the Spirit is least known to our culture and often be interpreted mistakenly.

As we journey in the Holy Spirit, let us remember that Pentecost is not simply an event of the past, confined to the first followers of Jesus in Jerusalem two thousand years ago. Rather, Pentecost is for us to share the Spirit of the risen Jesus here and now. Pentecost reminds us that we are the people with gifts our neighbors need desperately. Pentecost reminds us that we are the people who can heal the world, our communities, and our families. *Veni, Sancte Spiritus.* ✝

[Pentecost (A), 14th OT (A)]

THE MOST HOLY TRINITY SUNDAY (C)

(Proverbs 8:22-31; Romans 5:1-5; John 16:12-15)

Triune God and Christian Life

"The love of God has been poured into our hearts through the Holy Spirit" (Rom 5:5). This scripture passage from the second reading is the basis of one of our favorite prayers: "Come Holy Spirit, fill the hearts of your faithful and enkindle in them the fire of your divine love." God has poured His love into our hearts, so that the Holy Spirit actualizes this gift of God within us. It is one of St. Paul's famous exhortations on the Holy Trinity.

The doctrine of the Holy Trinity says that God the Father has given Himself, once and for all, to humanity through His Son, Jesus Christ with the help of the Holy Spirit. The silent and incomprehensible God creates and redeems the world in the power of the Holy Spirit through the Word Incarnate. The doctrine is about how God forgives, heals, and transforms, that is—how to save all human beings. It is the grammar of how God reconciles the world to Himself (2Cor 5:19). The doctrine of the Holy Trinity says that God is above us as the Father, among us as the Word, and within us as the Spirit. Simply put it, God is for us.

As we celebrate the Feast of the Holy Trinity today, let us reflect on three Trinitarian virtues—poverty, chastity, and obedience. They are contraries to and opposites of our most fundamental, and yet dangerous desires—money, sex, and power. Thus poverty, chastity, and obedience provide a key to a healthy Christian life anchored in the Holy Trinity.

Poverty relates to a special trust in the providence of the Father. The Beatitude begins with the virtue of poverty: "Blessed are you who are poor, for yours is the kingdom of God" (Lk 6:20).

Chastity concerns special dedication to the Son. Chastity is the center of Christian life and helps us maintain the human dignity based on true freedom. It is sad and shocking to say that in the world we live in the word chastity is rapidly disappearing from our dictionary.

Obedience involves special devotion to the Holy Spirit. The word "obedience" comes from the Latin word meaning "to hear." Religious sisters, monks, and priests, by taking a vow of obedience, dedicate themselves to the Holy Spirit, who speaks through their superiors.

Moreover, these three virtues—poverty, chastity, and obedience—are the same virtues against which Jesus was tempted. Right after the baptism, Jesus was led by an angel into the desert (Mt 4:1-11). There, Satan asks Jesus to convert stone into bread. He wants Jesus to be rich, instead of being poor. Next, Satan asks Jesus to throw himself from the Temple of Jerusalem. He wants Jesus not to embrace chastity. Finally, Satan takes Jesus to a high mountain overlooking all the kingdoms of the world. He wants Jesus not to be obedient to the Father, but to pursue his own power.

Christian life is a Trinitarian life rooted in poverty, chastity, and obedience—trusting the Father, following the Son, and being docile to the Holy Spirit.

The Holy Trinity is a practical doctrine for us to genuinely experience the living God, who is already-always present in anything and everything we do in life. To be a human is to be in relationship with God, whether we realize it or not. The doctrine of the Holy Trinity is the dynamism of God's grace, offering Himself to all of us and inviting us to partake in His divine life. To be a human is to be in God's grace all the time. Surely, we are more than what we merely are, because God has come to us in Jesus Christ and poured the Holy Spirit of love into our hearts.

Trinitarian virtues—poverty, chastity, and obedience are for all Christians. In this world of materialism, we need to live in accordance with the will of the Father. In this world of individualism, we need to follow Jesus Christ as he commands: "Love one another as I have loved you" (Jn 15:12). In this world of secularism with numerous options and choices to choose, we need to listen to the Holy Spirit.

Let us conclude with the Sign of the Cross, a Trinitarian action: "In the name of the Father, and of the Son, and of the Holy Spirit, Amen." ✝ [1st Lent (C), Christ King (C), Holy Trinity (A, B)]

The Most Holy Body and Blood of Christ Sunday (C)

(Genesis 14:18-20; 1 Corinthians 11:23-26; Luke 9:11-17)

The Sacrament of Ongoing Christian Life

There is a cathedral in Germany that has four front doors. Something unique about the doors is that each door has a sculpture referring to an event found in the Gospels.

The first door shows six water jars, Jesus and Mary, and some other people. It is about the miracle in Cana. The second door shows Jesus sitting with twelve disciples. It is about the Last Supper. The third door shows Jesus at a table with two people. It is about Jesus having dinner with two disciples on the way to Emmaus. The fourth door shows five loaves of bread and two fish, with Jesus and a lot of people around him. It is about Jesus feeding the five thousand, as we have heard in today's gospel reading. All four doors lead to the altar, on which the Eucharist is celebrated.

On the altar, a piece of bread and a cup of wine are consecrated (spiritualized and personalized) by the power of the Holy Spirit and are transformed into the body and blood of Christ. We continue the death and resurrection of Jesus through the mediation of the Last Supper. The risen Jesus wants to be with us so intensely that he comes to us in the form of the bread and wine; he makes us holy through the consecrated bread and wine.

What a comforting thought to ponder that we can be in union with the risen Jesus! However, the union with Jesus requires sacrifice in this fallen world filled with division and hatred and fear. God's love and mercy come only at the expense of sacrifice. Jesus broke the bread and then gave it to his disciples in an anticipation of his impending sacrificial death on the cross. In an imitation of Jesus' sacrifice, the priest breaks the bread at Mass before he gives it to us.

We remember the story of the two disciples on their way to Emmaus (Lk 24:13-35). Jesus suddenly appeared to those frustrated disciples and explained that the Messiah had to suffer and die. Later, when Jesus broke the bread, they recognized Jesus as the Christ and, at that very moment,

Jesus disappeared. "Where did he go?" we wonder. "When will he come again?" we ask. Actually, the risen Jesus disappeared within the two disciples when they ate him, the consecrated bread.

In the same way, when we break ourselves, that is, when we sacrifice for others, the risen Jesus appears among us. This is the way the Eucharist builds the Church: "The Church draws her life from the Eucharist" (*Ecclesia Eucharistia*, #1).

During Communion, when the Eucharist minister says, "the body of Christ," we respond, "Amen." What does this "Amen" mean? Of course, it means that the Eucharist we are about to receive is the body of Christ, the risen Jesus. Going beyond this reality, we must internalize this sacred reality and live it fully in our daily lives.

By saying "Amen," we identify ourselves as members of the mystical Body of Christ, the Church. St. Augustine said in his sermon, "What you receive is what you yourselves are (Sermon #229).... So become members of the Body of Christ, in order to make that Amen true" (Sermon #272). Therefore, by responding "Amen," we affirm we will be transformed into Christ. This is why we often see the image of Christ in the faces of our brothers and sisters. The horizontal and the vertical are inseparably linked in the Eucharist. The Eucharist is the sacrament of ongoing Christian life.

In a few minutes, we will come to the altar to eat the bread and drink the wine of the risen Jesus. We will share the one body and one blood of Christ, who is love par excellence. On one hand, we are not worthy to receive the risen Lord. On the other hand, we are very worthy, because God is love.

So we will be loved once again, and we will be fed once again. We will then be sent forth into the world to live that love, as the body of Christ. Christ comes to us so that we may become another Christ. ✝

[Corpus Christi (A, B), 14ᵗʰ OT (C), 19ᵗʰ OT (B)]

SECOND SUNDAY IN ORDINARY TIME (C)

(Isaiah 62:1-5; 1 Corinthians 12:4-11; John 2:1-11)

Sharing in God's Work of Creation

We are created in the image and likeness of God, so that we continue to do God's work of creation. Artists create beautiful images from seemingly ordinary objects. Musicians create joy and happiness with harmonious sounds. Scientists create theories about what is going on in nature. Businessmen create new jobs. Lawyers create social values more advanced than before. Doctors create better quality of life. All of us create something valuable for the advancement of humanity.

Even saying simple "Hellos" to our neighbors or picking up a trash in a street creates something good to humanity. In fact, the goal of life is to create something good and positive to humanity.

Among all these creative acts, a wedding ceremony marks the recognition for a bride and a groom to participate in God's creative work. It is one of happiest and most privileged moments of life.

In today's gospel reading, Jesus performs his first miracle at the wedding in Cana. When they run out of wine, Mary first notices it and informs Jesus. Reluctantly, Jesus converts the water in six large stone-jars into wine. The water reserved for Jewish ceremonial washings is converted into a choice wine in super abundance, almost two hundreds gallons. And the wedding feast continues.

It is interesting to reflect upon Jesus' words to his mother: "Woman, how does your concern affect me?" Jesus calls his mother "woman." This sounds arrogant, if we put too heavy emphasis on Jesus' humanity. It is not just Mary, however. Both the Samaritan woman (Jn 4:21) and Mary Magdalene (Jn 20:15) are called woman. In John's Gospel, Jesus, the Son of God, uses the language inclusive to all women.

Jesus also says to Mary, "My hour has not yet come." In John's Gospel, Jesus predicts his being lifted up three times (Jn 3:14, 8:28, 12:32), whereas in the Synoptic Gospels, Jesus predicts his passion and death three times (Mk 8:31, 9:31, 10:33). The "hour" is the time for Jesus' passion, death, and resurrection as one great event. At the hour when Jesus is lifted up on the cross, the glory of God appears. The miracle at the wedding in Cana is an anticipation and preview of the fullness of God's glory.

Accordingly, this miracle in Cana reveals the power of God, signaling the messianic age. And the wine at the wedding in Cana is a foretaste of the wine Jesus will bless at the Last Supper and will eventually be transformed into the blood of Jesus Christ. It is the whole new way of saving God's people. This is why, when we drink the consecrated wine during Mass, we drink the blood of Christ.

Last Sunday, we celebrated the Baptism of the Lord, which marks the beginning of the Ordinary Time. Hence, the sign at Cana invites us to reflect upon how we can drink the wine Jesus blessed at the wedding in Cana. In other words, how we can continue to share God's creative work throughout the year.

A plausible answer to these questions comes from the second reading. After Paul founded the church in Corinth, an affluent city in Asia Minor, the Corinthians became enthusiastic and somewhat disorderly. They liked exotic spiritual gifts, such as speaking in tongues. Paul insisted that the source of all spiritual gifts is Jesus Christ. They have different gifts but the same Holy Spirit dwells within them, uniting all of them totally to God. Therefore, rather than boasting individual identity and accomplishments, they must go down deeper into their hearts and encounter the risen Jesus there.

That same teaching is applicable to us today. Every one of us is unique and performs different aspects of God's creative work, yet it is one God who inspires all. We are one in Christ. Mother Teresa put it nicely: "You can do something I can't do. I can do something you can't do. Together let us do something beautiful for God." All of us make up one proud community of Jesus Christ. Let us continue to do the creative works of God. For Jesus says later on in the Gospel, "I came so that they might have life and have it more abundantly (Jn 10:10). ✝

THIRD SUNDAY IN ORDINARY TIME (C)

(Nehemiah 8:2-4, 5-6, 8-10; 1 Corinthians 12:12-30; Luke 1:1-4, 4:14-21)

The Word of the Lord

"One Word the Father spoke; it was His Son. The Word speaks always in eternal silence. And in silence the Word should be heard by the soul." This quote is from St. John of the Cross (*The Ascent of Mount Carmel*, Book 2, *22*, #4).

God spoke through the prophets before. Now God has spoken His final word through His Son, Jesus Christ (Heb 1:1-2). God has spoken all at last; God has no more to say. God is eternally present in the person of Jesus Christ, who is the fulfillment of the times (Mk 1:15).

In the gospel reading, Jesus returns to his hometown after being tempted in the desert. He attends the synagogue on the Sabbath day. A scroll is presented to him, and he gets up to read Isaiah from the scroll. After Jesus reads the passage, he sits down. "The eyes of all in the synagogue looked intently at him." Then, Jesus says, "Today, this scripture passage is fulfilled in your hearing." It means that Jesus is the fulfillment of the prophecy of Isaiah. Jesus is the Messiah. That is all Jesus has to say. It is the shortest homily ever delivered. Jesus has revealed precisely who he is—the eternal Word.

The Word was made flesh, and thus we often experience the presence of God in our daily lives. We feel God's presence when we are possessed by the remarkable wonders of nature. We feel God's presence when we forgive someone, with no expectation of returning gratitude. We feel God's presence when we experience the terrible gulf between what we desire and the reality of life. We feel God's presence when we are utterly faithful to the depths of our consciences, even when everyone rejects our opinions. We feel God's presence when we finally accept sheer loneliness. We feel God's presence in all of these moments, because the Word was made flesh.

The first reading describes a moving scene of how the Jews in Jerusalem after the Exile celebrated the Liturgy of the Word. Ezra the priest-scribe read the words of the law "in the presence of the men, the women, and those children old enough to understand," and then, "all the people were weeping."

We also listen to the Word of the Lord during Mass. The Church teaches that "Christ is present...when the holy scriptures are read in the Church" (*Sacrosanctum Concilium*, #7). We are attentive to the Word of the Lord and affectively moved by it. And the Word of the Lord culminates with the Eucharistic celebration, where we encounter the risen Jesus in his flesh and blood.

How, then, can we listen to the Word? We first listen with the ear of the mind. We become attentive and make God's words intelligible. This is the intellectual approach, and it doesn't have to be academic or scholarly. We then listen to the Word with the ear of the heart. By connecting the Word with our life experiences, we attain affective knowledge and encounter the living God in faith. The love of God moves our hearts, and we find that the eternal Word is not somewhere far away, but resides in the depths of our beings. Thus, we become mystics in our own unique ways.

In the second reading, Paul talks about the unity in diversity of the Christian community. We have different and distinct roles and functions in this community, but we are brothers and sisters of the One Lord, the eternal Word. The Word was made flesh, so we are sons and daughters of God and members of one body of Christ.

God spoke through the prophets before. Now God has spoken His final Word through His Son, Jesus Christ. God has spoken all at last; God has no more to say. God is eternally present in the person of Jesus Christ, who is the fulfillment of the times. "One Word the Father spoke; it was His Son. The Word speaks always in eternal silence. And in silence the Word should be heard by the soul." ✝

[Pentecost (B), 4th Adv (B), 4th OT (B), 15th OT (A), Christ King (C)]

FOURTH SUNDAY IN ORDINARY TIME (C)

(Jeremiah 1:4-5, 17-19; 1 Corinthians 12:31-13:13; Luke 4:21-30)

Jesus Is Love Incarnate

Throughout history, there have been people ahead of their time. Their ideas were so advanced and often unpopular that people rejected them. As a result, they led miserable lives full of suffering. They were considered crazy, even though their ideas were accepted later in history. For example, Vincent van Gogh, the famous Dutch painter, earned very little money from his paintings in his lifetime. Now, his paintings are worth several hundred million dollars.

When Jesus came to his hometown, his own people rejected him, as we heard in today's gospel reading. Perhaps they didn't accept Jesus' claim of being the Son of Man. Perhaps they expected Jesus to perform miracles as he had in Capernaum. So they dragged Jesus away and almost threw him off a cliff.

Jesus was rejected in his hometown because he is Love Incarnate. St. John, after reflecting upon what happened since the creation of the world and what Jesus did, concluded that God is love.

In the same way, Jesus' earthly life makes him the Love Incarnate. Jesus has created a new meaning of love for all human beings. This is the reason why Jesus was rejected in his hometown.

We know that love is the most precious and powerful thing in life. We long for love that lasts forever and satisfies all the time. But there is no such perfect love. We only catch a glimpse of perfect love, at best. We always search for it, but never grasp it completely.

It is not easy to define what love really is. Scripture does not define exactly what love is either. As we heard in the second reading, Paul says to the Corinthians, "Love is patient, love is kind. Love is not jealous; love is not pompous...." Here, Paul tries to explain what love is in terms of more than a dozen virtues. This means that love is the mother of all virtues. All virtues are grounded to love. Without love, no one can attain any virtue. Therefore, to have a virtuous life, one must first love.

We may ask, "How can this be so?" Before we try to answer this question, let us look closely at the linguistics of love. In English, we have only one word for love. In Greek, there are several words for love: *agape* for the love of God, *eros* between man and woman, and *philia* among friends. Moreover, we usually consider *eros* apart from *agape,* and *agape* apart from *eros.* Against this dualism of love, Pope Benedict XVI issued his first encyclical letter, *God Is Love* (*Deus Caritas Est*). He says that God's desire to glorify mankind is so intense that the incarnation is the manifestation of God's *eros.* And God's love to follow his Son even unto his death is so sublime that the cross is the climax of God's *agape.*

It is surprising to learn that God's love, which I believed to be *agape,* can be *eros.* And man's love, which I believed to be *eros,* can be *agape* too. Therefore, *eros* and *agape* are two distinct dimensions of love, rather than two different types of love. Love is one reality. In Jesus Christ, *eros* and *agape* are combined and make up one and the same love. By contrast, our human love is basically self-centered. And if *eros* is left alone, an undesirable situation will develop due to its destructive nature. To have a holy and virtuous life, therefore, our self-seeking *eros* must mature and be purified into self-giving *agape.*

Jesus Christ has shown us "that love comes from God and that love unites us to God." Jesus Christ is the condition necessary for us to love. Jesus Christ is the source of the one reality of love. Jesus Christ has created a new meaning of love for us. Therefore, in Jesus Christ and through Jesus Christ, we can purify and transform *eros* into *agape.* In fact, how we manage to love and to be loved, by purifying *eros* to *agape,* decides whether we attain salvation or not.

We give thanks to Jesus Christ, who has shown us that God is love and thus changed the very meaning of love. Jesus Christ is the Love Incarnate. Therefore, those who truly follow Jesus are likely to be rejected, even by his own people. **✝**

[7th Easter (B), 30th OT (A)]

FIFTH SUNDAY IN ORDINARY TIME (C)

(Isaiah 6:1-2, 3-8; 1 Corinthians 15:1-11; Luke 5:1-11)

God's Call in the Postmodern Age

Called by God, we gather here in this sacred place to celebrate the Holy Mystery. Strange as it may sound, however, we cannot recall exactly how it was when God first called us.

God calls us in a warm spring breeze. God calls us among brilliant stars at night. God calls us among the unspoken faces of loved ones. God calls us in loneliness at night. God calls us through frustrated conscience in hope. God calls us at the early departures of beloved ones. When God call us, however, He rarely uses a direct human voice. This is why we cannot describe precisely when and how God has called us. But we know for sure that God has called us.

When God calls prophets and apostles in the Bible, His call is usually described in a way that is esoteric, irrational, and mystical (*The Idea of the Holy* by Rudolf Otto).

In the first reading, Isaiah experienced a heavenly vision of God in a temple. God was like a warrior Lord on a high and lofty throne guarded by angels who cried out, "Holy, holy, holy is the Lord of hosts." (Holy here means God's transcendence.) This imagery of God was further accentuated with smoke and earthquake. Isaiah was overwhelmed by his unworthiness and responded, "Woe to me, I am doomed, for I am a man of unclean lips." God purified him, and Isaiah accepted God's offer, saying, "Here I am."

Jesus calls Peter and his fishing companions in the same way. Peter, an experienced fisherman, cannot catch any fish all night long. Suddenly, Jesus appears and asks him to put the net in a deep-water. Peter does it reluctantly. Then he catches a great multitude of fish, to the point of tearing his nets. Peter knows this miraculous catch of fish means that God's promise has been fulfilled, as well as God's judgment being at hand. Thus he cries out, "Depart from me, Lord, for I am a sinful man." Jesus calms him down: "Do not be afraid, from now on you will be catching men."

(God's call and the disciples' responses are in a dynamic relationship. God reveals Himself, and they recognize their inadequacies or unworthiness. God assures His fidelity, and they follow Him.)

Jesus calls us, too. However, Jesus' call for each of us seems to be less dramatic than those for the prophets or apostles. Perhaps because we are influenced by modern science and technology, we cannot easily describe Jesus' call if it comes through esoteric or mystical language. But we know for sure that Jesus calls us.

God is the Holy Mystery. We can know something about God but never understand God. We can feel God's love, but never fully. God is always present with us, but we cannot grasp it completely. This mystical and transcendence of God is quite fitting for our age.

We live in an age called "postmodernity." To be more precise, we are in transition from modernity to postmodernity. Postmodernity is a sort of "protest" against modernity, which has been characterized by intellectualism, positivism, and microchip technologies. One of the most important aspects of postmodernity is the emphasis on irrational and transcendental knowledge that comes from the heart, rather than from the mind (intellect and reason). Postmodernity also respects individual experiences with varying habits and cultures.

We welcome postmodernity. God reveals Himself in a postmodern way. God, who is the Absolute, the Other, or the Holy Mystery, is beyond our logical description and rational knowledge. This is why Isaiah and Peter, when called by God, were terrified and then cried out their unworthiness and inadequacy. This is why we do not remember clearly how and when God has called us.

Postmodernity is an ideal time to be religious and to become disciples of Jesus Christ. Postmodernity is a good time to open our hearts to Jesus Christ, who is the same yesterday, today, and tomorrow (Heb 13:8). ✝

[10ᵗʰ OT (A), 16ᵗʰ OT (B)]

SIXTH SUNDAY IN ORDINARY TIME (C)

(Jeremiah 17:5-8; 1 Corinthians 15:12, 16-20; Luke 6:17, 20-26)

Blessings and Curses

As we come to know Jesus more clearly, we boldly, and often spontaneously, speak out our Christian values. This tends to spoil the atmosphere at a party or gathering. As a result, we are blessed with Christian values, but often cursed by the world.

The first reading and responsorial psalm speak of blessings and curses. Those who trust in God are like trees planted near running water. They will thrive even in hard times and will be a source of life for others. In contrast, those who trust in humans are like the barren bush in a desert. They may live for now, but will disappear in hard times.

Moses set forth the same blessings and curses to the Israelites when they were about to enter the Promised Land: "I have set before you life and death, blessings and curses. Choose life so that you and your descendants may live" (Dt 30:19). Blessing and curse are often indistinguishable or inseparable.

One intimate occasion that is both blessing and curse involves the blessing we give to our sons and daughters when, for example, we send them off to colleges or universities. They are adults now and need to face the world by themselves. So we bless them and hope that they may not be cursed by the world.

Jesus provides us with these same blessings in the gospel reading. He goes out to the mountain to pray and chooses his twelve disciples (Lk 16:12-16). He comes down with them to a plain where many people gather, including the Gentiles from Tyre and Sidon. He then blesses the people by way of the Sermon on the Plain.

(In Luke's Gospel, Jesus comes down from the mountain to the plain where all the people of the world gather, and gives the Sermon on the Plain. By contrast, in Matthew's Gospel, Jesus and his disciples go up the mountain to pray, and there Jesus gives the Sermon on the Mount (Mt 4:23–7:29). Luke's Gospel was written for Gentile Christians, whereas Matthew's Gospel was written for Jewish Christians.)

The Sermon on the Plain sets forth the ethics in the kingdom of God. Jesus so loves us that he gives us the code of conduct that is necessary to live the life of God in this world.

The Sermon on the Plain also focuses on the primacy of God rather than the things of this world. God is the source and ground of all things. If we choose God, we will be blessed. If we choose the world, we will be cursed.

The Sermon on the Plain, however, turns everything upside down. For example, what does it mean that the poor or the hungry are blessed? Jesus knows very well that poverty and hunger are evils must be eradicated. Why, then, are the poor blessed? The poor are blessed because they are not attached to things of this world. The rich are cursed because they worship worldly possessions, not God.

The world in which we live is finite and temporal, and nothing in this world will genuinely satisfy our souls. Once we have achieved a certain goal in life, another one lurks at the door. Once we have accumulated some money, more money is needed. We long for and pursue honor, glory, fame, status, and love; we can never grasp and attain them fully. We cannot be completely and permanently satisfied with things of the world. Our souls desire and yearn for God. We are made for eternity.

We must make a choice, therefore. We must ask ourselves: What is the most important thing in life? What is the central point of life? What is the ultimate concern for us? What is the final fulfillment for us? Our answers to these questions decide whether we will be blessed or cursed. The answer for us, of course, is Jesus Christ, who has revealed God for us by his life, death, and resurrection. Only in Jesus Christ, can we live the life of God, with hope for the resurrection. ✝

[4th and 30th OT (A)]

SEVENTH SUNDAY IN ORDINARY TIME (C)

(1 Samuel 26:2, 7-9, 12-13, 22-23; 1 Corinthians 15:45-49; Luke 6:27-38)

Love Your Enemies

"Love your enemies." This is one of Jesus' most paradoxical teachings. All religions have moral and ethical instructions pertaining to justice and peace. And so the ancient Jews were taught not to mistreat the enemy (Prov 25:21). However, only Jesus insisted on *loving* the enemy—one of the most important but paradoxical teachings.

Most of us have enough difficulty loving our own family and friends. To love those who hate us, to bless those who curse us, and to pray for those who don't like us do not appeal to our common sense. Still, it is the main point of today's gospel message.

In the gospel reading, we have also heard the golden rule: "Do to others as you would have them do to you" (Lk 6:31, Mt 7:12). Just imagine what a wonderful world it would be if everyone practiced this rule. We would be kind, loving, and considerate to whomever we meet. In return, others would treat us in kind, loving, and considerate ways. If everybody practiced this rule, the entire world would exist in perfect peace and harmony. We would never have international conflicts and wars. We would never experience racism and human abuses of all different kinds.

If we look at this golden rule carefully, however, it is limited and aimed at self-preservation. In fact, we treat others well in order for ourselves to be treated well. The golden rule is short of perfection, especially if compared to Jesus' teaching of "love your enemies."

Jesus teaches that, by loving our enemies, we follow the example of God, who is "kind to the ungrateful and the wicked." God is kind and merciful to both the righteous and the wicked: "God makes his sun rise on the evil and on the good, and sends rain on the righteous and on the unrighteous" (Mt 5:45). Therefore, Jesus challenges us "to be merciful, just as God the Father is merciful." Jesus asks us to look, not from our human perspectives, but from God's perspective.

Yes, indeed, we shall act as God acts because we live in the kingdom of God. This is the ultimate goal in Christian ethics and morality. We must always remember that for us to attain God's divine nature, the Son of God has become fully human by taking on human flesh and *has shown* us how God acts.

In the second reading, Paul explained that both the earthly man (the first Adam) and the heavenly man (the second Adam) dwell within us. Accordingly, we must detach ourselves from the first Adam by denying our egos and selfishness, and, at the same time, we must attach ourselves to the second Adam by letting Christ be formed in us (Gal 4:19). God's love poured into our hearts through the Holy Spirit helps us to cultivate the second Adam within us (Rom 5:5).

Naturally, we are baptized into Jesus' death and share in the life-giving Spirit that flows from Christ's resurrection, which points at our own resurrection. Our final state is not death, but eternal life with God. We belong to the new humanity in a new age. This is another reason why Jesus teaches us to forgive our enemies.

Today's first reading shows that David passed up an opportunity to kill King Saul. The reason, if we interpret the Bible literally, is that Saul was God's anointed. This is indeed what David said. At a deeper level, however, it was not because Saul was anointed, but because David was graced by God and became as holy as God (Lv 11:45). David became as merciful as the Father (Lk 6:36), so he was able to love his enemy. David was able to see with God's eyes, by forming Christ within him, so he loved his enemy.

We love our enemies because they are created in the image of God as we are, and because they will be raised as we will be. To achieve this ultimate goal of Christian ethics, however, we need to empty ourselves and let Christ be formed within us, so we can see with God's eyes. ✝

[6th Easter (B)]

Eighth Sunday in Ordinary Time (C)

(Sirach 27:4-7; 1 Corinthians 15:54-58; Luke 6:39-45)

We Become What We Do

"Hypocrite, remove the wooden beam from your own eye first; then you will see clearly to remove the splinter in your brother's eye." This aphorism, although much exaggerated, rings true. We judge others on their seeming evils, all the while hiding or neglecting the evil within our own selves. Evil always coexists with good. Therefore, the evil within us must first be recognized.

We find several more aphorisms in today's readings. One from the Gospel reads, "A good man produces goodness from the good in his heart; an evil man produces evil out of his store of evil." Another, from the first reading, states, "A man's speech discloses the bent of his mind." These two aphorisms suggest that the heart is the source of man's deeds. If we are good persons, we perform virtuous deeds. If we are bad persons, we perform evil deeds. What kind of hearts we have decides what kind of persons we are and, subsequently, what kind of deeds we perform.

Let us consider what heart is and how important it is. In the recent history of civilization, we have made heavy use of intellect and will. We always think hard; we always reason accurately; we always judge perfectly. As a result, our heads have grown much too big. Our hearts have become too small. And we are not easily convinced by things that are non-logical, non-rational, or non-reasonable.

On the other hand, there are such things as beauty, love, and wisdom in life. How to describe beauty in a computer program? How to formulate wisdom in a mathematical equation? How to express love using human logic? We know and love not only with intellect and will, but also using hunches, feelings, and intuition. Indeed, we experience "woman's intuition" and "man's gut." There are things in life we cannot say or write precisely; only the heart can know and understand guts and intuitions.

St. Augustine, in an attempt to understand the Trinity, searched for images of God based on human psychological makeup, such as memory, intellect, and will, and lover, beloved, and love. By combining these two triads, intellect, heart, and will make up three distinct, not separate, aspects of consciousness (intentionality). Intellect is the basis of thought, cognition, and reason. Heart is the source of feeling, affection, love, and wisdom. Will is the basis of freedom, choice, and volition (action).

Consciousness operates as a combination of all three distinct faculties of intellect, will, and heart. As we cannot isolate one person of God (in the economy of salvation) of the Holy Trinity, so we cannot isolate heart alone from intellect and will. Heart cannot function alone. Mind (intellect and will) must help heart develop harmonious dispositions and habits.

Oftentimes, we consider heart to be simple emotion or affection. In Scripture, heart is the soul of conscience and the center of inner being. Sometimes heart is equivalent to unconscious in modern psychology. Heart is man's inmost being where the Holy Spirit dwells. Heart knows the language suitable for encountering God. Therefore, a person possessing a big heart performs virtuous acts naturally. A person with a warm heart loves God and his neighbors, as he is naturally formed by love.

In today's gospel reading, Jesus asks us to strive for big and warm hearts. He says, "A good man produces goodness from the good in his heart; an evil man produces evil out of his store of evil." So we ask ourselves, "How can we be persons with big and warm hearts?" The answer is by doing good and virtuous acts. We become what we do. If we keep stealing from a shop, we will soon become thieves. If we keep attending Sunday Mass conscientiously and pray to God honestly, we will soon become holy.

We encounter God in our hearts. We listen to God's words with our hearts. We pray to the Sacred Heart of Jesus. Heart is where we are alone with God. Heart is the source of love, wisdom, and holiness. ✝

[1ˢᵗ Lent and 4ᵗʰ Lent (A), 6ᵗʰ Easter (A), Holy Trinity (A), 8ᵗʰ OT (B)]

(1 Kings 8:41-43; Galatians 1:1-2, 6-10; Luke 7:1-10)

Faith, Faith, and Faith

"Lord, I am not worthy that you should enter under my roof, but only say the word and my soul shall be healed." We recite this prayer right before we receive the Blessed Sacrament during Mass.

This prayer comes from the centurion's statement to Jesus in today's gospel passage. A centurion, the officer in charge of one hundred soldiers, was a powerful force in the Roman Empire. But this particular centurion is a humble man. He respects the Jewish custom that forbids Jews to enter a Gentile's house, and sincerely begs Jesus to save his servant's life. The centurion, who represents Caesar, has faith in Jesus, who represents God the Father.

Faith is defined in the Scripture as "the assurance of things hoped for, the conviction of things not seen" (Heb 11:1). Faith refers to confidence in hoping for things of tomorrow and, at the same time, certainty of seeing what cannot be seen. Faith concerns with things beyond our ordinary senses and intelligence.

We are bodily creatures grounded on earth, but we are capable to transcend our limitations toward eternity. We always desire something true, something beautiful, something divine, and something everlasting. We are spirits in the world.

Karl Rahner wrote a short article concerning Heidegger's existential philosophy; it was about the transcendental nature of man, being in the world and ultimately facing death (*Being And Time*). At the end of the article, Rahner mentioned that the final option of man is either for God or for nothingness. In other words, at the deepest level of human existence man has a choice to be either profoundly religious or radically atheist. Ultimately, faith determines man's destiny—either eternal life or eternal darkness. This is what it means when Jesus says to his disciples, "Whoever is not with me is against me, and whoever does not gather with me scatters" (Lk 11:23, Mt 12:30).

Faith is beyond human reasoning based on ordered intellect and systematic knowledge. Faith is to believe with heart (Rom 10:10). "Faith is an encounter with the living God" (*Lumen Fidei* #4).

Faith allows our souls to transcend human limitations in this world and soar into the eternity of God. Faith allows us to assent to the supernatural Revelation. (By contrast, belief is more to do with natural and rational grounds. A. Hincks, *America*, 9/22/2014) If we have faith, we can transcend ourselves and have dispositions to eternal life. Conversely, if we don't have faith, we are possessed by things of this world and have dispositions to eternal darkness.

Therefore, in faith, we hope for things of tomorrow. Through faith, we see things we cannot see. With faith, we hear what we cannot hear. If we have faith, we find God in all things, and life is meaningful and fruitful. This is what Jesus means when he says, "If you have faith the size of a mustard seed, you could transplant a mulberry tree in the sea" (Lk 17:5). We conquer the universe with faith. If we don't have faith, we are controlled by our primitive and ambitious egos, and life is void or filled with envy and greed.

In reality, however, it is hard for us to be always faithful. Faith seems to dwindle away on a cloudy day. Faith flickers in a strong wind, as we step back and forth from belief to disbelief. Faith has its day of brightness on the mountaintop and its day of darkness in the valley. Faith requires continuous struggles in trusting God. Our journey of faith never ends.

Whenever we recite the prayer, "Lord, I am not worthy that you should enter under my roof, but only say the word and my soul shall be healed," we ought to do it humbly and faithfully. The Blessed Sacrament we are about to receive is precious nourishment for our souls, and allows us to encounter the living God truly present. The Blessed Sacrament we about to receive is the body and blood of Jesus Christ.✝

[12ⁿᵈ OT (C), 14ᵗʰ OT (B), 19ᵗʰ OT (C)]

TENTH SUNDAY IN ORDINARY TIME (C)

(1 Kings 17:17-24; Galatians 1:11-19; Luke 7:11-17)

We Can Be an Apostle Like Paul

St. Paul never met Jesus in person. But he called himself an "apostle" equivalent to St. Peter (1 Cor 15:5-8). In his letter to the Corinthians, St. Paul said humbly, "I handed on to you what I had received" (1 Cor 11:23 and 15:3). This is what is called "the Apostolic Tradition."

We may ask, "When and from whom did Paul receive the Apostolic Tradition, even though he never met Jesus in person?" The answer to this question is found in today's second reading. Immediately after his conversion on the way to Damascus, Paul stated, "I went off to Arabia (the Syrian Desert), and later I returned to Damascus. Three years after that I went up to Jerusalem to get to know Peter, with whom I stayed fifteen days; but I did not see any other apostles except James the Lord's brother." Thus, St. Paul learned the Apostolic Tradition from James, the powerful apostle in Jerusalem, in the late 30s, a few years after the death and resurrection of Jesus.

As an apostle, St. Paul did not just theologize Judaism; he did not simply invent Christianity. He understood the righteousness of God from the death and resurrection of Jesus and responded to God's call for the new creation. He spread the Good News of Jesus Christ throughout the world and lived the life of a new humanity rooted in God's love. Without Paul, Christianity could not have spread like a wildfire. As Jesus is the Word Incarnate, so Paul is the Word Promulgated.

St. Paul died in Rome, as did St. Peter. This makes Rome and, subsequently, the Bishop of Rome very important in the history of Christianity. The bishop of Rome, usually called the Pope, sits on the chair of Peter, with the charisma of Paul.

Paul said, "Be imitators of me (1 Cor 4:16)." So we follow his footsteps. Unlike Paul, we may not be able to declare to others, "It is no longer I who live, but it is Christ who lives in me" (Gal 2:20). We, at least, try to understand that God, who is love, has infused His love into our hearts through the Holy Spirit (Rom 5:5).

We heard in the first reading that Elijah raised the widow's son from death. Jesus also raised the son of a widow from death in Nain. Both miracles are indicative of God's intervention in our earthly affairs, demonstrating God's power in a new age.

This brings us to an important point. The miracles of Jesus are not events that took place two thousand years ago and then ceased. They are taking place today. Jesus continues to raise people to a new life today, just as he raised the widow's son. The only difference is in how Jesus does this. He does it not by reaching out his own hands to people, saying, "I tell you, arise!" Rather, he does it by inspiring us to reach out our hands to people, saying, "I tell you, arise."

In other words, Jesus shares with us the power to raise people to a new life emotionally by our love and compassion, spiritually by our prayer and sacrifice, and socially by our mercy and generosity.

This is what we celebrate in today's liturgy. Jesus is still performing miracles today in our midst. Jesus still raises people from death to life, just as he raised the widow's son two thousand years ago. But Jesus does all this, not with his own hands and voice, but with our hands and voices. We are his heart; we are his voice; we are his hands. We can be apostles like Paul. This is what we celebrate in today's liturgy.

It is good to be with Jesus Christ and taste the love of God in this sacred place. Like the apostle Paul, we never met Jesus in person, but we are disciples of Jesus. We spread the Good News; we heal the sick; and we raise the dead in this world. ✝

[13th OT (A, C)]

ELEVENTH SUNDAY IN ORDINARY TIME (C)

(2 Samuel 12:7-10, 13; Galatians 2:16, 19-21; Luke 7:36–8:3)

Sin Is the Mystery

What would we do if a woman came into our sanctuary, went to the altar weeping, bathed the cross with her tears, dried it with her hair, and then set a bouquet of flowers in front of the altar? We would get upset and drag her away from the altar, like Simon the Pharisee in today's gospel passage. She has broken our liturgical law, and we will judge her according to rumor and gossip.

And yet, isn't it true that, when we listened to the gospel story about the sinful woman a little while ago, we identified with her? We were glad to see Jesus forgave her. We, too, forgave her.

We don't practice what is in the Bible. And it is very difficult to maintain a clear, straight conscience. It is easy to find a sinner out there, rather than to recognize our own sinfulness. It is easy to identify sins with someone else, rather than to identify them with our own self.

To know that we are sinners is important because, by knowing who we are, we can come to closer to God. King David is a good example of this. He was one of the most terrible sinners in human history. He committed not only adultery, but also premeditated murder. Even though he sinned, he was chosen by God and became the hero of the people. Furthermore, one thousand years later, the Jewish people anticipated the Messiah like David. Why? They did so because King David had turned from his sin.

This story of David points out the mystery of sin. Sin is the mystery because we cannot talk about our sinfulness apart from the love and mercy of God. And human sinfulness is always measured against God's absolute goodness. According to St. Thomas, sins make no difference to God, only to our own proper good. The psalmist says, "God does not deal with us according to our sins, nor repay us according to our iniquities (Ps 103:10)." Sin is the mystery.

The parable in today's Gospel reading illustrates the mutual relationship between man's sinfulness and God's goodness. Two persons who are in debt owe different amounts: one owes five hundred days' wage and the other fifty. Both debtors are equally forgiven by God, regardless of the amount of debt owed. This is so, not because God preferentially loves one person over the other, but because one person feels more of God's love than the other. God is unaffected by our sins. God does not remember our sins (Is 43:25). Man's sinfulness is revealed because of God's goodness.

Sin is the refusal to let God be God. Sin is to violate the transcendence of God. Sin is the mystery. As long as we live, we cannot avoid sinning. We live in a fallen world. We participate in sin with Adam and Eve. We are sinful.

Another remarkable aspect of sin is that, although it sounds strange, we can take advantage of our sinfulness. By realizing and repenting our sins, we can get to know a different dimension of God. Therefore, in order to love God, it is necessary for us to be aware of our sinfulness.

Still another aspect of the mystery of sin is that the closer we come to God, the more deeply we feel our sinfulness. We often see that many holy men and women are not really confident of their holiness. Instead, they still depend on God with their utmost humility, simply because they are aware of their genuine sinfulness.

God invites us on the journey with Christ Jesus toward the New Heaven and New Jerusalem. We must experience the forgiveness of sins and find an ever new face of God. By repenting, we become loved sinners, and we get to experience a different dimension of God. The sacrament of reconciliation leads to a new understanding of God. We repent, and we become holy.

We are graced sinners and loved sinners. Because we are sinners, our souls are always inflamed with the love of God. ✝

[10ᵗʰ OT (A), 10ᵗʰ OT (B)]

TWELFTH SUNDAY IN ORDINARY TIME (C)

(Zechariah 12:10-11, 13:1; Galatians 3:26-29; Luke 9:18-24)

Faith and Discipleship

We believe in Jesus Christ, the Son of God, and we follow him. The first statement shows faith, and the second statement shows discipleship in action. Faith and discipleship are not separated from each other. They form a unity in distinction.

In today's Gospel, Peter confesses that Jesus is "the Christ of God." Then Jesus explains to all disciples what it means to have faith in him and follow him. Jesus says, "If anyone wishes to come after me, he must deny himself and take up his cross daily and follow me. Whoever wishes to save his life will lose it, and whoever loses his life for my sake will save it." This is one of the central and most characteristic scriptural passages of the Synoptic Gospels (Mt 16:24-25, Mk 8:34-35, Lk 9:23-24). Today, we will reflect upon faith and discipleship, and how they are related each other.

Recently I went to a funeral service at a local Baptist church. It was an opportunity to listen to the minister's sermon. As usual, sadness for the dead and encouragement for the living were addressed with hope for both the dead and the living. But one theme repeatedly resonating from his sermon was that one must believe in Jesus in order to have eternal life in heaven. In other words, to save the immortal soul, one must believe in Jesus.

Until very recently, the slogan, "To save the immortal soul believe in Jesus" has been popular. Obviously, no one wants his or her soul to go to hell. This slogan, coupled with serious and somewhat threatening, words such as death and judgment, heaven and hell, has been an effective tool to attract people to the church, subsequently bounty money baskets also.

Actually, heaven and hell have something to do with what is going to happen at the end of tomorrow. Tomorrow starts today; without today, there will not be tomorrow. And what happens at every present moment of today is projected into the end of tomorrow. On the other hand, our primitive and ambitious ego is always looking forward the heaven. Therefore, blind and somewhat selfish expectation for tomorrow can make today relatively unimportant. Whether or not there is life after death seems to be out of our hands. Jesus Christ did not "open the gate of heaven" so that our souls would go there when we die; Jesus Christ "brought the life of heaven to earth" (McCormack, *America*, 9/10/2012).

Let us also remind ourselves that the heart of the Gospel does not concern going to heaven but establishing God's kingdom here and now (Gal 6:15, 2 Pt 3:13). Jesus is the perfection of humanity and, by being such, has shown us the human face of God. Thus our understanding of God comes not just from words of Jesus, but from both words and deeds of Jesus.

This brings us back to the sermon of the Baptist preacher, which showed a separation between faith and discipleship. The minister put too much emphasis on faith. In contrast, today's Gospel reading provides a clue as to how faith in Jesus results in discipleship. Faith is not merely accepting or affirming Jesus as the Christ. Faith is following Jesus in action. Faith is discipleship.

To be disciples of Jesus, we must deny ourselves. To deny ourselves is to be responsive to Jesus Christ alone, by abandoning attachments to things of this world. When we deny ourselves, only then are we ready to take up the cross for Christ's sake. Self-emptying and self-transcending are the consequence of carrying the cross. If we are selfish and hold on to something as our own, we will lose it. By contrast, if we give our life to others by carrying the cross, we will gain it.

To be disciples of Jesus is to participate in the personhood of Jesus Christ, who was rejected and suffered on the cross. Insofar as we partake in his cross, we are his disciples. For those who are stubborn and self-absorbed, it can be difficult to be disciples of Jesus. By contrast, for those who are gentle to the Holy Spirit, the yoke is easy, and the burden is light (Mt 11:30). And Jesus asks nothing from us without giving us the strength to follow him (1 Jn 5:3). ✝

[11ᵗʰ OT (A), 23ʳᵈ OT (C)]

Thirteenth Sunday in Ordinary Time (C)

(1 Kings 19:16, 19-21; Galatians 5:1, 13-18; Luke 9:51-62)

"Follow Me!"

We are the disciples of Jesus; we are on a journey to Jerusalem together with Jesus. This journey is not like taking a family vacation and then coming home. It involves constant movement toward an ultimate destiny, to which God calls us. We journey toward our death and resurrection.

Today's readings are all about how to take this journey. The first reading shows that when Elijah called Elisha, Elisha responded gladly and got rid of his oxen and farm equipment. Before he joined Elijah, however, Elisha was able to bid farewell to his family.

In the gospel reading today, three persons wanted to follow Jesus on the way to Jerusalem. To each of them, Jesus explained what following him entailed. The journey would take them far away from their comforts and security. It would require more than an essential duty of the society, such as burying the dead. It was urgent enough to justify not bidding farewell to their families.

Let us also remember that when Jesus called Simon, Andrew, John, and James, they followed Jesus "immediately," without even cleaning up their fishing gear (Mt 4:18-22). The disciples responded to Jesus' call immediately, without bidding farewell to their families. Why? The disciples followed Jesus not because they had heard of Jesus' miracles, but because the call came from the Son of God. Jesus didn't say, "If you want to find the meaning of life, follow me." Jesus didn't ask, "Would you like to follow me?" Jesus simply said, "Follow me!" And the disciples immediately followed Jesus for the sake of the call. Otherwise, they could not follow him.

When Jesus calls us, he calls us to our true home. It is like a scene from our childhood. When we played outside with our friends until dark, our mothers called us home for supper. In the same way, Jesus calls us home, to where we naturally belong. Our discipleship leads to Jerusalem, where our death and resurrection await. This is another reason why Jesus doesn't ask our opinions when he calls us.

Discipleship is not our consent; it is God's gift for us. Discipleship is neither acquiring knowledge about Jesus nor embracing his ideology. Discipleship is trusting in God's saving grace in and through the person of Jesus Christ. Discipleship is following Jesus, the parable of God. Therefore, discipleship requires that we walk in Jesus' footsteps and accept the consequences of that option.

God has taken on humanity in the body of Jesus, who needs other human bodies to build the kingdom of God. Thus the disciples of Jesus must live and suffer in bodily communion with Jesus, including the cross. Discipleship is an embodiment of the person of Jesus.

In reality, however, we live on the margin of faith. We are still figuring out what we believe and why we believe. We are always free, but our freedom is often fragile. We talk a lot about what the Church should do. We expect from the Church more than we give. On the other hand, we would really like to follow Jesus. The more deeply we think about our lives and destinies, the more closely they should resemble the life of Jesus.

For most of us, the discipleship neither demands death nor requires leaving our families. It is precisely within our families and our society that the discipleship finds its meaning. Jesus does not ask us to leave home. Instead, Jesus asks us to think about those who have no home. Jesus does not require that we bury the dead. Instead, Jesus asks us to think about whether those already born can have a chance in life. We are asked to take up our own cross.

In today's gospel reading, Jesus begins his journey to Jerusalem, where his death and resurrection await. In the Gospel of Luke, this journey covers eleven long chapters (9–19). We, too, have a long journey ahead through the hot Texas summer until the season of Advent. We pray that our journey to Jerusalem with Jesus will be meaningful. ✝

[13ᵗʰ OT (A), 15ᵗʰ OT (B), 18ᵗʰ and 33ʳᵈ OT (C)]

FOURTEENTH SUNDAY IN ORDINARY TIME (C)

(Isaiah 66:10-14; Galatians 6:14-18; Luke 10:1-12, 17-20)

The Body of Christ

The central message of the Gospel is that God the Father at last reclaimed the whole world as his own through Jesus Christ. Jesus' response to God's call was to establish the kingdom of God on earth. Now human beings can share God's divine life in His kingdom.

In today's Gospel reading Jesus sends out 72 disciples, in addition to 12 apostles already sent, to preach the kingdom of God and to lay out its foundations. The kingdom of God is the sacred dwelling place for all human beings, allowing them to see in God their own destiny and goal.

The kingdom of God is for the here and now. It also is the future in the sense that it is always capable of becoming "more" and "better." For example, when we pray, "Thy kingdom come," we are praying that God's justice and peace will be done on earth as it is already done perfectly in heaven. There will be always a room for the kingdom's more intense presence in this world.

Jesus Christ has laid out the foundation for building the kingdom of God according to the will of God the Father. On the other hand, there are some people, if not most, want to build the kingdom of God according to their own will. History reminds us how dangerous it is, if a group of people claims to know the will of God, forgetting God's infinite incomprehensibility. So, it is worthwhile to take a close look at the current status of the kingdom of God, because we must understand a deeper meaning of God's kingdom with intellectual honesty.

For example, in political arena harsh words surrounding the racism simply go well beyond the normal. It was in the year of 1979 that US Bishops labeled racism "a sin" and a violation of "the fundamental human dignity of those called to be children of the same Father" (*Brothers and Sisters to Us*). We are appalled for the presence of the evil of racism in this the most advanced Christian nation.

Actually, racism is a part of the original sin, because the slavery casted the shadow of hypocrisy over the Declaration of Independence which proclaimed the rights to life, liberty and the pursuit of happiness. Therefore, as long as there is racism, there is no kingdom of God. As long as there is no fundamental equality for all human beings, there is no kingdom of God. As long as there is no sanctity and dignity for all forms of human life, there is no kingdom of God.

In reality, the kingdom of God is 'horizon'—the horizon from which the hidden knowledge of God slowly revealing and—the horizon towards which our true selves awaken every morning. No matter how fast we walk towards the horizon, it always remains far away. The kingdom of God is already here with us, but it has not yet been completed. God's kingdom constantly invites us to grow beyond who we are. We are always on a journey of faith in God's kingdom. We cannot grasp or possess things of God firmly and definitely. Our faith has not matured yet. We must trust God and His kingdom.

God's kingdom will be completed at the end-time. This means that God will complete his kingdom in his way, not in our ways. We live between the Book of Genesis and the Book of Revelation. In the beginning, God created us. And until the end-time comes, we pray, "Come, Lord Jesus."

The kingdom of God is a pure gift of God, but it is always subjected to our self-conscious freedom in action. We cannot escape from our responsibility, because Jesus Christ has shown us how to build it. We cannot be simply satisfied with who we are, contending with God's grace. The more God's grace abounds, the more should we be responsible for building God's kingdom. Like those 72 disciples sent by Jesus, we must do our share by following Jesus in his life, death, and resurrection.

We are called to build the kingdom of God. We have responded to this call, as we have gathered here in this sacred place, worshiping God and celebrating what God has done for us. So we sing, "Let all the earth cry out to God with Joy." ✝

[Christmas Day, Corpus Christi (ABC)]

313

Fifteenth Sunday in Ordinary Time (C)

(Deuteronomy 30:10-14; Colossians 1:15-20; Luke 10:25-37)

Who Is Our Neighbor?

Who is our neighbor? As Christians, we love God and we love our neighbors. But who is our neighbor?

Jesus faced the same question from a scholar of the law on the road to Jerusalem. The ancient road from Jericho to Jerusalem was nineteen miles with a steep elevation of 3,600 feet. In places, it twisted around huge boulders, and it was dangerous because there were many robbers and bandits.

We are familiar with the story of the Good Samaritan in today's gospel reading. On the road from Jericho to Jerusalem, a man is left half dead, having been stripped and beaten by robbers. Then three different persons appear at the scene: a priest, a Levite, and a Samaritan. A priest is probably on his way to Jerusalem to worship in the Temple, and apparently he thinks that the bleeding man by the roadside is dead. Because he is not supposed to touch the dead, he simply passes by. Next a Levite (someone like a permanent deacon) comes. He also fears the "dead" man and passes by.

Finally, there comes a Samaritan. This Samaritan, however, is moved with pity at the sight of the wounded man. He carries him to an inn and gives enough money to the innkeeper to take care of him, promising to settle any additional expense on his return. At the end of the story, Jesus asks the scholar which one of the three is a neighbor. He tells Jesus, "The one who treated him with mercy." Jesus says to him, "Go and do likewise."

I would like to share with you my own story, story about my failure to be a Good Samaritan. Some years ago, I was returning home with my daughter from her music lesson. It was late evening and getting dark very quickly. We were late for dinner, and I was hungry. I was driving fast. Suddenly, I saw an elderly man on the roadside, standing next to his truck with its hood open. He was waving a jumper cable in his hand. Obviously, he needed to recharge the battery in his truck. I thought about what to do—to stop or to keep on driving. I was hungry and wanted to go home. On the other hand, I could have stopped for a few minutes for the elderly man who simply needed a little help. While debating to myself, I found I was already some distance away from the site.

Eventually, I decided to help him. When I returned to the site, however, neither the man nor the truck was there. "Has anybody already helped him?" I wondered, looking everywhere nearby. But there was no trace of both the man and his truck. I had to go home feeling empty, but no longer hungry. What was strange and, in fact, mysterious about that incident is how the man and his truck disappeared so quickly. Could he have been an angel? I thought so. That incident still remains with me; it is a dark spot in my heart.

Oftentimes, when we help our neighbors, we feel good and satisfied. This is so because, by loving our neighbors, we encounter the living God. The love of neighbor is the concrete realization of the love of God. Conversely, the love of God is the source of the love of neighbor. Therefore, the one who loves his or her neighbor already loves God. Love knows no boundaries. Love emanates from all of us in grace and reaches out to everyone in need. Love is the mother virtue on which all other virtues are cultivated.

We find stories in the Gospels that show us what love is in action. The Parable of the Good Samaritan, as in today's Gospel, the Parable of the Prodigal Son, and Jesus' washing of feet in John's Gospel are those stories through which Jesus wants to convey the meaning of love. Indeed, God is love.

Jesus Christ is "the image of the invisible God, the first born of all creation," as we have heard from the second reading. Jesus Christ is the sacrament of God and has shown us the face of God. Jesus Christ is the Sophia/Wisdom of God and has shown us the paradigm of true humanity. To attain eternal life, therefore, we must love God and our neighbors, as Jesus says at the end of the parable: "Go and do likewise." ✝

[15th and 31st OT (B)]

(Genesis 18:1-10; Colossians 1:24-28; Luke 10:38-42)

Mary versus Martha

Abraham was a man of hospitality, as we heard in the first reading. Abraham entertained three angels of God in such an extraordinary way that God promised Abraham and Sara a son, although they were much advanced in age. Such a story of hospitality should not stir up argument or generate suspicion, especially in the Bible. But it seems that we have heard otherwise in today's gospel reading.

On the way to Jerusalem, Jesus stops by the house of Mary and Martha, whose brother is Lazarus, a dear friend of Jesus. Martha welcomes Jesus and gets busy preparing a meal for Jesus. In the meantime, her younger sister, Mary, does something unusual. Instead of helping Martha, she sits quietly at Jesus' feet and listens to him. Shouldn't Mary share with Martha the responsibility for cleaning the house and preparing meals for their guest?

Martha, apparently tired of doing all the work alone, lets her feelings be known. Martha does not say anything directly to Mary, however. She tells Jesus to let Mary get to work. Surprisingly, Jesus tells her, "Martha, Martha, you are anxious and worried about many things. There is need of only one thing. Mary has chosen the better part and it will not be taken from her."

Some fifty years ago, this scripture passage was commonly interpreted as if Mary represented contemplative life for the clergy and the religious and Martha represented active life for the lay people. Such a "two-tiered" distinction, rather separation, in spirituality was originated from the dualistic thought-pattern of Greek philosophy, which values spirit over matter. Therefore, to be holy one must flee from the material, secular world and rise to the spiritual sphere of quiet prayers.

Nowadays, contemplation and action are combined as "contemplation in action," the trade mark of Spiritual Exercises of St. Ignatius, because we find

God in all things, an excellent example of non-duality. If God exists only for monks and nuns, such biased and discriminating God is irrelevant to us. Therefore, contemplation in action means every one of us is called to be holy.

This "universal call to holiness" is one of remarkable accomplishments of Vatican II. It states, "All in the Church, whether they belong to the church hierarchy or are cared for by it, are called to holiness" (*Lumen Gentium*, #39). We are called to be holy, uniquely and distinctively, in our ordinary and everyday lives. As Mother Teresa put it, "Holiness is not the luxury of a few. It is everyone's duty: yours and mine."

Holiness means to be taken up with things of God. Holiness is living God's life in and through Jesus Christ. Holiness means holding on our true selves before God. Therefore, holiness is not the privileged signature of the religious or spiritual elites alone. A young mother of many little children is called to be holy in her own way. A company executive who often deals with self-centered employees is called to be holy in his own way. All of us are called to be holy. All of us are meant to be holy.

Perhaps, the real point of today's Gospel reading is that the presence of Jesus is beyond the usual human etiquette and hospitality. Jesus does not criticize Martha's actions. And Jesus was on the way to Jerusalem and would not return to them again. So Mary was listening to Jesus' last words.

We, too, must pay attention only to Jesus. We live in a busy world. We recover our true selves when we find Christ in the depths of our being. We also forget that a lot of events in life are non-dualistic. For example, the good and the bad, the joy and the sorrow always exist together. In reality, however, we usually pursue only the good based on our own intellect and reason. If the apparent good turns into bad, then we become "anxious and worry about many things." Jesus was never a dualist. The parables he taught and the sermons he preached are always non-dualistic. We must learn from him (Mt 11:29). We must let Jesus be the focal point of our existence. Indeed, "there is only one thing necessary." We must locate Jesus Christ at the center of our lives. ✝

[5th Lent (A), 6th OT (A), 21st OT (C)]

SEVENTEENTH SUNDAY IN ORDINARY TIME (C)

(Genesis 18:20-32; Colossians 2:12-14; Luke 11:1-13)

"Our Father"

Jesus prays frequently in the Gospels. Jesus prays at his baptism, before choosing twelve apostles, during the Sermon on the Plain, at the Transfiguration, during the passion and, finally, at his death. In fact, Jesus always prays before major events in his ministry.

In the gospel reading today, one of Jesus' disciples saw Jesus in prayer and asked him to teach him how to pray. Jesus taught him the Lord's Prayer. (The Lord's Prayer in Luke's Gospel is shorter and may be older than the one in Matthew's Gospel. The Lord's Prayer, that we pray most frequently, is based on Matthew's version.) Today, we will reflect upon what to pray, how to pray, and why we pray.

The Lord's Prayer has been the most important prayer for Christians in the last two thousand years. Whenever we pray it, we also pray together with millions of other people, Christians and non-Christians. Sometimes we pray it alone, but it is not an individual prayer. Many saints and scholars have written commentaries on it (including Pope Benedict XVI and St. Teresa of Ávila).

In the Lord's Prayer, Jesus called God *Abba*. It was a tender and affectionate way of calling a father in ancient Palestine. At the time of Jesus, no Jews called God *Abba* (Joachim Jeremias). This means that Jesus had an extraordinary insight into the inner life of God. This also means that Jesus showed us God the Father, who is a affectionate father. God is not an old man with a beard who is always writing down our sins. Jesus wants us, children of God, to have a warm and personal relationship with his *Abba* (Lk 9:48).

Jesus teaches us to pray for the coming of God's kingdom. We don't know when it will come. We simply pray for its coming, knowing that the kingdom, which we can glimpse now, will be a full-blown reality some day. Jesus also teaches us to ask God to sustain our everyday lives, to forgive our sins as we forgive others, and to protect us during the boredoms and difficulties of daily life.

Having taught us what to pray, Jesus then teaches us how to pray with persistence and boldness. He says, "Ask and you shall receive; seek and you shall find; knock and it shall be opened to you." So we ask God what we want. Prayers of petition, however, must be a two-way (dialogical) conversation with God rather than one-way talking to God. We dare not try to change God's mind. Instead, we are to be converted and transformed through our prayers (the efficacy of prayer). Therefore, if we are earnest in what we ask for in prayer, God always listens to us.

For example, in the first reading Abraham pled his case to God and bargained with God. Abraham asked God earnestly and sincerely for what he wanted. Abraham knew how to pray.

Finally, Jesus shows us why we pray. We pray simply because we are human beings—God's creatures. In our dreams, in our hopes, in our imaginations and, of course, in our pain and troubles, God is always with us. Only if we accept the incomprehensible mystery of the self-communicating God, can we live true lives. Only if we look through God's eyes, can everything in life is intelligible. Only if we love others, can we live authentic lives. Therefore, whenever our minds are oriented to the mystery of God and our hearts are filled with love for others, we pray naturally and spontaneously.

Even with all the theories and techniques, prayer is simply a way of life, uniquely different for each one of us. We pray alone at home. We pray together as a community when we come to Mass. The birds in the sky do not need to come to Mass, because they always pray. But because we wear masks all the time, we have to come to Mass to pray. Because we have forgotten our true selves, we need to pray. Therefore, we look up the birds flying in the sky and say, "Blessed are you, birds, for you do not have to come to Mass to pray." Our blessing of the birds in the sky explains why we need to pray all the time. ✝

[14th OT (A), 17th OT (B), 29th OT (C)]

EIGHTEENTH SUNDAY IN ORDINARY TIME (C)

(Ecclesiastes 1:2, 2:21-23; Colossians 3:1-5, 9-11; Luke 12:13-21)

Death Is the Completion of Life

A friend of mine has coordinated a great many funeral arrangements over the last thirty years as a volunteer at the Korean Catholic Church in Dallas. According to him, the face of a dead person in a coffin is mostly serene and peaceful. Occasionally, however, he encounters a face with an irritated, unforgiving look, which appears to be a reflection of the person's clinging to life, rather than dying in faithfulness to God.

Death is unavoidable and comes at the end of life. But it is the completion of life. Death is a part of life. Whether death is considered to be the end of life or the completion of life makes a big difference in the way we live. If death is the end of life, one might say, "Vanity of vanities! All things are vanity!" On the other hand, if death is the completion of life, one tries to live fruitfully and meaningfully until the very last moment. Perhaps the deceased person with the irritated and unforgiving look struggled in his last hour.

All of readings today have something to do with how to live. In the first reading, Qoheleth says, "Vanity of vanities! All things are vanity!" In the second reading, St. Paul tells us, "Think of what is above, not of what is on earth." Finally, in the gospel reading, Jesus teaches us how to live by illustrating the Parable of the Rich Fool, who builds security and comfort in his life and then dies suddenly that very night.

Life is short. Life is limited in virtue and wisdom. Life is troubled by evil and injustice. Thus the psalmist says, "The days of our lives are seventy years, or perhaps eighty, if we are strong; even then their span is only toil and trouble; they are soon gone, and we fly away" (Ps 90:10).

The author of the first reading says, "Vanity of vanities! All things are vanity!" All are vanities; all are hot air; all are wind. This is not a naïve and pessimistic lamentation on life, but a wise and joyful enlightenment from a long-lived life.

In addition to life's existential anguishes, we live in a market-oriented and materialistic culture. One of the most prominent Protestant ministers lamented, "The means by which we live have outdistanced the ends for which we live. Our scientific power has outrun our spiritual power. We have guided missiles, and misguided men. Like the rich man before us, we have foolishly minimized what is interior in our lives and maximized what is exterior."

Yes, it is our interior life, not exterior life, which holds the key to how to live. Our interior life, however, depends on how we can free ourselves from selfishness and unite with the divine; as St. Augustine said, "You have made us for yourself, and our hearts are restless until they rest in you." We are made for God. We are made to search for divine beauty and goodness. We are made to be free from our self-centeredness and be united with God. This is why St. Paul suggests we "think what is above, not what is on earth." We must die to "the old self" in order to be born to "the new self."

Now that we have encountered the risen Jesus Christ, we need to sort out what is really important and lasting. Death is not the end of life; it is the completion of life. We must strive to be persons made for God, up until the very last minute. We must accept that the desire of the human heart cannot be satisfied by what is here today and gone tomorrow: one's life does not consist of possessions. Those who live in Christ will die with Christ.

Let us close with a poem.

> When I was a child, I laughed and wept. Then, time crept.
> When I was a youth, I became more bold. Then, time strolled.
> When I grew up, I became a man. Then, time ran.
> Finally, into a ripe, old age, I grew. Then, time flew.
> Soon I shall be passing on. Then, time will be gone.
> O, Jesus, when death comes, nothing will matter, but you. ✝

[11ᵗʰ OT (A), 13ᵗʰ OT (C)]

NINETEENTH SUNDAY IN ORDINARY TIME (C)

(Wisdom 18:6-9; Hebrews 11:1-2, 8-19; Luke 12:32-48)

To See Is to Believe

When I was a graduate student at Texas A&M University, I had an advisor who came from Missouri, the Show-Me State. Whenever I explained to him results of laboratory experiments in words, he said, "Show me!" In science and other professional fields, one often has "to see to believe."

Not everything in life, however, needs to be seen to be believed. When we look at the night sky, we see many stars, but there are many more stars than those we can see. The Milky Way alone consists of several hundred million stars (Hincks, *America*, 5/16/2012). When we listen to a symphony at Meyerson, we hear only certain sounds. But there are many more sounds, more than we can hear, that make up the intricate harmonies and the masterpiece as a whole.

Faith is like the stars at night or a symphony. Faith can be neither measured nor quantified. If we have faith, however, it allows us to see what we cannot see and to hear what we cannot hear. "Faith is the realization of what is hoped for and the evidence of things not seen." This is a definition of faith we heard in the second reading. In this definition, faith is intimately tied to hope. Thus faith and hope are inseparable. Faith is indeed more than simply believing or accepting.

Moreover, because the present and the future are separated in human time, but combined in God's time, faith allows us to transcend from human time to God's time. Therefore, faith is the conviction of things not certain at the present time and the assurance of things hoped for in the future. Faith carries over the present to the future.

The author of the second reading continues to convey the example of Abraham's faith. Abraham left his hometown and journeyed through foreign lands without knowing what he would find. He detached himself from things he was familiar with and simply believed God. He did not see, yet he believed. Also, he clung to God's promise to him, even though he was much advanced in age. His faith rested on a hopeful trust in God's promise. Abraham did not see, yet he believed.

The greatest and final test for Abraham's faith came when he was asked to sacrifice the very child who would fulfill God's promise. Abraham's faith allowed him to hold fast to the reality yet to come. Abraham did not see, yet he believed.

In the gospel reading today, Jesus asks his disciples to be faithful servants. He asks his disciples to seek not the security and comfort of this world, but treasures in God's kingdom. He asks them to be steadfast in their faith and tells them a story to explain what he means. Servants are entrusted with managing a household. They do not know exactly when the owner will return. When he returns, he will expect to find things in order. A wise servant will always be vigilant and greet the owner whenever he comes. Then the owner will give him an (eschatological) banquet. The faithful servant of Jesus is diligent in the present and has confidence over the future.

The same is true of faith in God. Faith is more than an internal conviction. Faith is more than accepting or believing in Jesus Christ. Faith needs to be understood in conjunction with hope and love, particularly within God's time. Faith is the assurance of things hoped for in the future and the conviction of things not certain at the present time. Faith is not a simple intellectual assent to God's Revelation. So faith is not a noun, but a verb.

Earlier, I spoke of my dissertation advisor at A&M, who often asked me to show him the results of experiments in writing, and I mentioned that he would not believe unless he saw. Actually, the real reason he wanted to see the results was that I did not speak English well. I am certain that, even now, some of you have the same difficulty listening to me preaching in English. I sincerely appreciate your patience and generosity. In a sense, you have been very faithful to the Church. I thank you again for that. ✝

[9th OT (C)]

<u>Twentieth Sunday in Ordinary Time (C)</u>

(Jeremiah 38:4-6, 8-10; Hebrews 12:1-4; Luke 12:49-53)

To Take a Stand

The Gospel of Luke is one of the most beautiful books ever written. The Infancy Narrative contains amazing Christmas stories to which our hearts can tune in any time of year. The Prodigal Son (Lk 15:11-32) is a wonderful illustration of God's love. The Good Samaritan (Lk 10:25-37) is an elegant instruction on how to put God's love into action; as Jesus says at the end of the story, "Go and do likewise." The Gospel of Luke, however, is a challenging book.

Today's gospel reading presents three puzzling sayings of Jesus. They are (1) he has come to light a fire on earth; (2) he will undergo the baptism of death; and (3) he will bring division, even among family members. What happened to angels singing "Peace on earth"? Where is Jesus, the Prince of Peace?

To understand these sayings of Jesus, we first need to understand that Jesus is on his way to Jerusalem, where he will face death. Under such an urgent and unavoidable situation, Jesus shows his ardent desire and longing. Perhaps this is similar to a father who is annoyed with his child because the father knows precisely what's going to happen to his son, if he does not listen to him.

Returning back to today's gospel story, the fire is the fire of the Holy Spirit (Acts 2:3). The baptism of death is the death of Jesus on the cross. And so, knowing his own death approaches, Jesus tells that the fire of the Spirit will come upon the earth after his passion and death and resurrection.

What about the divisions among family members, such as mother against daughter and son against father? Today's gospel story has to do with the urgency of Jesus' message. To follow Jesus, one must take action right away, not after burying a dead father, for example. It is not a matter of "maybe" or "thinking about." The disciples of Jesus followed him immediately when they were called.

Today's gospel story also has to do with the centrality of Jesus. The choice for Jesus is the choice against all that are opposed to him and against all that are incompatible with him. Jesus says, "Whoever is not with me is against me" (Mt 12:30). The choice for Jesus is so crucial that one must take a stand on moral and political issues of the society. To take a stand is to perform according to the dictates of conscience, where one is alone with God, even though it may expose one to shame, mistreatment, or even death.

St. Thomas More was Lord Chancellor in England in the sixteenth century. When Henry VIII divorced his wife and remarried unlawfully, the king circulated a document, swearing under oath that his remarriage was lawful. Anyone who refused to sign the document would be arrested for treason. One day his friend came to him with the document and said, "Oh, confound all this... I don't know whether the marriage was lawful or not. But damn it, Thomas, look at these names.... You know these men! Can't you do what I did and come along with us?" Thomas refused. He couldn't disobey his conscience. St. Thomas More took a stand against immoral Henry VIII. He was finally beheaded.

Sometimes, taking a stand puts us in opposition to even friends and family members. Sometimes, taking a stand causes us to be persecuted, as was the case with Jeremiah in today's first reading. Sometimes, taking a stand causes us to struggle, as the author of the Letter to the Hebrews did in today's second reading. So there is a strong temptation to retreat to one's own comfortable corner and refuse to take a stand on issues. If we do not take a stand on issues, however—such as respect for life and for human rights—our souls will be suffocated and perish.

God is the living God who is love and mercy. This does not mean that God brings us joyful and pleasing news all the time. Sometimes, we experience God in empty promise, in dark misunderstanding and in a lonely solitude. Nonetheless, God asks us to make a choice from our conscience and to take a stand. ✝

[13th OT (C), 29th OT (A)]

TWENTY-FIRST SUNDAY IN ORDINARY TIME (C)

(Isaiah 66:18-21; Hebrews 12:5-7, 11-13; Luke 13:22-30)

The Narrow Gate

Someone asks Jesus, "Lord, will only a few people be saved?" Jesus does not answer that question. Instead, he explains the difficulty of entering God's kingdom. Only those few who show constant fidelity and vigilance can enter God's kingdom through the narrow gate. And then, he calls to people from all over the world and invites them to enter the kingdom.

We hear a similar message in the first reading. The prophet Isaiah foretold that those Israelites who had already come to Jerusalem would be sent "to the distant coastlands that have never heard of God's fame, or seen his glory; and they shall proclaim God's glory among the nations." Isaiah continued to say that, by "bringing brothers and sisters from all nations," God would make some of them "priests and Levites."

These messages from both Jesus and the prophet Isaiah provide the foundation for the doctrine of universalism (*Lumen Gentium* #16). This doctrine says that God gives himself freely to all human beings and invites them to the banquet in the kingdom of God (1 Tm 2:4-6, Jn 12:32, Eph 4:6, Mt 19:28). God's grace is offered to everyone all of the time, not to some of the people some of the time. This doctrine has become an orthodox teaching of the Church since Vatican II. In a broad sense, universalism is about reaching out to all people on earth.

God wants every human being to be saved. But salvation is not at all automatic. We must earn it. We must be ready to receive the salvation from God as a gift. God is everywhere, but God is not anywhere we like to be. Jesus tells us, "Strive to enter through the narrow gate, for many, I tell you, will attempt to enter but will not be strong enough." The gate to God's kingdom is narrow, simply because it is not easy to pick up the cross and follow Jesus. To attain eternal life is not easy, not because God made it that way and only a few people could pass, but because *we* make it that way. We enter God's kingdom through the narrow gate.

Let us look at two possible examples where the gate to the kingdom is narrow. One example concerns "cradle" Catholics, baptized by virtue of being born in a Catholic family. They generally believe that God's grace is available mainly through the authority of the Church. They are slow in developing their own religiosity. As a result, cradle Catholics tend to possess religious values and practices handed down to them rather than "purchased" from their own personal experiences.

Another example relates to "stagnant" Catholics. They are blind to the signs of times. They generally insist on their own opinions and practices of yesteryears. And they have a strong nostalgic longing for bygone days. Perhaps they are like frogs living in a pond. As a result, stagnant Catholics insist strongly on their way of practicing the Neo-Scholastic theology of the nineteenth century.

Perhaps both "cradle" and "stagnant" Catholics are good candidates for not being able to enter the narrow gate to God's kingdom. God wants everyone to be saved. However, we cannot be complacent or self-sufficient with God's grace just because it is at no cost. We enter God's kingdom through the narrow gate.

While we prepare ourselves to enter God's kingdom, we shall not be concerned with things which only God is concerned with. The question on how many will be saved in today's gospel reading is a good example. Jesus does not answer that particular, and somewhat, silly question. Another example refers to the last day. Jesus simply says he doesn't know when the last day will come. Only the Father knows (Mk 13:32).

Some mysteries in life must be lived, not solved. Therefore, we must busy with the things that concern us, and let God be God. We must be faithful and thankful for the gift of salvation from God. We enter God's kingdom through the narrow gate. ✝

[16th OT (C)]

TWENTY-SECOND SUNDAY IN ORDINARY TIME (C)

(Sirach 3:17-18, 20, 28-29; Hebrews 12:18-19, 22-24; Luke 14:1, 7-14)

Humility

When we meet the Lord face to face, he will prepare the finest banquet we've ever seen. Jesus often talks about this banquet in the Gospels. It is an (eschatological) banquet to which we are invited when the kingdom of God is fulfilled.

In today's Gospel, Jesus asks his followers to invite to dinner the poor, the crippled, the lame, and the blind, rather than the rich and the famous. This is not what we normally do, however. We invite important and influential people so that we may benefit from them. We like to expand our personal relationships.

At the banquet of God's kingdom, not the rich and the powerful but the poor and the insignificant are exalted. Why is this so? Perhaps the reason is that the poor and marginalized depend on God, knowing full well their desperate situations. Because they are close to God, God is close to them.

On the other hand, the rich and powerful are self-sufficient and don't depend on God. They depend on themselves. They always want something else or something more out of their envy and desire. This mystery of envy and desire is the source of our sinfulness. For example, Adam and Eve wanted to be like God and, even after the Fall, blamed someone else for the consequences of their envy.

Envy is deeply entrenched in us. A child desires and envies another child's toy, even though there are plenty of them around. A housewife desires and envies her neighbor's new car. A professional desires and envies his colleague's promotion. In fact, human history is full of all kinds of desires and envies. We are so trapped by illusions and pretenses that we know not who we are; we forget that we are God's children. This is why we need to be saved and redeemed.

Theologians say that the original sin has to do with our intrinsic envy or desire. When we say that Mary was born without the original sin, it means that she didn't envy at all, as the supreme model of humility.

What is humility? What does it mean to be humble? Does it mean to lower ourselves? Does it mean to deny our true worth? No, humility does not mean we must lower ourselves. Humility does not mean we are okay with being belittled. Humility does not mean we should deny our true worth.

Humility is the virtue that allows us to know we are creatures of God. Humility is the right attitude of asking for, and depending upon, God's grace as creatures—God's children. Thus humility is the most fundamental virtue in Christian life.

A humble person knows he is created by God. He does not judge himself more or less than what he really is. He considers what he has as gifts from God. He does not envy or desire what others do or have. In doing so, he avoids despair and vanity as well as arrogance and pride. A humble person enjoys the freedom of being who he is. He empties himself easily, so that wonders of God can fill his heart. He is not troubled by accidental happenings in life such as failure, illusion, or reputation. Most of all, a humble person knows how to let God be God and respects God's transcendence, while remaining God's creature.

Let us return now to the main point of today's Gospel. The reason why the poor are welcomed to the banquet of God's kingdom is that they are humble and know who they are. They do not envy or desire others. They are pure in heart and depend upon God.

We are invited to God's banquet, partly because we are made in the image and likeness of God. And we are joyful at God's banquet, because we are redeemed by Christ Jesus. Therefore, we must be humble, instead of being prisoners of envy and desire. ✝

[5th Lent (C), 7th and 22nd and 26th OT (A)]

TWENTY-THIRD SUNDAY IN ORDINARY TIME (C)

(Wisdom 9:13-18; Philemon 9-10, 12-17; Luke 14:25-33)

Do We Believe in Jesus and Follow Him?

It was only about fifty years ago that we often heard from a pulpit words like heaven and hell, eternal life and damnation. Heaven was believed to be a blissful place for immortal souls, and in order to save one's soul, one had to believe in Jesus. It was a powerful tool for preachers to attract people to church. And people responded obediently in fear. Back then, Christianity was a necessity in life.

Nowadays, we understand those words differently. We cannot locate heaven and hell in the universe, which is expanding with the speed of light. At the same time, we are grounded to the earth so tightly that we have become efficient and pragmatic materialists. We have lost the sense of transcendence—the sense of God. Not many people talk about God; very few people talk to God. God is no longer a self-evident reality. Consequently, Christianity is an option, not a necessity in life.

Perhaps this is why pews are half empty on Sundays. Perhaps this is why evangelical Protestants and Pentecostals flourish, at least for the moment. And so we wonder: Why is Jesus still credible today? Why do we believe in Jesus and follow him? Answers to these questions are found in today's Gospel.

In today's Gospel Jesus says, "If anyone comes to me without hating his father and mother, wife and children, brothers and sisters, and even his own life, he cannot be my disciple. Whoever does not carry his own cross and come after me cannot be my disciple." This means that in order to follow Jesus we must completely detach from worldly possessions, including our fathers and mothers, wives and children, and even our own lives. Our ultimate goal is the communion with God, and we must attach ourselves to God alone—nothing else.

To attach ourselves to God alone is to carry the cross. To carry the cross is to live for others. To live for others is to suffer and sacrifice for others. This is the divine paradigm that Jesus has shown us in words and deeds.

If Christianity is only an option in life, then we don't need to carry the cross. If we don't carry the cross, Jesus is not necessarily the central point of life. If Jesus is not the central point of life, we no longer have the real joy that comes out of pain and suffering. Buddha left his palace and experienced hunger, sickness, and death. Had he stayed at the palace, shielded from pain and suffering, he would not attain enlightenment. In Christian terms, the cross brings in the resurrection.

The second reading shows how Paul lived his life, attaching himself to God alone. Paul met Onesimus, a runaway slave, in prison and convinced him to return to his master, Philemon. Paul appealed to Philemon to receive Onesimus not as a slave, but as a brother in the Lord. Paul also hinted that he would like to have Onesimus back as a coworker for preaching the Gospel. By calling the slave a "brother" and "coworker," Paul sent "his own heart."

This letter of Paul to Philemon is one of the most moving episodes in the Bible. It reminds us how early Christians were able to free from their own selfishness through the Gospel of Christ. It was not until the nineteenth century that slavery was abolished. Even in this twenty-first century, societies formed in the cradle of Christianity still struggle badly with human rights issues. Paul lived a blessed and happy life by carrying his cross! And we know that many holy men and women in the Church have done so. We, too, would like to have a blessed and happy life by carrying the cross. Therefore, Christianity is still credible in this day and age!

We do not believe in Jesus Christ merely so our souls can go to heaven. We do not follow Jesus Christ so that we may live forever and ever. Jesus did not "open the gates of heaven, so that our souls will go to heaven when we die.... Jesus brought the life of heaven to earth" (McCormack, *America*, 9/10/2012). We believe in Jesus Christ because he is the Savior, who has shown us the face of God and has lived most perfectly how to be a human being. ✝

[3rd Lent (B), 12th and 30th OT (C)]

331

TWENTY-FOURTH SUNDAY IN ORDINARY TIME (C)

(Exodus 32:7-11, 13-14; 1 Timothy 1:12-17; Luke 15:1-32)

Jesus Has Revealed That God Is Love

Jesus of Nazareth has revealed to us the face of God the Father. Today we are going to take a close look at what kind of God Jesus has revealed.

Today's gospel reading contains three parables about recovering what was lost: the lost sheep, the lost coin, and the lost sons. All three episodes point to God's willingness to recover what was once lost. The shepherd recovers the lost sheep, the woman recovers the lost coin, and a father recovers his lost sons.

The third story, often called the Prodigal Son, is better named the "Lost Sons" because both sons are lost—one physically and the other spiritually. Actually, the story is about their father, who shows them boundless and unconditional love.

The younger son is too impatient to wait for his father to die. He has asked for his share of the inheritance and squanders it away in "a distant country." He ends up in a farm where he "tends the swine." It is a terrible thing to do for a Jew. Suddenly, he realizes that, while "dying from hunger," the workers in his father's farm have plenty to eat. So he decides to go home to be one of "hired workers" for his father. As he approaches his father's house, the father sees him "a long way off" and runs to greet his son. The son tries to say something, but the father doesn't listen to him. Instead, the father embraces him and puts clothes on his body, shoes on his feet, and a ring on his finger. The father recreates the son in a new and elevated state rather than restoring him to the previous state. And the father holds a jubilant party with his friends and neighbors over a fatted calf, for "his son was lost and has been found."

In the meantime, the older son comes home that evening. He is furious at the seemingly unjust party. Filled with jealousy, he complains that he has never had a party with his friends, not even with a young goat. In his selfishness, he does not address his father as "father," and he calls his brother "this son of yours." But the father pours out the same love to him, saying, "Son, you are always with me, and all that is mine is yours."

The younger son loves the wrong things in life, whereas the older son loves no one. But the father shows what love is without even saying, "I love you." This compassionate father is God the Father Jesus has shown us. In order to appreciate this God of Jesus, we must review the image of God in the Hebrew Bible. In the Hebrew Bible God is slow to anger and rich in mercy. When God expelled Adam and Eve from the Garden of Eden, God prepared garments of skins and clothed their naked bodies (Gen 3:21). When Cain murdered his brother Abel, God cursed Cain to be a wandering nomad, but protected him by putting a mark on his face (Gen 4:15). However, the God of Israel, having similar temperaments as human beings, is often jealous and vengeful.

By contrast, Jesus calls God *Abba* Father, who is compassionate and merciful, not at all punishing and vengeful. God is the loving Father who "pitched his tent" among us. In the gospel story, the father did not say to the younger son, "If you work hard as a hired hand, then I will take you as my son." He did not say to the older son, "Take a young goat and have a party with your friends." God the Father Jesus has shown us penetrates deep into our agonies and struggles. God the Father Jesus has shown us embraces our faults and wrong-doings. God the Father Jesus has shown us is no longer God of the history of Israel, but God of the essence of life for all human beings.

Jesus has revealed his *Abba* and asks us to call Him "Our Father." Jesus has revealed God who does not love us simply because we deserve to be loved. God loves us even if we are guilty and sinful. Jesus has revealed God who does not forgive us if and when we repent. God forgives us even before we repent. This is God the Father Jesus has revealed to us. To describe this God of Jesus Christ, St. John said simply, "God is love"—the love that unites both human and the Divine as one. ✝

[3rd Lent and 4th Lent (C)]

TWENTY-FIFTH SUNDAY IN ORDINARY TIME (C)

(Amos 8:4-7; 1 Timothy 2:1-8; Luke 16:1-13)

Catholic Relief Services

When I was a little boy, I was often hungry. It was not just me, but many people were hungry. I even saw some people die from hunger. It was the time following the Korean War that brought the terrible shortage of food. One day a bag of flour came to us from the United States. The flour was so soft and white that I sifted it with my fingers before I scooped it. My mother made watery dumplings out of the flour. It was flour from angels, sent by Catholic Relief Services in the United States. It alleviated much hunger during and after the Korean War.

I have begun my homily with this memory of my childhood, because you are either those persons, or their sons and daughters, who sent money to Catholic Relief Services during the Korean War. Another reason is that today's readings concern money and spirituality—that is, how to live life fully and abundantly.

We live in a world of a free market economy; thus we desire to balance money and spirituality properly in our lives. In theory, very few people worship money. In reality, however, many people live as if the main goal of life is making money.

On the other hand, spirituality cannot flourish in a vacuum. For example, when we are very sick, we cannot pray. Our bodies need to get well before any meaningful prayer begins. In the same way, when we are hungry, we cannot pray. Healthy spirituality does not come from a hungry stomach. This does not at all mean that when we are rich, we pray better. The rich have their own problems. Therefore, how to mix money and spirituality is important in Christian life.

Eight centuries before Jesus Christ, the same problem existed. The prophet Amos called for the conversion of the people of Israel against their social injustice and religious arrogance, as we heard in the first reading. The rich had been taking advantage of the poor, to their own benefit.

334

Today's gospel reading is difficult to understand. It is somewhat paradoxical. The steward, who is on the brink of losing his job, turns around and makes bargains with his master's debtors. Jesus praises this steward not because of his dishonesty, but because of his practical wisdom (prudence). What Jesus asks from his disciples is to be prudent by following him, because they "cannot serve both God and Mammon."

Neither can we serve both God and money. It is true that none of us is truly the master of what we have. To worship money or to be a slave of money is a terrible thing. I have a friend who lost his health to make money, and then he lost money in restoring his health. When we are slaves of money, it is almost impossible to have a spiritual life. To seek satisfaction in money alone is to deny "there is only one mediator between God and the human race, Christ Jesus."

Furthermore, we know that God calls every man and woman to his kingdom. This is called "universal salvation." In the same way, material goods on earth belong to all people. They are not exclusive property for a group of developed countries alone. For example, Americans make up only five percent of the world population, but use twenty five percent of natural resources. We need to accept, therefore, that other people, particularly the poor in war-torn countries, have God-given rights to the goods on earth. Far beyond the boundaries of our families and our parishes, we are responsible for the resources of the good earth.

I began this homily with my personal story of hunger during the Korean War era. I will end now by expressing thanks once again to you for what you did through Catholic Relief Services more than half a century ago.

Let us also remember that there is still much hunger and starvation due to wars, violence, and natural disasters. And Catholic Relief Services is strong and active, performing humanitarian relief and development works in over ninety countries around the globe. †

[8th OT (A)]

TWENTY-SIXTH SUNDAY IN ORDINARY TIME (C)

(Amos 6:1, 4-7; 1 Timothy 6:11-16; Luke 16:19-31)

"It's None of My Business"

We often say or hear people say, "It's none of my business." This saying can be an excuse for not getting involved with affairs of others. Occasionally, it also can be a cold and shrewd declaration of self-protection or selfishness.

The story Jesus tells us today—the Rich Man and Lazarus—is about "It's none of my business." The rich man in the story enjoys an exceptionally extravagant lifestyle, while the poor man Lazarus, covered with sores, lies nearby, hoping some scraps to fall from the rich man's table. Lazarus does not have the strength to beg. One thing both men have in common is their mortality—the death. Perhaps the rich man is buried in the midst of much lamentation of his friends and relatives. And Lazarus, rolled in a sack, is thrown out of the city.

The Gospel continues with a narrative concerning what happens to their souls. The poor man is perfectly happy in Abraham's bosom. The rich man falls into hell and asks Lazarus to bring water to chill his burning tongue. Abraham tells him it is too late. Finally, the rich man asks Abraham to send Lazarus to his brothers on earth. Abraham replies that they should learn from Moses and the prophets. While alive, the rich man did not harm Lazarus; he simply enjoyed his own lifestyle. The point of the parable, therefore, is not what the rich man *did*, but what he *did not*. He did not pay attention to Lazarus, who was too hungry and too sick to beg. To the rich man, the poor and sick Lazarus was none of his business.

In any society, the rich, having almost everything in life, are self-sufficient and usually do not depend on God. But the poor, being deprived of many necessary things in life and having nobody to turn to but God, develop the virtue of gratefulness for what little they have. This is the mystery of poverty. On the other hand, the rich, using their natural instinct and greed, exploit situations and acquire power and wealth to the detriment of the poor. Moreover, the society tolerates certain socioeconomic structures built by the rich and the powerful. The poor simply do not have the same opportunities as the rich, resulting in a gap between the rich and the poor.

In the world we live many people live on less than a dollar a day. Among the total population in the world, the richest one-fifth has 82.7% of the world's total wealth, while the poorest one-fifth has only 1.4%. Among one hundred people of the world, 15 of them are obese, 20 of them hungry, and one of them is dying from hunger.

Because the rich and the poor are separated by such "a great chasm," the Church teaches that God has a preferential option for the poor. Of course, God does not side with some people over others. Just because human beings are greedy, ignorant, and unjust, God shows a special form of primacy to the poor. In fact, we know that Jesus protects the poor and that the entirety of Scriptures (the Magnificat, the Beatitudes, Jesus' sermon on Isaiah 61, and the Last Judgment) points at this doctrine. Therefore, in order for us to see through the eyes of God, we need to look through the eyes of the poor. This is another mystery of poverty.

The preferential option for the poor is not to turn ethics into religion, but to maintain the purity of heart. We will then hear the voice of God hidden among us. The preferential option for the poor is announcing the good news of Jesus Christ. We will then see how blessed are the poor, how blessed are those who mourn, and how blessed are the meek. The preferential option for the poor involves leaving the road we are comfortable with and responding to the Holy Spirit. We will then know that the love of neighbor and the love of God are the same. (At the same time, we will experience that tears and sorrow are not obstacles of joy and happiness.)

In the story Jesus told us, we don't know who the rich man is; he has no name but a loud voice. We know, however, who the poor man is; he is Lazarus with no voice. Perhaps this story suggests that we can identify ourselves with the rich man, either financially or intellectually or spiritually. If so, Lazarus must be someone nearby we know. Can we identify with this Lazarus today? ✝

[22nd OT (C), 23rd OT (A), 32nd OT (B), Christ King (A)]

Twenty-Seventh Sunday in Ordinary Time (C)

(Habakkuk 1:2-3; 2:2-4; 2 Timothy 1:6-8, 13-14; Luke 17:5-10)

Unprofitable Servants

Sometimes Scripture says something difficult to understand, perhaps even surprising and paradoxical. But if we listen closely, we find that Scripture speaks to our hearts, not to our ears.

Today's gospel reading is a good example. We tend sheep in the field all day long and come home at sunset. And then, we prepare the meal for the master and wait for him. Finally, we take a little bite of food before cleaning up the dishes. In spite of all these good things we have done for our master, he calls us "unprofitable or unworthy servants." This gospel message does not sound like the Good News we want to hear. We have come to this sanctuary to be nurtured by God's word. We have not come here to be called "unprofitable servants."

In order to understand the gospel passage properly, we have to understand the culture of two thousand years ago in Palestine. In old days, servants were the property of the master, not employees. And two-thirds of the population was either servants or slaves. The word "servant" had a warm and inclusive meaning. It also was the way people identified themselves with God, not as employees, but as members of the household of God.

In the Bible, Jesus taught his followers to be slaves of one another (Mk 10:44). The apostle Paul was happy to identify himself as a slave of Jesus Christ (Rom 1:1). Our religious ancestors were at home with the concept of servitude to God and to one another, although this concept is not convincing in contemporary culture.

Moreover, today's gospel story has to do with respecting God's freedom and sovereignty. We use our language to describe and to talk about God. Sometimes, however, we tend to describe something about God, forgetting that God is a totally incomprehensible mystery. As a result, we may violate the transcendence of God by not letting God be God. If we understand something about God, it already is not about God! God, by definition, is totally incomprehensible and totally the Other. God is the Holy Mystery.

For example, some people consider human lives to be mere matter and objects, devoid of soul and spirit. To abort unborn children in the name of free choice and individual privacy is to play the role of God. Therefore, when we pray for the respect of unborn lives, the aim is not to abolish or to get rid of abortionists in this world. It is to raise our conscience levels, and theirs, by cultivating human dignity and the virtue of love. It is to develop mutual, moral dispositions toward God's love and compassion, so that we may all begin to see that any form of human life is a gift from God and a reflection of God's human face.

We see a similar thing in today's gospel reading. When the disciples request Jesus increase their faith, Jesus gives them the example of a tiny mustard seed that can produce astounding results; even the tiniest bit of faith can move a mulberry tree into the sea. Jesus teaches them how to cultivate faithfulness—not faith itself, but faithfulness, a virtue to strengthen faith.

We need to leave God's affairs to God, regardless of whether or not God calls us worthy or unworthy. Letting God be God does not mean that we do nothing. On the contrary, it is precisely in the face of our unworthiness that we must rely upon God as we fulfill our responsibilities. Otherwise, the sheer pride of doing our work would certainly elevate us into demigods. We do not become more than we actually are by performing our work for God. We are servants of God, doing servants' work.

Scripture does not speak to our ears. Scripture speaks to our hearts. Scripture speaks to the centers of our beings. Let us live responsibly according to the Word in faith, hope, and love. God gave us the Spirit of "power and love and self-control." We are unprofitable servants. We do only what we are obliged to do. ✝

TWENTY-EIGHTH SUNDAY IN ORDINARY TIME (C)

(2 Kings 5:14-17; 2 Timothy 2:8-13; Luke 17:11-19)

"Thank You!"

We say "thank you" to one another many times a day. And we know that our gratitude ultimately stems from God's love and mercy.

Today's readings concern the gratitude and thankfulness of being healed rather than the healing itself. The first reading is the healing story of Naaman, the commander of the Syrian army. Naaman had a terrible leprosy. As suggested by his Jewish slave girl, he came to Elisha, who simply sent word through a messenger to wash seven times in the Jordan. Naaman was not satisfied with this directive because he felt he could do the same in a Syrian river. Eventually, Naaman overcame his pride and went to the Jordan to wash himself—and he was healed. And he began to worship the God of Israel.

The gospel passage describes another healing story. Ten lepers were healed by Jesus, but only one, the despised Samaritan, returned to Jesus to thank him. We don't know what happened to the other nine lepers who did not come back to Jesus. Perhaps they went immediately to a priest. Perhaps they went home in a hurry. To the returned Samaritan leper, Jesus asked aloud, "Has none but this foreigner returned to give thanks to God?" Jesus was clearly unhappy and disappointed.

Gratitude is a response to our gifts. A friend gives us a present. For that, we say, "Thank you." A stranger shows us the way to get to the destination. For that, we say, "Thank you." Our parents take care of us, educate us, and sacrifice for us. For that, we say, "Thank you." Even if things are not easy, we shall not grumble about thorns on our roses; we shall give thanks for the roses among thorns.

Gratitude is the memory of the heart. It is an expression of love and respect that soon transforms itself into deed. St. Paul begins his letters with thanksgiving. We, too, always begin our prayers with thanksgiving to God. We also teach our children to say "thank you" for the favors they receive: "What do you say, Jimmy, for the nice present Grandma gave you?" Children should be taught to be grateful from an early age. Gratitude is the first step that children take in forming their relationships with adults.

Sometimes we feel like we do not know how to pray. This is so, probably because we do not know how to be grateful to God. By giving thanks to God, we acknowledge that God is the creator and we are His creatures. That is, our relationship—our foundation—with God is correctly situated at the ground level and confirmed by our gratefulness. Based on this fundamental ground, a genuine prayer naturally follows.

We ought to give thanks to God for who we are and for what we have. Whatever we have is mostly given to us or garnered by sheer good luck. When the time comes for us to return to our true home, we cannot carry any of our possessions. We are lucky and grateful for who we are. We thank for the gift of life.

Saying "Thank you" is a nice way to express our humility. Saying "*Deo gratias*" is a nice way of being a Christian.

Let us end with a poem and give thanks to God for the gift of life.

> *I asked for health, that I might do greater things;*
> *I was given infirmity that I might do better things…*
>
> *I asked for riches, that I might be happy;*
> *I was given poverty that I might be wise…*
>
> *I asked for power, that I might have the praise of men;*
> *I was given weakness that I might feel the need of God…*
>
> *I got nothing that I asked for, but everything I had hoped for.*
> *Almost despite myself, my unspoken prayers were answered.*
> *I am among all men most richly blessed.* ✝

[14ᵗʰ OT (A), 29ᵗʰ OT (C)]

TWENTY-NINTH SUNDAY IN ORDINARY TIME (C)

(Exodus 17:8-13; 2 Timothy 3:14–4:2; Luke 18:1-8)

Persistence in Prayer

Prayer is the fundamental act of Christian life. Prayer is a means of maintaining our relationship with God. Whether we realize it or not, we are always connected to God. Otherwise, we cannot exist. So we pray all the time.

Prayer can be joyful thanksgiving; prayer can be sorrowful lamentation; prayer can be silent reflection. To some, prayer is the lifting up of minds and hearts. To others, prayer is listening to God. To still others, prayer concerns something we simply have to ask God. No matter what the prayer is, no matter how it is felt or defined, prayer is unique and special to each one of us. We pray all the time.

Prayer is also a means of making ourselves available to God. We don't pray to ask God to be present with us. God is already, and always, present with us. We pray to make ourselves present to God. The problem of presence during prayer is not with God, but with us.

I would like to suggest two important points concerning prayer. First, prayer allows us to maintain a close relationship with God, who is love, not a fearful judge. Second, when we pray, we must try not to violate God's sovereignty. The first point regards God's nearness or closeness (immanence), and the second regards God's distance and remoteness (transcendence). The burning bush that Moses saw at Mount Horeb provides a good example. God's nearness and revealing aspect are shown through the bush burning, whereas God's distance and concealing aspect are shown by the fire not consuming the bush. While praying, we do our best to be near God without violating God's freedom and sovereignty. We can sincerely ask God what we want. But it is always up to God to realize that prayer.

Today's readings are about the perseverance of prayer and about praying all the time. During the war with the Amalekites, Israel won whenever Moses raised his hands, that is, whenever Moses was in prayer. Moses' hands were bound to get tired, so his assistants, Aaron and Hur, kept his hands lifted up until the battle was won.

Today's gospel reading tells us of the defenseless and powerless widow who could wear down a corrupt judge through her persistence. In the same way, God hears our prayers and answers them because we pray all the times.

One practical point is that prayer helps us maintain our psychological and spiritual well-being. The world we live in is full of all kinds of noises, fantasies, temptations, and especially unwanted nerves and stimuli from TV, newspapers, cell phones, computers, and other telecommunication products. To maintain our minds healthy and spirits ordered, we must pray. As we take care of our bodies by taking showers or baths every day, so we must pray to cleanse our minds and purify our spirits. Without prayer, our minds get contaminated, and our spirits suffocated.

Finally, it is important to remember to pray simply and honestly. Beautiful prayer comes from the bottoms of our hearts and creates intimacy with God. One of Thomas Merton's prayers portrays this honesty in prayer: (from *Thoughts in Solitude* by Thomas Merton, p. 83.)

> *My Lord God, I have no idea where I am going. I do not see the road ahead of me. I cannot know for certain where it will end. Nor do I really know myself, and the fact that I think I am following your will does not mean that I am actually doing so. But I believe that the desire to please you does in fact please you. And I hope that I will never do anything apart from that desire. And I know that if I do this you will lead me by the right road, though I may know nothing about it. Therefore I will trust you always though I may seem to be lost and in the shadow of death. I will not fear, for you are ever with me, and you will never leave me to face my perils alone.* ✝

[14th OT (A), 17th and 28th OT (C)]

THIRTIETH SUNDAY IN ORDINARY TIME (C)

(Sirach 35:12-14, 16-18; 2 Timothy 4:6-8, 16-18; Luke 18:9-14)

Do I Need God in My Life?

When God speaks, he does so by asking questions. In the Old Testament, God asks Adam and Eve, "Where are you?" as they hide in the Garden. In the New Testament, Jesus asks, "What are you looking for?" when Andrew and another disciple follow him on the bank of the Jordan River.

Answers to these questions are important to our identity as Christians. So we follow Jesus, searching for answers to these questions.

The gospel reading today is called the Parable of the Pharisee and the Tax Collector. The Pharisees are religious people who strictly observe the Law and are highly respected by the people. They avoid sin, fast twice a week, and give one-tenth of their income. They are good and law-abiding people. Therefore, the Pharisee in the Gospel is not a hypocrite who provides only lip service to God. Or is he?

Let us find out what is really at stake here. The Pharisee is so confident and complacent in his relationship with God that he does not look at God. Rather, he is busy looking at himself. He prays, "O God, I thank you." Actually, he is talking to himself. He feels so safe and satisfied in front of God that he does not need God. He is self-sufficient. He has a non-repentant attitude toward salvation. Therefore, he does not realize that salvation is a free gift from God. Salvation can come neither from his own self nor from the world. It comes only from God. This is the whole point of the parable.

In contrast, the tax collector is a certified sinner; he not only works for the Romans but also makes an illicit profit off his own people. As a sinner, he knows that he depends solely on God, and thus he asks God's mercy at a distance. He dares not "lift his eyes toward heaven," because he is busy looking down into his own conscience, in the presence of God.

In our spiritual journeys, we search for God, who asks us, "Where are you?" and "What are you looking for?" At this stage, we try to build up our religiosity, using mainly speculative and rational knowledge. The Pharisee is at this stage of spiritual journey.

As the journey continues on, we realize that we cannot attain God's grace through our own efforts. And suddenly, we understand that God has been searching for us, rather than we searching for God. Therefore, in order to respond to the searching of God, we must first empty ourselves. We must be freed from ourselves and snatched from ourselves. At this stage, no more speculative knowledge is needed. The love, the heartfelt love from one's innermost being, is all that is required. This emptying of egos (self-transcendence) is what Jesus means when he says, "Those who want to save their life will lose it, and those who lose their life for my sake will save it" (Lk 9:24).

The tax collector is at this stage of spiritual journey. Simply because he has nothing but God to hang on to, he is already self-emptied. He is a man of humility. Therefore, the tax collector returns home justified, but the Pharisee receives no grace.

In the first reading, God hears the cry of the oppressed, the wail of the orphan, and the complaint of the widow. God raises the lowly and the poor, but leaves alone those who are self-sufficient and self-satisfied.

The world is composed of sinners and repentant sinners, not sinners and saints. Only those humble and poor in heart seek God. Those who are proud and self-sufficient do not seek God. Moreover, we become truly human only when we realize that God is our ultimate heart's longing. ✝

[9th OT (C), 22nd OT (C), 26th OT (A)]

THIRTY-FIRST SUNDAY IN ORDINARY TIME (C)

(Wisdom 11:22–12:2; 2 Thessalonians 1:11–2:2; Luke 19:1-10)

Today

$ome time ago, I read an interesting article about modern impressionist art, comprising artists such as Degas, Monet, Renoir, Cezanne, Van Gogh, and so on. The article stated that impressionism was born out of the invention of the camera. Before the camera was invented, artists reproduced objects just as they were. But the camera could do a better job, with only a click in time. Of necessity, artists had to learn the dynamic impression, rather than a static description, of objects. Cezanne said, "I see objects as they change, not as fixed. I see the tree is changing its shape moment by moment, as I look at it continuously."

Impressionistic paintings show hidden realities—beautiful and imaginative and transcendental. I wonder how Renoir or any other impressionist would paint Jesus' encounter with Zacchaeus, who is smiling on a tree, looking down at Jesus passing by.

Zacchaeus is walking along the road and sees the crowd lining up. He asks, "What is happening?" Someone says, "It is Jesus, the great Jesus of Nazareth. He is coming to town." Zacchaeus rushes to the roadside to take a glimpse of Jesus. But he is too short and cannot see Jesus. So he climbs up a sycamore tree. Surprised by such enthusiasm, Jesus invites himself to Zacchaeus' house by saying, "Today I must be at your house." Jesus does not say, "God loves you," as some modern preachers would do. At Zacchaeus' house, Jesus sits at the table and opens up conversation with him. Something quite transcendental, not unlike an impressionistic painting, happens between the two.

Zacchaeus finds out from Jesus that God accepts all men and women equally and wholly. Moreover, he learns that he can have a relationship with God. In short, through the humanity of Jesus, he has discovered the reality of God. Zacchaeus has seen the light of God shining upon Jesus' face.

Having discovered the saving act of God in Jesus, Zacchaeus is able to find his true self. God's love has freed him from himself; he has transcended himself toward God's boundless love. So he declares that he will give half of his possessions to the poor and be honest in his business dealings. Jesus is happy and says, "Today salvation has come to this house."

The word "today" is found in other places in Luke's Gospel. At synagogue, after reading Isaiah 61 from the scroll, Jesus says, "Today this scripture has been fulfilled in your hearing" (Lk 4:21). On the cross, Jesus says to the thief on his right, "Today you will be with me in Paradise" (Lk 23:43).

The word "today" means here and now rather than an uncertain time in the future and someplace else. It also means certainty over ambiguity, an affirmative pledge over lip service, and warm enthusiasm over cold indifference. It is an expression of the presence of God like the impressionistic paintings. Jesus is concerned with the here and now, rather than the there and then, and the next world or tomorrow (Mt 6:34). Those who hang on the past with nostalgias and those who hold on the unfounded future cannot live today fully.

The story of Zacchaeus shows us how to open our hearts to God and let them be filled with the Holy Spirit. This story is about conversion here and now. Perhaps most of us have not experienced such a dramatic conversion as Zacchaeus. Slowly and continuously, we change our attitudes and dispositions toward God and our fellow human beings. And we experience the reality of God and internalize gospel ideals and perspectives in our lives.

God loves us and calls us to be holy. God calls us to live the life of God—the life in Jesus Christ and with Jesus Christ. We are not saints yet; our faith journey is slow but continues. And we know that following Jesus is not unlike viewing a Monet or a Renoir. **✝**

[Christ King (C)]

THIRTY-SECOND SUNDAY IN ORDINARY TIME (C)

(2 Maccabees 7:1-2, 9-14; 2 Thessalonians 2:16–3:5; Luke 20:27-38)

Resurrection

We have journeyed together with Jesus toward Jerusalem for the last seven months. Finally, we have arrived.

Today's gospel reading shows that in Jerusalem Jesus is mocked by the Sadducees, who do not possess faith in resurrection. Jesus knows his own death approaches soon, so he wants to talk about his resurrection. It seems proper for us to reflect upon some aspects of the resurrection based on today's gospel reading.

The ancient Israelites did not believe that death would destroy a human being completely. They understood that the person who died went down to the shadowy underworld known as Sheol, where no relationship with God existed. They also believed that God was for the living, not for the dead. The idea of resurrection occurred only about two centuries before the time of Jesus. For example, the first reading describes the brutal martyrdoms of seven brothers and their mother, all of who believed in resurrection. Even at the time of Jesus the Sadducees, who accepted only the Torah, did not believe resurrection.

The gospel reading today is about the controversy between Jesus and the Sadducees involving the topic of resurrection. The Sadducees made fun of Jesus for his belief in resurrection. Using the fictitious story of seven brothers and one woman and applying it to Mosaic Law, they tried to point out the absurdity of resurrection after death. Jesus refuted them by saying that, after resurrection, there was no marriage, because there is no death for souls.

Jesus also pointed out that when God revealed himself to Moses, God claimed to be the God of Abraham, Isaac, and Jacob. This meant that these patriarchs were already raised from death. Contrary to the ancient Israelites' belief that God existed only for the living, Jesus showed that God dwelt among both the living and the dead. During his dispute with the Sadducees, Jesus also called the dead "children of God," establishing a covenant relationship even with the dead.

There is a story about twins in a mother's womb. The sister said to her brother, "I believe there is life after birth." Her brother protested, "No, I don't think so. This place is cozy and warm." The little girl insisted, "There must be something beyond this dark place. There must be a place with hope and light." Her brother complained, "I say again this is fine." The sister suggested, "If there is no tomorrow, how can we live today? Besides, we have stayed in the dark so long." Still, she could not convince her twin brother.

After some silence, the sister said, "I have something else to say. I think there is a mother." Her brother became furious, "A mother?!" he shouted. "Are you crazy? Who put the idea in your head? As I told you, this place is just fine. Why do you always want more?" The sister was quite overwhelmed by her brother's response and didn't say anything anymore.

Perhaps all of us live in mothers' wombs. Some of us are like the girl; others like the boy. We cannot prove the resurrection using logics or mathematical equations. We simply accept it in faith. And it is important to live today with hope for tomorrow.

Jesus Christ is "the resurrection and life" (Jn 11:25). The resurrection of Jesus has brought a new life for us. By virtue of the resurrection of Jesus, God has entered into our space and time. We must hope for our future resurrection, because Jesus, "the first fruits" of resurrection (1 Cor 15:20), has defeated death (1 Cor 15:26). In fact, not just human beings, but "the whole of creation is groaning in labor pains" for the fulfillment of salvation (Rom 8:23).

Finally, the faith in resurrection can only come from God's love. St. Paul says, "For I am convinced that neither death nor life will be able to separate us from the love of God in Christ Jesus our Lord" (Rom 8:38-39). It is love that understands the resurrection. ✝

[Easter (A)]

THIRTY-THREE SUNDAY IN ORDINARY TIME (C)

(Malachi 3:19-20; 2 Thessalonians 3:7-12; Luke 21:5-19)

As We Await a New World

The air is getting colder and the nights are getting longer. At this time of year, our Sunday readings are filled with scary themes such as earthquakes, famines, and plagues. We are about to begin a new liturgical year and another secular year. It is time to reflect upon what is passing by and what is coming soon.

While it is easy to observe the changes in the season and the liturgical year, it is difficult to face our own aging with the change of the season. To put it bluntly, it is good to see children and grandchildren being born and growing, but the same cycle of life that creates new life also reminds us that our time here on earth becomes shorter and shorter day by day.

How will we cope with the spiritual task of growing older? To get some answers to this question, we need to reflect upon today's readings, which are filled with harsh and demanding themes. The prophet Malachi from the first reading said, "Lo, the day is coming, blazing like an oven.... The day that is coming will set them on fire." This refers to the fiery judgment on the last day. Jesus says in the gospel reading, "There will be powerful earthquakes, famines, and plagues from place to place." Jesus does not tone down the severity of the final judgment.

The Gospel reading is called Jesus' "eschatological discourses." As we know, the early Christians were Jews and to whom the fall of Jerusalem at 70 AD was the most devastating event in history. They no longer had the temple where God dwelt on and where animal sacrifices were offered. Fortunately, however, they found the Messiah, the Son of God, whose voluntary death on the cross made animal sacrifices obsolete. While waiting for their final judgments in their dark and troubled life, therefore, they continued to hope for the future, by taking missionary effort in the new age of the gentiles.

Like the early Christians, we also live in a new age. We endure hardships and problems today, hoping there will be no more troubles or worries tomorrow. The old world is passing by and the new world has already come. Sometimes, however, it is not easy to let the old world go. We tend to hold on to it so tightly that it takes painful birth pangs to let it go. This is why earthquakes, famines, and plagues are actually needed. Our love must be shaken by earthquakes; our faith must be strengthened by famine; and our hope must be tested by plagues.

For example, in the second reading, the Christians at Thessalonica thought Jesus would come again very soon. So they stopped supporting their families and the community. Instead of working for bread, they acted like busybodies. Paul asked them to imitate him, as he supported himself without depending on the communities he established. As Christians, we must confront these issues, particularly unavoidable and often recurring questions of suffering and death.

In the gospel reading, Jesus encourages us to endure in faith, because his death will fulfill God's promise. Jesus also suggests that suffering can provide a means to purify ourselves. Jesus is central in Christian life, and central to Jesus are his death and resurrection. (This is why eschatological discourses appear in the Gospels immediately before the Passion.) Therefore, we must be familiar with the paschal mystery of Jesus.

To participate in Jesus' paschal mystery is the best way to let the old world pass and to welcome a new world. We need to die before we can live anew. There are many different forms of death—the death of ambition, the death of ego, the death of envy, the death of fame, the death of youth, the death of unnecessary material things, and so on. Within each of these deaths we are born into a new life. These deaths hold the key to letting the old world pass by, so that we may encounter a certain resurrection as a new world comes.

When the weather gets chilly we retreat deeply into our hearts, where the love of God has been poured into (Rom 5:5). This is the gift of encountering God through the Spirit of Jesus Christ. ✝

[1st Advent (C), 13th OT (C), 32nd OT (A), 33rd OT (B)]

OUR LORD JESUS CHRIST THE KING (C)

(Samuel 5:1-3; Colossians 1:12-20; Luke 23:35-43)

The Experience of God

On the hill of Calvary, Jesus is put on the cross with two convicted criminals. One thief on the left says to Jesus in anger, "Are you not Christ? Save yourself and us." The other thief on the right says with compassion, "We have been condemned justly..., but this man has done nothing criminal." He then makes the most of the little life left in him and offers a short prayer to Jesus: "Jesus, remember me when you come into your kingdom." This is all he can manage to do through parched lips and lungs short on air. And for this, he inherits the fullness of Jesus' promises: "Amen, I say to you, today you will be with me in Paradise."

Traditionally, this gospel story has been interpreted as that the good thief on the right is compassionate with Jesus. And Jesus grants him, as a reward, a divine forgiveness. The good thief will stay in Paradise—a primordial happy place, the Garden of Eden.

Upon a close look, however, we observe that the thief on the right calls Jesus by his first name and refers to Jesus as "this man." And the whole incident happens right before the death and resurrection of Jesus. In other words, the thief on the right, having not yet recognized Jesus as the Christ, simply expresses his honest opinion on the reality—an innocent man dying on the cross. The thief has a pure heart. This is why he is able to experience God when he encounters Jesus.

As we are know, Christianity was founded with profession of Jesus being the Christ. We also know that the central point of Jesus' preaching was not about himself, but about the in-breaking of God's reign. So, Jesus always points at God the Father: "He who has seen me has seen the Father" and "The Father and I are one." These sayings of Jesus show how he has experienced God.

The experience of God is the root of all our experiences. When we are in love, we experience God. When we are lonely, we experience God. The experience of God is absolutely necessary for us to know who we really are, although it is often coincides paradoxically with contingencies in life, such as the death in today's gospel. When Jesus says, "Today you will be with me in Paradise," it shows Jesus' being in union with God and the simultaneous realization of the kingdom of God. The word "today" means the time consciousness that is present-centered, rather than past- and future-oriented. It means just now, neither tomorrow nor yesterday. And paradise, of course, is not a faraway place above the sky, it is right here where we are.

We find more examples of the word "today" in Luke's Gospel. The angel of the Lord informs the shepherds, "Today, in the city of David, a Savior is born" (Lk 2:11). At the beginning of his ministry in the synagogue, Jesus says, "Today this scripture has been fulfilled in your hearing" (Lk 4:21). To Zacchaeus, who sits on a tree, Jesus says, "Today I must stay at your house" (Lk 19:5). And at his house, Jesus says, "Today salvation has come to this house" (Lk 19:9). Finally, on the cross Jesus says to the thief, "Today you will be with me in Paradise." In all these, the word "today" expresses the here-and-now.

In conclusion, when Jesus says, "Today you will be with me in Paradise," it means "Right now and right here, you are in union with God, as I am." "Now is the acceptable time. Now is the day of salvation (2 Cor 6:2). Therefore, the gospel message shows how to experience God here and now through Jesus, rather than confessing Jesus being the Son of God, and subsequently, receiving a divine forgiveness.

We are about to celebrate another union with God, the Eucharistic Communion. When we receive the body and blood of the Christ, it is the moment of experiencing God right-here-right-now. The Christ, whom we are about to encounter is the divine reality for all human beings. (In other religions, they simply call Christ different names: in Hinduism Isvara and in Buddhism the Buddha nature.) So let us then go forth and celebrate the death and resurrection of Jesus Christ to experience the goodness of the Lord. ✝

[28th OT (A), 33rd OT (B), Holy Trinity (C), 3rd OT (C)]

Printed in the United States
By Bookmasters